THE LATINO EDUCATION CRISIS

THE LATINO EDUCATION CRISIS

The Consequences of Failed Social Policies

Patricia Gándara

Frances Contreras

Harvard University Press

Cambridge, Massachusetts

London, England

Printed in the United States of America

First Harvard University Press paperback edition, 2010

Library of Congress Cataloging-in-Publication Data

Gándara, Patricia C.
  The Latino education crisis : the consequences of failed social policies /
Patricia Gándara, Frances Contreras.
      p.   cm.
  Includes bibliographical references and index.
  ISBN 978-0-674-03127-2 (cloth : alk. paper)
  ISBN 978-0-674-04705-1 (pbk.)
  1. Hispanic Americans—Education.   2. Hispanic American students—
Social conditions.   I. Contreras, Frances, 1972–   II. Title.

  LC2669.G36 2008
  371.829′68073—dc22   2008024118

To the Latino students who shared their lives, their hopes, and their dreams with us—our future is in the hands of their generation.

—P. G.

To those who advocate for the services and needs of disadvantaged children—especially my late sister Lupe M. Contreras, who encouraged children to believe "all things are possible."

—F. C.

CONTENTS

THE **LATINO**
EDUCATION
CRISIS

Introduction:
A Call to Action

In 1983 the nation was called to action with the admonition that "if an unfriendly foreign power had attempted to impose on America the mediocre educational performance that exists today, we might well have viewed it as an act of war."[1] With these words a newly formed federal commission launched a generation of attempts to reform and improve American public schools. By any measure, this is an unfinished agenda. In fact, gaps in opportunity and educational outcomes are greater between racial and socioeconomic groups than when the Commission on Educational Excellence made its provocative pronouncement twenty-five years ago.

Today the most urgent challenge for the American educational system has a Latino face. Latinos are the largest and most rapidly growing ethnic minority in the country, but academically, they are lagging dangerously far behind. As has been thoroughly documented, a college degree is increasingly a prerequisite for a middle-class job and middle-class income; the gaps in earnings and opportunity between those with college degrees and those without have widened dramatically since 1983. But about half of all Latino students fail even to graduate from high school, and while all other ethnic groups—including African Americans—have gradually increased their college graduation rates, Latinos have seen almost no such progress in three decades.

Adding to the significance of the problem is that Latinos are becoming an increasingly large percentage of the U.S. school-age population. As we write in early 2008, Latinos make up about 48 percent of public school students in California, about 46 percent in Texas, and about 20 percent in New York State. If these children's educational futures prove to be as discouraging as those of their older brothers and sisters, or of their parents, the economic and social consequences for them, and for the country as a whole, will be grave. This book is a new call to action.

Is There Really an Education Crisis?

Some have argued that the exceptionally low educational achievement of Latinos is a disturbing but passing phenomenon, the result of the large recent influx of undereducated immigrants. They find reassurance in the fact that previous generations of immigrants have consistently exceeded their parents' and grandparents' social and economic status. We argue, however, that the current data do not give cause for optimism, for they show that the demands of contemporary American society are outpacing the ability of post-immigrant generations of Latinos to overcome the educational and socioeconomic barriers they confront.

The Latino education crisis is not simply a result of immigration. In fact, some scholars have noted that on the contrary, Americanization is bad for immigrants. For example, based on his data from over 2,400 eighth and ninth grade immigrant students in the San Diego area, in which immigrant students who were learning English tended to outperform native-born students with greater facility in English, Rubén Rumbaut concluded that "Americanization processes, all other things being equal . . . may be counterproductive for educational achievement."[2]

A number of other studies have similarly found what is often referred to as "immigrant optimism," a factor that helps account for the surprisingly higher educational achievement of many immigrant students in comparison to that of their native-born co-ethnic peers.[3] Russell Rumberger and Katherine Larson studied academic achievement among Mexican American students in a large urban school district. They found that bilingual students—generally immigrants and children of immigrants—earned better grades and accumulated more course credits than either students who were still learning English or the native-born Mexican American students.[4] Rumberger and Larson speculated that the bilingual students simply had more social capital—access to more supportive networks—than either of the two groups. Nonetheless, the overwhelming majority of Latino students are native-born and in spite of the recent large increase in Latino immigration, the Latino native-born population is still growing at a faster rate than is the Latino immigrant community.[5] Therefore, the low educational attainment of Latino students cannot be attributed solely, or even largely, to factors associated with immigration; rather it is the result of circumstances encountered in this country.

Some studies are optimistic.[6] Philip Kasinitz and his colleagues show that immigrants in New York City are incorporating into the economic mainstream in much the same way that prior generations did, learning English and finding jobs. It is notable, however, that the proportion of unauthorized immigrants in New York City is effectively half that of Los Angeles, the metro area with the largest number and proportion of Latino immigrants. Because unauthorized immigrants have less access to social services and postsecondary education, their job options are more limited and they may be less able to incorporate successfully into the broader community. Moreover, whether the trends observed among immigrants in New York will be sufficient for them to catch up with the accelerating educational demands of the twenty-first century is not altogether clear.

In contrast to the more heterogeneous Latino population studied by Kasinitz, Gretchen Livingston and Joan Kahn analyze income over the generations for Mexican-origin wage earners specifically. They conclude, based on an analysis of the 1989 Latino National Political Study and the 1990–1991 Panel Studies of Income Dynamics, that Mexican immigrants, both male and female, experience either steady or declining wages across the generations when education level is controlled, thus rejecting for this group the "linear assimilation hypothesis"—that successive generations experience ever greater assimilation.[7]

Joel Perlmann weighs in on this issue in a comparative study of the second-generation educational and economic progress of southern, central, and eastern non-Jewish European (SCEN) immigrants during the period 1890–1914 and that of more recent descendants of Mexican immigrants.[8] While he, too, finds some basis for optimism in the data, he notes that

> even at the lowest SCEN ratio, the second generation advantage then over the Mexican relative position today is not inconsequential. . . . Part of the reason the wage handicap is greater for today's second generation is the [Mexicans'] relatively lower educational attainment. Larger differences in educational differences also matter more today than they would have mattered in the 1940 to 1960 period.[9]

There is little dispute that successive generations of Latinos tend to outperform their parents, if those parents are very undereducated.[10] In twenty-first-century America, however, it is not sufficient for each generation to advance from, say, a sixth grade education to an eighth grade education. Latinos for the most part are now stalled at the level of high school completion, with dropout rates remaining very high across generations. Only one in ten Latinos has a college degree, compared to more than one in four white Americans and more than one in three Asians. The Latino share of college degrees has not increased for more than two decades, while for all other groups the percentage of the population with degrees has increased substantially over that period.

If the Latino population were a small percentage of the overall population, this trend might be unfortunate, but not terribly consequential, for society as a whole. But because Latinos are the nation's largest and fastest-growing ethnic minority group, it matters very much to everyone how well these students fare in school. The Center for Public Policy and Higher Education has projected that if California does not immediately begin preparing more underrepresented students for higher education, by 2020 the state will experience an 11 percent drop in per capita income, resulting in serious economic hardship for the state's population.[11] California is likely to experience the steepest drop because of its very large and undereducated Latino communities, but Arizona, Texas, and other states with high percentages of Latinos are also projected to see declines in per capita income over the period. To understand the effects of such a decline in per capita earnings, it is useful to know that the present-day economy of California is in fact the result of a 30 percent increase in per capita income since 1980.[12] With no evidence of an imminent turnaround in the rate at which Latino students are either graduating from high school or obtaining college degrees, it appears that both a regional and national catastrophe are at hand.

Among those who assert that there is indeed a serious problem, even a crisis, regarding the education of Latino students, the solution is usually couched in language about school reform—better schools, better teachers, better curriculum, schools reorganized to provide small learning communities, or other more effective organizational arrangements. The No Child Left Behind Act of 2001 has even fostered the idea that by testing these students repeatedly and holding their schools accountable for those test scores, schools can rise to the challenge and do a better job—as though students were failing simply because no one had pointed it out.[13] Some believe that just teaching these students English as quickly and efficiently as possible will close the gaps in their educational achievement. Over the past ten years, several statewide ballot initiatives have been implemented to curtail the use of native language instruction, with no evidence that these policies have increased students' achievement relative to their English-speaking peers.[14] Some education pundits even believe that if we were to only raise our expectations for Latino students, they would, more or less on their own, perform at much higher levels.[15]

Whatever the solution, most supporters of education reform agree that the problem is fixable if only schools can muster the will, the resources, and the talent to address it. We agree that schools can do a great deal more to improve the achievement of Latino students. And clearly many American schools, especially those serving the majority of Latino students, are in desperate need of reform. But the crisis in Latino education goes beyond what schools can do, even if they were given far greater resources than taxpayers appear to be willing to commit or politicians are willing to request. Instead, the increasing failure of Latinos to achieve the American Dream is embedded in the very origins of that dream: the American mythology that everyone can make it in this country, no matter the circumstances they encounter, if they simply work hard enough.

Whom Is This Book About?

Writing about Latinos as a group, given the diversity among Latino subgroups, presents special challenges to researchers, policymakers, and journalists. Although Latinos may be of any racial background, may hail from many different nations, and may hold very different positions on the social ladder, they are bound together by a shared language, and to a more limited extent, a shared cultural heritage. Individuals of Mexican origin make up 64 percent of all Latinos in the United States, followed by Puerto Ricans, the next largest subgroup, who account for 9 percent of the Latino population. Hence together these two groups alone make up almost three-quarters of all Latinos. Cubans are a significant cultural and economic force in Florida and parts of New Jersey, but they represent only 3.4 percent of all Latinos, and Dominicans, who cluster in the Northeast, form less than 3 percent of the group. Both Central and South Americans outnumber Cubans and Dominicans by almost 100 percent, with each representing between 5 and 8 percent of the Latino population.[16] But Central and South Americans are also extremely heterogeneous, varying from a largely mestizo population in much of Central America to European stock in Argentina and a majority indigenous people of Bolivia. These groups are as diverse as any on the planet and they tend to be more dispersed across the nation than are other Latino subgroups. Yet in spite of subgroup differences, the great majority of Latinos in the United States encounter surprisingly similar educational challenges, as well as many of the same limitations on their aspirations for a better future.

Given the numerical as well as the historical dominance of Mexicans, Latino culture in the United States is marked in many ways by their presence. The American Southwest was, until 1848, part of Mexico. Tacos, piñatas, mariachis, margaritas—many of the cultural artifacts that Americans think of as Latino are, in fact, Mexican. Even in communities with different Latino subgroups, the Mexican cultural influence is often so strong that other groups become "Mexicanized," participating in Mexican cultural traditions and even, in some cases, adopting a Mexican accent or characteristics of a Mexican lifestyle.

Moreover, many studies of Latinos and education do not disaggregate data by subgroup. Thus the category of "Latino" becomes a catchall for all Latino subgroups, the largest of which is usually Mexican. Consequently, this book relies to a large extent on data regarding Mexican-origin students and on studies that have been conducted in California, where almost 11 million people of Mexican origin live and where they represent 83 percent of the Latino population (as well as 36 percent of the state's total population).[17] Where possible, we show data for other groups—data that show clearly that Puerto Ricans, like Dominicans and others who have relocated to the United States as economic refugees, share many of the same social and educational obstacles as Mexican-origin students, and experience similarly dire educational outcomes.[18] Thus while we acknowledge a range of Latino experiences, a guiding principle for the data and interpretations presented in this book is that the experiences of Mexican-origin individuals are common to most, though certainly not all, Latinos.

Will Solving the Immigration Problem Resolve the Education Crisis?

It is impossible to discuss the education of Latino students without also mentioning immigration policy. The backlash against the increased undocumented migration of Latinos from Mexico and Latin America in recent years colors almost every conversation about Latinos in the United States. Many Americans are concerned about this issue and some believe that undocumented immigration is the source of almost every social ill, from overcrowded schools to increases in crime rates and overstretched social service budgets. A recent *Los Angeles Times* poll found that 81 percent of respondents considered immigration to be either an "important" issue (54 percent) or "among the most important" issues (27 percent) facing the country. It is not so surprising that large numbers of respondents in Los Angeles would see the issue as important because the city has been at the epicenter of the new immigration. In 2004, Los Angeles was home to 3.5

million immigrants, one million of whom were unauthorized—twice as many unauthorized immigrants as any other metropolitan area in the United States. But even in areas with far fewer immigrants, feelings can run high. In Iowa, a state with relatively low rates of immigration, 67 percent of Democrats and 81 percent of Republicans in a recent poll noted that they thought immigration was a "key issue."[19]

Many voters, and even some academic researchers, claim that Latino immigrants cannot or will not assimilate into American society and therefore will fundamentally change the character of the nation in negative ways.[20] But these fears are largely groundless. Data from a number of credible sources, including the U.S. Census, demonstrate clearly that Latinos are acquiring English as rapidly as, or more rapidly than, past generations of immigrants. A recent report by the Pew Hispanic Center based on a series of surveys it conducted showed that while only 23 percent of Latino immigrants report being able to speak English very well, 88 percent of their U.S.-born adult children say they can.[21] Among later generations, the figure rises to 94 percent. Moreover, as fluency in English increases, so does the regular use of English at home and at work. Ironically, analyses of census data show that in fact most Latinos have lost fluency in Spanish by the third generation, an outcome that some social commentators lament.[22] The data suggest that, having come to the United States for work, Latinos work at least as much and as hard as native-born Americans. According to a recent Urban Institute report, 94 percent of unauthorized men—and 84 percent of legal immigrants—between the ages of eighteen and sixty-four are in the workforce, compared to just 82 percent of native-born men.[23] Disproportionately, the jobs held by Latino workers are low-wage and require little formal education.[24] As we shall see in later chapters, the strong loyalty to family among Latinos—an American value if there ever were one—can lead many to consider the opportunity costs of going to college too high.

The U.S. Constitution confers citizenship on anyone born in this

country. Unless the Constitution is amended to change this definition, the two-thirds of children of undocumented immigrants who
are born in the United States are legitimate citizens and are due all
the rights and privileges of any other American.[25] Moreover, that
smaller fraction of children of immigrants who were brought here by
their parents through no choice of their own are also guaranteed by
the Constitution, as interpreted in *Plyler v. Doe,* access to a full and
equal public school education in the United States.[26] In the majority
opinion, written by Justice Brennan, the U.S. Supreme Court justices
held that children should not bear the responsibility for decisions
that their parents make and over which they have no control, nor
should they be denied an education that "has a fundamental role in
maintaining the fabric of our society." As Justice Brennan warned,
"We cannot ignore the significant social costs borne by our Nation
when select groups are denied the means to absorb the values and
skills upon which our social order rests." Thus all of the Latino children in our schools, whether documented or undocumented, have
been determined to have an equal right to education.

This legal fact does not, however, address the sense that many
Americans have that these children and their parents do not truly
"deserve" taxpayer-funded services such as education. Many Americans believe that undocumented workers pay few or no taxes and
burden the nation's social service systems, including the schools. Although the costs and revenues generated by immigrants remain a
hotly debated issue among economists, and is far too complex a topic
to do justice to here, there are some findings that are relatively consistent. Immigrants, both documented and undocumented, use both
social and medical services at significantly lower rates than the general population and thus add little additional burden to the social
service system. There are many explanations for this difference, but
prominent among them is the fact that immigrants tend to be both
younger and healthier than the general population.[27] They also pay

more taxes into federal coffers than they take out.[28] The costs of schooling, however, fall to local governments, which because of federal policies are not compensated for the burden they bear. Of course, immigrants cannot be blamed for the way that tax dollars are distributed by the federal government. A number of researchers have also argued that without the taxes paid by immigrants—both legal and undocumented—the Social Security system in the United States would not be sufficiently solvent to support the now aging baby boomers.[29]

The most common complaints about undocumented immigration—that these people are criminals because they have "broken the law" by entering the country illegally—only point to the limited public understanding of the exceedingly complex system that governs U.S. immigration. The immigrant ancestors of the vast majority of native-born Americans were considered "legal" even if they entered the United States exactly as many Mexican and Latin American workers do today. The Chinese Exclusion Act in 1882 was the first attempt to restrict immigration to the United States based on race or ethnicity, and this affected only Asian immigration. Later, quotas were placed on Eastern and Southern Europeans, but the U.S. border patrol was not even created until 1924. Before this, immigrants moved relatively freely across the borders.

Since 1990 the United States has placed a heavy emphasis on admitting highly skilled workers—for instance, foreign-born doctors and scientists—but even for them, the demand for permits far exceeds the supply. Virtually no legal means of entry to the United States exists for the unskilled workers who are the majority of unauthorized immigrants. Yet as the data show, the U.S. economy has plenty of room for these millions of unskilled workers, and in fact is highly dependent on them. In a recent talk before a group of California legislators, Carlos González Gutiérrez, foreign minister in charge of the Office of Mexicans Abroad, painted a quite different picture of

Mexican immigration to the United States. Countering the U.S. perspective that Americans are footing the bill for illegal Mexican workers, he asserted that Mexico is subsidizing the American economy with cheap labor, without which large sectors of the American economy would falter. He also warned that the U.S. economy must soon wean itself of dependence on this inexpensive labor source, because the growth of the Mexican economy and the decline in the Mexican birthrate indicate that a severe shortage of such Mexican workers will occur within twenty years.[30]

Well-known scholars Doug Massey, Jorge Durand, and Nolan Malone agree on the negative effects on both the United States and Mexico of what they refer to as the "charade" of U.S. immigration policy:

> If there is one constant in U.S. border policy, it is hypocrisy. Throughout the twentieth century the United States has arranged to import Mexican workers while pretending not to . . . [and] politicians and public officials have persistently sought ways of accepting Mexicans as workers while limiting their claims as human beings. Only the formula by which the sleight of hand has been achieved has changed over time. . . . Despite these charades, the benefits of Mexico-U.S. migration have historically exceeded the costs for all concerned . . . [but] in many ways the United States is doing serious damage to the social and economic fabric of both nations.[31]

Immigration and Opportunity in a Globalizing World

The waves of immigration occurring around the world create cultural and economic strains and opportunities, but we are hardly alone in this experience. In a rapidly globalizing world, who wins and loses economically will depend on how successfully nations integrate new populations into existing societies. Such enormous changes require us to have a new vision of the possible. As Marcelo Suárez-Orozco notes,

> Immigration is now a global phenomenon and the United States is once again at the forefront of a new set of world-wide dynamics. But for the first time in human history all regions of the world are involved in large-scale migration—either as sending, transit, or receiving regions and sometimes all three. The largest migratory wave in history is structured by powerful global forces. Transnational labor recruiting networks, wage differentials, and family reunification ("Love and Work"), and war, are behind new migratory practices that cannot be easily contained by the apparatus of the state. Hence [there are] growing numbers of unauthorized migrants world-wide. Leicester, England, will be the first European city with a non-white majority before the end of the decade. Frankfurt today is about 30 percent immigrant; Rotterdam is 45 percent immigrant. Amsterdam will by 2015 be 50 percent immigrant. Sweden has 1 million immigrants. . . . In all of these countries immigrant children are a fast growing sector of the child and youth population. . . . Failure to properly address the realities of immigration in the global era and failing to educate and ease the transition of the unauthorized children of immigrants will strongly shape their transition to citizenship and the labor market, and their long-term patterns of adaptation in all advanced post-industrial democracies. The immigrant achievement gap is now global.[32]

Education is the single most effective way to integrate the burgeoning population of Latinos into the U.S. economy and society. Thus, if the high dropout rates and low educational achievement of Latino youth are not turned around, we will have created a permanent underclass without hope of integrating into the mainstream or realizing their potential to contribute to American society. If we find a way to educate them well, their future and ours is bright. Regardless of how they got here, Latino children are America's children and America's future. This book suggests how we might choose the brighter path, challenging our schools, our politics, and our society at large to envision a more inclusive American Dream.

CHAPTER ONE

The Crisis and the Context

Carlos's parents were worried. Immigrants to the United States, they had worked hard as a day laborer and a housekeeper to earn enough to buy a modest home in a not-so-good neighborhood that harbored several street gangs. The house wasn't much, but it was a lot more than they could have hoped for in their native Mexico, and they were proud to call themselves homeowners—*dueños de su propia casa.*[1] In many respects the Rodriguez family was an American success story—they had come to this country with nothing more than what they could carry in a knapsack, and now they were genuine title-holders of the American Dream. But they worried about their son, and not without reason. Unlike his parents, Carlos had a shot at an education that could bring better options than they had, but he was vulnerable to the distractions of the street and often found himself cutting class and getting into little problems at school—problems that seemed to grow as he developed a reputation as a "troublemaker."

Andrés was in many ways Carlos's opposite. Andrés's family wasn't as successful as Carlos's. His mother was born in the United States, graduated from high school, and attended a couple of years of community college. But after three children, her first marriage had ended in divorce. She remarried an undocumented European immigrant who had difficulty finding steady work. With the family depending mostly on her income from a paper route and a fast-food job, they struggled to stay afloat economically. Andrés often woke up in the early hours of the morning to help his mother with the paper route, then went to school with barely four or five hours of sleep. Nonetheless, he maintained a high grade point average and appeared to be headed for a bright future. He wanted to go to college and vowed to help his friends get there with him. Few people worried about him— he was level-headed, responsible, and focused on school.

Carlos and Andrés would come to have much more in common, however, than most people might imagine. Growing up Latino and working-class or poor in the United States means that opportunity can be more apparent than real and that opportunities offered almost every middle-class kid from the suburbs could be out of reach for a *chamaco* from the barrio. What happens to Carlos and Andrés, however, is increasingly important for everyone else sharing this nation with them, because this country's future is predicated to a large extent on how well or how poorly these young people fare in our education system.

A little more than a generation ago, most U.S. students were of European background and went to school mostly with other students like themselves. In 1972, almost 80 percent of K–12 students were reported to be non-Hispanic white; African Americans accounted for about 15 percent of the school-age population, and were still highly concentrated in the South. With a few exceptions, Latinos were mostly unheard of outside the Southwest and a few pockets in the East, and less than 1 percent of the K–12 population was Asian. The baby boomers were moving through high school and into college in unprecedented numbers, and they were pressuring society to take the first real steps toward acknowledging and accepting ethnic diversity. Sweeping civil rights laws had recently been passed, and many youth had coalesced around their opposition to the war in Vietnam, as well as what they perceived to be other societal injustices, including racial discrimination.

Fast forward to the beginning of the twenty-first century. The baby boomers are now all grown up with a new generation of children of their own completing high school and going on to college in unprecedented numbers. In 2005, less than 58 percent of the K–12 population was of European descent. African Americans had increased slightly from 15 percent to about 16 percent of the K–12 population, but the Latino population had quadrupled—from about 5 percent to almost 20 percent—and Asians had become a significant national presence, now 3.7 percent.[2] By the last decade of the twentieth century, virtually all of the major urban school districts had become "majority minority"—overwhelmingly black and brown. Moreover, in 2003 the West became the first region in the United States to be majority minority, with a majority that is largely brown. Only 46 percent of school-age children were European American, while 54 percent were minorities. By 2025, the U.S. Census Bureau predicts that one of every four students will be Latino, and that the population will continue to become more Hispanic. Latino youth are inextricably linked to the nation's future.

The history of the United States is one of different groups—often immigrants, but not always—finding their place in society and the economy. For most, there has been a period of difficulty and adjustment during which both the ethnic group members and the existing society adapted to each other. And the adjustment has been more difficult for some groups than others. Italians, for example, fared much more poorly in school than many other immigrant students, and for a time there was considerable concern about whether Jewish immigrants would be able to compete academically.[3] Yet these groups were eventually integrated into the mainstream society and those students are at no greater risk academically than any other European-origin group.

The situation is not as hopeful this time around. Evidence suggests that there may be real reason for concern—even alarm—about the state of the growing Latino school-age population. Latino students are underachieving at high and consistent rates, and while children of immigrants, and their grandchildren, do indeed improve their educational attainment with each generation, there appears to be a ceiling effect that results in little or no improvement after the third generation (and a number of researchers argue after the second) for some Latino immigrant groups.[4] At a time when college has become the new critical threshold for entry into the middle class, the overwhelming majority of Latinos do not attend degree-granting colleges—and those who do attend, often don't graduate. Thus Latinos remain the most undereducated major population group in the country. In making this statement, we acknowledge fully the great diversity in the group labeled "Latino," and note that Cuban Americans actually outperform white students in college attainment. Individuals of Mexican origin, however, who comprise about two-thirds of all U.S. Latinos, fare exceptionally poorly in the public schools, as do Puerto Ricans, the second largest subgroup. Never before have we been faced with a population group on the verge of becoming the majority in significant portions of the country that is also the lowest performing academically. And never before has the economic structure been less forgiving to the undereducated.

The Achievement Dilemma

Achievement differences among ethnic groups are consistent and large at the earliest stages of formal academic assessment. For example, in a national sample of America's kindergartners, African American, Latino, and Native American children were found to be much more likely to score in the lowest quartile on a test of early reading and math skills than either white or Asian students.[5] And with the exception of Native American students, Latinos were the most likely of all groups to fall into the lowest quartile of performance (see Table 1.1).

According to U.S. Department of Education researchers, children's academic performance increases as a function of mothers' education across all ethnic groups. But Latino mothers have much less education than mothers from all other major groups (see Table 1.2). Thus the lower educational background of Latino youngsters' parents appears to be a significant factor in these children's early low academic performance, and continues to affect their achievement throughout their later education.[6]

The National Center for Education Statistics conducts a periodic assessment of academic achievement of the nation's fourth-, eighth-, and twelfth-graders. Known as the Nation's Report Card, the National Assessment of Educational Progress (NAEP) tests a repre-

Table 1.1 Percentage of kindergartners scoring at highest and lowest quartiles in math and reading, 1998

	Reading		Math	
Ethnic group	Highest quartile	Lowest quartile	Highest quartile	Lowest quartile
White	00	10	02	10
Asian	39	13	38	13
Black	15	34	10	39
Latino	15	42	14	40
Native American	9	57	9	50

Source: West, Denton, and Germino-Hausken 2000.

Table 1.2 Mothers' education level, by ethnicity, 1998

Ethnic group	High school or more (%)	Less than high school (%)
White, non-Latino	94	6
Black, non-Latino	83	17
Asian	86	14
Latino	67	33

Source: West, Denton, and Germino-Hausken 2000.

sentative sample of students in all fifty states in reading and math. Scores on NAEP exams are categorized into three levels: basic, which signifies rudimentary, partial mastery of the subject at grade level; proficient, which represents full mastery of the subject at grade level; and advanced, which is superior performance normally considered above grade level. Table 1.3 shows the percentages of fourth grade students from different ethnic groups who scored at or above proficient in reading and mathematics in 2005. The discrepancies by ethnicity found here are similar to those noted for kindergartners. While 41 percent of white students in the fourth grade scored at or above proficient, only 13 percent of African Americans and 16 percent of Latinos reached this level of competency in reading. Again, Latinos' mathematics scores paralleled their reading scores, and are very different from the scores for white and Asian students.

Another recent national study that looked at the educational progress of "at risk" students in Title I schools—those schools designated as needing special help because of poverty conditions and overall low academic performance—found similar ethnic discrepancies in both reading and mathematics on the Comprehensive Test of Basic Skills (CTBS).[7] But the most troubling finding of this study was the extent to which low-income students continued to disengage from school throughout the elementary years. That is, their achievement declined with each succeeding year. The researchers noted that among chil-

Table 1.3   Percentage of fourth grade students proficient in reading and math, by ethnicity, 2005

Ethnic group	Reading	Math
White	41	47
Asian	42	55
Black	13	13
Latino	16	19
Native American	18	21

Source: Perie, Grigg, and Donahue 2005; Perie, Grigg, and Dion 2005.

dren who were the highest achieving when they entered school, "the process of disengagement begins at first grade and continues through the sixth grade [and] . . . African American students who began third grade at or above the 50th percentile disengage at a significantly faster rate than comparable White students."[8] These researchers focused on schools with high percentages of black students and did not investigate the academic achievement of Latinos separately, but it appears likely that this pattern would hold for academically talented Latinos, because they tend to score similarly to blacks and experience many of the same schooling conditions.

By the eighth grade, scores for all groups drop, but Latinos remain significantly behind most other groups; 39 percent of white students score at or above proficient, whereas only 15 percent of Latinos are able to reach this level of reading competence. NAEP mathematics scores for 2005 reveal an even more troubling picture. While 39 percent of white students and 47 percent of Asians scored at or above proficient, only 9 percent of African Americans and 13 percent of Latinos scored this high (see Table 1.4).

Although grade point averages are known to vary greatly among schools that are more and less rigorous in their demands on students and the difficulty level of the courses they offer, it is nonetheless a useful measure of comparative performance among groups.[9] While minority students—and Latino students in particular—tend to go to

Table 1.4   Percentage of eighth grade students at or above proficient in reading and math, by ethnicity, 2005

Ethnic group	Reading	Math
White	39	39
Asian	40	47
Black	12	9
Latino	15	13
Native American	17	14

Source: Perie, Grigg, and Donahue 2005; Perie, Grigg, and Dion 2005.

schools and be assigned to classes where standards are often lower and teacher and other resources weaker, they also receive lower grades than either white or Asian students (see Table 1.5). Why would this be so if the classes, on the whole, are easier? A history of underpreparation is undoubtedly part of the problem, but also likely to blame are lowered aspirations and little understanding by Latino students and families of the connection between good grades and future opportunities.[10] Whatever the cause, persistently lower grades result in fewer opportunities for students and lower their chances of gaining access to college and other sources of postsecondary education.

The high school dropout rate is yet another indicator of the relative educational performance of students from different ethnic groups. But there are many ways to count dropout students (or the inverse—graduates), and most data on this topic are suspect because of variations in reporting among schools, districts, and states. The National Center for Education Statistics tallies dropouts and graduates several different ways, using the Common Core of Data reported to the Department of Education; it estimates that in 2005 about 70 percent of Latinos (Hispanics) graduated from public high schools in the United States after four years in high school, an increase from the rate of about 56 percent documented in 1972.[11] These figures, however, do not take into account those students who drop out even before ninth grade, and as noted earlier, they rely on reporting systems that are sometimes suspect. For example, recent

Table 1.5   Grade point averages for high school graduates, 2000

Ethnicity	High school GPA
Asian	3.20
White	3.01
Latino	2.80
Black	2.63

Source: U.S. Department of Education, Institute of Education Sciences 2000.

analyses of dropouts in the Boston public schools show that from 2003 to 2006, between 3 and 4.8 percent of Latino students dropped out annually in the sixth through eighth grades. That is, as many as 14.4 percent of these students had exited before ever entering high school.[12]

Analyses reported by the Civil Rights Project at Harvard University and the Urban Institute, too, call into question the more generous graduation estimates and further suggest that improvements over time may, in fact, be illusory.[13] Using what they contend is a superior method of data collection, which "chases" students who have left school but were formerly unaccounted for in the dropout numbers, these investigators argue that an estimated 68 percent of all students who begin high school in the ninth grade in the United States graduate with a regular diploma four years later. For white students the rate is about 75 percent, but for Latinos, it is only about 53 percent. That is, almost half of Latinos do not receive a diploma four years after entering high school. (Consistent with many other studies, they find the African American dropout rate to be almost the same as that for Latinos.) These dropout estimates raise serious questions about the efficacy of the entire public school system for Latino (and black) students.

The poor achievement record of Latino students in K–12 is reflected in the rates at which students begin and complete college. Although in a recent study of Latino college-going rates Richard Fry argued that Latinos "go to college" at rates comparable to other students, his analysis is based on those students who actually complete high school, a percentage that we noted earlier is probably at least 25 percent lower than for white students.[14] Moreover, "going to college" means very different things for the average white and Latino high school student. Nationwide, 72 percent of white students, and about 54 percent of Latinos, go directly to college after high school graduation. Of those white students who went full-time to college in 2002, two-thirds (65 percent) enrolled in a four-year college, while only about half (51 percent) of Latino college-goers enrolled full-time in a four-year college that year.[15] Half (49 percent) of Latinos attended two-year colleges after high school, from which they would have to successfully transfer in order to earn a bachelor's degree. Most never do. Among those Latino students who go to two-year colleges, many attend part-time, live at home, and work.[16] All of these factors are associated with a lower chance of college completion.[17] In California, the state with the highest number and percentage of Latinos, fully 75 percent of Latino students go directly to community college, where their likelihood of completing a bachelor's degree is much lower than if they had attended a four-year college or university from the start.[18]

Latinos complete bachelor's degrees at less than a third the rate of white students. Table 1.6 shows the percent of students ages twenty-five to twenty-nine in each of the three largest ethnic groups who completed a college degree during the thirty years leading up to 2005. While there has been substantial growth in college degree completion for other groups, Latino degree completion has been stagnant.

Figure 1.1 shows white-Latino K–12 enrollment compared to bachelor degree attainment for the period 1975–2005. While white enrollment drops substantially over the thirty-year span and bachelor's degree attainment rises to narrow the gap between enrollment and bachelor's degree attainment, the opposite is true for Latinos.

Table 1.6 Percentage of population ages 25–29 with bachelor's degree or higher, by ethnicity

Ethnicity	1975	1985	1995	2000	2005
White	24	24	29	34	34.1
African American	11	12	15	18	17.5
Latino	9	11	9	10	11.2

Source: U.S. Department of Commerce, Census Bureau 2005.

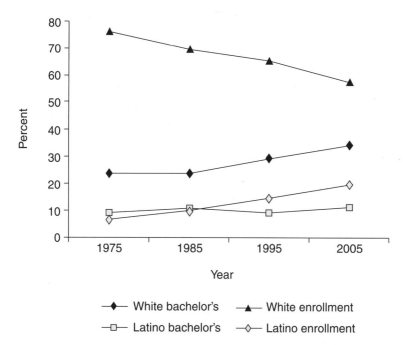

FIGURE 1.1 White and Latino bachelor's degree (or higher) attainment versus school enrollment, 1975–2005. (Data from U.S. Department of Commerce, Census Bureau 2005, and U.S. Department of Education, National Center for Education Statistics 1999, table 5–1. School enrollment data for 2005 are based on enrollment projections.)

In 1975, Latino K–12 enrollment and bachelor's degree production were quite close and in fact Latinos received somewhat more bachelor's degrees than would be predicted by enrollment. In 1985, by contrast, the lines cross over and begin to head in different directions, with K–12 enrollment outpacing the achievement of bachelor's degrees. This result can be explained by both demography and social policy. Latino immigration since 1980 has increased dramatically, exacerbating a situation in which school systems have proven to be ill-equipped to address the needs of this population. But just as important, policies developed in the 1970s to recruit and support Latino college students were curtailed in the 1980s, and financial aid and other supports for desegregating public higher education institutions have been replaced with policies that actively work against bringing more Latino students into higher education. We return to this topic later.

The Problem of Gender

As disturbing as the picture is for Latinos as a whole, the situation is even more serious for Latino males. In most areas of schooling, females now outperform males, a trend that is even more pronounced among Latino students. Since the early 1980s Latinas have been completing high school at higher rates than Latinos, and since the 1990s they have entered and completed college at significantly higher rates than their male counterparts.[19] In 2000, almost 59 percent of Latinas graduated high school, compared to 48 percent of Latinos.[20] Latinas also work harder in school, taking more academic courses than Latinos, and they have higher grade point averages.[21] For example, for the 2004 SAT cohort, Mexican American females in the top quintile had mean GPAs of 3.87 compared to 3.64 for their male counterparts.

These gaps in achievement occur across ethnic groups and begin as early as kindergarten.[22] For example, in a recent study using the National Education Longitudinal Study (NELS) and Early Child hood Longitudinal Study (ECLS) datasets, white girls started kindergarten with reading scores about two points higher than those of white boys, an advantage that increased to five points by the third grade.[23] By the end of the third grade, Latinas outscore Latinos by 4.7 points in reading. In math, Latinas outperform males by 1 point going into first grade but quickly lose this advantage. There are no significant differences in NAEP math scores at either fourth or eighth grade, but Latinas go on to earn science and engineering degrees at higher rates than Latinos. In 2000, Hispanic females garnered 7.8 percent of science and engineering bachelor's degrees, as compared with just 6.6 percent for males.[24]

An emerging literature on boys and education has blamed the gender divide on feminized schools, and on learning environments that privilege girls, who tend to be able to sit quietly for longer periods than many boys can.[25] Critics claim, for example, that society is at "war against boys" and that the schools are driven by "misguided feminism."[26] In reality, however, schools have for at least the last century been feminized institutions, with female teachers far outnumbering male teachers, and yet during most of that time boys held an achievement advantage over girls. It seems clear that rather than the school environment, societal expectations have changed: girls are now expected to do well in school and prepare for a career. Indeed, most of the gender divide is not caused by boys losing ground so much as by girls gaining it. For example, the proportion of boys who go on to college has not changed appreciably in the last few decades; what has changed is the proportion of females who attend, which has increased greatly. The increases have been especially dramatic for women of color (Latinas and African Americans) because they started from such a low base. No doubt some boys are intimidated by the potent competition that ambitious girls represent, and this may cause them to lose confidence or characterize school as "girl stuff," but the fact remains that schools haven't changed a great deal—society has.

Tom Mortenson notes, somewhat tongue-in-cheek, that at the rate that the gender gap is increasing, the last male to be awarded a bachelor's degree will receive it sometime in the middle of the twenty-first century.[27] Oddly, one of the last places that Latino and other males hold an advantage over women is on the SAT and GRE exams, even though women have higher grade point averages.[28] Evidently the college admission tests measure something different than what is required to do well in the classroom, where women appear to excel.

We have painted a picture of a group—soon to be the largest of all students in many parts of the nation—that is underperforming at alarming levels. Every measure, beginning with kindergarten readiness and extending through high school completion and postsecondary education, shows a consistent pattern of under-achievement, especially for males. As we discuss later, billions of dollars in federal programs and remedial education programs at the state and local levels no doubt have influenced the achievement of Latino students. But the gaps between their performance and that of both white and Asian students remain large and persistent. Why?

Conditions that Contribute to Poor Achievement

It would be simplistic to suggest that a single cause or even a combination of factors could entirely explain the low level of achievement of many Latino students. The situation is far more complex than a simple cause-effect model. Some students in terrible situations excel, while others who are apparently ambitious and have caring, involved parents fall through the cracks and fail to achieve. Nor are all Latinos poor or educationally disadvantaged. In fact, some Latinos perform at exceptionally high levels. Certainly some portion of academic achievement is due to personal characteristics, but these attributes alone cannot explain group trends. Instead, personal characteristics intersect with group factors, which in turn encounter broader social and schooling conditions that all add up to patterns of achievement. To make sense of the achievement patterns of Latino students, we will later explore in detail the multitude of factors that influence them. Here, however, we provide a brief overview of the major contributors to achievement gaps among ethnic groups. The most often cited, and best researched, of all factors affecting achievement relates to the student's experience within the family and community.

There are huge variations by ethnic group in the amount of education parents have completed, which leads to parents having dramatically different levels of knowledge about how to navigate successfully through the U.S. school system. Table 1.7 shows the high school and college completion rates of parents of the three largest ethnic groups of U.S. public school students in 2005.

Table 1.7   Parents' education level for public school children ages 6–18, by race/ethnicity of the parent, 2003 (percentages of children)

Parent and race/ ethnicity	Less than high school completion	High school completion[a]	Some college or associate's degree	Bachelor's degree or higher		
				Total	Bachelor's degree	Graduate degree[b]
Mother						
Total[c]	14.8	29.4	30.3	25.5	18.6	6.9
White	5.9	29.0	33.4	31.7	23.0	8.7
Black	18.2	34.4	32.2	15.3	10.6	4.7!
Hispanic	41.3	28.6	20.2	9.9	7.7!	2.2!
Asian/Pacific Islander	16.0!	22.2!	17.1!	44.7!	32.9!	11.8!
American Indian/ Alaska native	11.9!	31.3!	48.4!	8.4!	3.9!	4.4!
Father						
Total[c]	13.6	31.0	25.8	29.7	18.7	11.1
White	6.9	30.6	27.4	35.1	21.8	13.3
Black	11.5	41.8	29.5	17.3	13.0	4.3
Hispanic	41.5	28.1	19.0	11.4	8.0	3.4
Asian/Pacific Islander	8.5!	25.3	18.5	47.7	26.7	21.0
American Indian/ Alaska native	14.9!	40.1	32.9	12.1!	8.4!	3.7!

a. Includes high school diploma or equivalency.
b. A master's, doctor's, or first professional degree.
c. Total includes persons of more than one race, not separately shown.
Source: U.S. Department of Commerce, Census Bureau 2005.
Notes: Parents include adoptive and stepparents but exclude parents not residing in the same household as their children. Race categories exclude persons of Hispanic origin. Detail may not sum to totals because of rounding. An exclamation point (!) following a figure indicates that data should be interpreted with caution.

A very large body of literature has pointed to the strong correlation between education and income of parents and the achievement outcomes of their children.[29] Here we do not attempt to explain why this is so, but only call attention to the very large discrepancies between the educational backgrounds of Latino students and others. While nearly 40 percent of Latino students come from homes in which parents have not completed even a high school education, this is true for only about 4 percent of white students. Similarly, while almost four in ten white students can count on the higher education experiences of their parents to help guide them through college, this is true for only about one in ten Latinos. An important aspect of formal education is the cultural capital (knowing how things work) and social capital (having access to important social networks) that are acquired while earning a diploma or a college degree; this knowledge and access help students succeed.[30] Latino parents, with their relatively low levels of formal education, have far fewer of these important assets to assist—and pass on to—their children.

Community contexts and resources are also very important to student success. Safe environments versus dangerous ones surely affect the health and welfare of young people and consequently, their ability to do well in school. But the availability of parks, libraries, youth entertainment, and social services are important as well. The degree to which neighborhood characteristics contribute to schooling outcomes is widely debated, and is not easy to separate from family background and resources, but a growing literature suggests that these may play a far more critical role than once believed.[31] Of course, a critical component of communities are the families and peers who live in them. The availability of adult role models in the community—individuals who exemplify educational, occupational, and social success—as well as peers who are supportive of educational achievement, is important for students. There is currently a considerable debate about the extent to which students of color in general, and Latinos in particular, are captive to the idea that doing well in school means one is "acting white"; the theory is that such students may be reluctant to try hard in school because they feel doing so will cause them to lose status among their less academically ambitious friends. Nonetheless, there is a compelling body of literature that points to lowered expectations among Latino youth and therefore to a culture of low achievement that, whether overt or more subtle, operates to dampen the achievement of some members of this group.[32]

Residential and school mobility also appear to affect Latino students disproportionately. Low-income Latino families (and especially immigrants) are more likely to change residences than other groups and as a consequence, Latino students tend to change schools more often for reasons unrelated to grade promotion.[33] That is, Latino students are more likely than others to change schools as a result of their parents' changing jobs and moving, or due to disciplinary actions—a change that interrupts learning and instruction as well as disrupts personal relationships.[34] Taken together, challenges presented by one's family background, communities and neighborhoods, peers, and frequent moves can be powerful forces in the lives of young people. When one or more of these challenges are present in the lives of these students, research shows that they can be at risk for school failure, and when inequalities in schooling are added, the impediments to academic success can become daunting.[35]

It has often been observed that two students—one majority, one minority; one poor, one middle-class—attending the same school may interpret their experiences completely differently.[36] In fact, it is almost as though they attend different schools. And in many ways, they do. Low-income and minority students are less likely to gain access to college preparatory, honors, and Advanced Placement classes than other students, and they are more likely than nonminority students to be placed in the low, non-college-bound track, independent of their actual academic achievement.[37] Once on a low curriculum track, they find it very difficult to change tracks and catch up to higher-performing peers because the curriculum in remedial courses and non-college preparatory classes is generally at a slower pace or the curriculum is watered down; in addition, less is expected of these students.[38] It is also well documented that the schools most Latinos attend have fewer resources, are more crowded, and have teachers who are themselves less skilled; such schools are also more likely to have high teacher turnover and teachers with less experience (because the more skilled and experienced teachers often leave these challenging environments to seek jobs elsewhere).[39] In sum, there are great inequalities in schooling resources and experiences between Latino (and some other minority students) and white and Asian students in the United States.

It is also true that Latino students are more segregated than other students, and therefore more likely than students in any other group to go to school with others like themselves.[40] In such settings, Latinos are isolated and do not interact with mainstream students, nor are they exposed to the differences between groups in expectations and aspirations. They may not know what a typical student in a suburban school reads in the tenth grade, or what command others have of math concepts. They may not know that in some schools science laboratories are standard and six foreign languages are taught, or that there are opportunities to study in places where those languages are spoken. Being isolated from the experiences of middle-class students can lead to a distorted view of the world and a very limited vision of the possibilities that exist in it.

For many Latino students, limited use of English outside the classroom adds to this isolation and reduces their access to educational opportunity. Most Latino students are born in the United States, and are not immigrants themselves. But two-thirds of Latino students have at least one parent who was born outside the United States.[41] For this reason, we estimate that as many as two-thirds of Latino students come from homes in which another language—generally Spanish—is spoken. About half of all Latino students begin school—at whatever grade they enter—speaking primarily Spanish, and therefore access to the English curriculum can be problematic for them. The half of Latinos who must learn English while simultaneously attempting to learn the regular curriculum also experience a significant challenge. The U.S. Supreme Court acknowledged this problem in its dramatic 1974 *Lau v. Nichols* decision:

> There is no equality of treatment merely by providing students
> with the same facilities, textbooks, teachers, and curriculum; for
> students who do not understand English are effectively foreclosed
> from any meaningful education. . . . Imposition of a requirement
> that, before a child can effectively participate in the educational
> program, he must already have acquired those basic skills is to
> make a mockery of public education. We know that those who do
> not understand English are certain to find their classroom experi-
> ences wholly incomprehensible and in no way meaningful.[42]

In spite of the rather commonsense finding of the Court, that a
student who does not speak English cannot make sense of what he or
she is being taught and that it is unreasonable to expect that such a
student would have to learn English before being taught the regular
curriculum, there has nonetheless been a protracted debate in the
United States about how best to educate these students. Bilingual
education, a pedagogical strategy that employs two languages for
instruction, has been a lightning rod for controversy in this debate.
Although it has been shown to be a viable and often superior form
of instruction for both English learners and English speakers, some
states have moved to ban its use.[43] Others merely ignore it as an
option and opt to place English learners in English-only settings with
very few, if any, additional resources or supports. It is not surprising, then, that under these conditions, Latino students who are not
proficient in English fare poorly in U.S. schools, never really catching
up with their English-speaking peers, and thus are prone to drop out
of school.[44]

The Politics of Ethnicity and Achievement

In a world with limited resources and a commitment to the idea that
educational opportunity should be distributed according to "merit,"
the definition of who is merit-worthy is a constant point of political

contention. For some, only legal citizens are worthy of particular educational opportunities regardless of how hard they work or how well they do; for others only those students with the highest grades are worthy of college admission, regardless of extreme differences in opportunity to learn; and for still others, only those who speak English should be given access to such opportunities, regardless of whether they actually know more than their English-speaking peers, but are unable to express that knowledge in English. Citizenship, grades and test scores, and English-speaking ability have all been at the center of recent political battles that have implicated Latino students and their access to education. As Latinos make up an ever larger proportion of the school-age population, such debates rage ever more intensely. Not surprisingly, the initial site of many of these battles is California—the state with the highest percentage and largest number of Latinos, and one with an initiative process that allows anyone with enough money to create his or her own laws through the ballot.

Citizenship and Access to Education and Basic Services

In 1994 the citizens of California, spurred on by then-governor Pete Wilson, passed Proposition 187, which intended to ban any individual who was not a legal resident of the state from receiving any nonemergency state services. Thus children of undocumented workers drawn to California by the ample—if low-wage and back-breaking—work available in the state's fields and factories were to be denied schooling, as well as other social services like basic health care. A disproportionate number of individuals targeted by Proposition 187 were of Mexican origin, because they made up most of the undocumented immigrants in the state (a fact not lost on the voting public).

One by one, however, the courts struck down the various provisions of Proposition 187, finding them illegal because the U.S. Constitution does not protect "citizens," but "people," against discriminatory treatment. With respect to education, the Supreme Court had already found in *Plyler v. Doe* that punishing children of un-documented immigrants for their parents' transgressions by denying schooling violated the Fourteenth Amendment.[45] In 2004, Arizona, in a similar initiative process, passed a ballot measure modeled after Proposition 187 that was followed by several more ballot measures—to deny immigrants' ability to post bail, bring a civil law suit, and take adult education courses (including English classes), and to declare English the official language of the state. The federal courts have not yet clarified the extent to which all of those measures will be enforceable.

Plyler v. Doe notwithstanding, undocumented students often encounter barriers to schooling in the United States because of their tenuous legal status. Some school districts illegally advise parents that their children cannot be enrolled without showing evidence of legal residency, an effective scheme given that immigrants often do not know their rights.[46] At the level of postsecondary education, many students are denied access to public universities because *Plyler* did not address the issue of higher education, and in cases where these students are able to gain admission, they are often not able to afford the tuition because they are categorized as foreign students and therefore must pay the extraordinarily high costs levied against students who come to study from abroad. The Dream Act, which has been stalled in Congress, would confer temporary-resident status on undocumented students who have graduated from U.S. high schools and demonstrated good moral character, allowing them to pay resident tuition and providing for permanent resident status if they complete at least two years of college or military service within six years.[47] It would also make such students eligible for some federal financial aid. Those who favor such policies argue that the development of human capital is in the interest of all; to deny education to individuals who are going to continue to live in the United States only reduces the quality of the American workforce with negative consequences for almost everyone. Those who oppose such measures, by contrast, argue that providing any benefits to undocumented individuals only encourages more illegal immigration.

The Campaign against Affirmative Action

Affirmative action is, without a doubt, one of the most contentious and politically divisive topics in American society. Thousands of books and articles have been written on the topic and, like other hot-button social issues, it incites deep emotions. The two sides appear to be irreconcilable. The 2003 affirmative action case in Michigan, *Grutter v. Bollinger* (described in detail later), brought the topic of affirmative action in university admissions back to center stage, and numerous polls were conducted during the period to gauge public sentiment. A 2003 national Gallup poll found that only 44 percent of whites favored affirmative action in university admissions, while 63 percent of Latinos and 70 percent of blacks did. These figures roughly parallel the different groups' views of whether blacks and Latinos experience racial discrimination. Opponents of affirmative action have argued that it discriminates against nonminorities by offering opportunity on the basis of the color of people's skin rather than on merit. They have invoked the words of Martin Luther King Jr., who famously envisioned a society in which people would be judged "not by the color of their skin, but by the content of their character."[48] The goal of civil rights legislation, they argue, should be a color-blind society, not one that uses color to distribute benefits. They worry that affirmative action can stigmatize people of color, so that they are perceived as less capable than they may actually be (because there will always be doubt in their own minds, and in the minds of others, about how they have come by their achievements).[49] Shelby Steele has argued passionately that affirmative action causes minorities to adopt the role and status of "victims," causing psychological damage to its recipients, lowering their motivation to compete on a level playing field, and ultimately reinforcing low achievement because they believe they do not have to meet the same standards as others.[50] And Linda Chavez, the most vocal of the Latino anti-affirmative-action activists, has asserted that the measure holds Latinos back from assimilating into American society by perpetuating stereotypes about them.[51]

Opponents of affirmative action have likewise argued that affirmative action hurts those it is intended to support because preferences place individuals in contexts for which they may be ill prepared. This is what Sigal Alon and Marta Tienda refer to as the mismatch hypothesis.[52] Many of these arguments are, in fact, testable hypotheses, and we offer some of the research that speaks to them later, but ultimately the arguments against affirmative action boil down to a sense of unfair advantage, that beneficiaries of affirmative action are receiving something they don't deserve and didn't work for. This argument is difficult to refute because it is based on people's conception of fairness and "merit." As such, it is useful to remember how the notion of affirmative action came into being. While some historians have traced the concept and the language back to John F. Kennedy, the policy in fact took shape in President Lyndon Johnson's commencement address at Howard University in 1965. In this address Johnson intoned,

> You do not take a person who, for years, has been hobbled by chains and liberate him, bring him up to the starting line of a race and then say, "you are free to compete with all the others," and still justly believe that you have been completely fair. . . . We seek not just legal equity but human ability, not just equality as a right and a theory but equality as a fact and equality as a result.[53]

In this speech, President Johnson made clear that the policies of the Great Society he was intending to construct would look not just to words, but to actions, in pursuit of equity: it was not enough to say that the United States stood for equal opportunity; it had to demonstrate the possibility of equality of outcomes for all groups. This vision departed fundamentally from historical notions of equality in America and would come to be one of the most controversial legacies of Johnson's Great Society.

In 1995, a new chapter in the debates over affirmative action was opened in California, and eventually spread across the country. An African American regent of the University of California, Ward Connerly, spearheaded a drive that had been launched by the then-governor (and aspiring presidential candidate) of California to abolish the use of affirmative action in admission to the University of California. The argument he made for abolishing affirmative action was that it was unfair to white (and Asian) students because a student of color with lower grades or test scores might be given preference for admission over a white or Asian student who was actually more qualified. The student with the absolute highest grade point average or test scores was assumed, by this logic, to be the most qualified. An important strategy of the Connerly campaign was to feature white students who had been denied admission to the university while "less-qualified" minorities had been accepted. In fact, the incident said to be the precipitating event behind the anti-affirmative-action drive was a white applicant's denial of admission to medical school at the University of California, San Diego. When the parents of the applicant investigated the grade point averages and test scores of the minority students who had been admitted, they found that some had scores lower than their son's. The family called regent Connerly and threatened to sue the university. Connerly and his supporters quickly seized on the incident as a platform on which to build the anti-affirmative-action campaign. They did not question whether the university might have a compelling reason for wanting a more diverse medical school class than would have resulted from simply taking the highest scorers across the board. Nor did they consider whether there were attributes applicants might possess besides test scores and grade point averages that could uniquely qualify them to study medicine—or anything else. They certainly did not question the implicit assumption that anyone with a 4.0 grade point average was inherently more qualified to deliver a baby than someone with a 3.9. If they had done so, they would have found that there is no evidence to support this position. After a campaign that included unprecedented arm-twisting, threats, and cloakroom politics, the ban won approval of a majority of the regents and affirmative action was abolished at the University of California.[54]

The following year, the campaign was extended to the entire state of California and in 1996 a wide majority of the electorate agreed that it was time to end the practice. The voters of California were convinced that a person's race, ethnicity, or gender was irrelevant to his or her chances of becoming adequately prepared to compete for a public-sector job or admission to the state's most selective public educational institutions. And the argument that a diverse college class afforded any benefit to society as a whole was never articulated in a compelling way. The playing field was, de facto, ruled to be level, and affirmative action was deemed to be unfair to all but students of color. In the year after the passage of Proposition 209, Latino and African American undergraduate admissions and enrollments fell precipitously—by about 50 percent at the flagship campuses of UCLA and Berkeley. Professional schools were hit even harder. Even today, enrollments have not recovered to pre–Proposition 209 levels, even though the very low representation of black and Latino students was an issue of grave concern at the time.

The battle over affirmative action, launched in California in 1995, continued to be a major social issue across the nation. In 1997, the

Fifth Circuit Court of Appeals ruled in favor of Cheryl Hopwood, who had been denied admission to the University of Texas Law School. She argued that she was discriminated against because minority applicants who were less qualified had been accepted. The court's decision was interpreted by the attorney general of Texas as outlawing race or ethnicity as a factor in admission, financial aid, and retention and recruitment programs in all institutions of higher education within the Fifth Circuit. Texas, too, suffered a radical reduction in black and Latino students at its flagship institutions. In 1998, the State of Washington followed the example of California and passed Initiative 200. Michigan's Proposal 2 (2006) bars the consideration of race or ethnicity in college admissions decisions within that state. The sum total of such policies has been a decline in admissions to the institutions from which Latinos are most likely to graduate and prepare for graduate education and professional careers. In other words, the academic pipeline for Latino students is much narrower and more tenuous today than it was thirty years ago.

Affirmative Action and the Educational Establishment

There is broad consensus among higher education leaders that something must be done to equalize access to college education for many students of color. A review of press accounts of statements by college presidents during 1996–1997, in the aftermath of several of the highly publicized anti-affirmative-action decisions, yielded well in excess of three hundred articles appearing in newspapers, magazines, and other journals in which university CEOs addressed the issues raised by these initiatives and legal decisions.[55] A surprisingly strong consensus in favor of affirmative action emerged among the CEOs of the nation's colleges and universities. The leaders of both public and private institutions of higher education were virtually unanimous in their support of the policy as a tool to achieve some measure of diversity in the nation's colleges. The chancellors of all nine University of California campuses, who were compelled to abandon affirmative action in the face of the passage of Proposition 209 and the 1995 University of California regents' decision, were also vocal in their repudiation of the university's board of regents' stand against affirmative action.

University presidents' positions on affirmative action were based on two major principles: first, that colleges and universities that more accurately reflect the state or national population provide greater equality of opportunity for all members of society; and second, that diversity is intellectually healthy because it brings students and faculty into contact with a broad mix of perspectives. Most of the rhetoric in the press considers the intellectual benefits of diversity, perhaps because this interpretation is viewed to be the least politically charged, and the most defensible on purely academic grounds. Moreover, the beneficiaries of this position would appear to be the majority population whose intellectual perspectives are presumably enhanced by diversity among faculty and students. Perhaps one of the best examples of this perspective was articulated by Neil Rudenstine, then president of Harvard University, who asserted that students are challenged

> by a diverse educational environment . . . to see issues from various sides, to rethink their own premises, to achieve the kind of understanding that comes only from testing their own hypotheses against those of people with other views. Such an environment also creates opportunities for people from different backgrounds, with different life experiences, to come to know one another as more than passing acquaintances, and to develop forms of tolerance and mutual respect on which the health of our civic life depends.[56]

The other principle, that of equality of opportunity, was candidly described by the departing chancellor of UCLA, Charles Young, who was not shy in disagreeing with his own regents' decision to abandon affirmative action in the university.

> What we're really trying to do is provide an opportunity for groups that have not been able to participate equitably in our society to make the kind of contribution they should, to reap the benefits they should, and to receive the education which will enable them to do so. We are trying to make enrollment in the university look more like the breakdowns in the population—not because that in itself is some ideal, but because those great disparities indicate serious problems.[57]

Both President Rudenstine's and Chancellor Young's comments also made reference to the general welfare of society as a whole. Rudenstine referred to "the health of our civic life" and Young alluded to "serious problems" in our society. These concerns are no doubt on the minds of many university CEOs: how does a nation, or a state, reconcile the enormous disparities in education and opportunity that result from university admissions criteria that effectively, and systematically, shut out large sectors of the population? What are the consequences for race relations of these disparities? How is the social contract that guarantees equal opportunity in the society renegotiated as a result? And over the long run, how do they affect the social and economic health of the states and the nation?

William Bowen, former president of Princeton University, and Derek Bok, former president of Harvard University, entered the fray in 1998 with *The Shape of the River.* This book advanced a third major argument in favor of affirmative action: that "race-sensitive admissions" produce an important social good. In a study that documented outcomes spanning two decades for more than 45,000 students from twenty-eight selective colleges and universities, they found that African Americans who had been the beneficiaries of such race-sensitive policies went on to make greater contributions to their communities in the form of public service and volunteerism than did white graduates of the same institutions. Moreover, both black males and females were more likely to be involved in leadership roles in civic organizations than were their white peers, thus adding substantially to the social capital of their communities.

Contrary to the argument made by such critics of affirmative action as Abigail and Stephan Thernstrom, that affirmative action stigmatizes its recipients, Bowen and Bok found that black graduates contended that the benefits of race-sensitive admissions far outweighed any potential stigma attached to them.[58] Black graduates of these institutions earned far more than black college graduates nationwide, and were far more likely to attend graduate and professional schools. In another important myth-countering finding, Bowen and Bok concluded that the more selective the institution, the greater the likelihood that African Americans would complete their degrees. This notion flies in the face of the oft-repeated criticism that admitting minorities who are "less qualified" (according to grade point averages and test scores) than their white peers only results in disillusionment and self-disdain when they find they are unable to compete.[59] Of course, Bowen and Bok were quick to point out that these students were highly qualified for the universities they attended; they did not have test scores and grades that were as high as those of their white peers, on average, but they had high enough scores to allow them to compete ably. In these selective institutions there was a greater concern shown for the students' academic welfare than in less selective, often overcrowded institutions that rely on a certain attrition level to maintain acceptable enrollment levels. It must be noted that while the Bowen and Bok study made a major contribution to the discourse on diversity in higher education, the study did not include an analysis of Latino education. By overlooking this group, an important opportunity was lost to broaden the discussion beyond a black-white paradigm.

In 2003 the Supreme Court delivered a nervously anticipated decision in the case of *Grutter v. Bollinger,* in which a white applicant to the University of Michigan Law School claimed she had been denied admission while minorities who were less qualified (that is, who had lower test scores) had been admitted. The case directly challenged the *Bakke v. Regents of the University of California* decision of 1982 in which the University of California Davis School of Medicine was sued for the same ostensible reason. In that case the Court confirmed the value of diversity and held that race could be considered as one factor among many others in admissions, but it also determined that a college could not set quotas or reserve seats specifically for minority students. The outcome of the *Grutter* case effectively affirmed the earlier *Bakke* decision and left it standing. Justice O'Connor, writing for the majority, found that diversity is a compelling interest of the state and that all students benefit intellectually by being educated among a diverse student body; consequently, absent quotas, race could be taken into consideration.

Diversity in public education went to court once again in 2007. *McFarland v. Jefferson County Public Schools* and *Parents Involved in Community Schools v. Seattle School District No. 1* were ruled on jointly by the Supreme Court, and while the Court struck down the voluntary desegregation plans that these school districts had devised to increase diversity in their classrooms, it did note that its determination in the *Grutter* decision—that diversity was a compelling interest in higher education—still held. The Court maintained that diversity does continue to be an important goal of public education, but that racial diversity cannot be achieved by considering race as a sole or even primary criterion for assigning students to particular schools. The ruling in the Jefferson County and Seattle cases will almost certainly make it more difficult for Latino students to be educated with non-Latino peers, thereby limiting these students' access to an equitable education unless some other effective means of desegregating students that does not use race primarily can be found.

Proposition 227 and Native Language Instruction

Following what had by now become a routine among California voters, a new proposition, this one aimed at restricting the use of Spanish in the classroom, was passed and became law in 1998. Proposition 227 declared that English learners in California were to be taught English by teaching them in English and that placement in a special "structured English immersion" class should not normally last more than one year, after which students would be placed in mainstream classrooms. Effectively, this measure was a return to the old "sink or swim" approach in which students were mixed in classrooms with teachers who could not communicate with them, and would hopefully acquire English before falling so far behind in school that they would give up and drop out. Although dropout data for English learners have been notoriously difficult to acquire, transcript data from Los Angeles City schools allowed an analysis of graduation rates in 2004 for those English learner students who were enrolled in the ninth grade in 2000 under the new restrictive language policy. Of those students, only 27 percent remained in school and graduated with their class in the district in 2004. In other words, 73 percent of those English learners did not graduate with their class. Some may have graduated from a school outside the district or stayed behind, but it is safe to assume that most simply dropped out.

The sponsor of Proposition 227 had a great deal of money but no experience in education, nor in the instruction of English learners. He had never been in a bilingual classroom, though his initiative was designed to curtail bilingual education because he considered it a failed instructional method.[60] Since the passage of Proposition 227, a number of researchers have tracked its effects on students. The general consensus is that there has not been much change in the test scores of these pupils—the overwhelming majority of whom (about 85 percent) are Latinos. Scores for English learners did rise somewhat in the first years after passage of the proposition, but they rose for all students—English learners and English speakers alike—presumably because of reform efforts such as class size reduction, teacher professional development, and increased investment in education generally, all of which were occurring simultaneously. The gap between the performances of English learners and English speakers showed negligible change.[61]

The lack of significant changes in test scores is understandable: prior to the passage of Proposition 227, approximately 29 percent of English learners were in a program that offered some kind of primary language instruction. After the passage of Proposition 227, ultimately just under 10 percent remained in such programs, so that only about 20 percent of English learners were eventually affected by the proposition. Most continued more or less in the same program they were in before the new law, although they were now mainstreamed more rapidly into classrooms where teachers had little or no training to teach them.[62] Indeed, the researchers contracted by the State of California to track the progress of these students noted that there was a slight test score advantage for those students who had been in bilingual programs prior to the passage of the initiative and who remained in those programs afterward.[63]

A provision in Proposition 227 that teachers could be personally sued by parents if they were found to use a student's primary language for instruction triggered a lawsuit by the California Teachers' Association. The association claimed that the law did not specify what would constitute a sufficient amount of non-English and so made it impossible for teachers to know how to protect themselves from legal action. The association lost, but Judge Tashima of the Ninth Circuit

Court of Appeals dissented with the opinion, noting that "if teachers must fear retaliation for every utterance, they will fear teaching."[64] In fact, several studies of the implementation of Proposition 227 showed just that: teachers were confused by the law and feared retaliation for inadvertently failing to comply with it.[65]

Both Arizona, with Proposition 203 in 2000, and Massachusetts with Question 2 in 2002, took a page from the political history of California and passed similar initiatives, although another measure was stopped in Colorado in 2004 after a successful counterinitiative campaign was launched. The evidence suggests that students will probably not fare much worse—or much better—as a result of these political initiatives, given that those states did not have well-developed bilingual programs serving large numbers of students.[66] Considering the extremely low test performance of English learners in California (see Figure 1.2) and their high dropout rates, the focus on how much or how little damage has been inflicted by the loss of primary lan-

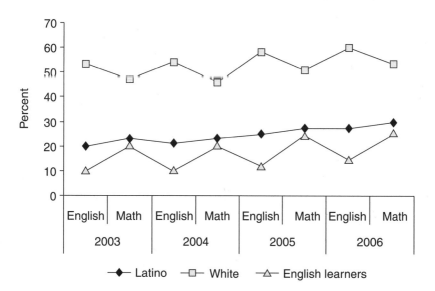

FIGURE 1.2 Percent of Latino and white students scoring at proficient and above on California standardized tests, 2003–2006. (Data from California Department of Education 2006.)

guage instruction distracts from the more critical issue: what must be done to increase the achievement of this population?

Figure 1.2 illustrates the very large gaps between Latino (English proficient) and white (English-speaking) students, and between English learners and English speakers. Given that these English learners comprise a significant portion of the Latino student population (about 50 percent in California), and that the population of both English learners and Latinos is growing rapidly, these data lend urgency to the challenge.

Finally, in 2002 No Child Left Behind, the reauthorization of the federal Elementary and Secondary Education Act, took effect with far-reaching consequences for all low-income students. NCLB was a double-edged sword for Latino students. For the first time, schools across the nation were required to report information about the educational progress of all students, broken down by subgroup categories including race/ethnicity and English learner status. No longer could schools bury the inequalities in student outcomes within test score averages. This change brought almost immediate attention to the very large gaps in performance among subgroups of students. Interestingly, the law also included language to protect students who did not speak English from being tested with measures in English that were not reliable or valid for their purpose. Unfortunately, however, the federal government did nothing to enforce this language, and the high stakes testing required by the law came down especially hard on Latino students who were just learning English but were required to demonstrate what they knew on a test in English they could not understand. In California the *Coachella Valley Unified School District et al. v. the State of California et al.* lawsuit sought to prod the state to adhere to federal guidelines for testing English learners, and allow appropriate testing accommodations and/or testing in the language that the students understand. The case is currently on appeal, having lost on the first round at the state district court in June 2007.

In addition to the problems created by testing students in a language they do not understand, NCLB required that all students be proficient in core subjects by 2014, and that annual progress toward that goal be demonstrated on standardized achievement tests. If annual progress was inadequate for more than two years, schools were sanctioned and could ultimately be disbanded if they did not improve. Of course the schools that have failed to make adequate yearly progress have been disproportionately those with large populations of Latino and English learner students. Thus many of the schools that serve these students have been labeled as failures, which has demoralized and created anxiety among parents, teachers, and students. Stories abound of students who worry about beloved teachers losing their jobs because the students were unable to perform adequately on a test that was unintelligible to them. There is widespread consensus that NCLB has done more to hurt poor and minority students than to help them, even though this was certainly not the intent.[67]

In sum, there has been a political assault over the last several years on the Latino population in the United States, and especially in the Southwest, that has had enormous consequences for the way in which Latino students are educated. The assault began with attempts to deny schooling and other services to undocumented students (who are largely Latino). This was followed by initiatives that reduced access to higher education through bans on affirmative action in California, Texas, Washington, and Michigan. Next, in several states English learners were subjected to a policy of "sink or swim" that had been outlawed by the Supreme Court decision *Lau v. Nichols* in 1974. Then a high stakes testing regimen was established that resulted in these English learners having to meet impossible standards on tests in English that they could not understand. Finally, voluntary measures that reduced ethnic and linguistic isolation in public schools were ruled unconstitutional by the Supreme Court. Taken together, these policies and decisions have restricted options for educators, created ever higher educational hurdles, fostered a chilly environment for K–12 educators, and impeded access to higher education for Latino and other minority students.

Class, Language, and American Education

The idealistic American belief that (almost) everyone deserves a second chance, and the myth that the American Dream can be achieved by anyone who is willing to work hard, have always been in tension with class privilege. Contrary to the perception of many Americans, the United States has less income mobility then most other developed nations and it is increasingly difficult in this country to ascend in the class structure.[68] Everyone has heard of a poor immigrant student who becomes valedictorian of her class and goes on to Harvard, or a Latino entrepreneur who builds a small chain of *tortillerías* and becomes a wealthy businessman. In some ways this makes it even more difficult to confront class and racial privilege. The stories that stem from a "second chance" school system where a student can drop out of high school and still end up with an Ivy League degree, or where an immigrant can build a business and become a millionaire, obscure the reality that this rarely happens—and undermine efforts to really make good on the American promise of equality.

While measures such as providing basic social services (as other modern nations do without question), employing affirmative-action principles to broaden the pool of applicants for jobs or college admission, and offering bilingual instruction to ease the transition to a new culture and language (and possibly maintaining a cultural and intellectual asset) only minimally improve access to societal benefits, they are often framed as creating "unfair advantages" for minorities and immigrants. The prevailing mythology is that the society is open and welcoming of all who are willing to work hard and play by the rules. But of course, Americans have ironically never been very welcoming

of immigrants, and racial and ethnic tensions have not been eradi-
cated from this nation. Now there is mounting evidence that the
intergenerational mobility of Mexican immigrants may not follow the
path of earlier immigrants for a variety of social and economic reasons.[69] Moreover, recent anti-immigrant sentiment, which has led to
increased sanctions on undocumented workers and attempts to withhold basic services, may further slow the social and economic integration of the children of immigrants who are born in the United
States.

Parent education is a powerful predictor of student performance
not just because parents with little education cannot help their children at home—many wealthy parents are not able or inclined to help
their children at home either. But parent education is essential because it is tied to class, and class privilege is tied to social and cultural
capital—access to power and authority, to networks of influential and
informed friends and colleagues, to the understanding of the work-
ings of "the system" that allow those with privilege in society to maintain it. And the reason that the middle class is so reluctant to even the
playing field is not just that its members truly believe that things as
presently structured are indeed equal, but also because in a highly
competitive society in which opportunity is rationed, there can be
very real personal consequences to releasing one's grip on class privilege. Perhaps especially in a society where class distinctions are not
as rigid, the stakes are higher. Accounts of attempts to truly restruc-
ture opportunity in schools, for example, are rife with examples of
middle-class parents organizing effectively to prevent more equitable
redistribution of school resources.[70]

A few years ago one of us was doing research in a school district
that served two very different populations. On the hillsides above
the school lived the children of prosperous businesspeople—lawyers,
doctors, and other professionals—who were almost exclusively white.
In the valley below lived very low-income, largely Mexican migrant

workers and others who tended the crops. In the hillside community the children spoke English; in the valley they spoke Spanish. A very enterprising and innovative young principal saw an opportunity in these differences and decided to create a dual-language school where the children from the hills could learn Spanish alongside the children from the valley who would learn English. The school was very successful, the PTA parents were delighted, and it even earned a blue ribbon award from the state for being one of its highest achieving schools. When the principal teased apart the achievement data, however, he found that the students from the hills were, indeed, performing at very high levels while learning a second language, but that the students in the valley had not made nearly as much progress, and many continued to perform at unacceptably low levels in both languages. He surmised that the problem was that the students from the valley came to school in kindergarten far behind their affluent peers, that they had few educational resources available to them when they returned home at the end of the day, and that they needed additional instruction to catch up. His proposed solution? To use funds that were earmarked for desegregation to provide an all-day kindergarten for the valley students. He did not have enough money to provide all-day kindergarten for all students, so because the affluent children were not only excelling in school but also had many other educational and recreational opportunities outside of school, he decided to focus the limited funds on the valley students.

The hillside parents, hearing that the students in the valley were going to get a whole-day kindergarten, and their children, who already bore the burden of being bussed to the school (about a thirty-minute trip) would not receive this benefit, organized and threatened to remove their children from the school if their children were not given the opportunity to attend the full-day kindergarten, thereby putting in jeopardy the desegregation funding that paid for the program. The principal was forced to acquiesce. The full-day kindergarten was opened to all students on a first-come, first-served basis so that only some of the valley children were able to attend along with children from the hills, and the disparities in achievement continued relatively unabated. Perhaps the parents from the hills cannot be blamed for wanting for their children all that the schools had to offer. They were not trying to create a disadvantage for the children from the valley; they were only trying to secure a benefit for their own children. But in the end the outcome was the same: it was not possible to redistribute resources in a way that would allow the Latino students, whose parents were politically powerless, to catch up to peers whose parents were far more savvy about how to pressure the system.

Later in this book we will revisit Carlos and Andrés, whom the reader met at the beginning of this chapter, and some of their peers. Both of these young men began high school full of hope and high aspirations. They were identified by a college access program as "high potential," with good test scores and an articulated desire to "go to college." The program intervened on their behalf and provided them with additional counseling and a better curriculum than they would probably otherwise have been exposed to. But as we will see, they will still encounter many hurdles. Students who attend poor schools in risky neighborhoods are likely to have peers who, even when they are supportive of their friends' academic achievement, have little to offer in terms of academic help or advice. Their parents, too, often do not have the social capital—knowledge of the educational system and the critical actors in it—to guide their children. And these students are products of a political environment that erodes opportunity and limits the options of both teachers and students, ultimately affecting the educational outcomes for many Latino students, even those who do not appear to be "at risk."

CHAPTER TWO

On Being Latino or Latina
in America

To an outsider, Carlos and Andrés may have seemed like quite different students in the tenth grade: Carlos was getting into trouble and letting his grades slip, and Andrés was working hard to get good grades and help his mother raise his younger brothers. But in fact, they had much in common. Both boys had two parents at home, which actually provided advantages many of their peers did not have: only 65 percent of Latino children live in a two-parent household compared to 78 percent of non-Hispanic white youth.[1] And with respect to educational background, both Carlos and Andrés mirrored national statistics fairly accurately; they appeared to be following in their parents' educational footsteps. Andrés's stepfather had the equivalent of a high school education, but his mother had finished high school and completed a couple of years of community college— Andrés too appeared to be headed toward college. Neither of Carlos's parents had finished high school, and Carlos's track record could easily lead to his dropping out of high school as well. In addition, both sets of parents, regardless of educational background, struggled to work at any job they could find to support their families.

Both of these young men were growing up in barrios, or Latino neighborhoods largely inhabited by other Mexican-origin families like their own. In fact, their communities were ethnically isolated; that is, very few non-Latino families lived there. Much of the time they heard only Spanish on the street and in the neighborhood, and what they knew of the world outside their immediate environment was brought to them largely by the television set, because neither boy had ventured far. The social context in which they were growing up and that was shaping their vision of the future would exert heavy pressures on both. Among those pressures were some created by neighborhood peers—some of whom disparaged the idea of doing well in school and being a "schoolboy," and others who, seeking a sense of safety and belonging in a society that they felt had rejected them, had joined gangs that would lead them into the world of the criminal justice system.

In this chapter we explore the social context in which young Latinos grow up in the United States, and how this social context shapes their ability to navigate successfully through school and on to college. We are acutely aware that by pointing out the multiple ways in which Latinos are disadvantaged in American society, and implicating these factors in their educational achievement and attainment, one could conclude that schools can do nothing to improve these students' outcomes. Worse, some might conclude that Latino culture is to blame for their situation and that the students themselves are "defective." This is neither our belief nor our intent. There are many examples of both schools and communities attempting to respond to these challenges, and there is abundant evidence of the extraordinary resilience of many Latino students. We do, however, argue that powerful and negative social and economic forces limit both institutional and individual agency.

We leave Andrés and Carlos for the time being, returning to them in Chapter 5, where we will examine their particular circumstances in detail. Here we introduce other students whose social circumstances probably should have precluded college, but who have managed to successfully enroll in competitive four-year universities. Alex, Amalia, and Leticia share aspects of their lives that illuminate the challenges so many Latinos face.[2]

All children require substantial investment in order to grow and develop normally, to avoid problems with the law, and to become productive members of society. They need good nutrition, health care to address medical needs, a safe and decent place to live, and nurturing families and communities in order to develop both cognitive and noncognitive skills, healthy self-concepts, and a desire to do well in school (and later, in a chosen occupation). Most middle-class children arrive at school already having been heavily invested in by their families and communities. The majority are born to mothers who had consistent prenatal care; their own nutrition is at least adequate; they have visited doctors and dentists regularly where any acute medical problems have been attended to; and if they have had vision problems, they have likely been corrected. They are also very likely to have had safe areas to play, educational toys to play with, and caregivers who were skilled at introducing them to the rudiments of literacy and numeracy.

Many poor children, however, have had little investment in their development aside from the care that their families are able to provide with very limited resources. They may have inadequate nutrition or lack medical, dental, or vision care—that is, they may come to school hungry, they may be unable to see the board at the front of the class or the writing on the paper in front of them, and they may have toothaches or ear infections that interrupt their ability to attend to lessons. They may return home every day to a community that lacks safe places for children to play and so their parents may discourage normal neighborhood exploration. In addition, the toys they play with are not likely to be of the sort that will prepare them to succeed in school; their harried parents may have turned instead to television as an affordable babysitter that occupies them for an average of four hours a day or more, robbing them of time for reading and active play.[3] Poor children are less likely than their middle-class peers to have many books in the home, and they are less likely to be read to by parents or caregivers, or to observe those adults reading for enjoyment.[4] If they are undocumented, their families may live in fear of separation and deportation; if they do not speak English, they are likely living in a community in which English is seldom heard, and they are also likely to move frequently in search of affordable housing. These children are dependent on the schools and society to invest in them in areas where their parents cannot.

But Americans tend to believe that people are supposed to make it on their own, to "pull themselves up by their bootstraps"; meaning, in part, that public support is to be provided only on an emergency basis, and increasingly, only for legally documented residents.[5] The American Dream, after all, is about hard work and not depending on anyone else for a handout. That so many people are effectively shut out of the American Dream because of an inability to access very basic resources is not dealt with effectively either in American mythology or American social policy.[6] In fact, a failure to succeed in American society is typically attributed to individuals, who are thought through laziness or squandering of opportunity to have created their own fate.[7] This belief is so strongly held that even the poor often blame themselves for their own condition.[8]

Figure 2.1 illustrates the social context for youth development, where developmental needs, family conditions, and community and neighborhood environment all contribute to the growth and development of Latino youth.

Poverty and economic insecurity are constants throughout the social context in which many Latino youth are born and grow up. While it does not appear in every box in Figure 2.1, for many Latino chil-

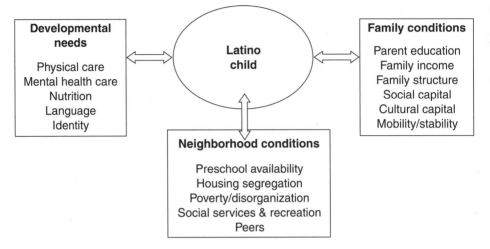

FIGURE 2.1 Social context for Latino youth

dren it underlies—and undermines—every facet of life, disproportionately affecting their personal development. While many Americans probably believe that the United States has the highest standard
of living in the world, this is not the case. It is true that the middle
and upper classes in the United States have material benefits that ex-
ceed those of most other nations, but the United States also suffers
from extremely high rates of child poverty. That is, Americans live in
a highly polarized economy in which a few hold great wealth, many
are modestly comfortable, and a substantial percentage live in circumstances significantly more difficult than they would find in almost any other first-world country.[9] The Luxembourg Income Study,
which has tracked poverty in fifteen wealthy nations (twelve European countries, Canada, Australia, and the United States), has concluded over two decades that among all these countries, the United
States has the highest rate of child poverty—just over 20 percent in
1997.[10] The Luxembourg definition of poverty is having an income
"below one-half of the median equivalent income . . . so low that
these children and others in their family were not able to partici-

pate enough in community activities to be perceived, by both themselves and others, as regular members of society."[11] The official U.S. poverty classification is far below this level.[12] About 9.5 million people, 17 percent of whom were children, went hungry in America in 2003.[13] And these were disproportionately African American and Latino children.

Latino Poverty and Children's Developmental Needs

The Luxembourg Income Study's figures on Latino poverty in particular are alarming. The study found that in 1997 nearly 37 percent of Hispanic (Latino) children were living in poverty in the United States, compared to about 12 percent of white children—in other words, the poverty rate for Hispanic children was three times that of white children. While the U.S. Census and the Luxembourg study have different definitions of poverty, both sets of data show that Latino children are at much greater risk for poverty than white children. In 2005, the U.S. Census reported a poverty rate for all children under age eighteen of about 18 percent. The poverty rate for Hispanic children under age eighteen, by contrast, was more than 28 percent, double that of white children, of whom 14 percent lived in poverty.

Another way to measure poverty is by students' eligibility for free and reduced price lunches at school. The National School Lunch Program (NSLP) was first established in 1946 to provide free meals for children living in impoverished homes. The criterion for eligibility for free lunch is family income no higher than 130 percent of the federal poverty guidelines; for reduced price lunch, students must come from homes with incomes no higher than 180 percent of federal poverty guidelines. These criteria are in line with international poverty thresholds such as those used by the Luxembourg Economic Study. In 2005, 73 percent of Latino (Hispanic) fourth-graders in the

United States were eligible for the NSLP. This was higher than for any other group of children in the public schools. Among white students, 24 percent were eligible for the program.[14]

The situation for very young Latinos is even worse than for older children. Looking at children under six years old, the U.S. Census reports that more than 31 percent of Hispanic children, compared to 17.5 percent of white children, were living in poverty in 2005. Among Hispanics, the two most numerous subgroups—Mexican origin (64 percent of all Hispanics) and Puerto Ricans (9 percent)—were also the most likely to be living in poverty. Immigrants and children of immigrants comprise roughly one-half of the Latino population in the United States and although almost all young children of immigrants (93 percent) are citizens themselves, more than one-quarter have parents who are not documented, and 56 percent live in families designated "low-income" (because they earn less than double the federal poverty level).[15] In short, young children of immigrants have higher levels of economic hardship than children in native-born families. In addition, these children of immigrants receive lower levels of benefits than do children of native-born parents. Randy Capps and his colleagues at the Urban Institute attribute this phenomenon to the fact that young children of immigrants tend to live in mixed status families. That is, some members of the family have legal status while others do not because the families move back and forth across the U.S.-Mexican border.[16]

Alex, an undocumented student who has lived on both sides of the border with his parents and four siblings, described how his family came to have mixed status.

> My three other siblings were born here because my parents came here legally to work. Then they went back to Mexico and we, my brother and I, were born there. So when things started to get bad in Mexico and they wanted to return, it meant us coming over ille-

gally while the rest could cross. The crime rate in Mexico is so high; I always lived afraid that someone [would] come and kidnap me. People are just afraid. That is why families try to find a safer environment.

Alex went on to describe that his family did not have health insurance. "Luckily, I have not ever been very sick in my life. But the times that I needed to go to a clinic it was the farm workers' clinic in Yakima. My mom managed to get us some coupons, but we did not have health insurance."

There are many reasons why children of immigrants may not receive publicly funded benefits such as welfare (Temporary Assistance for Needy Families, or TANF), food stamps, and Medicaid. Perhaps the children are undocumented and so are ineligible for these programs. Maybe they are documented, but live in a state where even documented immigrants are not eligible for TANF and Medicaid. Or perhaps, as is the case for many eligible citizen children, they do not receive services because their undocumented parents either do not know about the availability of such services for their children or fear that using public services will jeopardize their own legal status.[17]

Poverty is measured fundamentally by a lack of money. But the effects of poverty, especially on children, extend far beyond the stretched budgets of the poor. Children who live in poverty lack not only material comforts and a sense of possibility; many also lack attention to basic needs that will condemn them to repeating the cycle of undereducation and poverty that they are born into. Many poor Latino children also lack basic nutrition. Fresh fruits, vegetables, and healthy sources of protein are among the most expensive foods for sale, and because fewer chain supermarkets and discount stores choose to locate in areas heavily populated by minority and low-income groups, there is often little competition to drive down prices. Consequently, the poor often pay more for the same or lower-quality food products available elsewhere.[18] Many families must make do with low-cost, carbohydrate-heavy diets that fill the stomach but deprive the developing mind and body. While simple vitamin and mineral supplements provided by schools can improve student performance, many schools forgo breakfast programs for students who qualify because it is so difficult to organize these programs in the morning before school.[19] Michael Martinez cites a number of experiments in the United States and abroad in which vitamin and dietary supplements have been shown to significantly increase the mental capacity of poor children. For example, in a carefully controlled study of California secondary students reported in 1991, those receiving 100 percent of recommended daily vitamin requirements outperformed controls on both reading and math CTBS scores, and students with particularly low concentrations of required vitamins, on receiving supplements, gained an average of 8.1 IQ points over the control group.[20] One has to question why more low-income youth have not been helped by such simple vitamin supplement programs.

In a nation with such abundant food, it is sometimes difficult to imagine that there are children in the schools who actually go without, but Amalia, a Mexican American student, recounted how getting enough food for the family's dinner was a daily struggle. Born in Phoenix, Arizona, the daughter of a Mexican immigrant woman, Amalia moved with her mother to Southern California in order to flee her mother's abusive husband. Amalia was only nine years old, the oldest of four children. Her mother had gained legal resident status, but had only a sixth grade education and no work skills. Amalia, her three siblings, and her mother lived in one room of a home they shared with another family. In exchange for a place to live, Amalia's mother handed over her welfare check to the primary renters of the house. She recounted how the family of five lived on food stamps as well as whatever her mother could earn from selling on the streets—*elotes* (roasted corn ears), ice cream, trinkets. The children, Amalia explained, would often "sneak food from the cafeteria line to bring home for dinner. . . . When I think about it, I don't know how we survived."

Many poor Latino children also come to school with vision problems that prevent them from participating fully in classroom instruction. Some studies have found that more than 50 percent of urban poor children have correctable vision problems—importantly, not just distance vision, but problems doing close-up work—that are often overlooked in mass screenings available in some schools.[21] Dental care, too, can be a luxury if there isn't enough money for food or rent. Nothing is more distracting than a painful toothache, and dental cavities are three times as prevalent among poor children as among middle-class children with consistent dental care.[22] Leticia, a young undocumented student who came to the United States as a young child with her parents, explained how any kind of dental care depended on the legal status of the family member.

> The first time I ever went to a dentist, it was at school. If something hurt, you just used home remedies. My brothers and sisters who were born here, they can get dental care. But I was eleven years old the first time I saw a dentist and I didn't go again until college.

Although immigrants and the poor can have difficulty getting medical and dental services, they can also be unwittingly recruited for unscrupulous schemes by people trying to scam government programs. Amalia recalled spending a lot of time at a dentist's office when she was a child, receiving "treatments that we probably didn't need. But they gave us coupons for free dinners if we would go to the treatment. And so we were always at the dentist; it was a way to get dinner."

There are several medical conditions associated with poverty that can affect learning in chronic, negative ways. Prematurity and low birth weight, asthma, and otitis media (infection of the middle ear) all occur disproportionately among the poor. Asthma in particular appears to be epidemic among inner-city poor children. For reasons presumed to be associated with poorer environmental conditions in low-income urban neighborhoods, one in three Puerto Rican children in Chicago suffers from asthma, and as a result is more likely to miss school than his or her middle-income peers.[23] While otitis media commonly afflicts all children between birth and three years of age, it is more likely to go untreated in poor children—and the hearing loss associated with untreated ear infections has been associated with reading problems in school as well as the development of attention deficit disorder.[24]

Diabetes has reached epidemic proportions in the Latino community. Latino children in general, and Mexican-origin children in particular, are especially susceptible to developing type II diabetes, which has devastating long-term effects on health status and can impair learning. Latino children are 90 percent more likely than white children to develop diabetes, the highest rate for any ethnic group. Multiple factors are responsible for this high risk, but prominent among them are obesity and lack of exercise.[25] One study conducted in the 1990s found that 29 percent of Mexican-origin girls ages six to eleven were overweight, compared to 23 percent of white girls.[26] Overweight is of course related to both diet and exercise, as well as to genetic makeup. Ironically the prototypically healthy diet of Mexican immigrants that contributes to their unusually good health in the first generation—corn, beans, rice, fruits, and small amounts of meat—converts to a high fat, high sugar (low cost) fast food diet in the United States—where fast foods are an inexpensive alternative to fresh fruits and vegetables, and where, at least in low-income urban neighborhoods, opportunities for active play and recreation are limited, and where schools often lack the time or the facilities for sports and physical education.

Of course, not all poor Latino children suffer from these medical conditions, but taken together, the higher incidence of these conditions introduces large, additional educational risks into the lives of all poor Latino children. For in addition to the risks that arise from failing to treat the children's health problems, there is an ever-present risk to the family's livelihood if a parent gets sick and either cannot access health care or cannot take the time away from work to be treated. Lack of dependable health care, then, is a family problem that can undermine support for children in both direct and indirect ways.

In response to the question "What did you do when you were sick?" Leticia smiled and said,

> You just wait until you get well. There was nothing else to do. My father worked several jobs every day; he had to carry heavy stuff and he had two hernias, but he'd say, "How are we going to pay the rent if I go to the hospital?" So, they got worse. He finally had surgery after twenty years.

The United States has a meager safety net for children who are born into poverty.[27] According to the Census Bureau in 2005, more than one-third of all Latino families are without any health insurance compared to approximately 11 percent of white families.[28] Consequently, Latino children are less likely to have health insurance than any other ethnic group, and without insurance, they are less likely not only to visit a doctor, but also to even have a health care provider.[29] County health care offices may provide some basic services for the uninsured, but using them requires that parents be able to navigate the system, find transportation and childcare, take time off work, and often wait many, many hours to be seen: an impossible scenario for many low-income parents. Routine vision and dental checkups are anything but routine when a parent must give up a day's wages or even risk losing a job to keep such an appointment.

Amalia was a determined young woman who had overcome enormous odds to earn a college degree. She could not recall anyone else from her neighborhood who had gone on to a four-year college. She thought back to when she was in grade school and the storefront medical clinic where she and her family went whenever they had a medical need.

> The place was run-down and you would wait all day for a doctor to see you because no one had an appointment, everyone was waiting, watching the novelas on the TV. . . . One time my brother needed an X-ray and they told us we had to go somewhere else, across town, to get it. But since it was far away and we didn't have any way to get there, we just couldn't go. So he just never got the X-ray.

Undocumented parents, even if their children are citizens, may also be reluctant to engage with government-sponsored health and social services for fear of being reported. Thus the task of addressing the basic or chronic medical needs of poor children—needs that surely affect students' ability to focus on school and succeed academically—often falls to the schools themselves, which are generally unable to answer the challenge.

Family Socioeconomic Conditions

The very large differences that we saw in the test scores for Latino students compared to others—even at the beginning of kindergarten—can be attributed to a number of factors that are strongly associated with poverty and its immediate consequences. A national study of the characteristics of entering kindergartners found that Latino children are much more likely than white or Asian children to have five risk factors for school failure at the point of school entry: poverty, a single-parent household, a mother with less than high school education, a primary language other than English, and a mother unmarried at the time of the child's birth.[30] Whereas only 6 percent of white children and 17 percent of Asian children had two or more of these risk factors, fully one-third (33 percent) of Latinos had two or more risk factors. In addition, Latino children are much less likely to go to preschool, where some of these risk factors might be ameliorated.

Family Structure

An analysis of the National Early Childhood Longitudinal Study of 1998 shows that among all Latino kindergarteners who entered school in that year, only 65 percent were living with both biological parents. By contrast, 74 percent of that year's white kindergarteners were living with both biological parents.[31] The disparities are likely to grow in the coming years, because out-of-wedlock births are increasing at a faster rate for Latinos than for any other group.[32] For example, the out-of-wedlock birthrate for Latinos doubled between 1980 and 2004 from 23.6 percent of all births to 46.4 percent. The proportion of white out-of-wedlock births grew more steeply between 1980 and 2004 (from 9.6 percent to 24.5 percent), but has not accelerated at the same rate in recent years. Out-of-wedlock births are a concern because women raising children without partners are much more likely to be poor and to experience psychological stress and depression, factors that affect parenting—and the development of the child.[33]

Family Cultural and Social Capital

A number of studies have found that ethnic minority families have uniformly high aspirations for their children.[34] But not all parents are equally endowed with the skills and resources to help their children realize these aspirations. Low-income and minority parents often lack the cultural capital (knowledge of how the system works and what it values) and social capital (access to important social networks) that are such an essential part of how middle-class white and Asian parents support their children's academic achievement.[35] Even modest differences in education and income among lower-income families can be associated with enhanced academic outcomes for their children. One study investigated a sample of 154 former Head Start students who were functioning at high academic levels and found that mothers with only somewhat more education and resources were able to confer intellectual advantages on their children that marginally less well-educated and somewhat poorer mothers were not.[36]

Cultural capital also takes the form of knowing how to manage public resources, like school curricula, to the advantage of one's children. Annette Lareau has demonstrated how middle-class parents effectively "manage" the school system and its resources through active engagement with school staff to afford the best opportunities for their children, while low-income parents tend to refrain from interacting with teachers and school administrators, accepting the school's decisions at face value.[37] In another study of middle-class cultural capital, Elizabeth Useem showed how well-educated parents, keenly aware of the implications of taking algebra versus basic math in junior high school, actively intervened when they disagreed with their children's placement. In contrast, parents with lower levels of education were largely unaware of the implications of being tracked into a low math course and tended to trust the school personnel's decisions.[38] Even among middle-class parents from underrepresented communities of color, cultural capital may be in short supply. Often these families represent the first generation in the middle class, so they do not have these middle-class experiences in their own backgrounds to draw on as they guide their children. In addition, they may still have many lower-income family members who depend on their resources, which lowers the available resources to spend on the child.[39] Clearly, attitudes, tastes, and dispositions develop over generations and result from exposure to particular cultural experiences that are unique to class categories; consequently, the more generations that a family belongs to the middle class, the more cultural capital they are able to accumulate.

Research has also converged on a particular parenting style that appears to be associated with the majority culture and a middle-class orientation. Parents who are classified as "authoritative"—firm in their expectations of their children yet warm in their relationships with them, giving them significant autonomy—are most likely to have children who do well in school.[40] Yet many Latinos are accustomed to parenting in a more traditional, "authoritarian" style, in which parents set inflexible boundaries and young children are discouraged from exploring their surroundings. This parenting style, however, may be essential in other ways. Latino parents may be responding well to their particular sociocultural circumstances, adapting their parenting style to the realities of their situation. Higher-risk urban environments may call for a disciplinary style in which young people are not allowed to "explore" their less secure neighborhoods.[41] Indeed, many academically successful minority students credit their success to not being allowed to participate in activities or socialize with their peers from the neighborhood because it may have distracted from their focus on school.[42] As Amalia pointed out, "It was probably because I was always having to take care of my brothers and sisters, I never had a chance to hang out with the other kids in the [projects] where I grew up." Unfortunately, however, this parenting style may not foster the kinds of behaviors that are prized in American classrooms, where autonomy in problem solving is expected.[43]

Family Mobility

Family residential mobility can also play a large role in the educational achievement of children. School changes are frequently related to family income, because low-wage families are less likely to be able to own their homes, and renters, especially low-income renters, move more frequently than home owners.[44] A study of low-income, urban elementary students found that those who changed schools within the first five grades were also more likely to have behavioral problems, be held back a grade, and have poorer attendance.[45] Changing schools often means lost time and lost learning because students must adjust to a new curriculum and a new peer group—a process made more difficult because frequent moves also mean that few people in the school know the student, or his or her family's needs. Both young children and adolescents can be negatively affected by moves that result in school changes; young children are more likely to have school adjustment problems and older children are more likely to drop out of school altogether.[46] Robert Ream and Ricardo Stanton-Salazar describe the effects of high mobility on a propensity to drop out as being associated with the increased likelihood of hanging out with students who have dropped out of school: "Mobility tends to disrupt the social root systems of academically oriented friends who would otherwise fortify school success, [and] it simultaneously . . . strengthens the social root systems of dropout friends who disrupt others' success in school."[47]

In schools with high proportions of low-income and minority youth in particular, multiple school changes, especially at the secondary level, can also be the result of school practices that transfer students who are perceived to be problems. Often these children are among the brightest in their classes, but have difficulty "fitting in" at school.[48] About half of school changes at the secondary level are actually student-initiated, because of difficulties the student is experiencing in school. Marginalization almost certainly contributes to these difficulties for many Latino students.

Mexican-origin youth change schools about twice as often as non-Latino white students, and immigrant youth are even more likely to change schools.[49] This is due in part to unstable economic conditions in families that can require parents to move to seek work, as well as the high cost of housing and the difficulty of locating rental units that will accommodate large numbers of family members. There is also evidence of continuing discrimination in the housing market, in spite of long-standing fair housing laws. Latinos, and especially Mexican immigrants, are sometimes not steered toward available housing in nonminority neighborhoods, and some landlords refuse to rent to them.[50] In any case, residential and school mobility are most often associated with negative circumstances and take a disproportionate toll on the achievement of low-income and Latino students.

Neighborhood Conditions

There is considerable debate in the literature about the relative effects of a neighborhood, as distinct from the influence of family or peers, on student achievement. But at least two theoretical models help to explain how neighborhoods can affect the development of youth in ways that in turn help determine their schooling outcomes. Neighborhood Resource Theory argues that the quality of local resources available to families (such as parks, libraries, and child care facilities) affects child developmental outcomes. Because poor children's neighborhoods have fewer of these supportive resources than neighborhoods in which middle-class children grow up, researchers conjecture that low-income children receive less exposure to developmentally supportive and enriching activities.[51] Of course, even when such resources are available, a family's access to them is still mediated by the parents. Parents who are better educated and better informed are more likely to access whatever resources exist. Thus methodologically, it can be difficult to distinguish the influence of neighborhoods from the effects of parenting.

Neighborhoods provide another important resource to children—role models—and a second theory, Collective Socialization Theory, argues that more affluent neighborhoods generally provide more successful role models as well as stronger support for behaviors associated with school success.[52] Thus middle-income students are more likely to encounter both adults and peers in their communities who are supportive of high educational goals and can even assist young people in achieving them. While both theories make intuitive sense and almost certainly contribute to development in some ways, Collective Socialization Theory, like Neighborhood Resource Theory, is plagued by methodological problems that make it difficult to prove the independent effects of neighborhoods. For example, Nancy Darling and Laurence Steinberg note that it is difficult to separate the influence of peers in these neighborhoods from the effects of the neighborhoods themselves.[53]

A third aspect of neighborhoods that almost certainly affects children's development and therefore their academic performance is safety. When simply coming and going to school is risky for children because gangs in their low-income neighborhood may assault them, or when staying after school for extracurricular activities is out of the question because traveling through the neighborhood after dark is not safe, children's educational opportunities are limited. Impoverished neighborhoods are also known to be more associated with juvenile delinquency and teen childbearing—two powerful inhibitors of social mobility—and Latinas have higher rates of teenage pregnancy than any other ethnic group.[54] Neighborhood factors, then, may help continue the cycle of poverty and undereducation, given that teenage mothers often lack the skills and resources to prepare their own children for success in school. A report by the National Academy of Sciences on the problems of adolescence argues that too much emphasis is placed on "high-risk" youth, and not enough on the high-risk settings in which they live and go to school.[55]

Low-income neighborhoods not only represent increased risks for youth; they are also sites of more limited opportunities. Part-time jobs (which if limited in hours have been shown to support healthy development in young people) are less plentiful in low-income neighborhoods.[56] In fact, middle-income high school students are more likely to hold a job than low-income students, precisely because so few jobs are available in low-income neighborhoods. Moreover, transportation to where the jobs exist is also harder to come by in low-income neighborhoods. Fewer people have cars at their disposal, and public transportation is less available.[57] Thus opportunities to earn money and to become familiar with potential career and job opportunities are often foreclosed in the neighborhoods that Latinos inhabit.

Housing Segregation

Housing segregation is intimately related to school segregation, because schools tend to draw students from their surrounding communities. Moreover, in minority-segregated school communities, the segregation of the school can help keep neighborhoods segregated because nonminority home buyers are reluctant to purchase homes in neighborhoods where the local schools are largely minority—and so perceived to be weak. Additionally, the weak market for homes in these segregated communities keeps their value relatively low and makes home ownership in these areas less of an asset that can be drawn on to advance family fortunes, such as helping to pay for college tuition. Research points to other reasons for housing segregation as well. For Mexicans in particular, lack of economic mobility (jobs without any mobility potential), barriers faced in accumulating intergenerational wealth, and persistently low education levels appear to make it harder for them to move out of ethnic enclaves into the mainstream.[58] Perhaps not surprisingly, then, between 1980 and

2000, Latino housing segregation increased substantially, especially in the West.[59]

In addition, a new pattern of segregation has been developing in metropolitan areas throughout the country. As suburbs that were once the haven of white families have become increasingly Latino, they have been partitioned to maintain separation between white and Latino families, and consequently the schools that serve the two groups.[60] Segregation at the neighborhood level means that the social and cultural capital among families—and among schoolchildren—continues to be unequally distributed.

Housing segregation has particularly onerous effects on Latino students learning English. When students lack appropriate language models and individuals with whom to interact in English, their acquisition of academic English is delayed. As a recent evaluation of the state of linguistic isolation among California's Latino students concluded,

> Our analysis of the hypersegregation of Hispanic students, and particularly Spanish-speaking ELLs [English-language learners], suggests that little or no attention has been given to the consequences of linguistic isolation for a population whose future depends on the acquisition of English. . . . For ELLs, interaction with ordinary English-speaking peers is essential to their English language development and consequently to their acquisition of academic English.[61]

Lack of Peer Support for Achievement in School

Adolescent peer groups are commonly portrayed as having a negative influence on the values and behavior of youth. Drug and alcohol use, gang membership, and a culture of underachievement have been shown to be associated with peer influence.[62] But peers can also have a positive influence on each other. They can support academic goals and serve as important sources of information for upward mobility. In his study of Latino high school youth, for example, Ricardo Stanton-Salazar found examples of students with little traditional social capital who nonetheless supported each other and built important social networks with knowledgeable agents in their school.[63] This phenomenon, however, appears to be most common among Asian students.[64]

Students who hang out with low-performing friends tend to perform at lower levels as well, and those whose friends are dropouts are at higher risk for dropping out themselves.[65] Latino students, who like other ethnic groups tend to hang out with friends who are their own ethnicity and who live in their neighborhoods, are more likely to be with students who are low performing or dropouts.[66] Based on a survey of more than twenty thousand adolescents, Laurence Steinberg reported that one in five of his respondents said that his or her friends make fun of students who do well in school, and this was particularly true for Latino students.[67] Those Latino students who aspire to high achievement sometimes report being accused by lower-performing peers of "acting white" or acting like a schoolboy.[68] Such peer pressure during adolescence may be especially persuasive for minority youth, who are often excluded from mainstream peer groups.[69]

There also appears to be a gender difference. In a study of how Latino and other youth develop and change their aspirations for the future, we found that while relatively large percentages of urban Latina high school students professed they wanted to be known as a "good student," very few Latino males in either the low-income urban or rural high schools studied said they wanted to be identified this way.[70] Substantial numbers of Latino males conceded that neither they nor their friends "care about school at all," and in this study more than any other group, they contended that their friends influenced their behavior "a lot"—and often in the direction of antischool behaviors.

In an ethnographic study of Latino students in a high school English Language Development (ELD) class, Clayton Hurd found further evidence of Latino students' disaffection with schooling and with their peers who were trying to do well.[71] He describes the following scene:

> During a math lesson the teacher asked the students to name opposite integers. Alejandro (YSA-1), sitting at a table with a group of other boys, volunteered a correct answer. Immediately, the boys in his group broke out in a chorus of "schoolboy, schoolboy," followed by the comment, "now you think you are smart."[72]

Such taunting from peers is bound to shake the confidence of—and discourage participation by—all but the most resilient of students.

Beyond Poverty

Not all Latinos are poor, and not all disadvantage is directly associated with poverty. Slightly less than 28 percent of Latino families have incomes of $60,000 or higher, a reasonable threshold for a family of five to be considered middle class in 2005.[73] The percentage is virtually identical for black families. Half of white families and nearly 60 percent of Asian families, however, have incomes above this mark, and their average family size is smaller by at least one person than that of Latinos.[74] For a family of five, this income, without accumulated wealth, is no guarantee of economic security, nor for Latinos does it guarantee that the family will live in a middle-class neighborhood. In fact, low-income white families are more likely to live in a middle-class neighborhood than are middle-income Latinos.[75] Nonetheless, there are risks to youth that are associated with simply being Latino of whatever class. These include risks associated with mental health and identity development. When socioeconomic status is held constant, but important outcomes are consistently more negative for Latinos than for other groups, some researchers conclude that racism may be a factor, either directly or indirectly. In a recent study of intergenerational mobility among Mexican Americans, based on interviews of more than 1,400 individuals, half of whom had participated in a seminal 1970 study, Edward Telles and Vilma Ortiz found not only a lack of intergenerational mobility, but actual downward mobility over generations. Family members in the third and subsequent generations were, on average, faring worse than those in the second, when parents' socioeconomic resources and other factors were controlled for. The authors concluded that the lack of mobility was related to poor-quality schools and the racialization that occurred there, cementing Mexican Americans' low status in American society.[76]

Mental Health

Depression is a serious mental health problem that leads to lowered motivation, loss of focus, and often underachievement, and Latinos appear to be particularly prone to it. One large study that analyzed the Early Childhood Longitudinal Study (ECLS) national data set found that Mexican-origin young children were judged by their teachers to have better overall mental health than other racial and ethnic groups; other researchers, however, have found exceptionally high rates of depression for Latino youth and adults.[77] Perhaps the lower reported incidence in the early years can be explained by evidence that teachers are less capable of judging certain personality characteristics in Latino youth than in others, presumably because of a difficulty in bridging cultural and linguistic divides.[78] Alternatively, depression may develop over time as a realistic response to the harsh conditions and stress, in part due to racism, that this population faces in the United States. In any case, there is consensus in the literature that Latino youth on the whole suffer disproportionately from depression and that it is more likely to go untreated, leading to social and academic problems.[79]

Identity Development

It has been long understood that adolescence is a period when young people spend a lot of time and energy exploring their identities. Consequently, adolescents are extremely vulnerable to the perceptions of others. How well students do in school, and how others view this academic success or failure, will influence the developing identities of most adolescents. Likewise, ethnic identity formation is often a central feature of adolescence and one that is bound up with a youth's identity as a student. The perception that Latinos are not "smart" or not good students will have to be confronted by students who are both Latino and striving to be a good student. David Hayes-Bautista provides ample evidence of the perceptions that non-Hispanic whites have of Mexican-origin people.[80] He describes a series of focus groups in which white subjects were asked their opinion of a television commercial that was part of a publicity campaign to improve the image of Latinos in the southern California area. The commercial had shown images of Latinos in a variety of situations intended to convey to white audiences that they are "just like us"—medical researchers, soldiers, businessmen, students graduating from college—and ended on a patriotic note that Latinos see themselves as Americans too. But the white audience had difficulty identifying with the message. Over and over they commented that the people in the ad weren't what Latinos are really like. "I got this sense of looking for the Latinos in the picture, and I couldn't find them," said one respondent. Another offered, "In political culture, we don't talk about the middle-class Hispanic. We talk about the barrios, and gangs and the violent, the people who don't have opportunities."[81]

As the focus group facilitator noted, the white participants "had articulated that a key element of the American Dream was the desire to achieve more, to accomplish more, to better oneself [and] they were not sure that Latinos really wanted to progress, particularly into the middle class."[82] This is the perception against which Latino youth must attempt to construct an identity as a good student and an aspirant into the American middle class. For many Latino students, the struggle to reconcile the perceptions of others will result in their rejecting either their ethnicity or the role of good student, neither of which augurs well for healthy personal or psychological development.[83]

Claude Steele has advanced a theory of "stereotype threat" to explain why many blacks, or other minorities, may perform poorly or choose not to participate at all in academic endeavors.[84] He contends that many minorities worry that if they engage in academic competition, they run the risk of confirming the stereotype that they are intellectually inferior if they do not perform at superior levels. According to Steele and others, the pervasive societal belief in the inferiority of some groups weighs heavily on their members when they are confronted with tasks that could result in failure. A number of researchers have extended Steele's work to incorporate studies of Latinos in particular. For example, one such study showed that Latinos, like blacks, also score lower on tests when primed with the idea that their group does not do well on this kind of material.[85] The explanation is that the students feel performance anxiety in settings where any mistake can be seen as an affirmation of the stereotype that Latinos are not as smart as whites. Moreover, Steele showed that, in an effort to protect themselves from stigmatization for low performance, minority students may "disidentify" (that is, plead lack of interest) with academic goals. He argues that such disidentification can lead to disengagement from academic endeavors as well as depressed performance on tests. These findings help to explain why we have found in our own research that so many Latino males, in particular, contend that neither they nor their friends "care about school."[86]

Clayton Hurd described the plight of Carlos M., a high-achieving student taking Advanced Placement courses who nonetheless felt he had to contend with stereotypes in his high school about Latino males.[87] Expressing deep concern about how white students saw him, and how he might feel about asking a "stupid question," he said:

> [All] the little gangs are Mexican, and I get pretty embarrassed. It's my race, you know. And you know how some people can stereotype you? I don't want to be stereotyped as a gangster or nothing. . . . Like in classes you don't want to be judged as a stupid person, like a gang [member]. Like maybe you wear the color or you ask a stupid question—"oh, he is a gang member." Saying "a gangster" doesn't seem like an insult right now, but it's the thought of "oh, he is Mexican, he's gotta do this" . . . that "he is ignorant and stupid just like the other Mexicans that are in gangs." You don't want to be compared like that.[88]

Taken together, all of these social and background factors can, and do, have an enormous influence on the school achievement and educational aspirations of Latino youth. In Chapter 1 we discussed the dismal statistics on educational achievement for low-income Latino youth. Yet many of the effects of poverty and disadvantage continue to affect the performance of these students long after they have entered the middle class. Table 2.1 shows that low-income white students perform nearly as well as upper-middle-income Latino students on the SAT college admissions test. The difference between the average score of low-income white students and upper-middle-class Latino students is a relatively insignificant twenty-five points, or about one-eighth of a standard deviation on a scale that runs from 400 to 1600. By contrast, the differences between white and Latino students are great whatever their socioeconomic situation. White low-income students outscore Latino low-income students by 127 points, or almost two-thirds of a standard deviation. Likewise, middle-class Latinos perform about one-third of a standard deviation (67

Table 2.1 Mean total SAT score by ethnicity and income, 2004

	Income	
Ethnicity	Below $35,000	Above $70,000
Latino	857	1009
	(36%)	(12.5%)
White	984	1076
	(10%)	(33%)

Source: Data from College Board 2004.

points) below middle-class white students, again a significant difference.

If social-class differences between white and Latino students have such powerful effects on achievement, what accounts for the continuing differences in academic performance even when social class is controlled? One answer is that social class as measured by gross categories of income and parent education is so broad a construct that it obscures as much as it reveals, and that low socioeconomic status, especially for people of color, has a continuing legacy. (Of course, as we have suggested earlier, racial discrimination cannot be entirely excluded as having at least indirect effects on some social and educational outcomes.) Movement into the middle class does not overnight erase all the vestiges of low-income disadvantage. Because correlations between academic outcomes (and many other behavioral indicators) and social class (defined as parent education and income) are so high, researchers generally find the measure useful. But it is in data like those reported in Table 2.1 that one can see the serious limitations of the construct. More than one-third of all Latino students taking the SAT come from low-income homes, compared to only 10 percent of whites, and within the low-income category, many more Latinos are clustered at the bottom.

The clustering effect brings up the question of what is truly meant by "low-income." Clearly, low-income Latinos are actually poorer than low-income whites as a group. Latinos also come from larger families so that, in general, they actually have much lower per capita incomes.[89] Moreover, because Latinos, on average, earn less than white workers (and all other ethnic groups), more work hours and more family members working are required to produce the same income.[90] Significantly, these additional hours at work also limit disproportionately the time that Latino parents have to support their children's education.

Ideally, the understanding we have of Latinos' economic situation would encompass meaningful information on wealth, not simply income, which although easier to measure captures only a part of the total picture. Homeownership, for example, which is lower for Latinos than for whites, is not included in income data but certainly affects total wealth, as does the ownership of other property, the assets of relatives, and inheritance. Heather Johnson, in a detailed ethnography of how families from different social classes make choices about their children's schooling, describes how the assets of grandparents in some white families can make a powerful difference in the choices available to them compared to families of color who are ostensibly from the same social class, but without the resources of multigenerational wealth. For example, even though parents may be of modest means, grandparents may have put aside funds to pay for their grandchildren's college education—a not uncommon scenario among families with multigenerational assets.[91] In addition, because most Latinos have historically been low-income, those in the middle class are much more likely than whites to be the first generation to have acquired this status. As such, they have little family wealth to rely on, and often must share their assets with extended family members who have less than they do. Thus, family income may be shared with not just a larger nuclear family, but also grandparents and other extended family members.[92]

Parental education, as measured in most studies of social class, is reported by students about their parents (such as in SAT questionnaire data) according to broad categories such as "less than high school," "some college," or "college degree." But as we will show in Chapter 3, all education is not equal, and the schools that even middle-class Latinos attend are more likely to be segregated and of lower quality than those that white students attend. Hence, the average white parent who has completed high school is likely to have had a qualitatively different education than the typical Latino parent who is a high school graduate. Likewise, Latinos on average attend less selective colleges than whites and complete fewer years when they do attend. At every level of education, then, the experiences of Latino parents—however these experiences look on paper—are likely to have been qualitatively inferior to those of white parents, which results in less educational and social capital available to pass on to their children.

As important as income, wealth, family size, and quality of parental education are to shaping the social and educational opportunities available to children, there are many other differences in the experiences of white and Latino children of the same apparent social class that result in distinct educational outcomes. For example, many studies have shown that teachers hold lower expectations for students of color than for white students and that these lowered expectations can result in diminished achievement.[93] As mentioned earlier, Latino parents also have less access to information about schooling and other social resources because of more limited social networks and language differences, even when they are ostensibly from the same social class as white parents. And if they are undocumented, they have much less access to social and health services than a similarly low-income white family. Further, Latino parents across social classes are less likely to have experienced in their own families the kinds of socialization practices that provide an academic edge for children from the mainstream culture; they haven't been exposed to the same academic "priming," storybooks, and cultural knowledge. Many have not learned the same language. They are much less likely to have attended preschool than white children from their same social class. And when all is said and done, racial and ethnic discrimination—not just by teachers in the classroom, but in the culture at large—still negatively influence the development of Latino youth and their perceptions of themselves and their abilities.

The Role of Schools

Although the problem of educational achievement and attainment gaps is laid almost exclusively at the feet of the public schools, and the solutions to such unequal schooling outcomes are virtually all centered on school reform, a relatively small percentage of young people's lives is actually spent in school—on average, only a little more than a thousand hours a year.[94] That means that 80 percent of students' time is spent outside school, in the home and in the neighborhood, engaged in activities that have little to do with school. Schools alone, then, cannot possibly be expected to completely resolve the profound inequities in children's lives.

Even so, certainly one of the most effective ways of reaching school-age children and their families with health and social services is in the schools themselves. Schools cannot be expected to do this within existing budgets, with existing staff, or within existing time frames, however. Moreover, coordination of social services for students and families with existing school activities and personnel can be fraught with problems if not implemented very carefully.

Although the odds are stacked against them, a small percentage of low-income Latino students manage to do well in school and go on to attain academic success. These students tend, like other academically successful students, to come from homes with relative advantages. They are somewhat more likely to live with both parents, to have parents who have had some success in school (perhaps they attended community college), and they are more likely to attend non-public schools.

Perhaps surprisingly, however, they are also less likely to be the same students who began kindergarten performing at high levels. That is, schooling itself has a bigger influence on academic outcomes for Latino students than for middle-class white students who have substantially more resources outside school.[95] For this reason, it is critical to examine what goes on in the schools that most Latino students attend. What will Carlos, Andrés, and their friends encounter as they journey through the public schools? How will the daily impediments they encounter in segregated, low-income communities affect their school experience? Will the schools be able to counter the tremendous negative effects of poverty and disadvantage that these Latino youth face?

CHAPTER THREE

American Schools and the Latino Student Experience

During the second half of the twentieth century, the population of Latinos in the United States grew from 4 million to 40 million. In 2000, one in five children in the United States was the child of an immigrant, and two-thirds of these children were Latino. Children of immigrants made up an even greater proportion of low-income American youth—one in four.[1]

Most Latino students are either children of immigrants or immigrants themselves. For these students the public schools are not only critical to their future occupational opportunities, but also key to becoming socialized into American society. Even the many third- and fourth-generation Latino youth whose families have failed to achieve significant educational or occupational mobility must rely on schooling for admission into the middle class.[2]

For many low-income Latino students the schools are also the first response system for any kind of social, medical, or psychological problem or disability. But by and large, those schools that serve Latino students in neighborhoods of concentrated poverty are much like the students themselves—lacking in resources and the social know-how needed to garner more. The evidence suggests that rather than addressing the disadvantages these students face, the schools perpetuate it.

Figure 3.1 illustrates the schooling context for Latino youth. The box labeled "school resources" includes the school's facilities, curriculum, skilled teachers, technology, and special programs. These are the tangibles on which the education budget is spent. The next box includes those things that contribute to campus climate, or what one feels when stepping on the campus. Is it inviting? Does it feel safe? Are activities and spaces organized to include all students, or do they serve to separate and segregate them? Are there people on the campus who can communicate with students or their parents if they do not speak English? The last box, on the right, refers to the peer context: who are the other students on the campus? What kinds of activities are organized by the school to bring students together and make them feel a part of the school and connected with one another?

Most American public schools provide relatively little in the way of support for children's healthy development. For example, in California in 2007 there was only one school counselor for more than

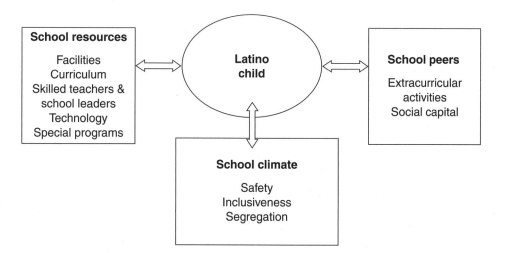

FIGURE 3.1 Schooling context for Latino youth

eight hundred students, and these counselors were disproportionately spending their workdays arranging the class schedules of high school students, a largely bureaucratic job that utilizes few of the unique skills that counselors have. Little time is allotted for meeting personal counseling needs.[3] Few of these counselors speak Spanish, though no data are collected by the state on the language or cultural competencies of counselors or other support personnel. If students have some kind of psychological problem, or need assessment for learning difficulties, one psychologist was available for every 1,383 students in 2007. And few of these overworked psychologists are competent to assess or provide psychological services for a Spanish-speaking child.

In the California public schools in 2007, there was also only one librarian for every 5,123 students to help guide them toward books that could support their learning or inspire their imaginations. The lack of librarians may have made little difference to Spanish-speaking students, however. Few libraries in California schools even have books in Spanish that students can read at school or take home to read with their parents. Books in Spanish that did exist for students in California were commonly packed away or discarded after the passage of Proposition 227 in 1998.[4]

Other supports were also meager, at least as of 2007. If a child had need of some immediate medical attention at school—an earache, a toothache, the flu—there was one nurse for every 2,242 students and so the likelihood that one would be available at the child's school site was very, very slim. Finally, should a student and her family need to be connected to a social support system, the chances of encountering a social worker within the schools were extremely remote. There was one social worker for every 18,117 students in the California schools in 2007.[5] In sum, when children come to school in California, they are pretty much on their own, with only the teacher, facing the largest class sizes in the nation, to intervene on their behalf.

Some states and communities provide greater social supports than

California: New York and New Jersey, for example, ranked third and fourth in the nation in 2006 in average student expenditures, according to the National Educational Association. But some states actually are worse than California, and no states employ enough school personnel who have the language and cultural skills to meet the needs of immigrant and non-English-speaking parents.

Not Enough Preschool

Brain researchers have recently argued strongly that early educational experiences are essential to optimal intellectual development, and that preschool attendance may, in fact, be most critical for children from low-income backgrounds. They contend that low-income and working-class students encounter, on average, one-half to one-third fewer words by age three, resulting in these children's hearing and learning far fewer words at that early age than their middle-class peers.[6] Furthermore, because learning is sequential and builds on earlier skills and understanding, such gaps may continue to grow, and inadequate neural patterns may be established that may actually limit the child's capacity for learning over time.[7] At the same time, other researchers argue for the plasticity of the human brain, and especially of children's brains, providing evidence that enriched education in the early years can make up for a lack of cognitive stimulation in the home.[8] Hence, preschool education has come to be viewed as a critical component of the education of low-income Latino children. Yet most do not attend.

Fifty-seven percent of all three- to five-year-olds nationwide attend some kind of preschool (in 2005, approximately 66 percent of black children, 59 percent of white children, and 43 percent of Latino children participated in early childhood programs).[9] Middle-class children enroll in a wide variety of private preschools as well as publicly supported programs in the community. Moreover, many of those middle-class children who stay at home receive enriched educational opportunities in more informal contexts. Low-income, and especially

Latino, children, however, have many fewer options for early childhood education in their neighborhoods. Although considerable research evidence exists for the short-term benefits of a high-quality preschool education on children's cognitive functioning, health status, and socioemotional adjustment, for low-income children, both the opportunity to attend preschool and the quality of the experiences they will have there are much more limited.[10] Head Start is the primary federally sponsored program for low-income preschoolers, but it is able to serve only about half of all eligible children and recent cuts in its budget threaten to reduce that figure.[11]

Bruce Fuller and his colleagues have explored the reasons that Latino children are less likely than other children to be enrolled in preschool. Although the low attendance of Latino children in preschool is often portrayed as arising from a culture that does not support sending young children to school, these researchers did not find this to be the case, at least not primarily. Through surveys and collection of data on existing programs, these researchers found that the primary reasons that Latino children did not attend preschool were, first, that fewer programs are located in their neighborhoods than in other areas; and second, that many parents in their study were concerned that traditional values, such as respect for elders and authority figures, and use of the primary language, were not being taught at preschool.[12] Thus if high-quality preschool programs were available, affordable, and culturally sensitive, there is no reason to believe that Latino parents in general would withhold their children from them.

The pattern of differences in preschool attendance can also affect the ways in which some children may be at a higher risk than others for school failure. Table 3.1 shows the rates of preschool attendance for three- to five-year-old children in the United States by ethnicity.

Latino students are the least likely to be enrolled in center-based preschool programs. In 2005, only 43 percent of Latino children

Table 3.1 Percentage of U.S. three- to five-year-olds in center-based preschool by
ethnicity, select years, 1991–2005

Race/ethnicity	1991	1996	2001	2005
White	54	57	59	59
Black	58	65	64	66
Latino	39	39	40	43

Source: U.S. Department of Education, National Center for Education Statistics 2006.

were enrolled in these programs, which provide the foundation for skill development in kindergarten. Interestingly, although Latino children are much less likely to be in a program than all others, they are more likely to go to kindergarten at an early age than other groups; that is, Latino children are much more likely than black or white children to be found in kindergarten at ages four and five. Early enrollment in kindergarten, however, is associated with a higher risk for less positive educational outcomes, especially when kindergarten has not been preceded by preschool attendance.[13]

The effects of these different preschool experiences, combined with different patterns of risk, begin to have consequences early in the educational careers of students. Almost all first grade teachers, for example, group students for reading instruction. The skills that children bring with them to first grade will normally determine the group to which they are assigned, and in spite of the best intentions of teachers, the boundaries between reading groups formed early in the first grade often become insurmountable barriers to advancement among reading groups thereafter.[14] In other words, students have a strong tendency to stay in the groups into which they are initially placed.

Other factors tend to keep children "tracked" in a certain level of learning. Those students who arrive at school ready to read, for example—usually those who come from more advantaged homes that have encouraged early literacy and who have attended high-quality preschools—tend to maintain their advantage over time. This occurs in large part because low-level reading groups cover significantly less material than high-level reading groups, and the interpersonal dynamics in high-level groups are more supportive of achievement. That is, the high-performing groups rarely have students with behavior problems, and successful students tend to be more engaged in the lesson. Taken together, these factors increase the gaps in curriculum content among different reading groups over time. Thus teachers' early judgments at the beginning of schooling, based in part on preschool experiences, can presage the educational path of students for the balance of their K–12 careers.[15]

Inadequate School Facilities

In a recent Public Broadcasting System documentary produced by John Merrow, the viewer was given a tour of what Merrow referred to as a school system that went from "first to worst" over twenty-five years. This was a study of the California schools, in which today the single largest group of students is Latino, and which educate more than one-third of all Latinos in the nation. By most measures that matter, California schools are near the bottom of rankings—teacher/ student ratios, class sizes, counselor/student ratios, and academic proficiency scores. Yet even among these troubled public schools, there are very good schools and there are very inadequate schools. The very good schools are attended largely by white, Asian, and middle- and upper-income students, and the very inadequate schools are virtually always overwhelmingly attended by students of color.[16] Because in California African Americans make up only about 8 percent of the student population, and Native Americans make up only 1 percent, this means that the very inadequate schools are almost always those in which the student population is largely Latino. They tend to be urban and overcrowded, and they are often on year-round schedules that allow the schools to cram as many as four thousand students onto a single elementary school campus by cutting short the school year to 163 days and cycling both students and teachers through on multiple tracks.[17] Many campuses have had to defer maintenance both because of lack of funds and lack of downtime to get the jobs done, a situation that has taken a terrible toll on school facilities. Merrow films the nonfunctioning drinking fountains and bathrooms, broken windows, falling ceiling tiles, leaking roofs, filthy grounds, and unkempt landscape of the schools serving California's poorest children. It was these same conditions that in 2000 launched the lawsuit *Williams v. State of California* on behalf of poor children who were being asked to learn in what were referred to by the plaintiffs as "conditions that shock the conscience."

California is not alone in underfunding education for its Latino population. Other states with very large Latino populations are in similar situations. Texas, with the second largest school-age Latino population—half of its incoming kindergarteners are Latino—ranked thirty-fourth in the nation in per-student spending in its K–12 schools, and thirty-second in its compensation of teachers.[18] Not surprisingly, Texas faces a teacher shortage, and especially a shortage of bilingual teachers.[19] Arizona, one of the two fastest growing states in the nation, with one-third of its student population Latino—and with Latino students projected to be the majority within ten years—ranks fiftieth in per student expenditures, according to the same National Education Association rankings. Arizona has fought the courts for more than a decade and a half, attempting to avoid funding the education of its English learners, who are virtually all Latino, at appropriate levels. The plaintiffs in *Flores v. Arizona* asserted in 1992 that the state was shortchanging the education of these students, and U.S. District Court Judge Alfredo Marquez ruled in 2000 both that the state provided a funding level for English learners that was arbitrary and capricious and that it failed to provide enough teachers, teachers' aides, classrooms, materials, and tutoring for these students. At this writing, the Arizona legislature continues to drag its feet while a new judge has threatened to fine the state millions of dollars daily for failing to comply with the court's ruling that it adequately fund the education of English learner students.[20]

The *Williams* suit in California was settled out of court in 2004, when a new governor decided not to defend the condition of the schools as the prior governor had. Instead, a certain "floor" was established for all schools: schools were given five years and a billion dollars to fix the bathrooms and leaking roofs, get a textbook for every student, and phase out the practice of shortening students' academic year in order to accommodate more students on a campus.[21] In reality, however, the focus was on the lowest-performing third of schools; the difference in per-student expenditures, which collectively amounted to considerably less than 1 percent of the annual education budget, was hardly noticeable.

While it has been difficult to establish a firm link between the quality and condition of school facilities and the educational outcomes for students—largely because the quality of school facilities is so highly correlated with the wealth of the students and communities that schools serve—there is considerable consensus that it is difficult to teach or learn in grossly inadequate facilities.[22] Equally important, poor conditions lead to higher teacher turnover. Teachers do not want to teach in dirty, dangerous, and uncomfortable conditions, and so they leave when they can.[23] In fact, recent research suggests that working conditions influence teachers' decisions about where to teach more than do salaries.[24] Given that it is exceptionally difficult, if not impossible, to effect school reform without a stable base of teachers, it is hard to deny the important, if indirect, role that school facilities play in student achievement.

In California, approximately 85 percent of English learners are

Spanish speakers, or Latinos. Therefore, data on English learners are a rough proxy for at least one portion of the Latino student population—the lowest-income group—because those who do not speak English well are most likely to be immigrants or the children of immigrants. Patricia Gándara and Russell Rumberger have collected a great deal of data on the learning conditions of these English learners in California, which confirm that the poorest schools are disproportionately the same ones to which Latino students—especially English learners—are assigned. The Early Childhood Longitudinal Study (ECLS) data set, collected by the U.S. Department of Education, yields state-specific data on subgroups. Gándara and Rumberger examined teachers' and principals' evaluations of their school facilities, and found that more than a third (35 percent) of principals in schools with higher concentrations of English learners reported that their classrooms were never or often not adequate, compared to 8 percent of principals with a low concentration of English-learner students. Similarly, teachers with larger numbers of these students in their classes were significantly more likely to report they had seen evidence of rats and other vermin at school and that school bathrooms were either unclean or not open throughout the day.[25]

Technology and the Schools

A few years ago there was great concern about the "digital divide," or the differential access to technology by race and income. Technology is expanding rapidly, however, and the concern appears to be abating. This is no doubt in part because of the rapid spread of computers into most schools in the nation. For example, in 1993, only 52.3 percent of Latino elementary students used computers in their schools, compared to 72.6 in 2003.[26] Yet computer access to the internet for information seeking is perhaps the most powerful use of the technology, and connectivity is not evenly distributed across groups. According to the U.S. Census more than half (54 percent) of white students used the internet at school, compared to only 37 percent of Latinos in 2003.[27] How technology is used in low-income versus middle-class schools can differ radically as well. Overcrowded schools without sufficient space for computer labs or areas, schools with limited resources that do not allow them to buy proper software or maintain and update hardware, schools with classroom management problems and under-prepared teachers, are all unlikely to use technology effectively, and these are precisely the same kinds of schools to which so many Latino students are assigned.[28]

Importantly, students from different backgrounds use technology differently outside school, in ways that schools do not normally equalize. For example, Latino students have much less access to the internet at home than do white students (37 percent versus 54 percent) and are more likely to use technology for games and entertainment than for information seeking.[29] Middle-income students are more likely to have parents who can guide them in their use of the computer as an information-seeking tool.[30] In a recent dissertation study, Melanie Jones has found that low-income parents of African American students were much less likely to be able to help their children find information about applying to college than middle-income black parents, who used the internet extensively to support their children's college application process.[31] Such differences in technology use are no doubt related to the fact that greater access to computers and the internet are correlated with better schooling outcomes. For example, Robert Fairlie found that high school–age children with computers in the home were more likely to be enrolled in school than those without computers, even controlling for socioeconomic factors and motivation.[32] Another study investigated why computers may have this effect and, once again controlling for several aspects of socioeconomic status, found that students with access to computers at home were six to eight percentage points more likely to graduate from high school than those who do not, a finding that appeared to be related to a reduction in "non-productive" activities.[33]

Inadequate Instructional Offerings

Beginning in elementary school, children are grouped by reading ability. Children from middle-class homes whose parents speak English as a native language, and who have read the classic children's literature to them—those who are already familiar with the adventures of Babar the Elephant and the misadventures of Curious George, and who can recite the story of the Little Train That Could—are placed in the higher-level reading groups, while Latino students begin to be tracked into the lower-performing groups. The lower reading group will cover less material, read fewer words, and spend more time in remedial activity.[34] Moreover, the students in the lower reading group will come to see themselves as slower and not as smart as the students in the higher reading groups.

Clustering Latino students into the lower-level curriculum groups is a common practice in U.S. schools, and documented in many ethnographic accounts of schooling. The practice, known as "tracking," usually begins in the early grades when students, especially those whose English verbal skills are not as developed as their mainstream peers', are placed in the slower groups "to help remediate their deficiencies," setting them on a pathway that becomes glaringly unequal in secondary school.[35] Students from college-educated families are routinely placed in a track that will lead to college preparation, and those whose families lack such educational backgrounds are significantly more likely to be placed in lower-level curriculum tracks even when their test scores are identical to their more socioeconomically advantaged peers.[36] Deep inequalities in education result both from different curriculum placement in the same schools, and assignment to different schools that serve very different student population groups.

Tracking and the High School Curriculum

The particular high school that a student attends determines in part whether the student can take the courses that are needed for college admission. Schools in more affluent neighborhoods, and that serve more socioeconomically advantaged students, have been shown to provide more rigorous college preparatory and honors courses than schools in lower-income communities that largely serve populations of underrepresented students. For example, a recent study of California schools found that only 52 percent of classes in the lowest-income (and highest percent Latino) schools met college-preparatory requirements, whereas 63 percent of courses in the highest income (and highest percent white) schools were designed for college preparation. These researchers also found that "the median high SES [socioeconomic status] school has over 50 percent more Advanced Placement courses than the median low-SES school."[37]

A recent study in the Los Angeles schools found that Latino students had far less access to Advanced Placement and honors classes than white students, even when such courses were offered in their high schools. As an example, Latinos constituted 78 percent of one school's enrollment, but only 13 percent of Advanced Placement class enrollment. Similar patterns of ethnic disparities in enrollment in Advanced Placement courses were found at all of the high schools the researchers examined. They referred to this phenomenon as a "school within a school," where Latino students occupy a lower-achieving track than non-Latino peers within the same high school.[38]

Clifford Adelman, a longtime analyst with the U.S. Department of Education, has argued that the rigor of the curriculum to which students are exposed is more predictive of long-term academic outcomes than even the powerful variable of family socioeconomic status. That is, Adelman argues that the greatest amount of the variance in long-term academic outcomes among ethnic groups can be explained by differences in the groups' exposure to high-level curricula—most particularly to advanced mathematics courses, which black and Latino students are least likely to take.[39] Of course, there can be a simplification in this logic that makes it difficult to address from a policy perspective. Without a considerable redistribution of resources it would be impossible for Latino students to take highly demanding courses: many schools serving Latino students are simply not prepared to offer such courses, and most Latinos are not prepared in their earlier school years to take advantage of them.

Programs like Gifted and Talented Education (GATE) are important precursors to gaining access to high-level, college preparatory courses and operate as "rewards" for having performed well very early in one's school career. The cause and effect relationship between assignment to gifted classes and access to high-level curriculum goes two ways. Doing well in school as early as kindergarten can place children on a path to participate in GATE, and being in GATE results in greater access to honors and Advanced Placement classes later in high school. Perhaps most important, students selected for such classes are labeled "smart" and, by default, those who are left behind are viewed as not as intelligent. Latinos are significantly underrepresented among the students selected as "smart." Table 3.2 shows the latest data available on national participation in gifted and talented classes. In 2002 when these data were collected, Latinos, like African Americans, were significantly underrepresented in these classes.[40]

A National Academy of Sciences report computed the odds ratios for minority students to be selected as gifted, based on data collected in 2002 by the National Center for Education Statistics, and found that Latino students were half as likely as white students to be nominated for a gifted and talented placement, while Asian students were

Table 3.2   Percent participation in K–12 gifted and talented classes by ethnic group, 2002

Ethnic group	Percent of own population group in gifted/talented classes
White	7.8
Black	3.1
Hispanic	3.7
Asian	11.1
Native American	4.9

Source: U.S. Department of Education, National Center for Education Statistics 2006.

almost three times more likely than Latinos to be identified for the program. As mentioned earlier, the opportunity to be identified as gifted and talented can be critically important for putting students on a pathway to college preparation. Analyses of data from the 1988 National Educational Longitudinal Study shows that students who are elected to participate in gifted and talented classes are also more likely to be assigned to algebra in the eighth grade, thereby setting them up for the college preparatory academic track in their high schools.[41] At what point in their schooling do Latino students first become shunted into a parallel, lower-track curriculum?

Stereotypes and Self-Fulfilling Prophecies

Robert Crosnoe studied three domains of development in children of Mexican immigrants (physical health, mental health, and cognitive development), as well as three contexts of development (home, preschool, and school) in an analysis of the federally sponsored Early Childhood Longitudinal Study–Kindergarten (ECLS-K), begun in 1998. This work helps us to understand how the process of lower achievement begins to unfold for Latino students in the early elementary school years, and how the curriculum they receive fails to prepare them to succeed or excel in school over the longer term. Crosnoe was particularly interested in those factors in children's backgrounds that were associated with early performance in mathematics—an area of academic performance that he argues is essential for students' eventual academic outcomes because it largely determines their access to higher-level curricula. Across the board, he found that Mexican immigrant children perform poorly in math at the beginning of school compared to all other ethnic groups, including other Latino students. Not surprisingly, he also found that the gaps in their math achievement widened over time. Crosnoe presents a scenario by which this increasing academic disadvantage occurs:

> Even more worrisome is the potential for U.S. educators, on the basis of their early evaluations of these entry level skills, to shape the instruction and placement of children in self-fulfilling ways. For example, a teacher views a gifted Mexican immigrant child to be unintelligent because of her difficulty speaking English, and consequently recommends that this child be placed in remedial coursework that provides no intellectual stimulation or challenge for that child and eventually causes her to disengage from school and do poorly. In this way, the low level of English proficiency and early math skills characteristic of children from Mexican immigrant families could even trump their actual aptitudes and abilities.[42]

It is important to note that the children he chose to study—children of Mexican immigrants—were also the most economically disadvantaged of all population groups in the study, with nearly one-half of all of these families reporting incomes below the poverty line. This was in spite of the fact that most (78 percent) were two-parent families with the majority of fathers and about half of the mothers working outside the home. To briefly summarize, Crosnoe found that Mexican-origin children had poorer physical health than other children (not surprising given their low incidence of health care); that

English was seldom spoken in the home; and that these parents, while concerned about their children's academic performance, did not engage as much as other parents did in activities at home or at school that supported achievement in U.S. schools.

The observation that low-income Latino parents exhibit different child-rearing practices is not new. Luis Laosa found in 1978 that low-income Mexican American mothers used different teaching strategies than either middle-income Chicanas or white mothers.[43] Low-income Chicana mothers were more prescriptive in teaching their children new skills and tended to allow fewer opportunities for them to perform tasks on their own. In general, they did not encourage exploration or autonomy in their children, dispositions that are viewed as critical to high academic achievement in middle-class communities.

Crosnoe also found that Mexican-origin children were much less likely to attend preschool (as we noted earlier), and much more likely to be assigned to schools that had several undesirable features: they were segregated by poverty and minority status, they were larger and more crowded than the typical school, their teachers were relatively less experienced, and they were located in "disorganized communities." In other words, these students were attending the poorest schools with the fewest social and educational resources.

There are multiple ways to think about remedying the problem of some parents' inability to prepare their young children for school. For example, there have been consistent calls from educators for low-income and minority parents to become more involved in their children's schools and schooling, and to support their children's academic development through reading and other activities in the home. When these calls to action are more than just nagging complaints about the parents, they generally translate into "parent training programs" in which parents are exhorted to read and speak to their children in English (even if they do not speak or understand English) and to attend parent meetings in which they are taught that they should model middle-class behaviors that may not relate to their own life circumstances. Certainly it makes sense to help parents be more supportive of their children's learning. But schools as well must find ways to respond to the needs of students whose parents simply do not have the resources (educational, linguistic, or financial) to deliver their children to the school fully prepared for American schooling.

The Critical Importance of Well-Prepared Teachers

Perhaps the most essential resource needed by Latino students is high-quality, stable teachers who are well trained to address their learning needs. To get at the question of whether minority students in general are receiving the high-quality teaching they require, an Illinois study evaluated teachers in the field using a teacher-quality index that included five attributes associated with highly qualified teachers, then cross-tabulated this with types of schools in which teachers at each quartile taught.[44] Researchers found that in the highest-minority schools (those with 99 percent or more minority students in their populations), 88 percent of teachers scored in the bottom quartile for quality. By contrast, the schools with the lowest percentage (less than half) of minority students had only 11 percent of teachers who scored in the bottom quartile of the teacher-quality index. Numerous studies have shown a clear relationship between the quality of teachers and the achievement of their students, and the quality of instruction has also been shown to have the greatest impact on the academic achievement of students of color.[45]

One important way in which even "highly qualified" teachers can inadvertently affect their students' achievement is through the expectations they hold for them. Teachers' beliefs about children's abilities can either enhance or reduce their school performance, and teachers' assessments of student potential begin at a very early age.[46] One study of low-income minority students in Baltimore demonstrated that social distance (that is, difference in social and economic status) between first-graders and their teachers was correlated with lower expectations and lower assessments of maturity and behavior for low-income students. Moreover, these early assessments resulted in lower academic achievement in subsequent years.[47] Teachers can be very effective at sending nonverbal messages to students about the amount of confidence they have in their abilities. For example, research has shown that teachers will wait longer for an answer from a student whom they believe knows the answer than they will from a pupil in whom they have little confidence. If the teacher has little confidence in the student, he or she is instead more likely to provide the correct answer, or move quickly on to another student.[48] This finding has direct implications for Latino schoolchildren. A 1973 study of four hundred classrooms in the Southwest, conducted by the U.S. Civil Rights Commission, found that Latino students consistently received less praise and encouragement from their teachers than white students, and more recent studies of teacher and other school personnel attitudes toward Latino students in Texas high schools confirm the continuing existence of such inequalities in the classroom.[49] Recent research on teachers' beliefs about their ethnic minority students has found that cultural differences between students and teachers also contribute to teachers' unfairly low opinion of these students' academic abilities.[50] Even well-intentioned teachers who perceived their students to come from "broken" or troubled homes tended to focus on creating a nurturing rather than a rigorous academic environment for their students.[51] Robert Ream refers to this as negative social capital, when teachers of Mexican American students lower their standards or implement a less rigorous curriculum out of a desire to not "make the students feel bad."[52] He argues that this form of negative social capital is a significant feature of the downward educational mobility of Mexican-origin students.

Students have been shown to be very sensitive to these subtle teacher behaviors; they "read" their teachers' attitudes quite accurately.[53] It also seems likely that students internalize these attitudes in ways that can reduce their achievement long-term.[54]

Further complicating matters, Angela Valenzuela argues that a different understanding of "caring" on the part of teachers and students is at the root of many Latinos' lack of enthusiasm for what goes on in the classroom. She notes:

> The predominantly non-Latino teaching staff sees students as not sufficiently caring about school, while students see teachers as not sufficiently caring for them. Teachers expect students to demonstrate caring about school with an abstract, or aesthetic commitment to ideas or practices that purportedly leads to achievement. Immigrant and U.S. born [Latino] youth on the other hand are committed to an authentic form of caring that emphasizes relations of reciprocity between teachers and students.[55]

Patricia Gándara found direct evidence of this phenomenon in an unpublished study conducted when she was working in the 1990s with Jaime Escalante, the famed Latino math teacher profiled in the movie *Stand and Deliver.* At the time Escalante was teaching in Sacramento, California, and had far more ethnically diverse classes than those he became known for in East Los Angeles. Gándara was interested in knowing how students of all ethnicities evaluated the teacher's influence on them. In a short survey of all of Escalante's students that year, she asked the simple question, "If another teacher in this school were able to teach you as well or better as Mr. Escalante, would you be willing to change classes?" White and African American students were somewhat divided in their responses, but Asian students almost all marked "yes" and Latino students all marked "no." The Asian students appeared to share the "aesthetic" (instrumental) view of caring described by Valenzuela. But independent of how well they were doing in class, Latino students felt they had an authentic relationship with their teacher and this was a powerful motivator for them. He bantered with them, scolded them at times (teasingly calling them "burros"), but more than anything was a strong father figure, asking students how things were going in their personal lives, inviting them in to talk before and after school, taking them to sports activities, or paying them to work on math over the summer. His behavior with students of other ethnic groups was not demonstrably different, except where the students indicated by their own behavior that they did not want such a personal relationship, but Latino students (and some black males) gravitated to this teacher who seemed to instinctively know how to communicate with them in an authentic way.

Importantly, though he became in the mid-1990s a spokesperson for the antibilingual initiative in California, Escalante also used his Spanish-speaking ability to communicate with both students and families. He would explain things in Spanish to students whose English-language skills were weak. When confronted with the apparent contradiction between his own use of Spanish with students and his position against bilingual education, he simply noted that "if all bilingual teachers were as effective as me, I wouldn't have a problem with it." In interviews with some of his Latino students, it was clear that they were working hard at math perhaps more in an attempt to not disappoint their teacher than because they understood the value of the subject matter for themselves.

Sometimes, however, even teachers' best efforts at caring are frustrated by adolescents for whom school has already become a battleground, or a stage on which to act out their desperate need to claim an identity that counters that of "failure." Clayton Hurd described a high school English-language development classroom in which all of the students were Latino, and one student, baiting others, called out profanities while the teacher was trying to read to the class. Soon other students were joining in as the class began to spiral out of control. One young woman, interviewed after class, commented,

> Poor her. She cares about us a lot, but we haven't shown that we care about her. It is the worst class, but it is also the one where she does the most things for us, the most field trips and stuff. It is because she does not want to send us to the office. In order not to get us into trouble in the office, she tells people to calm down, but they do not understand.[56]

Secondary teachers who have little time—usually a fifty-minute period—to develop authentic personal relationships with their students are at a serious disadvantage in breaking through the tough exterior that many Latino youth have developed after years of feeling inadequate in school. Even Escalante did not reach all of the students assigned to him. He did not tolerate misbehavior and had the authority in his school to refuse to teach students who did not meet his behavioral expectations. So authentic relations in his class were based on a reciprocal notion that in exchange for my caring about you, you will care about, and respect, me. Most secondary teachers are not given the authority to demand this kind of reciprocity, nor the time and resources to nurture these relationships.

Many of the problems of cultural mismatch, lack of understanding of students' social and educational circumstances, and inability to communicate with students and parents who do not have a good command of English could be ameliorated if the schools had more well-trained bilingual and bicultural teachers. In fact, the inability to mount strong bilingual programs for Latino (and other) students has long been attributed to insufficient numbers of highly qualified bilingual teachers. In a country of immigrants in which large percentages of young people speak Spanish (and other languages) at home, it is hard to understand why it could be so difficult to recruit and train bilingual teachers. A nation that could decide to go to the moon, and do it within a decade, could certainly decide to recruit and educate sufficient numbers of teachers for its English-learner students so that they might have a better chance of succeeding in school. Clearly, doing so has never been an educational or budget priority for either the states or the federal government—even as these governmental bodies use the lack of sufficient teachers as their excuse for not providing programs that would truly support the academic progress of many Latino students.

High Mobility among School Leaders

A culture of caring among students and teachers in schools begins with good leadership. From district leadership to school leadership, students in poor neighborhoods not only lack access to quality teachers; they also attend schools with higher teacher and administrator turnover than schools that serve more affluent students.[57] Poor schools and school districts also have more difficulty than affluent schools attracting both teachers and principals. As Cynthia Prince reports,

> Higher salaries, better benefit packages, signing bonuses, newer facilities, smaller classes, more resources, more opportunities for professional development, and bigger budgets for aggressive recruiting campaigns give wealthier districts overwhelming advantages that further stratify the rich and the poor.[58]

A meta-analysis of twenty-seven studies that examined the relationship between district leadership and student academic achievement (2,817 school districts and the achievement scores of over 3.4 million students) confirms this observation. Among the findings of the study were that stability of leadership, student achievement, and superintendent length of tenure positively correlated with student achievement.[59] In other words, more stable leadership appears to result in more stable, better functioning schools that in turn lead to higher performing students. School leaders are responsible for reducing the achievement gap between advantaged and disadvantaged students, and for convincing affluent parents that the additional efforts to reduce the achievement gap for Latino students will not take away from the education of their own children. To succeed, they must be skilled in the politics of equitably distributing limited resources and garnering others. But since principals and superintendents tend not to stay as long in low-income Latino schools and districts, they are less likely to have acquired the requisite political capital and skills.

It is well established in the research literature that strong superintendents are essential to recruiting and retaining highly skilled principals, and that skilled principals, in turn, are critical for the optimal functioning of schools, including most importantly the recruitment and retention of highly qualified teachers—the sine qua non of an effective and just school.[60] While the research remains unclear about whether teachers and administrators from the same ethnic background as their students are more educationally effective with these students, there is considerable consensus that teachers and administrators who know and are engaged with their students and communities are more effective than those who are detached from them.[61] Certainly, teachers and administrators from the students' own community are more likely to understand the issues that students and their families face, and to be familiar with both problems and resources in those communities. They are also more likely to speak the language of the families they serve. But for a long time, the nations' students and their teachers (as well as their administrators, who are normally pulled from the teacher ranks) have generally been from different ethnic backgrounds. In 2004, for example, nearly 19 percent of all students nationwide were Latino, but only 6 percent of teachers were also Latino. Yet while just 58 percent of students were white, 83 percent of all teachers were white. The problem of training and hiring Latino teachers stems from a serious "pipeline" problem that afflicts other college-degree-dependent fields. Not enough Latino students become eligible to become teachers by gaining a college degree, and often for the relatively few who do reach such academic heights, other opportunities are plentiful and more attractive than teaching. In short, the crisis in the education of Latino students is reflected in the absence of Latinos from the teaching force.

Safety Concerns

It is difficult to teach and to learn in an environment that does not feel safe—either physically or psychologically. School violence can make students fearful and affect their ability to learn, and concerns about vulnerability affect the entire school climate.[62] Both black and Latino students are significantly more likely to report that they do not feel safe at school, or on the way to school, than white students. For example, in 2005, 10 percent of all Latino students nationally reported that they were afraid of being attacked at school or on the way to school, compared to just 4 percent of white students. And students who attended urban schools were twice as likely as students from rural schools to report this level of fear.[63] Poverty and neighborhood disorganization are also correlated both with race and ethnicity and with higher incidences of violence on school campuses.[64] A recent study of successful students from "bad" neighborhoods concluded that neighborhoods alone held relatively little explanatory power about which students would excel and which would fail, but that bad neighborhoods in combination with safety concerns at school did, indeed, predict for poorer academic outcomes.[65]

Gang membership can be a threat to students' sense of safety both at school and in the neighborhood. While it is not as pervasive a feature of Latino adolescent life as sometimes portrayed in the media, it does, in fact, affect some Latino youths' sense of well-being and eagerness to attend and participate in school. Many believe that between 4 and 10 percent of Latino students in the twelve- to eighteen-year-old age range are members of gangs, and these students are inclined to engage in both bullying and overtly violent activities.[66] Of course, another unknown number of students are affected by the presence of gangs in their neighborhoods without actually being members themselves. In fact, staying out of gangs is a regular challenge for some Latino youth.

Surveys of students indicate that fear of violence actually decreases with age, with elementary school students more fearful of violent acts than are high school students, even though more acts of violence occur at the secondary level. It may be that violent acts are less noticeable to students on large high school campuses than on smaller elementary campuses, or that adolescent bravado limits how much older students are willing to admit, even to themselves, the level of fear they experience. Nonetheless, fully 10 percent of Latino students worry about their own physical safety at school, which no doubt affects their learning and their attachment to school. Victimized students have been shown to be more likely than others to be truant or drop out of school altogether.[67]

Physical safety is not the only kind of safety that matters at school. Even students who do not fear for their physical well-being can experience the psychological fear of being ostracized, marginalized, and excluded. Especially for adolescents, for whom the need to belong is so powerful, being excluded can be more painful and debilitating than being physically attacked, as Diego Vigil illustrates in a quotation from a young gang member he interviewed:

> When I joined the barrio I was jumped in [initiated with a beating]. I remember the older guys looking me over real hard. When they started hitting me from all over, the older guys gave me the

best shots to make sure I could take it. But after, they made me feel like I belonged and every time I'd see them I felt good because of it. I was part of the barrio. I belonged. I was somebody.[68]

A study of a high school program called Puente, in which Latino student participants were grouped together for part of the day, found that in these contexts the students claimed to feel "safe." The Puente classroom was a place where they could talk about personal matters like undocumented immigration, or parents and family members who could not speak English and who perhaps had never even gone to school, without worrying about being misunderstood or laughed at by white students.[69] A similar finding is reported in a study of the role of migrant student centers where many Latino students—migrant or not—cluster to feel psychologically safe in a large high school in which they often are made to feel they do not belong.[70] Such "home bases" appear to be necessary for students who are often marginalized by their newcomer status, their lack of fluent English, or the fact that they look or dress differently. Unfortunately, few schools create such sanctuaries for these students.[71]

Segregation within and between Schools

Latinos are more likely than any other ethnic group to attend racially and ethnically segregated schools in the western and southwestern states in which they predominate and these segregated schools are disproportionately low-income schools.[72] For example, in 2005, 49 percent of Latinos, compared to only 5 percent of white and 16 percent of Asian students, were enrolled in schools with the highest measure of poverty (schools in which more than 75 percent of the students are eligible for free and reduced price lunch).[73] This intense clustering of poor children puts enormous pressures on the resources of schools whose parents generally have little time or resources themselves to help support the children's school experience.

Schools with few poor children can often rely extensively on parents to support extracurricular activities as well as to provide extra volunteer help in the classroom. Not so in very low-income schools.

Inequalities in educational opportunity between segregated white schools and segregated schools with students of color have been well documented, and led to a decades-long experiment with desegregation and busing.[74] That experiment has been dealt a very serious blow, however, with the *Parents Involved in Community Schools v. Seattle School District* and *Meredith v. Jefferson County Board of Education* decisions in June 2007. Today, Latino students attend schools that have become increasingly segregated since data were first collected in the 1960s. In 1997, 35 percent of Latino students were attending schools that were 90 to 100 percent minority; today 39 percent do.[75] And as Gary Orfield has pointed out:

> Low-income and minority students are concentrated in schools within metropolitan areas that tend to offer different and inferior courses and levels of competition, creating a situation where the most disadvantaged students receive the least effective preparation for college. A fundamental reason is that schools do not provide a fixed high school curriculum taught at a common depth and pace. The actual working curriculum of a high school is the result of the ability of teachers, the quality of counseling, and enrollment patterns of students.[76]

Approximately half of all Latino students in Texas and California attend intensely segregated (90–100 percent minority) schools, and more than three-quarters of these schools are also high-poverty schools—that is, they serve a high percentage of students who are eligible for free and reduced price lunch.[77] High-poverty schools notoriously do not offer the same quality of education that middle-income schools do. Many, if not most, of their students perform below acceptable academic standards.[78] Moreover, Latinos who are also English learners—about half of this student population at any one time—are also heavily segregated by language. Across the nation, more than half of all English learners are in schools in which more than one-third of their fellow students are also English learners.[79] Put another way, 70 percent of English learners attend 10 percent of all schools in the country.[80] In California, the scale of the problem is even more dramatic: 38 percent of English learners attend schools in which more than half of the students are also English learners, and more than 75 percent of English learners attend just 39 percent of all California schools.[81] This stark segregation by native language means, in part, that Latino students who do not speak English well or at all have few opportunities to interact with native English speakers or to be surrounded by the sounds of English being spoken among their peers. One result of this isolation is that English learners have the lowest achievement-test scores of any group in the schools except for special education students, and drop out of school at least double the rate of Latinos in general.[82]

Even within nominally desegregated schools, ability tracks often work to segregate students. The effects of both subtle and obvious means of separating Latino students from the mainstream school community are truly inescapable.

The Problem with Extracurricular Activities

An important aspect of school life for many students, and one in which they form important relationships with other students, is extracurricular activities. Studies have shown that students who participate in extracurricular activities are more likely to feel attached to school and to do well there.[83] In particular, Latino students whose primary relationships are at school, as opposed to away from school, are more likely to persist and not drop out.[84] But there is evidence that Latino students are less likely than other students to participate in extracurricular activities for multiple reasons, including costs associated with some of these activities, lack of transportation, afterschool jobs and other responsibilities, and feelings of marginalization. Of these, feelings of marginalization may be the most influential. Students who do not feel like they belong at school, as many Latinos report they do not, are disinclined to join clubs and other activities, and are less likely to be chosen when they do make the effort.[85] To address this issue, Patricia Gándara and Margaret Gibson have argued that it is critical that schools act to make more extracurricular activities "curricular"—that is, part of the school day—so they will be more accessible to Latino students and so the schools can better orchestrate the inclusion of all students.[86]

As long ago as the 1960s, James Coleman found that peers were perhaps the greatest single influence on a student's academic achievement. Minority students, for example, clearly demonstrate higher academic achievement in largely middle-class, white schools than when they are surrounded by other poor and minority children.[87] A number of studies over the years have pinpointed why this is so. They found, in part, that white, middle-class students draw more resources to a school. But it is also true that teachers, parents, and students in these schools have higher aspirations for students' futures and therefore demand more of themselves and the schools. Several studies have shown that Latino students have lower expectations for themselves after high school than do other student groups.[88] The explanation for this is not hard to find. Latino students simply know less about what is possible because their families have much less experience with education, and they have less confidence that education will make a big difference for them.[89] Many also have concerns that they cannot afford to go to college, or sometimes even finish high school, and they know little about where to turn for financial support.[90] Such gaps in knowledge stem, in part, from school environments where Latino students have little contact with other students who might share this critical information with them.

Social Capital and Latinos: Missing the Inside Story

Racial and ethnic segregation continue to affect not only the quality of the physical plant and the resources of a school, but the social capital that students are able to access as well. Middle-class and ethnic majority students and their parents simply know more about opportunities: what kinds exist and where and how to access them. They tend to know more about which classes prepare one for college and which do not; which teachers are the better instructors; and what kinds of extracurricular activities will provide an advantage in school and beyond. They also know how to approach school authorities to extract the most resources from the institution and they are more likely to exercise influence with these authorities.[91] Thus when Latino students are segregated from their peers and the adults in their peers' lives, they are also shut off from powerful means of social mobility and sources of support for their academic achievement.

In a study of high-achieving Latino students, Gándara interviewed a young woman who explained how critical it was that she had the opportunity to share a class with white students, even though she attended a largely internally segregated high school:

> It was in the band. As a result of being with the white students, having to sit next to them . . . so I learned a lot about the academic situation and how I wasn't reading Steinbeck, how I wasn't reading novels, and how I wasn't taking the same courses that my peers were taking. And consequently that was real instructive to me, figuring out how I had to take chemistry, so I did take that on my own. . . . I would say that had the biggest impact, being in the band and seeing what I wasn't getting from school.[92]

A powerful illustration of the value of knowledgeable peers—those with significant social capital to share—is found in an interview with a Latina who eventually earned a Ph.D. but initially had no aspirations for higher education:

> I had to go to school to register and there was this huge line and I was by myself, so I got in line because I found that this was where you got in line if you wanted the general course which was to prepare you just for the basics. The girl in the other line was a girl I had gone to school with, her name was Rema, she said, "Don't get in that line, get in this line; this is for college prep." I told her that was not for me, and she said, "Yes it is," and so I went with her because I didn't want to be alone. . . . She talked me into it by saying, "Don't stand in that line because you will learn the same stuff you learned in seventh and eighth grade, just reviewing the same stuff."[93]

The Mixed Results of Intervention Programs

Resource-strapped schools and districts commonly attempt to address equity gaps between minority students and their more advantaged peers through targeted special programs. Ironically, the same schools that lack sufficient funds to recruit or retain strong teachers or school leaders may be able to access special state or federal funds that have been earmarked for specific intervention programs. For example, at both the elementary and secondary levels, afterschool programs have gained considerable political support in recent years. In California, $550 million of state funds were dedicated to afterschool programs in 2006.[94] These programs served as a venue for school staff or community agencies to provide tutoring and academic enrichment for youth who need additional support. But evidence of the effectiveness of afterschool programs remains mixed and context-specific.[95]

Thomas Kane summarized the results of four evaluations of large-scale afterschool programs, including: 21st Century Community Learning Centers (21st CCLC), the After-School Corporation, Extended-Service Schools Initiative (ESS), and San Francisco Beacon Initiative (SFBI). He concluded that none of the evaluations showed a statistically significant improvement of participants' achievement scores, although he did find that afterschool programs appeared to promote greater parental involvement in school, higher levels of student engagement, and improved student commitment to homework—all of which are associated with higher achievement over the long run.[96]

Los Angeles's Best program is an afterschool program designed to raise student achievement levels for K–5 students, and it is focused largely on Latinos. One study of sixty-nine sites throughout the greater Los Angeles region assessed its effects on participants who had been involved in the program at least four years. Among the key findings of the study were that the 4,312 children who participated in the program demonstrated significant gains on standardized achievement tests and increased school attendance in comparison with their 15,010 peers who had not; participants were also more likely to report that they hoped to go to college.[97] Two common problems with these programs, however, are first, that they serve only a small portion of the students who could benefit and second, that they usually struggle with inadequate financial resources, staff, and space to conduct their activities. Consequently most programs are short-lived.[98]

Other popular interventions include "college access" or "college preparation" programs. Although couched in terms of college preparation, many of these programs count themselves successful if they help to ensure that "at risk" students make it successfully through high school graduation. The goal of college may be as modest as enrolling at the local community college. Even though there has been an explosion of college-access programs in recent years across the nation—one study concluded that virtually every urban high school in the nation appeared to have at least one—it has been estimated that still no more than 5 to 10 percent of students who could benefit from such a program are able to gain access to one.[99] But the pressure is on to change this situation. With those students who are the least prepared to attend college—Latinos and African Americans—now the majority population in all major urban areas and many states, and with the demise of affirmative action as a tool to help underrepresented students obtain a higher education, such programs are playing an ever larger role in attempting to increase access to college for Latino students.

While few of these school-based programs focus specifically on Latinos, the Puente program, located in thirty-six high schools across California, does target Latino students. Puente consists of a three-pronged effort to help Latino students from across the achievement spectrum go to college: intensive college-preparatory English classes; a college counselor; and a mentor. An evaluation of Puente showed that students who participated in the program through the first two years of high school were nearly twice as likely to go to four-year colleges as demographically similar students who had not been in the program.[100] (A follow-up of the initial evaluation study yielded evidence that some of the students "slipped back"—leaving their four-year colleges to return to the local community colleges—though it was not possible to say what percentage did so because it was difficult to locate all of the students from the initial sample.[101])

Overall, then, it appears that very good programs that also meet stringent evaluation criteria are able to just about double the college-going rate for some underrepresented students in general, and Latinos in particular.[102] The extent to which these students attend four-year colleges, however, or successfully transfer from two-year colleges— as well as the extent to which they stay in college and complete degrees—remain open questions. Moreover, whether "going to college" means more than simply enrolling in a single course at a local community college is largely unknown. Certainly, the data for Latinos on dropping out of college, going to college, and completing a college degree do not suggest that major inroads have been made yet in changing the educational trajectories of Latino students. Additionally, such programs are vulnerable to the criticism that resources applied to the few students who are targeted for intervention may keep schools from investing in changing the fundamental conditions of schooling for the majority. The criticism would have merit: many of the practices that double the college-going rate for the few should be part of every student's schooling.

Helping More Latinos Beat the Odds

As we've learned, Latino students typically experience a host of impediments to success in school. Any one of these barriers is daunting, but to be challenged simultaneously by multiple obstacles and a lack of social, psychological, and educational support at school and in the community can and does limit the potential of many Latino students. That they survive these various hurdles to meet minimum demands of schooling and become competent citizens is a testament to human fortitude. To expect that they would demonstrate high levels of intellectual competence or aspire to go to college would seem overly optimistic. Yet some of these students do defy the odds by demonstrating superior intellectual competence in school settings and going on to college.[103] This phenomenon is explained by some psychologists as resilience, or the normal developmental process of "self-righting."[104] Contemporary resilience theorists tend to emphasize that resilience is not a "trait" but a "state" that can be nurtured and supported, and that it is evident in some circumstances and not in others.[105] From this perspective, failure to perform at high levels in school, given the enormous barriers that Latino children face, is not evidence of a lack of intellectual ability, but proof that educational support systems are not in place to help these students succeed.

CHAPTER FOUR

Is Language the Problem?

There is a widely held perception that language difference is the primary cause of educational difficulties for Latino students, and if that problem were addressed, the education crisis would be resolved. How did this opinion emerge, and to what extent is it true? How effective have second-language interventions been for Latinos? And in what ways has second-language instruction been shaped by political expediency and pandering to anti-immigrant sentiments?

Language as a Civil Rights Issue

Although Latinos have suffered many of the same inequities as blacks and other minority groups in schooling—inadequate and overcrowded facilities, underprepared teachers, inappropriate curriculum and textbooks, and segregated schools—the civil rights focus in education for Latinos has been primarily the issue of language. Latinos entered into the civil rights struggles for desegregated schools even before *Brown v. Board of Education* was heard. In 1946, in *Mendez v. Westminster,* the U.S. District Court found that the segregation of Mexican children into Mexican schools was arbitrary and discriminatory and outlawed the practice. Two years later, in *Delgado v. Bastrop Independent School District* in Texas, the courts again found the segregation of Mexican children into schools that separated them from white students to be arbitrary and discriminatory and ruled they could not continue. Nonetheless, districts in both California and Texas (as well as elsewhere in the Southwest) continued to segregate Mexican-origin students with impunity.[1]

By the 1960s, however, the major civil rights issue for Latinos had become not school inequality or segregation, but language of instruction. In some ways this was a natural progression: language had been a primary rationale for segregating Latino students and for marking them as inferior (because they could not perform in English, a language which many did not understand). But there are several other possible reasons why language has remained the focal point of the battles over equitable education for this group even though most Latino students are not limited English proficient (LEP), at least as measured by the schools.[2] First, an inability to speak English is the barrier to equitable schooling that is most obvious to many people, especially non-Latinos. The most obvious explanation, however, may not be the most accurate. A recent poll conducted by the Pew Hispanic Center and Kaiser Family Foundation found that almost two-thirds of white and black respondents thought language was the primary barrier to academic achievement for Latinos, while fewer than half of Latinos agreed with this position.[3] As the 1974 *Lau v. Nichols* decision pointed out, if a student does not speak English, that student's access to American schooling is effectively foreclosed. Moreover, because a typical response to the language needs of Latino students has been to place them in English classes until they have learned the language well enough to join mainstream classes, their general educational progress is often slowed considerably, which not surprisingly has led to very high dropout rates.[4]

Second, language is inextricably bound up with identity, and Latinos have sought to reinforce their common identity by asserting their language within an American culture that often rejected them.

Where languages compete in the public sphere, they can become a critical marker of social and political status. Ronald Schmidt argues that "the dispute [over use of non-English languages] is essentially a disagreement over the meanings and uses of group identity in the public life of the nation-state, and not language as such."[5]

Third, language is a tangible and malleable characteristic, and is addressable in relatively straightforward ways. It is politically easier to address students' language needs than problems of racial isolation. During the civil rights period, the right to bilingual education was incorporated into federal civil rights legislation, and became in 1968 Title VII of the Elementary and Secondary Education Act. This "right" was relatively weak and its aim purposely vague, but it did provide a tangible means of addressing concerns of Latinos and a potential way to measure their progress toward gaining more equitable schooling.[6] By showing progress in these students' acquisition of English, schools could argue that they had been responsive to their needs. The evaluation of bilingual programs, therefore, became a key factor in the "bilingual wars" that would follow. The only outcome of policy interest in these evaluations was usually students' performance in English, rather than their bilingual competencies.

Finally, the focus on language met the objectives of a number of different political actors. Although Latinos had been at the forefront of desegregation efforts in the Southwest, the issue of segregation had been claimed by blacks, who had suffered under official apartheid in the South. Moreover, in the 1960s and 1970s, there was considerable concern on the part of Latinos that desegregation plans that moved Latino children out of their local schools could reduce the critical mass necessary to mount effective bilingual programs, thereby undermining their hard-won concessions on bilingual education. Language was an issue that could be owned by Latinos and by which they could measure their own political clout. And the Nixon administration was only too happy to align itself with Latino activists who demanded bilingual education as evidence that the federal government was paying attention to their needs. Gary Orfield recounts how the shift to a focus on bilingual education allowed the Nixon White House to reduce the pressure for desegregation and divide minorities on a reform effort that the U.S. Department of Health, Education, and Welfare was dedicated to derailing.[7]

The overwhelming focus on the limited English proficiency of Latino children, however, has led to a perception that inability to speak English is the cause of Latino underachievement—and that mastering English will solve these students' educational problems. Some have capitalized on this perception for political gain; note the recent antibilingual education initiatives in Arizona, Colorado, California, and Massachusetts. Yet millions of Latino students speak only English but perform at exceptionally low levels academically. Acquisition of English may be a challenge for some Latinos, but it is by no means the core educational problem for the majority of Latino students, or even, we would argue, for most English learners.[8]

A Narrow Definition of English Proficiency

Even to the extent that language is a critical issue for Latinos, the challenge it represents has been constructed so narrowly as to miss critical aspects of language learning that do contribute to underachievement. One is either proficient or not; one is either an English learner or a fluent English speaker. This dichotomy is forced on teachers because a student's program assignment and hence funding source are based on being either one or the other. In reality, however, most Latino students' English skills fall somewhere on a continuum between these two extremes: from speaking English as their first or primary language and being exposed to Spanish in the home or community, to speaking no English and living in a linguistically segregated, Spanish-only setting. While only those students who fail to pass a basic test of English proficiency are likely to be categorized as

English learners and placed in some kind of special program, it can be argued that most Latino schoolchildren probably need some kind of support or intervention to help them achieve commensurately with their native-English peers. If children are not exposed to the English of the classroom—the vocabulary and rhetorical style that make up academic English—they will find it very difficult to decipher academic texts and write persuasive essays.

Even those children who are considered English learners, and therefore placed in some kind of special program, seldom receive the kind of specialized language instruction and support that they need. A number of researchers have argued that the type of language instruction to which most English learners are exposed is inadequate to allow them to perform at high levels of achievement in an English curriculum.[9] Lily Wong-Fillmore and Catherine Snow argue that the reason for the weak instruction in English usage is that teachers, especially those trained in disciplines other than English, are not sufficiently prepared to teach students explicitly about language and its use across genres and disciplines.[10] For example, math teachers do not routinely point out to students how the words they use make sense in the context of math, but may differ in other contexts, or the ways in which forms of language use may differ within the discipline. English learners can be especially perplexed by phrases that sound alike, as in "the sum of the numbers" as opposed to "some numbers," and idioms like "it goes without saying." We do not routinely teach teachers these skills; instead we assume they are making these features of language transparent for their English-learner students.

Recent data from California support this claim. Astonishingly, although 66 percent of tenth grade English learners were able in 2006 to pass the state's English proficiency test at the level of early advanced or advanced (roughly equivalent to "proficient"), only 4 percent were able to pass the state's English Language Arts (ELA) test at a similar level of proficiency that year.[11] The English Language Arts test requires a much more sophisticated understanding of English than does the proficiency test, as well as exposure to and familiarity with literature in English, yet educators often fail to make distinctions between these two kinds of proficiency in their instructional planning for English learners. A debate has raged for some time over the importance of English Language Development (ELD) standards as markers of students' progress toward readiness to undertake the more demanding curriculum of English Language Arts. Those who favor rapidly mainstreaming English-learner students have argued that there should be no substantive difference between ELD and ELA standards.[12]

A singular focus on teaching students to decode written language, and to use simplistic forms of English, can lead educators to assume that students understand more than they do, and consequently to shortchange them academically. A recent study of English-learner education conducted in a Northern California school district known for its overall excellence found that during a typical school day, the average English learner actually used English for oral or written expression no more than two to three minutes over four hours of academic instruction. The highly qualified teachers in the district were generally aware of effective techniques for instructing these students but found it difficult to use these techniques in mainstream classes, where they were kept busy attending to students with many different needs. Not surprisingly, Latino English learners in this district fared no better academically than English learners in the lowest-performing schools in the state, even though their English-speaking peers were routinely admitted to the most selective Ivy League colleges.[13]

Second, the concept of language proficiency has been restricted to encompass only those students who are learning English as a second language, yet there are many students in American schools who come from non-standard English backgrounds who have many of the same needs as English learners. These students, often referred to as "standard English learners," could also benefit greatly from a curriculum that is rich in academic language instruction. Little attention is paid to this issue, however, because it does not fit neatly into the English as a Second Language (ESL) paradigm that drives funding and programming in public schools.

A third problem with the narrow construction of the concept of English proficiency lies at the heart of the great debates over bilingual education: the emphasis on pushing schoolchildren to acquire English skills as rapidly as possible, to the exclusion of any other learning. Most advocates for English learners interpreted the *Lau v. Nichols* decision to mean that it was not acceptable to just teach students English and ignore their other learning needs; consequently there was a major push after *Lau* to implement bilingual programs that taught subjects in both English and the students' primary languages. *Lau* did not specify that schools had to implement bilingual programs, only that students had to be given access to the same curriculum as their English-speaking peers, but for English-learner advocates bilingual education seemed the commonsense response to that challenge. The U.S. commissioner of education agreed with this conclusion and promulgated the Lau Remedies, which ordered bilingual education for students whose civil rights had been violated by not having access to the mainstream curriculum. But by 1978 the Congress had made clear that bilingual education was to be used only "to the extent necessary to allow a child to achieve competence in the English language."[14] It was not to be implemented for any of the other possible goals that a bilingual education might have, such as achieving literacy in the primary language or strengthening students' disciplinary knowledge. This narrow construction of language competence has led many schools to back away from using primary language instruction that can strengthen students' general academic skills. In fact, in 2008 the Arizona Board of Education promulgated a policy that requires all English learners to take four hours daily of English language instruction, leaving almost no time in the students' school day to study the other subjects they must master.

Bilingual Education: The Failed Experiment?

Teaching children in two languages so that they can be competent learners and successfully acquire English has become over time such a hot-button issue that many people are reluctant to use the term "bilingual education" for fear of inciting scorn or stopping a conversation cold. Researchers even counsel each other to avoid the phrase so as not to prejudice readers against their research. Yet while critics in the United States claim that bilingual education is a "failed experiment," most other modern nations consider it the norm and cannot imagine why Americans would prefer an education in only one language. What about the history of bilingual education in the United States has led to the emotional controversy surrounding the teaching of students in two languages?

For the last thirty years, with only brief exceptions, the only government-sanctioned justification for bilingual education in the United States has been as a means to transition students as rapidly as possible into an English-only school experience. The idea that a good bilingual education might actually produce students who are literate in two languages gained initial acceptance in the late 1960s and early 1970s. Ever since, however, programs have had to defend themselves against the accusation that they were "maintenance" programs, trying to maintain students' primary language as they became fluent in English, as though this were a terrible thing to do to a child. Like "busing," bilingual education has become a lightning rod for those who oppose policies designed to equalize (or enhance) educational opportunity for minority children. Social conservatives have very effectively branded as failures these policies that an abundance of research evidence shows have provided many black and brown children with educational opportunities that had been foreclosed to them.[15]

Educational evaluation was used very effectively in the late 1970s and early 1980s to undermine bilingual education as a pedagogical strategy. Two expensive, multiyear studies were commissioned by the federal government to answer the perennial (and ultimately unanswerable) question: Which is more effective, bilingual education or English immersion? (One reason this question is so difficult to answer is because there is great confusion about the goals of these programs—for example, should the goal be rapid transition to English? Grade-level academic achievement? In addition, the nature of the instruction is seldom carefully specified—it is often unclear whether it should entail, for instance, fully qualified bilingual teachers providing rigorous curriculum in two languages, bilingual aides helping to translate some portions of an English curriculum, or sink-or-swim immersion into English.) The first major study, released in 1978, found that "there had been no consistent significant impact" of Title VII bilingual education on English learners.[16] Critics of this study noted that it was impossible to know what the "treatment" had been in these bilingual and English-immersion classrooms; the researchers had simply taken at face value the label applied to the classes. In 1991 a second federally sponsored longitudinal study was released with similarly ambiguous results.[17] In this study, great care was taken to observe actual instruction in the classrooms. But although the principal investigator, David Ramirez, argued that the trajectories of student achievement strongly favored late-exit ("maintenance") bilingual programs, he conceded that the four-year duration of the study was insufficient to draw definitive conclusions. Importantly, the study also noted that in several cases programs had shifted their language emphasis and no longer looked distinctly different from other categories of programs. Criticisms of both studies focused on the insurmountable methodological challenges of trying to compare students and programs that are not truly comparable. Schools assign different types of students to English-only and bilingual programs (usually placing in the bilingual programs the students who are least English proficient because they are viewed as needing the most primary language assistance); teachers tend to rely on the language they feel most comfortable in rather than the language mix that is mandated by the program; and students in low-income schools come and go so quickly that few are still in the same school or program after only a few years, making long-term assessments of outcomes unreliable.[18] Moreover, those students who do not move are likely to be more advantaged than those students who are highly mobile, which also biases study outcomes.[19]

There has been no major empirical study of dual-language or "two-way" programs, those that mix English speakers and non-English speakers in roughly equal proportions with the objective of fostering full bilingualism and biliteracy in both groups. Smaller studies, however, suggest that this is the most effective strategy for educating both groups of students to become competent bilinguals without sacrificing English development.[20] In a major meta-analysis funded by the U.S. Department of Education that looked at bilingual and two-way programs compared to English-only programs for English learners, researchers concluded:

> Evaluations conducted in the early years of a program (Grades K– 3) typically reveal that students in bilingual education scored below grade level (and sometimes very low) and performed either lower than or equivalent to their comparison group peers (i.e., ELL [English-language learner] students in mainstream English, SEI [structured English immersion]/ESL [English as a second language], or EO [English-only] students in mainstream classrooms). Almost all evaluation of students at the end of elemen-

tary school and in middle and high school show that the educational outcomes of bilingually educated students, especially those in late-exit and two-way programs, were at least comparable to and usually higher than their comparison peers. There was no study of middle school or high school students that found that bilingually educated students were less successful than their comparison peers.[21]

These findings are important because they may explain results of short-term evaluation studies in which students in bilingual programs sometimes score lower than others in English-only programs when tested early on and only in English. It seems that students require more time to become competent in both English and the primary language.

Dual-language, or two-way, programs have the added advantage of helping to reduce the linguistic isolation that so many Latino students experience. The strategy has its own challenges, including the need to cluster the appropriate numbers of both groups and protect against the social power imbalances that can occur in these settings, but their potential for increasing the academic success of English learners (as well as English speakers) would appear to far outweigh these potential pitfalls.[22]

The federal government has also sponsored research syntheses. The first of these, requested in 1980 by the U.S. Department of Education's Office of Planning and Budget, was charged with reviewing the research literature on the effectiveness of bilingual education.[23] Keith Baker and Adriana de Kanter conducted a simple meta-analysis on twenty-eight studies of bilingual education that they considered sufficiently methodologically sound, and concluded that there was not enough evidence in favor of transitional bilingual education to mandate it as the favored approach for educating English learners. The study was cited widely for many years afterward, as bilingual education came under increasing attack during the Reagan administration. The Baker and de Kanter study itself, however, was widely criticized for being biased in the studies selected and methodologically weak in its simple "up or down vote" methods. Questions about their meta-analysis gave rise to a series of re-analyses by other researchers, most of which concluded that when strict methodological criteria were applied to the selection of the studies, such as only including studies that had well-defined control groups, bilingual programs tended to show better outcomes than English-only programs.[24]

In the mid 1990s, in an effort to find definitive answers, the National Research Council commissioned a major study of what was known about educating language-minority students.[25] It concluded, "When socioeconomic status is controlled, bilingualism shows no negative effects on the overall linguistic, cognitive, or social development of children, and may even provide general advantages in these areas of mental functioning." In addition, "use of the child's native language does not impede the acquisition of English."[26]

A subsequent study also commissioned by the National Research Council on preventing reading difficulties in young children concurred: "If language minority children arrive at school with no proficiency in English but speaking a language for which there are instructional guides, learning materials, and locally available proficient teachers, they should be taught how to read in their native language."[27] More recently, a synthesis study commissioned by the U.S. Department of Education and the National Institute of Child Health and Human Development also concluded that it was generally preferable to teach Spanish-speaking students to read in Spanish where possible. The Bush administration, however, refused to release it with its imprimatur in spite of two peer reviews that concurred with its findings.[28] Thus while the debates over primary language—or bilingual—instruction have continued unabated, the major research syntheses that have been commissioned by the federal government have increasingly concluded that use of the primary language in instruction probably holds certain benefits, and at a minimum does not impede English learners' achievement in English. These findings suggest that English-only efforts are likely based on something other than a simple concern for these students' academic welfare.

Policymakers have presumed that if bilingual education is not shown to be systematically superior to English-only instruction with respect to achievement outcomes measured in English, then preference should automatically be given either to English-only programs, or to transitional programs that incorporate the least primary language for the shortest period of time. On its face, there is no particular logic to this conclusion. If both programs had more or less equal results in English, but one had the added benefit of teaching some competence in another language, shouldn't that program be considered the superior one? For the most part the answer to this question has been framed as one of cost. Critics of bilingual instruction have long assailed the programs as being a "costly" waste of the taxpayers' money. Consider the preamble to Proposition 227, California's anti-bilingual ballot initiative that largely prohibited bilingual education:

> (d) Whereas, The public schools of California currently do a poor
> job of educating immigrant children, wasting financial resources
> on costly experimental language programs.[29]

In fact, there has not been a great deal of research on the costs of bilingual education as compared to any other kind of intervention for students who are limited in English. The two studies that have been conducted, however—both by large, reputable research organizations—came to similar conclusions: bilingual education is in fact generally among the least expensive models for meeting the needs of English learners because it requires only that one teacher in a classroom be able to provide instruction in two languages (or two teachers who trade classes for part of the day). Other models, such as separate ESL pull-out programs or primary language aides who provide educational support, require additional personnel, which increases these programs' cost. Moreover, bilingual teachers tend to be less senior than other teachers, having been hired in larger numbers more recently, and so their pay level, on average, is lower.[30] Program costs, then, appear to be more of a red herring than a real issue in the debates over language education.

Because earlier studies of language instructional models had not been definitive, proponents and opponents of the different models used these earlier evaluations to make whatever point they chose. On one side are those who assert that English-only instruction not only is more efficient in teaching English learners because students are exposed to more English, but also does not waste valuable time instructing in a language that they do not "need to know." The primary argument for this position is that more "time on task" (learning English) will result in greater and more rapid acquisition of English.[31] It is an argument with intuitive appeal.

On the other side of this debate, however, are researchers who argue that a fundamental principle of learning is that students learn best when the teacher builds on frameworks of knowledge—or "schemata"—that students already possess. That is, teaching is most effective when new learning is tied to what students already know.[32] Thus by teaching students concepts in a language they understand, one can advance the learning in other subject areas while also teaching students English. In fact, as noted, studies comparing bilingual education with English-only approaches consistently find little or no difference in the rate at which students acquire fluency in English. Reading skills (in English), however, do appear to be enhanced by initial instruction in the primary language, suggesting that learning that occurs in the native language is not "wasted." Hence the earlier-mentioned study commissioned by the U.S. Department of Education and the National Institute of Child Health and Human Development found: "Where differences were observed [in studies comparing English-only and bilingual instruction] on average they favored the students in the bilingual program. The meta-analytic results clearly suggest a positive effect [on reading scores] for bilingual instruction that is moderate in size."[33]

Although well-implemented bilingual programs can claim a "moderate" advantage over English-immersion instruction, no language intervention has erased the gap between English speakers and English learners, or between native-English white children and Latinos. Clearly, other factors are essential to the academic achievement of English learners. Unfortunately our cultural obsession with whether to pursue English-only versus bilingual education has obscured the more critical social and pedagogical issues that need to be studied and understood.

Understanding Second-Language Learning

In addition to large-scale studies of program models, other research has been conducted in the fields of second-language acquisition, cognitive science, sociolinguistics, and sociocultural studies that can provide guidance on best practices for educating English learners. Understanding how students learn a second language is critical. For example, do students transfer what they learn in one language to another, or must they relearn what they have been taught in the first language? Does learning proceed in all languages in a more or less similar pattern? Is all language learned in the same way, or are there different types of language that require different instructional approaches?

In the early 1980s, some of the answers to these questions emerged with the research findings of James Cummins, who has been exceptionally influential in developing theory in second-language acquisition. One of his primary contributions has been to elaborate a theory that multiple languages occupy a common underlying proficiency in the brain, suggesting that knowledge acquired in any language is shared with other languages that an individual knows.[34] He has also theorized that language can be organized into two types—basic interpersonal communicative skills and cognitive/academic language proficiency.[35] Though not without its critics, this model presaged what would become an increasingly important area of research one and two decades later, as educators began to note that students who appeared to have good conversational English skills were not necessarily capable of using the language in cognitively demanding ways in the classroom. The distinction regarding skills has come increasingly into focus with the pressures of accountability testing: as we noted earlier, many students who pass English-language proficiency tests at high levels nonetheless fail grade-level tests of English Language Arts, both because the constructs of language proficiency and language arts that are assessed are different and because they call on different linguistic skills.

In the realm of sociocultural factors that influence the educational progress of English learners, studies find that attitudes toward language learning do, indeed, affect acquisition and that teachers are influenced by the primary language (or dialect) that students speak, holding higher expectations for some language groups than others.[36] Peer attitudes, too, can affect students' acquisition of English if learning environments are psychologically threatening, making English learners reluctant to use English for fear of being teased or ridiculed.[37] Researchers have also found that immigrant language-minority students hold more positive attitudes toward schooling than subsequent generations and as a result often outperform native-born members of their own ethnic group scholastically—even when the native-born group is more proficient in English.[38] Reasons given for this counterintuitive finding focus on the negative effects of socialization into low-income and low-status communities, and the loss of

hopefulness that comes when second and third generations fail to realize the American Dream and are left behind in an unforgiving
economy.[39] Researchers have also concluded that intergroup relations
can be positively affected by educating students in contexts in which
the first and second languages share equal status, such as in dual-
language classrooms.[40]

Three primary questions of particular policy importance that have
come out of the area of cognitive sciences are first, whether bilingualism or biliteracy confers special cognitive advantages; second,
whether additional time on task results in more rapid or better acquisition of a second language; and third, whether younger children are
better or more rapid learners of a second language. Given the importance of the topic, it is surprising that relatively few studies have been
conducted on the cognitive advantages of bilingualism and biliteracy.
There is some evidence in the literature, however, that individuals
who have command of more than one language gain specific cognitive advantages—creativity, problem solving, and perceptual disem-
bedding, as well as cognitive flexibility.[41] But because these attributes
are seldom tested in schools or, sadly, even considered very important in assessing the outcomes of the educational system, it is not
known to what extent they provide achievement advantages in subjects such as math or reading.

Other explanations have been offered for the unusual finding that
first- and second-generation bilingual Latinos are more likely to achieve
at high levels than their native-born, English-only co-ethnic peers.
Some believe that speaking Spanish marks one's proximity to the traditional culture, and the greater the influence of that traditional culture, and therefore parental authority, over students, the more likely
it is that they will perform well in school to please their parents. The
loss of a student's ability to speak Spanish, by contrast, may signal that
the student is now more attuned to the norms of his or her peer
group, which in many low-income, barrio settings is not especially

supportive of academic achievement.[42] It seems that Americanization is not very good for immigrant students.

If spending more minutes or hours in the day studying in English to learn English results in superior and more rapid acquisition of English, then this would argue for English immersion. But if bilingualism or biliteracy confers cognitive advantages, then this strengthens the case for bilingual or dual-language education. The first question has been pursued for years, but without sufficiently stringent methods to answer definitively. Neither of the major federal studies testing bilingual versus English immersion mentioned earlier could find a significant difference in the ultimate rate or quality of acquisition of English by program type, and studies of rate of acquisition of English proficiency similarly find little difference with respect to the type of educational program to which students are assigned.[43] Socioeconomic status and prior exposure to English are generally better predictors of rate of acquisition.[44] Of course, this "non-finding" is actually of enormous importance. If there is no discernible advantage to English-only programs in the rate of acquisition of English, it should mean that there is no cost to providing students with an education that allows them to learn in their primary language—either for short-term academic catch-up or longer-term mastery of the language.

Studies of which program is most efficient for teaching English bring up the question: how long should it take to learn English? The answer is necessarily related to the age of the student, his or her exposure to English, the availability of academic supports outside of school, and a host of other variables.[45] But holding as many of these things constant as possible, there is a consistent finding that it takes at least five to seven years for the typical English learner to learn the language well enough to be considered fluent.[46] Nonetheless, there is great skepticism in public policy circles on this issue, in part because the finding appears counterintuitive to many general observers.

Most children who begin school without knowing English learn to communicate in English relatively quickly, creating the impression that they are "little sponges" and acquire fluency rapidly. This observation has also lent support to the idea that there is a critical period for second language learning and that young children are better learners of language than older children or adults. Whether there is a critical period for second language acquisition can take on considerable importance from a policy perspective: if such a critical period exists and it occurs early in a child's life, then it would be important to introduce the second language early, perhaps in preschool, before she or he begins formal schooling, or certainly in kindergarten.

It turns out, however, that there is no truly critical age for language learning. Some researchers have found that older persons are more "efficient" learners of second languages, given that they already have considerable language knowledge to build on.[47] Moreover, young children simply have fewer words and less complex linguistic constructions to learn, since language in young children is far less developed than in older persons. (Most studies do, however, conclude that younger learners can acquire completely unaccented speech, whereas this is far less common among older learners. Even so, unaccented speech can give the impression of greater knowledge of a language than actually exists.[48]) Thus while exposure to a second language at a young age can provide certain advantages, it is by no means critical for long-term second language development, and educators should be very mindful with young children that they not lose the primary language in the process of gaining a second, because parents will need to use the primary language to support their children's social, academic, and psychological growth.

Notwithstanding the rapid progress that many English learners make in acquiring a conversational level of English, many will remain in the category of English learner for seven or more years. A recent study found that the typical English learner in California schools had only a 40 percent chance of reclassifying to a fluent English speaker by high school graduation.[49] The primary problem is that while many English learners appear to be orally fluent in English, they lack facility with reading comprehension, vocabulary, text analysis, and writing. In fact, the problem for many so-called English learners is not an inability to communicate orally in English, but an inability to pass grade-level tests in the use of the language in academic contexts.[50] Unfortunately, the labels English learner and limited English proficient conjure up visions of a student who cannot speak English, obscuring the real problem of inadequate instruction.

The Big Dilemma

One of the major dilemmas in the education of English learners arises from the fact that it takes many so long to become reclassified as "fluent English speakers." This issue was raised prominently in the campaigns to pass antibilingual initiatives in several states. Ron Unz, the backer of the antibilingual initiatives, was quoted often as making the claim that bilingual education was a failure because 95 percent of English learners fail every year to become fluent—referring to the 5 percent in California that he erroneously claimed were reclassified to English proficient each year.[51] (The figure was actually about 7 percent of all English learners, including those who had been in school one day or one month.) Notwithstanding the Unz rhetoric, the "reclassification" rate of English learners remains a conundrum for educators: is it better to reclassify these students more quickly and move them into the mainstream where they will receive little or no special attention or support, or to keep them in some kind of special program with instruction geared to their language needs, but where they may be denied access to the regular curriculum and mainstream peers? Students remain in the classification of English learner because they cannot pass tests of English proficiency or academic achievement that suggest they have sufficiently developed skills to survive in a regular setting, and trends that show declining academic performance a few years after students are reclassified as English proficient give educators reason for concern.[52] But interaction with mainstream English speakers, in classes with the standard curriculum, can also be an important impetus to learning.

The apparent answer to the conundrum would seem to be something in between—earlier mainstreaming into regular classes with consistent and targeted support. But the organizational challenges to doing this, especially with an insufficient supply of teachers who are well trained to meet these students' needs in mainstream classes, make such a strategy difficult, if not impossible, to implement. Another option is to provide more two-way learning opportunities for these students.

Assessing English Learners

Related to the issue of language of instruction and reclassification of students is that of language of assessment. No Child Left Behind (NCLB), with its focus on accountability and testing of all students, has resulted in much needed attention to the academic plight of English learners, but it has also placed inordinate pressure on schools and teachers to raise test scores at almost any cost.[53] Although NCLB encourages states to test English learners "in a valid and reliable manner . . . including, to the extent practicable, assessments in the language and form most likely to yield accurate data," states that were not prepared to test students who had been instructed in their primary language have largely ignored this provision of the law.[54] No state has been cited by the Department of Education for failing to adhere to this rule. Moreover, where students in bilingual programs have to perform on English-only tests, many programs curtailed instruction in the primary language in favor of test preparation in English only.[55] Some states, such as New York and Texas, have maintained primary language assessment for purposes of accountability under

NCLB in mathematics, science, and social studies, although the requirement that they test in one language only still leaves many students who are learning in two languages unable to express all that they know. Both Texas and New York have also been attempting to reconcile their systems with NCLB requirements to include all English learners in tests of language arts and not just English proficiency in the first years of instruction. Overwhelmingly, however, states are simply including their English learners in the regular testing regimen with minimal and often unrelated accommodations that do not address the problem of being tested in a language that the student does not understand.[56]

The Movement to Dismantle Bilingual Instruction

If bilingual education has a moderate advantage over other forms of instruction for English learners, is no more costly, at the very least does not harm these students, and can provide students with competence in two languages, why has it been so maligned? Many scholars have noted that language is intimately bound up with identity and that the choice of whose language will be used in the public sphere is also about political power and "belongingness." If one's language is accepted, there is a tacit understanding that the speaker of the language is also accepted. The United States, a nation founded by immigrants, nonetheless has an uneasy relationship with them, and whenever immigration has risen to between 10 and 15 percent of the population, Americans have been quick to wage campaigns against more immigration and to pass laws that make life harder for the immigrants who are here.[57]

Inevitably these laws or policies turn to language since it is a critical marker of the immigrant population. No less a liberal stalwart than Arthur Schlesinger wrote in *The Disuniting of America* in 1991, "Bilingualism shuts doors. It nourishes . . . racial antagonism. . . . Most ominous about the separatist impulses is the meanness generated when one group is set against another."[58] With these words Schlesinger echoed the assertions of the English Only movement, which claims that admitting other languages will tear the nation apart politically, and that English is the glue that unites the many different peoples of the United States together. Critiques of this philosophy, however, have argued that nothing is more disuniting of a nation than denial of the human rights of subgroups, including their right to their language. The drive for secession of Quebec has been popularized in the United States as resulting from French nationalists who pushed their own hegemonic agenda to the point of fracturing the country. But scholars have interpreted it as resulting from the repression of the French culture and language and economic domination by Anglophones, not an overly liberal language policy.[59] The "danger" of proliferating non-English languages is a recurrent theme in the anti-immigrant ethos of the nation, yet there is no evidence that this has ever been a serious threat. English is too valuable as an economic asset and all the polls show that immigrants are anxious to learn it. But many do not understand why they must lose their own language in order to do so.[60]

In 1998, Ron Unz, a Silicon Valley entrepreneur who had aspirations for political office but absolutely no experience in education or the education of English learners, seized on the controversial topic of bilingual education as a vehicle to carry him to statewide visibility. He was nothing if not astute in this regard. He was able to capture inordinate press attention, aided by his fax machine, which sent out daily bulletins on the campaign against bilingual education to every major newspaper in the country. At debates on the topic and other media events, Unz was the darling of the press; they hung on his every word. Outrageous assertions, such as that most bilingual programs did not teach English, went unscrutinized by members of the press, who printed them as though they were facts.[61] In one televised debate on the topic, Unz, after admitting that he had never been in a bilingual classroom, said he based his ideas about the failure of bilingual education on things he had read "in junior high school." When a researcher countered Unz's observations with facts based on numerous research studies, the moderator opined, "It isn't possible to resolve these issues here," thereby cutting off a true rebuttal.[62]

This incident was not unique. Jeff McQuillan and Lucy Tse analyzed research and media accounts of bilingual education between 1984 and 1994, focusing on studies reported in academic journals versus newspaper opinion pieces on the topic. They found that whereas 82 percent of journal articles reported favorable outcomes for bilingual education, only 45 percent of editorials and other opinion pieces in five major national newspapers were favorable to it.[63] Such a media bias against bilingual education would help to explain why so little critical attention was given to Unz's claims.

In the entire campaign against bilingual education, little or no attention was paid to the fact that the overwhelming majority of English learners, who were said to be failing as a result of bilingual education, were not even in bilingual education programs. In 1997, the year prior to the passage of the Unz initiative, only 29 percent of English learners in California were in bilingual programs of any sort. More than 70 percent were in English immersion programs, or nothing at all. The absurdity that bilingual education could be faulted for the educational failure of children who had never experienced it was not raised during the campaign. Moreover, comparisons to English-speaking Latinos and poor black students, who also fared very poorly in school but spoke English, were not raised by the press as counter-examples to Unz's claims.

After Proposition 227 passed with 61 percent of the vote, James Crawford, a former education reporter himself, analyzed how events had unfolded. He faulted, in addition to an uncritical press, a sophisticated campaign strategy paid for out of Unz's own pockets, and a failed countercampaign that fractured over whether it was possible to educate the public in sound bites about the real social and educational problems that confronted low-income English learner students. The countercampaign concluded it couldn't be done in ten-second sound bites and effectively gave up trying to defend the program.[64]

After winning in California, Unz succeeded in Arizona in 2000, and Massachusetts (a state with only 5 percent English learners) in 2002. His campaign was finally stopped in Colorado, which voted down the initiative in 2002 after launching a carefully crafted counteroffensive, paid for in large part by a wealthy Anglo parent of a child in a dual-language program.[65]

One of the keys to understanding why bilingual education is so maligned can be found in the messaging work that was done by the political consultants in Colorado, who had carefully studied what had happened in the other Unz initiative states. One of the chief strategists for the Colorado anti-Unz campaign was quoted as saying, "If this is about being Mexican, about Mexicans, it is gone. It's got to be about Coloradoans."[66] There were two messages in this quote: that an effective campaign had to be perceived as a local issue, and that Coloradoans would vote against a proposal they believed would benefit Mexicans. In other words, racism would play a role in how people voted.

The Bottom Line: Inequitable Education

The problem of English learners' underachievement, like that of other Latino students, is more likely related to the quality of education that these students receive, regardless of the language of instruction. Even though these students need more instructional attention and time than others (because they have more tasks to master and usually have fewer educational supports in their homes and community), they almost always receive less. A recent study on the conditions of learning for English learners in California found that these students were consistently underserved in comparison to other students, even similarly low-income students:

> They attend more segregated schools where facilities and conditions are demonstrably worse than in middle-income schools.

> They have teachers with less training and who receive very little professional instruction for teaching English learners.

> They have inadequate books and materials and are assessed with tests (developed for English speakers) that distort or fail to capture what they know.

> They have insufficient time to learn the curriculum they must master.

> Their academic year is often cut short by days and weeks as administrators work to find the correct placement for them.

> Daily instructional time is lost while they wait for someone to explain the lesson that the rest of the class is receiving.

> The likelihood that they will have a teacher who can speak to them or their parents in a common language, or instruct them by building on what they already know in their native language, is very small.[67]

As a result of these factors, the educational achievement of English learners is lowest of all groups of students in the public schools except for special education pupils.[68]

Nothing in schooling is more important than the quality of teachers. Good teachers prepare students for successful futures, whereas poorly prepared teachers can have devastating long-term effects on the academic achievement of students.[69] Some researchers have argued that after three consecutive years with ineffective teachers, pupils may never be able to recover academically.[70] Yet students with limited English proficiency are the least likely of all students to have a teacher who is actually prepared to instruct them.[71] No Child Left Behind requires that all pupils have "highly qualified" teachers, yet there is no mention of setting standards for highly qualified teachers of English learners. Moreover, we have seen in our research that highly qualified teachers for mainstream students may be completely inadequate for the task of educating English learners.

In a series of studies, Patricia Gándara and her colleagues investigated the preparation of teachers for students who are English learners in California. In one recent study we found that teachers' own sense of their ability to teach English learners was related to their degree of specialized preparation and skills: those teachers with bilingual teaching credentials were most confident, those with some training in cultural and linguistic diversity felt moderately capable, and those without appropriate specialized credentials felt the least competent.[72] How teachers feel about their ability to teach students has been shown to actually predict their success in the classroom, so these attitudes are important.[73] Many teachers in this study of 5,300 California educators said they needed a great deal of help, but that little was forthcoming.

Another recent study of California teachers similarly found that teachers cited the skills to successfully instruct English learners as one of their areas of greatest need.[74] Nationally, a survey of services provided to English learners in 2003 found that more than 40 percent of teachers nationwide had English learners in their classrooms, yet only about 10 percent reported that they were proficient in reading and writing the language of their students. Over a period of five years, these teachers had received only a median of four hours of training in teaching English-learner students.[75] Teachers who care but are not supported seldom succeed. Studies have shown that teachers who lack the skills to teach the English learners in their classrooms are frustrated and feel incompetent.[76] The belief that they are not effective at their job is a prime reason that teachers burn out and leave the field.[77]

There is a solution to many of the challenges of effectively educating English learners: hiring qualified teachers from students' own communities. Such teachers not only better understand the challenges that students face and the resources that exist in those communities; they are also more likely to speak the language of the students and be able to communicate with them and their parents. Moreover, teachers who come from the same community in which they work are more likely to stay in the job over time, developing valuable experience and expertise that has been shown to enhance the achievement of their students.[78] Unfortunately, only about 5 percent of the teachers of English learners across the nation are certified bilingual teachers, and only about 6 percent of teachers nationally are Latino (compared to 20 percent of students).[79] But there has never been a concerted effort to recruit and train teachers from these underrepresented communities. The costs associated with such an effort, even if it involved paying the full costs of teachers' college educations, would be well spent. Research has shown that government recoups the cost of a college education in a little over nine years after a student's graduation through increased tax revenues generated by enhanced earnings.[80] Moreover, given that these teachers have a much greater likelihood of staying in the schools with high percentages of English learners (where there is such a high, and costly, turnover of personnel), significant cost savings could be realized by their schools. This local-recruitment strategy would also be an important mechanism for getting more Latinos (and members of other underrepresented groups) into the higher education pipeline.

Redefining the Bilingual Issue

It is ironic that Latino civil rights in education became defined as access to bilingual education given that ultimately the biggest problem for Latino students in the schools is and was the inequitable education they receive, regardless of the type of language program offered. In many ways, the controversies and debates over language have distracted the Latino community from the essential inequities they face.

Approaches toward educating English learners in the United States have been driven more by political expediency or ideological bias than by solid research on effective practice. Moreover, the single most critical element of these students' education, qualified teachers, has received hardly a policy nod. Due in large part to the highly politicized nature of language use, the federal government has missed the opportunity to spearhead the critical research on how best to educate the teachers who teach English learners, and how to most effectively tailor instruction for these students. The federal government has wasted time and money on studies that asked the wrong question and avoided the important ones. Millions of dollars have been spent, and great amounts of political capital squandered, on attempting to determine which program is most effective—bilingual education or English-only instruction—without bothering to ask for whom and under what conditions. When the question is appropriately reframed, it becomes apparent that the goals of instruction also require definition: are they English proficiency, biliteracy, grade-level achievement, or something else? Research focusing on the critical competencies necessary for teachers of English learners has not been conducted, and the essential content of teacher preparation and professional development programs remains unknown.

Richard Ruiz has argued that the "problem" of limited English proficiency is, in fact, a social construction.[81] He contends that by framing the condition of English-learner pupils as having a "language problem," policy becomes skewed toward transitioning these students as quickly and efficiently as possible from their native language into English. If, as Ruiz suggests, programs for English-learning students were instead based on the belief that language is a resource, then they would look very different. Such programs would make full use of the primary language and attempt to build on it, and there would be more political support for, and a greater emphasis on, academic achievement, rather than merely acquiring English.

When our approach to language education involves eradicating a student's native language in an effort to transform their identities, the results are predictably negative. Moreover, shifting educational policies at both the state and federal level, which have been driven by political rather than pedagogical considerations, have undermined opportunities to improve the education of English learners. If more attention were given to broader social and economic goals, biliteracy—which is achievable for most English speakers and English learners at little additional cost—would likely be a national priority.[82] Instead, it is viewed as a threat to national unity. And Latino students have been left largely empty-handed, with access neither to the most effective language education, nor to an equitable education in English.

CHAPTER FIVE

Inside the Lives of Puente Students

Between 1994 and 2002, as part of a larger study of a college-access program called Puente (in Spanish, "bridge"), we followed the lives and academic experiences of twenty-eight Latino students, all of Mexican origin. Although the program operates in thirty-six high schools in California, we selected three, located in different areas of the state, from which to select our sample. The larger study involved approximately two thousand students from whom we collected attitudinal data about school, college plans, peer influences, and the like, and another smaller group of 144 (program and control) for whom we tracked grades, test scores, college acceptances, and other quantitative data. The smaller sample of twenty-eight, however, was studied intensively to understand how students in the program made decisions about school and college, and what kinds of circumstances and life events shaped those decisions. We met with students several times each year of high school; talked with their friends, teachers, counselors, and mentors; observed them informally on campus; and surveyed them periodically.

Puente is a unique program in that it focuses specifically on Latino high school students, drawing on resources in the students' own communities in an attempt to provide them with both the skills and the desire to continue on to college.[1] The program is based on the belief that solutions to the underachievement of Latino students lie at least partly in a stronger connection with both positive community elements and the intellectual traditions of the Latino culture. It has three basic components: a two-year, intensive college-preparatory English class that emphasizes Latino literature and sociopolitical circumstances, critical thinking, and intensive writing instruction across various genres; college and personal counseling; and mentoring. There is a preference for both counselors and especially mentors to come from the students' own community and to be able to communicate with parents in Spanish. The program attempts to serve a broad range of learners, and is very explicit about the types of students who are selected to participate. Puente tries to focus its efforts on students who demonstrate a sincere desire to improve or excel in school and who "buy into" a college-preparatory ideology. That is, it seeks students who can not only articulate that they want to go to college, but also see college as a vehicle for personal and social change. Commonly, students are nominated by teachers and counselors from the sending middle schools, and students are then selected based on how they fit one of four categories of effort and achievement.

Category 1 students are high achievers with good grades, generally good test scores, and other evidence of good effort. Category 2 students are commonly referred to as "high potential," as demonstrated by high test scores, grades, or recommendations, but they have shown lower motivation than a Category 1 student (for example, somewhat more erratic school performance). Category 3 students are those who put forth a great deal of effort, but have lower grades. A student in this category, for example, will demonstrate a strong desire to excel, but may not have been consistently successful in school. Finally, Category 4 students commonly have a history of low performance as well as low effort, but their teachers or counselors believe that, with help, they are capable of performing at a higher level. The program model assumes that recommendations for such students are based on evidence that a student sincerely wants to improve his or her performance, but sometimes students are recommended because they are perceived by others as needing an intervention to help turn things around.

Our twenty-eight students were selected at the beginning of ninth grade in consultation with teachers in the program. We also observed students in the classroom, and on the basis of observations, and discussions with teachers, we settled on the twenty-eight. Males and females were equally represented in the group, as were students from each school who fell into the four different categories. Significantly, very little was known about these students' personal lives at the point of selection. They were new to the school and their teachers knew little more than their prior grades, test scores, and general deportment in class. Thus, the experiences of these students over the next four years were as surprising as they were informative about the challenges that low-income Latino students face.

Most of the original twenty-eight students remained in the study through the first two years after high school. Unfortunately, however, funds ran out then; it was not possible to follow students all the way to college graduation, if it occurred. In addition, some students were lost right after high school graduation or even earlier, due to multiple moves and no forwarding information. We were able, however, to gather information about college outcomes for some students who had maintained contact with their counselors. For an overview of the group, see Table 5.1.

Although the high schools that these students attended were similar in size—between 1,800 and 2,000 students (a typical size for California)—they are located in three very different parts of the state. North High School is located in an urban area in the north. It is in a densely populated neighborhood with many apartment dwellers and is situated alongside a major four-lane highway. The school had long

Table 5.1   Sample Puente students

Category (number of students)	8th grade GPA	12th grade GPA	Percent held back in school	Percent going to four-year college	Percent going to two-year college	Percent going to military or other job
1 (8)	3.5	2.87	88	50	12.5	37.5
2 (7)	3.0	2.82	100	71	29	0
3 (7)	2.5	2.96	100	33	50	17
4 (6)	1.67	2.2	50	0	33	66

Source: Gándara 1998, p. 94.

suffered from a reputation as a "bad" school characterized by a lot of gang activity and occasional violence on the campus, although more recently the school had begun to turn its reputation around. By the time the Puente students were in the twelfth grade, nearly half of the school was Latino, 40 percent was Asian, and African American and white students made up the balance. The Latino students were largely of Mexican origin, and the Asians were primarily Southeast Asian—with a preponderance of Vietnamese. North High School touted that it had sent students on to prestigious colleges such as Yale and Harvard; overall achievement at the school, however, had historically been low, and Mexican American students ranked at the lowest levels academically.

The second school, South High School, is located within the suburban sprawl that extends between Los Angeles and Orange County. The school is framed by largely lower-middle, and working-class, single-family homes. Houses in the neighborhood are modest but well cared for. Like the rest of the Southern California region, the demographics in this area have been shifting rapidly. Once a largely European American area, it has become increasingly Mexican American. During our study, white and Latino students each made up about 40 percent of the school population, with the balance being made up of Asians and a very few African Americans. The school is typical of many other high schools in the state with respect to academic achievement; some students go on to four-year colleges, while most transition directly to work or two-year colleges. At South High School, like at other high schools around the state, the Mexican-origin students are the least likely of all groups on campus to go on to four-year colleges.

The third school in the study, Frontera High School, is located a few miles from the California-Mexico border. Not surprisingly, it has the highest percentage of Mexican-origin students, and a very high percentage of these are immigrants themselves, or the children of immigrants. The school does not keep track of immigration status, but clearly a significant proportion of the students come from homes in which some members of the family are undocumented—a situation that often stresses students and families in particular ways. More than 80 percent of the students are of Mexican origin, and the balance of the students are either European American or black. Spanish is spoken as frequently as English in informal conversation on the campus. Test scores at Frontera High School are below state and national averages. Some students excel and go on to four-year colleges, although the overwhelming majority do not. Unlike at the other schools in the study, however, those students who do excel at Frontera High School are likely to be Mexican American, and often from immigrant families.

Category 1 Students: Starting Out High

Seven of the original eight Category 1 students remained in the study through high school graduation. Four are females and three are males. (One male student dropped out of school rather suddenly and somewhat unexpectedly in the spring of 1997. Although a very capable student, this young man began working more and more hours until school no longer fit into his schedule.) The Category 1 students had an average grade point average (GPA) of 3.5 when they began high school, but by eleventh grade this average had dropped to 3.2, and they graduated with an average GPA of just 2.87—a considerable slide downward from their lofty beginnings. There is tremendous variability in the performance among this group of students who were high achievers at the beginning of high school. About half remained strong students and continued to excel through the eleventh grade, but by twelfth grade only two of these students had maintained a GPA above 3.0. The others, meanwhile, encountered problems or significant distractions—mostly outside school—that derailed their ambitions. In a general sense, the backgrounds of these students were not different from the backgrounds of the students in the other categories: six of the eight families either spoke only Spanish or used both Spanish and English in the home, whereas only two were primarily English-speaking families. A couple came from single-parent families and half had parents who were not educated beyond elementary school. Only two of these students came from homes in which the parents had gone as far as junior college. These were the same two students who continued to excel through the end of high school.

All students in this study were asked to rank the importance of their family, school, friends, boyfriend/girlfriend, work, sport, or other significant activity in their life. Seven of the eight Category 1 students ranked school either first or second, competing only with family. Interestingly, even the student who dropped out of high school ranked school second in importance in his life, right behind family. An important distinguishing characteristic of those students who remained among the highest achievers in this group is that they maintained close relationships with other students in the Puente program, often studying together and supporting each other socially and emotionally. All of these students aspired to attend four-year colleges and universities and had taken all of the required college entrance exams by eleventh grade, suggesting that they were on track to realize their ambitions. As a group, however, they experienced the most serious declines in both aspirations and performance. Two students from this group stand out as powerful examples of the life circumstances that can intervene in the lives of low-income Latino students.

Andrés

We introduced Andrés in Chapter 1 of this book. A tall and lanky young man, with straight black hair, intense black eyes, and a serious demeanor, Andrés attended Frontera High School. When we first met he was very shy and it was difficult to get him to say more than a few words at a time. Not having seen his records, we assessed that he was probably an above-average student, but struggling in some areas. When asked how he was doing in school, he said, "OK, but there are things I don't understand in my classes. I have to listen hard, pay a lot of attention." We assumed that Andrés was like many other Latino students, wanting to do well, but barely staying afloat in some of the more rigorous courses, perhaps with some problems due to language. As we probed further, it was evident that this early assessment was wrong. Andrés had completed his freshman year with a 4.04. He had earned all A's and two A pluses. He was taking a regular college preparatory curriculum and had selected German to meet his language requirement. Asked why he was taking German, when Spanish would have seemed the more obvious choice (he was a native Spanish speaker), he said he liked the challenge. And besides, he liked German.

Andrés was the oldest of three children when he began high school. By the end of his sophomore year, his mother had had another child—a fourth boy. Of his two other younger brothers, one was four years younger, and one was ten years his junior. The middle brother, at ten years old, was already showing signs of not liking school, and was getting into trouble. Andrés's household included his mother, a Mexican immigrant who had attended junior college but married and had children before she completed her studies, and a stepfather, a working-class man who had immigrated from northern Europe. Because the stepfather was undocumented, it had been difficult for him to find work, and the mother had supported the family of five with a paper route and part-time work at a fast-food restaurant. When she had her fourth child, however, she had to give up the fast-food job and just concentrate on serving a larger paper route. Andrés helped many mornings, getting up at two or three in the morning to prepare papers and help deliver them. He then came home and slept for a short while before going to school.

Andrés's mother and biological father had divorced when he was only a few years old. His father, a Chicano with a bachelor's degree in computer science, had since remarried and moved to a nearby state. During his freshman year, Andrés spoke positively about his father and looked forward to spending time with him. After his freshman year, however, Andrés returned from spending part of the summer with his father and reported that things had not gone especially well. He did not feel comfortable with his father's new wife, and he had begun to feel pushed aside in his father's life by the demands of the new family. This sense was confirmed in his eyes when after his sixteenth birthday, with his new driver's license in hand, he went to visit his father for the summer. Returning to school in the fall, Andrés reported that his father had not had time to make a promised road trip through the Southwest with him. Andrés's disappointment was palpable, but he made excuses for his father. He said he understood.

Serious tensions began to arise between father and son, however, as Andrés became increasingly aware that his father did not pay any child support for his brother and him. With a new baby in the home, and with his mother cutting back to only one job, finances were exceptionally strained. His father explained that he could not help out financially because of his own pressing needs. Moreover, each time that Andrés's mother suggested that the father might provide money to support his three sons, he reportedly threatened to seek custody of the boys, throwing the home into turmoil. These tensions began to erode the father-son relationship and by the end of high school, Andrés had only sporadic contact with his father.

From our first meeting in ninth grade, Andrés was certain of what he wanted to do for a career. He wanted to be in some kind of law enforcement, and joining the FBI was an ultimate goal. Asked about his interests, he offered that he was "a little obsessed with weapons." Asked why, he replied, "So I'll know how to use them when I'm an FBI agent." Andrés claimed not to romanticize the job. He said, "I know it's also a lot of paperwork, but I like the idea of capturing criminals and putting them behind bars to make the world a better place for my children." Andrés already had a grown-up sense of responsibility and a drive to right the wrongs he saw around him. In an essay he wrote in the ninth grade, he expressed this grown-up understanding of the problems his mother faced, displaying a sober view of the world that is uncharacteristic for a young adolescent. He wrote, "My younger brother does not see all of the positive things about my mom . . . [he] only sees my mom's struggles as a piece of cake, but my mom's problems are not a piece of cake. . . . I understand why my mom is strict. She is like that so when she dies we would already be in [the] habit to clean up or cook for ourselves."

In his freshman and sophomore years, Andrés reported not having a girlfriend. He hung out with the same best friends throughout high school—a small group of boys, only one of whom seemed to share his academic ambitions. In his junior year, he had a rather intensive relationship with a nineteen-year-old girl who was not from his school that caused his grades to slip considerably. Another transition came in his senior year: he reported then that he no longer had a girlfriend and was spending more time at his church. "I help out at the church by setting and cleaning up after a service. I've become very involved in the church. It is a support system for me. I've acquired a second family through the church. I can really relate to them. We can talk about our problems."

Andrés stood out among his peers in a very important way. He had gathered a group of Puente students around him, none of whom performed as well as he, and he tutored and encouraged them to push themselves in their studies. One morning when we met to talk, Andrés was clearly tired. He expressed that he had had little sleep the night before because he had been up almost all night helping two of his Puente friends finish papers for their classes. He was proud that they had completed three papers on one computer during the all-nighter. While Andrés pushed himself by taking every Advanced Placement and honors course that he could, he also vowed to make sure that all the Puente students in his study group would have the grades they needed to go to college.

Andrés graduated from high school with a 3.74 and an 1120 on the SAT: respectable grades, but less than the nearly 4.0 he had sustained for most of his high school career. Nonetheless, because of his rigorous high school course of study, and the significant hardships that he had overcome, Andrés was a good candidate for a highly selective university with considerable scholarship support. But he was very worried about leaving his mother alone with her heavy responsibilities. Consequently, even though he had always voiced the intention of going to college after high school, and even though his counselor and teachers had pressed him hard to apply to the closest highly selective four-year campus as a way of reducing his concerns about leaving home, Andrés opted to join the Marine Corps Reserves upon graduation. He reasoned that the Marines would help him pay for his college education when he enrolled and that he could simply defer college for the time being. His concerns about money and being available to help his family were ultimately the biggest factors in his decision.

When we last heard from Andrés his educational plans had been delayed by a year because of his service commitments, but he was in his second year of community college. Importantly, he had selected that particular college because it had a Puente program and in high school he had been involved in all of the Puente activities and had considered it his primary source of moral support. He had changed his major from criminal justice to psychology, and had maintained a 3.5 GPA. His plans were to get his associate in arts degree within four years of graduating from high school, and then his bachelor's degree two years after that from the local state university. But all of that changed with his orders to go to Iraq. We lost track of him—and his family members—until he surfaced once again in the community college records one and a half years later. Now Andrés was taking only one course at a time, and had failed two classes—a shocking development for such a strong student. Five years after high school graduation, we were again unable to find him, although we do know that at that point he was still not eligible to transfer to a four-year institution. There is no more record of him in the community college system. It is more than possible that he was called back for a second or third tour of duty in Iraq. His whereabouts are unknown. Andrés was one of the brightest academic stars in his high school, and it seemed that for him, the sky was the limit. By the numbers, he should have been one of the big academic successes of the Puente program—full scholarship to a prestigious four-year college or university. But for Andrés, loyalty to family was more powerful than his personal ambitions, and then a war got in the way, and then . . . we just don't know. It is clear, however, that if he had gone straight to college after high school, statistically his chances of having earned a degree several years ago would have been very good.

Ofelia

Ofelia was in Andrés's study group at Frontera High School. She is a slightly plump young woman with dark hair and eyes and a pleasant, earnest face. Ofelia was born in Mexico and came to the United States when she was seven years old. When she began high school, she was living with her mother and brother, and the language of the home was Spanish.

Ofelia began high school with a 3.8 GPA and big ambitions. On her application to the Puente program, she noted that she wanted to be a doctor, a lawyer, or a CEO. When asked where she wanted to go to college, her choices were Harvard, Stanford, or Boston University— even though most of her peers did not know the difference between an Ivy League school and a community college. Ofelia selected her friends carefully from among the most ambitious in her school, and when asked the hypothetical question of whom she might want to change places with, she chose the student who was perceived to be the smartest in the class. She also rated school as the number one priority in her life, ahead of family, friends, and other activities. Of all of the students in the study, Ofelia was the most clear about her goals and the most knowledgeable about her options. Like Andrés, however, she was enamored of the idea of joining the military, or going to the U.S. Naval Academy, as a way to help pay for her college education.

Ofelia's parents separated when she was young and she had almost no contact with her father, although in an essay on people she admired, she listed him "because he is smart." Her father graduated from high school and went to seminary in Italy. Ofelia and her brother became separated from their mother after coming to the United States and they spent most of their childhoods with foster families. A couple of years before she began high school, however, she and her brother, who is four years older than she is, lit upon the idea of searching for their mother through a radio program that attempted to unite missing relatives. Incredibly, the mother heard her children's plea and the family was reunited. But life with Ofelia's mother was unstable. The mother has only an elementary school education and suffers from chronic health problems. When questioned about her family situation early in the study, Ofelia defended her mother and expressed the belief that it was her own responsibility to help out around the house and work to augment the family's income since her mother was usually unable to work. After her mother was incarcerated on drug-related charges during Ofelia's tenth grade year, it became increasingly difficult for Ofelia to defend her mother's actions, and the picture she had painted for outsiders of a courageous, hardworking mother became difficult to sustain. The situation was psychologically very stressful for her. She went to live first with her older brother who was also struggling to go to school and work, then later with the family of her boyfriend, a young Chicano who was an outstanding student at the same high school and who was headed for a highly selective college upon graduation.

Ofelia also took on several jobs to help support herself. She worked at McDonald's, cleaned offices in the evening, and sold food at a ballpark concession stand. The stress of her difficult home life and long hours at work took a toll on her health and her grades. She was taken to the hospital twice during her sophomore year for stomach pains that doctors ultimately attributed to stress. Her grades fluctuated wildly, from a high of 3.7 to failing all of her classes. Nonetheless, Ofelia maintained the conviction that she would go to college. She took night classes and summer school to make up failed courses and raise her GPA. She studied three and four hours a night, often with the Puente study group, even as she volunteered at the local hospital and library and tutored ninth-graders. She was also on the school's

Academic Decathalon team, which required many additional hours of study. In the eleventh grade Ofelia reported that she routinely slept only about three hours a night.

When during Ofelia's junior year Ofelia's mother was released from prison and asked that they live together again, Ofelia was reluctant. She noted that her mother was not supportive of her educational goals. She said, "My mom and I argue about school; she [thinks] my classes take up too much time." Ofelia became convinced that living with her mother, and the resultant pressures to work more and study less, would make her college goals impossible. She decided instead to move in with her boyfriend's family.

As energetic as Ofelia is, she still found herself at a crossroads at graduation. She graduated with a 2.4 GPA and a 900 on the SAT, a considerable accomplishment given the roller-coaster ride that her high school years had been, but far below what everyone acknowl-edged was her potential, and what she would need to enroll in a se-lective four-year college. Ofelia credited the support of her Puente study group and her boyfriend with her academic comeback. At this point, reluctant to be separated from her boyfriend who was attend-ing college, she sought information about community colleges in the same area. But by the summer after high school graduation, she still had no definite plan. With intervention by the Puente program, Ofelia was admitted to a state university campus and given sufficient financial aid to live and go to school.

After moving to college, Ofelia spent every weekend visiting her boyfriend, and failed to make friends with other students on her own campus. She felt isolated and alone, with no family or friends nearby, and gradually began disengaging from school. At the end of the first semester of college, it was clear that things were not going well and she wanted to leave. Puente staff intervened again, encouraging her to stay, and she hung on until the end of the year. By the end of her first year, however, Ofelia had decided to leave college and had returned home. Meanwhile, her boyfriend had also had a difficult year at college and took a leave of absence. The two enrolled in the local junior college, but Ofelia only enrolled part-time. We do not know if Ofelia ever completed any more college credits. Her trajectory at the point of last contact was not good, and she stopped calling her counselor who had been her primary link to college.

Half of the eight very high-achieving students in our study went on to a four-year college after high school graduation. The odds are high that those students did, indeed, complete their degrees though we do not have data on this. We followed both Andrés and Ofelia for some years after high school graduation because, with their drive and ambition, they initially appeared to be the most likely to complete college. Both had enormous potential. On paper, both began high school with the kinds of grades, test scores, and focus that should have predicted high achievement and an easy transition to college. Many people would—and did—argue that these were the kinds of students who did not need significant support to make it to college, and that resources would be better spent on students whose academic careers were more precarious. All the way through his senior year, Andrés still looked like a candidate for a highly selective university and appeared to have the drive and ambition to make this happen. Ofelia's difficult personal life made her an obvious risk for school problems, but her ambition, tenacity, and clear goals, in addition to her tendency to hang out with very high-achieving peers, seemed to bode well for a positive outcome. Yet for both of these students, complicated personal lives and responsibilities, as well as a lack of financial resources, made the road to a college degree rocky. For Andrés and Ofelia, the Puente program remained an important source of support and guidance after graduation. Without parents or family members providing emotional support and knowledgeable guidance, the obstacles they encountered were difficult to manage alone. The outcomes for these students are still unknown, but their journeys have been far more difficult than anyone had imagined.

Category 2 Students: Moderately High Achievers

There were seven students in Category 2, all of whom stayed with the study through graduation. These students all began high school with fairly strong academic records, but were viewed as underachieving in some respect. As a group they started high school with a mean GPA of 3.0 and maintained that level for most of their high school careers, dropping to a mean of 2.82 at graduation. As a group, they were actually somewhat more consistent than the Category 1 students, mostly getting B's and some C's, with no one at serious risk of failing out of school. Demographically, they look very much like the Category 1 students, whose academic histories were more variable, and the Category 3 students, who performed less well academically. Five of the seven came from homes in which the parents had achieved less than a high school education—generally, they had only completed elementary school. One had a parent with junior college experience, and one had a parent with a bachelor's degree. In only one of the homes was English the only language spoken. With their somewhat lower individual GPAs than the Category 1 students, these Category 2 students focused their ambitions on the state college system or on private four-year colleges that might be a little easier to gain admission to than the University of California. But they also kept open the possibility of aiming higher. One student with a 3.3 still had hoped to go to a University of California campus at the point of graduation, and all but one of the students took the SAT, which opened up the possibility of applying to more selective schools. As with the Category 1 cohort, the most successful of the Category 2 students tended to socialize mostly with other Puente students, and all but one maintained active friendships with other goal-oriented students. Two students who typify the profile of Category 2 students are Angela and José.

Angela

Angela is tall and light-skinned, with light brown hair and a broad, expressive face. She smiles easily and is well liked by her peers. She is also something of a social butterfly. Asked about who her friends were in various contexts, Angela proceeded to name a lengthy list of students with whom she interacted both in and out of South High School. In spite of generally good grades and a serious attitude toward school, she listed it as a low fourth priority behind family, friends, and boyfriend.

Angela is the oldest daughter and one of six children; her parents were both born in Mexico and were educated there only as far as the third or fourth grade. Angela's mother stayed home with the children and her father worked in a factory making automobile parts. Her relationship with her parents is interesting. While she reported tensions with her mother because she set strict rules for Angela—no boyfriends, no driving, a strict curfew—she also professed to admire her mother greatly. In fact, one of the characteristics she admired most about her mother was her ability to be "in control" of her life. Thus the very control that sometimes made Angela bristle was also a quality that she valued highly in her mother. Her father was much more supportive of Angela's independence and often allowed what her mother would not. Nonetheless, Angela's strongest bonds were with her mother.

Although she was a good student coming into high school (she had a 3.4 GPA), Angela was undecided about going to college and unsure of what she might do when she finished high school. Her professed vocational interests shifted over the first few years of high school from architect to teacher, to pediatrician, to nurse. These changes seemed to be guided largely by Angela's growing understanding of what was required to prepare for each of these careers. She pressed herself to take largely Advanced Placement and honors courses, although she did not always do well in them. Her stated goal was to get B's, but she frequently fell short of this, once getting an F in math that had to be made up in summer school. Math, in fact, was a major stumbling block for Angela and she dreaded her math classes. Nonetheless she completed the sequence through Algebra 2 because she was counseled that it was required for good four-year colleges. By the eleventh grade she had decided that as a result of her experience in Puente, she "want[ed] to go to college. I know that I can have a better future for my family." Angela's goal became to attend a university, live in the dorms (which her mother did not support), and become a nurse. She was focused on her goals and anxious to raise her GPA from a 3.0 to a 3.5 to make this possible.

But Angela also had a number of other competing responsibilities and interests. As the oldest child, Angela had to help her mother with her brothers and sisters. Throughout high school she had a job most afternoons caring for the children of two professionals who lived nearby (but in her words, "in another world" from her family). And she had a boyfriend who also took up time. Both her parents and her counselor worried that she might spread herself too thin. But the easiest responsibility to drop—the childcare job—Angela was not anxious to give up because she relished the contact with the children's family and the advice they gave her about how to achieve her goals.

Angela tended to hang out with other high-achieving young women from school, two of whom were headed for the nearest University of California campus. Angela, too, had thought this would be a good option. But several things conspired to change her mind: higher grades did not materialize, she began to think of how hard it would be to maintain her focus on school if she were to try to commute or live too close to her family, and she broke up with her boyfriend. She was never able to raise her GPA to the 3.5 she sought, but she did manage to finish high school with a 3.0 and 1000 on her SAT exam. This made it possible for her to enroll at a relatively selective state university campus farther from home than she had at first considered. Angela moved away from home and went to live in a college dorm—something her mother had initially opposed.

The summer before college, Angela was invited to attend a summer bridge program at the college she was going to attend. This turned out to be an especially important experience. Although the program was not particularly instrumental in helping her decide what she might major in, or in providing a strong academic foundation, it did help to orient Angela to the routines and expectations of college, and introduced her to a number of students who later became good friends. In fact, she contended that the friendships she formed in the summer helped her immensely in adjusting to college. Having never been away from home before, she had been concerned about whether homesickness would be a problem. She attributed her ability to overcome it to her tight network of friends. This was probably a reasonably accurate assessment on Angela's part, because some other students we followed did, indeed, leave four-year colleges to return to the local community college due to feelings of homesickness and isolation.

In spite of her participation in the summer bridge program, Angela was not well prepared to decide what to study at college. Her parents were not able to provide guidance about career choices, so Angela declared a major in biology as a way of advancing toward her one-time goal of becoming a pediatrician or a nurse. But biology in college was not at all what she had experienced in high school; the classes were demanding and competitive, and the subject did not interest her. She changed to psychology after struggling with a relatively low 2.3 GPA in her freshman year. Nonetheless, Angela remained confident that she would graduate from college within five years and she was happy with her college choice. She also maintained contact with a number of her Puente classmates who attended other colleges, as well as with her Puente counselor, who continued to advise and encourage her. At the end of five years Angela was headed for graduation.

José

José is a handsome young man with bronze skin, dark hair, and a well-groomed appearance. He has an outgoing personality and a quick sense of humor that are apparent in even a brief conversation. He began North High School with a good GPA—3.1—and continued to advance academically each year. At the end of eleventh grade his GPA was 3.6. José is the second-oldest child in a family of five siblings, and neither of his parents had a high school education. His father was a construction worker and his mother was a homemaker. The family spoke Spanish at home.

José jumped at the opportunity to take honors classes and enjoyed a challenge in school. By his junior year almost all of his classes were honors or Advanced Placement, and he was maintaining at least a B in all with very little real effort. In fact, his goal going into twelfth grade was to get a 4.0, which would have required only a little more study. When he began high school his goal was to attend a very prestigious private university and go into medicine. This was the path his older brother was following and he, as well as the rest of the family, was very proud of this brother. José, however, started a car detailing business at about the same time that he started high school. Initially, it was a small, part-time activity he engaged in after school and on weekends. As the years went by, however, each interview with José included more and more discussion of the job and revealed that he was spending an increasing amount of time on the job rather than studying.

José was well liked by the other students and he maintained some friendships among the Puente group, but he generally preferred to hang out with the *cholos* from his neighborhood—boys who would often cut school and showed little interest in studying. Nonetheless, his school performance was not affected by the lower aspirations of his homeboys. His other interests, however, did threaten to derail his ambitions. The auto detailing business grew and José enjoyed the income it provided. Unlike his brother who studied all the time and had no money, José was able to maintain a nice car and buy most of the things he wanted. As a result, he started to talk about not going too far away from home for college, and maintaining the job on the side. He continued to contend that he wanted to go to a good university, but he also expressed a desire to be close to home and near his fledgling business.

José graduated from high school with an SAT score of 1020 and a GPA of 2.96. His grades had fallen precipitously during his senior year as his attention turned away from school. He vacillated throughout his senior year about going to college or dedicating himself to his business. He did not apply to the highly selective school he had initially set his sights on, but was accepted at a well-regarded private university near his home, and he reported at the time that he had decided to accept the offer of admission and maintain his business on the side.

José did not, however, go to college. He changed his mind and decided instead to "take a year off" to dedicate himself full-time to his business. He contended that his older brother and he were equal partners in the business and split the profits, although José was the one who ran it since his brother was studying full-time at college. As José put it, "My brother is the studious one, so the way I see it, he'll be living out both of our dreams in terms of medicine." Two years after high school, José did enroll at the local community college part-time, taking largely business courses. He reported that he had about a 3.5 GPA in his courses, because "it's not too tough there." When asked when he thought he would graduate from college, he could not say. He simply noted that he wasn't "really thinking about that now. Actually I think of it as a waste of time. My business is doing great and we're about to expand. When the weather isn't good, I work at city college library and get paid over $12 bucks an hour. So, I'm doing pretty good right now."

Angela and José were both bright students, although school clearly came more easily for José, and while neither had parents with very much formal education, José's good record and high ambitions in the early years of high school seemed to indicate a more likely enrollment in a good four-year college. When asked in the eleventh grade what was most important to him or her at the time, José ranked school first, but just ahead of work; and Angela ranked school a low number four, behind family, friends, and boyfriend. For both students, however, these priorities changed radically between eleventh grade and high school graduation.

For Angela, breaking up with her boyfriend, putting her family's needs in greater perspective, and seeing her friends preparing to go off to college left her with school and college as her highest priority. It is important to recall that Angela's best friends always intended to go to college, and they frequently talked about going off together. The idea of college simply moved from the margins of her thinking to take center stage. Although Angela's parents had not been able to provide much guidance about college, she had been surrounded with supportive friends, teachers, and a counselor who kept close tabs on her. She is also a woman, and therefore statistically more likely to go to college than a Latino male.

José, by contrast, hung out with people very unlike himself. While he maintained cordial relationships with the other college-bound students he had met in Puente, his close friends were not interested in school and none went on to a four-year college. Therefore, it was not a disappointment to any of his friends when he chose to stay home and work. He did admit that he "got a lot of advice from everyone. Of course, they were all telling me about going straight to college, but I made a decision that was best for me. I knew what I wanted to do." Like Angela, José's parents were supportive of him, but unable to provide either firm or knowledgeable guidance about the benefits of a college education. Even his brother could not persuade him that a college degree would be the better long-term choice.

Category 3 Students: Modest Achievers Motivated to Improve

The six Category 3 students began their high school careers with less well-developed skills than the previous two groups and they continued through high school with more modest goals. The students in this group had an overall GPA of 2.5 at the beginning of high school, an average that dropped to 2.0 in the eleventh grade, but rose substantially during their senior year so that they graduated with a mean GPA of 2.96. Moreover, there were no dropouts in this group. While the first two categories of students studied an average of two to three hours per night, most of the Category 3 students claimed to study between thirty minutes to an hour each night (though we suspect that they increased their study time during the final year of high school). In the eleventh grade, none of these students considered school to be their top priority—the majority ranked family first. Demographically, however, they are very similar to other students in the sample. None of their parents had an education more advanced than high school, and most had less. Only one of these homes is exclusively English-speaking. By the eleventh grade, the Category 3 students were beginning to scale their ambitions to their academic situations and although all but one wanted "to go to college," they were not specific about which one. In addition, most acknowledged that they would need to go to a community college first before hopefully transferring to a four-year university. One significant difference between these students and the higher-performing students was that none of them hung out regularly with other college-bound students from the Puente program. All had chosen their primary friendship groups from among other, non-Puente students, and often away from campus.

Raquel and Carlos are perhaps emblematic of the Category 3 student: they both started high school with modest goals and grade point averages that did not reflect their abilities.

Raquel

Raquel is petite with long dark hair and huge sad eyes. She is the third and youngest child of parents who immigrated to the United States when she was in the fourth grade. Raquel explained that her father had a difficult life; his parents died when he was still in his teens and he was left to care for his five siblings. With so many responsibilities, he did not marry until he was older; in fact, he is considerably older than her mother. Neither of Raquel's parents had a high school education, and they spoke Spanish at home. Her mother worked as a seamstress, but at the time we met her, she was out of work. Her father worked in demolition, tearing down old houses, but by the time she finished high school he had retired from this work. Although the parents lacked a formal education, they did not lack ambition for their children. Raquel noted that they had come to this country so that their children could get a better education. In fact, in an essay she wrote in the ninth grade, Raquel described how her father was the person she admired most in the world because he had worked so hard to give his family a better life. She felt very indebted to her parents for the sacrifices she perceived they had made for her, and expressed concern at one point that if she did not go to college, all their hard work would have been for nothing. Not surprisingly, she marked family as her first priority and school as her second priority, followed by friends.

When we met Raquel, her sister was completing a teacher credential program at a state university in another city. Although the two sisters did not talk much, Raquel noted that her sister was supportive of her schooling. Her brother, one year older, was also headed for college, and by the time Raquel graduated, he had enrolled at the local state university. He contended that he wanted to study to be an engineer.

Raquel began high school with a respectable 2.6 grade point average and a desire to go to college. Her initial grade point average was probably affected by her newcomer status: she had been in the country barely five years when she started high school, and we know that most students take at least five to seven years before they are able to hold their own in an English-only class.[2] By the end of ninth grade, Raquel was feeling "freaked out" that her GPA had dropped to a 2.1. She had not anticipated that she would do so poorly in her first year of high school. But she also knew that the clock didn't really start ticking until tenth grade. After she received her freshman grades, she vowed, "I am really going to study. Besides, it's tenth grade that really counts." She also maintained that she still held hopes of going to a University of California campus, and she knew that those colleges were very selective.

Unlike some of the higher-achieving Puente students, Raquel did not routinely hang out with other Puente students, but she did have a strong support group of female friends—all Latinas, all Spanish speakers—who also purported to want to go to college. She did, however, study with Andrés, and she often commented on how she would go to him for help with chemistry, a subject that was difficult for her. Raquel's parents were very strict about her social life and her father did not like boys to even call at the house. Raquel said she found it embarrassing when her father would spurn boys' calls, because "he doesn't understand that boys can be friends." Her father's outlook no doubt contributed to the fact that she did not have any serious boy-friends during high school.

In spite of her difficulties with chemistry, and even though she earned a D in biology in ninth grade, Raquel generally liked school, especially math. After her sophomore year, she attended summer school so that she could take geometry and get on track to take calculus. Unlike most Category 3 students, Raquel routinely studied two to three hours every night after her initial fiasco in the ninth grade. Not surprisingly, she continued to raise her grades each year. She commented that the Puente program was very important for her, crediting it with improving her writing skills, making her aware of the importance of maintaining a high GPA, and providing her with important information about college. In fact, she noted that since her brother was also interested in college and was not in the program, she commonly shared this information with him.

By the time Raquel graduated from high school, she had nearly a 3.0, but the University of California was still out of reach. She would have needed at least a 3.3, maybe higher, to be accepted at the campus she wanted to attend, and her family could not afford it in any case. She settled on the local state university campus, where she entered as a business and criminal justice major. But she worried a lot about her ability to study with all the distractions at home. Her Puente counselor from Frontera High School helped her to set up a study plan that included uninterrupted time at the library and continued to provide guidance during her first year of college. Two years after high school, Raquel was doing well at the state college. She had a 2.8 grade point average and considered herself on track to complete her degree in business administration in four years. She still maintained occasional contact with her Puente counselor from high school.

Carlos

We met Carlos in Chapter 1. He was the young man whose immigrant parents were deeply worried about him, more because he did not appear to be *bien educado* in the Mexican sense of being well brought up, than that he didn't seem well educated in the American, academic sense. Carlos is tall and light-complexioned with sandy-colored hair, a quick sense of humor, and a charismatic personality that draws others to him. He began North High School with a 2.5 GPA and had been recommended for the Puente program by his teachers because he appeared to be a smart student who was significantly underachieving. His test scores revealed that he was probably capable of much more than he produced in the classroom, and he claimed that he wanted to become more dedicated to his schoolwork and go to college. In the first year of high school, he seemed to be on track to do just that.

While Carlos's parents worked hard to provide for the family, which included four sons, they also worked long hours that kept them sometimes unaware of what their sons were doing. All three of Carlos's older brothers had completed high school—barely—but none had an interest in college, and one brother, in particular, actively discouraged it. When Carlos told this brother he was studying hard to get into college, the brother reportedly said, "'Bull. Don't listen to them. Just go to the JC [junior college].' He feels like I don't need it. He found himself a good job and he didn't need a college education to get that job."

Carlos received a similar message from his parents about school and college, although it was probably inadvertent on their part. Carlos's parents were concerned that their son develop a strong sense of responsibility—to himself and to the family. He had been working a significant number of hours every week at different jobs from the time he was fifteen and both his parents and his older brothers demonstrated strong approval for this even though it often meant missing college field trips, skipping enrichment activities that might have given him a different perspective on opportunities, and not getting his homework done. In one conversation about work and school Carlos offered that he had missed a museum field trip, a field trip to a high-tech corporation, and a visit to a four-year college, and wouldn't be taking the SAT because

> Usually my [work] schedule [at a pizza parlor] is Mondays, Wednesdays, and Fridays, and weekends. Weekdays during school I work from 4:00 till 9:00, and on weekends from 12:00 till 7:00. . . . I give like $40.00 to my mom whenever I get a check. I buy food. It makes them happy so that's why I do it. I think they only care if the school calls them. I think that is when they get concerned.

In fact, Carlos's parents had received calls from the counselor about him not doing his homework and occasionally cutting class, a suspension from school because of "an attitude" in one of his classes, and a run-in with the police for driving without a license. By his junior year, in spite of all of his intellectual talent, he had a 1.0 GPA—not sufficient to allow him to graduate. When queried in the eleventh grade about his priorities, he ranked family first and school second, ahead of the girlfriend about whom he talked a great deal. It was hard to believe that school was actually that important to him, but the second-place ranking may have accurately characterized how much time he spent worrying about it. Carlos did worry a great deal about his low performance, and seemed genuinely puzzled about why he was so behind in school. He admitted to not turning in homework, but attributed it to "just forgetting" or not being "organized." In an essay about what constituted a good student, he wrote that good students "stay out of trouble . . . always do their own work, and are quiet. They are very organized and never lose anything. . . . It's just that kind of person isn't me." On a number of occasions he suggested that he thought he wasn't really capable of much more academically. When asked the hypothetical question of whom he would like to trade places with, Carlos responded:

> I think I would trade places with a smarter student, maybe. Because classes for them seem a lot easier for them because they're successful. I think I'm just a person to look at and say, "I'm just gonna graduate high school and that's about it." I'll be very lucky if I graduate!

Carlos's family also strongly supported his identity as an athlete. One of his older brothers had been a star athlete in high school, and for the whole family a favorite pastime was watching sports. Carlos was on the football team throughout high school, even though practice often conflicted with work and he was frequently punished by the coach for not showing up to work out with the team. In fact, between work and football—the two things that brought the greatest approbation in his home—there simply wasn't time for school. Carlos's life was filled with people whom he liked and admired who had never gone to college and who, according to Carlos, thought going to college "was a waste." Moreover, they all seemed to land jobs that appeared to Carlos to yield a perfectly good lifestyle. They worked in department stores, in car dealerships, as auto mechanics, or in construction. He noted that his girlfriend was "really into going to college because she wants to be a cosmetologist." When asked what he envisioned college would be like, his response was perhaps more telling than anything else he had to say about the topic of college. "Going to college would mean not seeing my friends. My friends would be at work." To Carlos, college seemed to be a kind of punishment that would separate him from family and friends who would be doing the kinds of things he really liked to do—working on cars and playing football.

Carlos did manage to graduate from high school, with barely a 2.0 GPA, and he credited the support (and nagging) of his counselor for this feat. But it was clear that his experiences in high school—always worrying about not passing classes and never feeling very competent in school—simply reinforced the idea that high school was enough. Carlos got a job doing construction work with a friend after high school and said he also had the opportunity to sign on as an assistant mechanic at a nearby shop if the construction job didn't work out. He wasn't worried about finding work, and the money he made working full-time seemed more than sufficient. He exuded a sense of relief when he reported that he had a good job and wouldn't be "going to college right away." The Puente program probably kept Carlos from dropping out of school, and certainly helped to get him back on track when he got into trouble, but it did not successfully instill in him a desire to go to college.

Raquel and Carlos started high school with vague ideas about going to college, but little sense of what that meant or what would be required to achieve that goal. Their early performance in school appeared to be much lower than their capabilities. Raquel appeared to be held back initially by her still-developing English skills, and Carlos seemed to be torn between the models his family and friends provided of hardworking people who brought home a paycheck, and the promise of going to college where he would be separated from the life that he knew. It proved easier to develop Raquel's English skills than to change Carlos's conception of what young men do with their lives. Like many Latino males, Carlos seemed to feel more conflict about his identity as a student than Raquel. The devoted encouragement and monitoring provided by the Puente counselor undoubtedly helped Carlos to graduate from high school and Raquel to find a focus in her studies and develop a plan to attend a local state university. We do not know if Carlos tired of the jobs he was able to get without any further education and decided to try college or if Raquel finished college and got a degree. Nonetheless, both students are success stories in comparison to many of their peers who started high school in similar circumstances and did not finish.

Category 4 Students: Low Achievers Who Want to Do Better

Category 4 students proved to be a challenge to the program. Some candidates for the program wanted to participate in the study to be with friends, but had little motivation themselves for schooling. Often these students' records were borderline because their families had moved frequently or been unstable—problems that often continue to impede students' education. Hence this is the "riskiest" category—not just because the students are at the greatest academic peril, but because they represent a very uncertain investment for the program (it was difficult to judge the level of commitment of the student and the family to the goal of college, or even of completing high school). Yet the program was committed to the idea that all students could be successful with the proper support, and that being immersed (albeit for only one period a day) with other students who were clearly college-bound could have an important effect on their motivation.

Only four of the original eight Category 4 students remained in school through graduation; two left school by the end of their first year of high school, one left in the tenth grade, and one more after eleventh grade. (Another student left but later turned up as a graduate of another high school in the district.) The group began high school with a 1.67 GPA and by the end of twelfth grade, with four remaining, had a group mean GPA of 2.2 (a larger gain than any other category of students). Of course, since attrition was so high for the group, the increase in GPA is at least in part a byproduct of the reduced sample size. Although when they were selected all of the Category 4 students vowed that they wanted to raise their grades, do well in school, and go on to college, the students invested very little time in their homework—on average either no time at all, or at most, a few minutes per day. Only one of these students took the SAT. For the most part they did not hang out with other college-bound Puente students and, unlike the higher-achieving students, they did not maintain regular contact with the Puente teacher or counselor. By the eleventh grade, none of them listed school as a first priority and only one student ranked it second in importance. Demographically, they were very similar to all other Puente students—one student had a parent with a bachelor's degree, but the rest had parents with less than a high school education. Spanish was the primary language in three of the homes; one home was bilingual, and in one, English was the only language spoken. All but one of the students had both biological parents living at home. Two students who exemplify the challenges faced by both the students and the program in working with the Category 4 students are César and Margarita.

César

César is lanky and athletic, and wears an expression that suggests there is much on his mind that he is not sharing. He is the youngest of three brothers and neither of his parents continued beyond elementary school. César's mother worked as a beautician and his father as a janitor. His two older brothers did poorly in school, dropped out, and in their early twenties still had not found consistent employment. According to César, they "mostly just hang around the house all day." Prior to Puente, César's parents did not attend school functions or show particular interest in his schooling. He noted, however, that since Puente, they had attended Puente workshops and his mother had been "on his case" about his schoolwork—a change that César seemed to like.

When César started high school he had a 1.5 GPA and a history of cutting school, but he also had high test scores and said he wanted to go to college. It was evident from essays he had written that he had good academic skills: they were easily as well written as those by students in Category 1. He claimed that he was determined to do better than his older brothers, whom he said looked up to him as a role model. César became active in baseball and football in high school; he was also a Puente class officer and well liked by his peers. His grades also began a steady progression upward. By the end of ninth grade he had a 3.5 GPA and was taking a full complement of college preparatory courses. In tenth grade his GPA slipped somewhat, down to a 2.92 due, in good part, to his cutting classes. Skipping school seemed to be driven in part by peer pressure—although he was liked by the other Puente students, he nonetheless maintained close friendships with students outside the program. At one point when asked who influenced him to cut school, César replied, "Myself mostly, but my friends too. If I don't cut with them, I would be thinking that they would be having all this fun without me. But school is important to me and if I want to go to class and not miss my assignment, I will."

When César was interviewed at the end of tenth grade, he was grateful for the boost that Puente had given him: "I think more about college but right now my grades have dropped a little and I am really concentrating to bring my grades back up . . . without [the program] I probably wouldn't have cared so much about college. And I wouldn't have a perspective about how I need to prepare for careers, and I know I would not have been taught as good." César contended that he was spending three hours a day on homework, but he confessed that when he needed help, "I am kind of alone and just doing my best to stay on task."

Staying on task seemed to be a broader problem for César. When asked in the winter of his junior year what the hardest thing about school was, he replied, "Being here is hardest, because doing your homework, you just have to get there and do it, but showing up each day—sometimes it's boring and sometimes it's just hard to be here." César expressed that if he didn't go on to college he would be letting a lot of people down—his parents, uncles, teachers, counselor—"it would be a big letdown if I didn't." But evidently César's resolve began to falter by spring of his junior year. He was involved in an altercation at school and was asked to leave. It was not clear if he had enrolled elsewhere, and the Puente counselor lost track of him for a period of time. He was counted as a dropout. Later, however, word reached the Puente counselor that César's name was indeed on a list of graduates from another district high school. According to César, he had fully intended to go to a four-year college in his junior year, but after the incident at school, everything changed.

While César was always polite and well-mannered in interviews and during classroom observations, he purportedly had a reputation for having a chip on his shoulder. Some might have called it pride. The altercation that derailed his schooling started when he was confronted by two teachers one morning as he arrived at school late. The teachers tried to search him, and César actively refused in a way that was later described as an "assault" on a teacher. He was suspended from school and transferred to a continuation high school for one semester. In his senior year, he transferred to a regular high school in the same district where he graduated with his class. The fact that he had returned to school and graduated with his class was an accomplishment that eluded half of the Category 4 students, and demonstrated a focus that others also lacked.

After graduation from high school, César enrolled in the local community college full-time. He had little idea of what he wanted to do, though he still harbored the thought that he would complete his general education requirements and transfer to a four-year college. His grades were largely C's. In his second year at community college, however, he took a pipe-fitter's examination (according to César this was similar to plumbing) and, much to his surprise, passed the difficult exam. He was pleased and encouraged to learn that by entering an apprenticeship based on his exam grade, he could establish a career for himself. His objective changed from going to a four-year college, to completing his associate degree—which he expected to do within three years of high school graduation—and going into plumbing. He thought he might "someday take classes part time at the state university," but this was a vague notion when we last talked with him. He credited Puente with helping him to think about college and he was eager to reconnect with his Puente mentor, since he needed to have a mentor for a new program for which he had signed up. The new program, he explained, "doesn't focus on going to college like Puente; it just focuses on graduating."

Margarita

Margarita is a very attractive young woman with long black hair and a beautiful complexion. She prefers to speak in Spanish and her English is lightly accented; her family immigrated to the United States when she was in elementary school. She is the fourth of seven children. Her oldest brother dropped out of high school when he was seventeen, in spite of his parents' pleas to finish, but another brother had gone to community college. Neither of Margarita's parents completed high school in Mexico, but both had mastered English and were reasonably well employed. Her mother worked as a cosmetologist and her father as a construction foreman. The family had moved to a new, larger home while she was in high school and seemed to maintain a middle-class lifestyle. Her parents are also very traditional culturally, and according to Margarita, very strict. She was required to take another sibling with her whenever she went out, and she was not allowed to date. She managed to get around this rule by taking her sister to parties, then "ditching her."

Margarita rated her highest priorities as family and her secret boyfriend, who appeared to take up a fair amount of her time. School was a distant fifth, even in eleventh grade. Her boyfriend was several years older and had completed high school, but did not attend college. The relationship eventually fell apart when Margarita became aware that he was "a drug addict, and I don't want to be messed up in that."

When Margarita began high school she had a 1.83 GPA and little focus. By her own admission, she rarely did homework. In fact, while Puente requires that students have a desire to go to college, she admitted later that she really did not care about even finishing high school until the Puente counselor convinced her that it was critically important for her future. In her freshman year she talked about becoming a pediatrician but she had no idea what that required in terms of education. After she became close to her Puente counselor, she decided she too wanted to be a high school counselor "to help other kids." In the eleventh grade, she explained, "I used to not care about school but that has changed by being in Puente, and I want to do good for the program." Soon afterward, Margarita decided that she wanted to be a legal secretary and her energy became focused on passing her classes and graduating. In typical fashion, however, she did not know what she needed to do to become a legal secretary, but said, "I guess I need to find out." She had not taken the SAT or made any preparations for going to college by the end of eleventh grade, but she had been successful in raising her GPA to a 2.4.

In the twelfth grade Margarita took the SAT, scoring 670, and graduated from high school with a 2.4 grade point average. She applied to a state university and was accepted. But they requested that she submit a social security number to enroll. Because her legal status had been in limbo, she was not able to produce a social security number. She agonized over this, and claiming that she did not know what to do, she did not enroll. When her social security number finally arrived in September after her high school graduation, she believed it was too late to do anything and instead of pursuing college found a job. Two years after high school graduation, Margarita was neither enrolled in school nor working. When we last saw her, she contended that she was going to find a part-time job and enroll part-time at community college as soon as the new semester began.

Both Margarita and César began high school with few prospects for a bright academic future. Their grades and aspirations were low and they lacked focus. Neither had any idea how to create a plan for a brighter future, and both saw little reason to apply themselves in school. Although both had contended that they wanted to attend college, Puente was the lifeline that kept them from dropping out of high school; college was never really more than a distant, and somewhat abstract, goal. César, after experiencing a certain amount of success in high school and gaining the knowledge that he was a capable student, managed to graduate on time despite an interruption in his schooling. Graduating from high school and going on to community college represented a significant achievement, given where he started. Moreover, the community college appeared to be opening the door to a successful apprenticeship that would afford him a future with a well-paying job. Margarita went from being an unfocused ninth-grader without even the ambition to finish high school to a young woman with a sufficiently strong high school record to provide her with some educational options. Unfortunately, her undocumented status and a reluctance to seek advice undermined her chance to go to college after high school. Puente was able to help ensure that she graduated from high school and that she was prepared to continue her studies, but it could not facilitate passage to the next phase of life for Margarita, whose long-term prospects remain uncertain. Problems of legal status continue to be a significant barrier for many Mexican-origin students in the United States, and such obstacles no doubt deplete the ranks of educated, well-prepared workers for the nation's economy.

Supporting Latino Students with Understanding and Mentorship

Of the eight students in our study profiled here, four did not go to college after graduating from high school, and of the four who did go on, none went to a highly selective institution. Two went to a community college, and two went to a state college campus (with one of those dropping back to a community college after one year). It is likely that only three, or at most four, of the eight will eventually complete a four-year degree. This is particularly distressing given that half of the group entered high school with 3.0 or better GPAs and decent test scores. Had they been middle-class children, it is virtually certain that at least half would have matriculated immediately to a four-year college, and that some portion would have found their way into a selective school. Moreover, if they had been middle-class and either white or Asian, even those attending community college would have had a good chance of making an on-time transfer into a four-year college and completing a college degree.

The Puente program figured importantly in the lives of most of the students we studied. Those who chose to stick with high school until graduation, to take the courses and exams necessary to apply to college, and to attend college credited the program and usually their Puente counselor in particular as being major influences on these positive decisions. At least half of the students continued to maintain contact with their counselor even years after they had finished high school. In fact, in a couple of cases, it was the high school Puente counselor who continued to provide support and advice after the student had gone on to college. Certainly, if support, caring, and influence on students' postsecondary choices are the measures of program success, Puente was extremely successful. Most of the students' lives were improved in one way or another as a result of contact with the program. Yet the goal of sending Chicano students to college was inordinately more difficult to achieve than perhaps anyone imagined, and while we do not know the fates of most of these students at this point many years later, it is probable that most have not acquired a college degree—the stated goal of the program.

Many students who appeared to be "shoo-ins" in the ninth grade— in fact the kind of students whom many believe do not need the extra help of such a program—failed to realize their potential, at least im- mediately. Others who appeared to need not much more than a boost over the final hurdles encountered more obstacles along the way. The students we chose to profile were selected early in their high school careers, before we had any idea what would occur in their lives. In fact, we anticipated that we would have a quite different story to tell about many of them. We were surprised that a 4.0 student decided to go into the service instead of college because of the pay, that another student's mother was jailed at a critical point in her high school ca- reer, and that lacking legal citizenship prevented a student from sub- mitting college enrollment forms. But among the poor, the undocu- mented, those families that exist on the margins of our society, such setbacks are in fact commonplace. Moreover, even an effective inter- vention program was relatively impotent to change these circum- stances in students' lives.

One central theme that runs through the choices that the Puente students made about going to college was allegiance to family. Much is written about the structure of Latino families and the deep bonds that sometimes result in decisions that are difficult for non-Latinos to understand.[3] The life stories of these individuals are powerful exam- ples of this ethic. Although Andrés could have received a scholarship resulting in a no-cost education from a selective university, he could not leave his mother behind with the heavy burden of supporting the family. Even though he was clearly a highly capable young man, Carlos's need for approval from his family (and friends) put the identity of "college student" out of reach. In American society, these kinds of choices are viewed as borderline dysfunctional. After all, by advancing their position, these young people would be advancing the whole family. But the bonds among family members are not just economic bonds, and among Latinos, the rewards of success are often measured more in the strength of family ties than the economic welfare of the family.

Another distinctive theme of these stories is time. Americans are known for their efficiency and the emphasis they place on doing things according to a predetermined schedule. Latinos are not. Latinos more often conceive of time as "event time." Event time—as opposed to "clock time," which measures time's passage by the clock—measures time by the passage of human events. Hence, thirty minutes is far less meaningful as a concept than the time it takes to put dinner on the table. Whatever amount of time is required to gather the family to dinner will supersede in importance the time on the clock.[4] It is the same with going to college. For many of the students whom we studied, going to college was a value that they came to hold, but it did not necessarily need to occur according to the same schedule that many Americans are used to following. But we have a reason for worrying about students' not enrolling in college right after high school. We know from a great deal of research that students who do not go directly to four-year colleges are less likely to ultimately complete a degree than those who do.[5] There are risks with delaying college entry, and there are risks with going to two-year colleges or studying only part-time. But many of these students are unaware of these risks, and resist reframing their concept of time to contend with them. For many of these students, the time it takes for the youngest brother to be old enough to help out around the house, or the time it takes for a mother to get a better-paying job, is more important than the concept of completing a degree in four or five years. Time was viewed as expandable to fit the needs of family.

Like all adolescents, Latino students do not experience life only through the perspective of their families. They too encounter the developmental pressures to pull away from family ties and begin to exert an independent self—although there is evidence that they express this in a very different way than their Anglo-American peers.[6] Common to all American adolescents' experience, however, are the influence of peers' attitudes, values, and mores, as well as the pressures of the greater society (which are communicated, in part, through advertising and the media). In spite of placing a very strong value on family, then, some Latino students succumb to peer or societal pressures that can derail their ambitions and undermine their relationships with family members.

The twenty-eight students in our study sample, especially the males, also often struggled with the task of creating and maintaining an identity as a student. Many of the young men held as a model the identity of a breadwinner, someone who took care of family members and made the family proud by achieving tangible markers of success. Thus Andrés was compelled to help provide financially and morally for his family, Carlos felt good when he had a job and could contribute to his family, and José obviously enjoyed the trappings of a young man with a nice car and some money in his pocket. The girls we studied appeared to feel much less driven by a need to contribute financially or have substantial disposable income. The difference may have been driven by gender stereotyping—with certain expectations held lower for them—but it seemed to work to their advantage academically. By freeing them from the responsibility of being a breadwinner for the family, they were much better able to pursue a college education.

In the eleventh grade we asked all of the students to look at a list of social pressures and indicate which ones they felt most. The findings were illuminating. While many students acknowledged the typical pressures that adults fear most—drugs, sex, gang activity, pressure to go along with peers—these were not the ones that weighed on them the most heavily. Specifically, the pressure to use alcohol was more intense for these students than was the pressure to use drugs. And as for sex, most students did not consider the pressure to engage in a sexual relationship to be a major concern in their lives. This may be because they had already crossed this bridge and were no longer worrying about it—research suggests that about half of Latino adolescents have engaged in sexual intercourse by the time they are seventeen—or perhaps it simply was not an issue in their lives yet.[7] For those students (39 percent) who did consider it a concern, however, most felt that it was a particularly intense one. The perception that peers are engaged in sexual behavior can place great pressure on Latino adolescents to engage in similar activities.[8]

Instead, the great majority of these students (74 percent) indicated that they felt the greatest pressure from their relationship with their parents—whether because of disagreements with parents or concerns about meeting their expectations. This result fits with students' self-declared, and very evident, focus on family. Almost all of the students (95 percent), even those who were neither high achievers nor very low achievers, felt equally intense pressure with regard to performing up to expectations academically.[9] This suggests that being in Puente, with the expectation that everyone would do well and go on to college, may have created a great deal of pressure for students. And although it is true that optimal pressure can lead to optimal outcomes, we do not know whether the pressure in this case was perceived as optimal by these students.

If there is any lesson to be learned from the experiences of these students, it seems to be that the need to monitor students, as well as actively and carefully guide them, does not diminish with time and does not vary greatly with their academic profiles. Many of the students continued to walk a fine line between success and failure all the way to the end of their senior year and beyond, and even some who appeared to be highly able and on track for college were surprised (and disappointed) with the unexpected decisions they made. Conventional wisdom is that the junior year of high school is the watershed year. Most students take their hardest courses that year and it is the year that is critical in determining college eligibility, largely because most serious college-bound students apply to college in the fall, before their senior grades are in. Moreover, if students have not prepared themselves for postsecondary education, twelfth grade is generally considered too late to start. As such, the senior year is often viewed as a "coasting" year—the pressure lets up and students just need to "maintain" their academic standing. We saw, however, that for some students twelfth grade can be pivotal: a few can turn things around then if there is sufficient support and encouragement, whereas some students who appear to be on track then can quite suddenly become derailed. Most of the Puente students, even in the twelfth grade, were still vulnerable to pressures that could undermine their ambitions. Moreover, their intense concerns about school and their unresolved issues with parents pointed to an unrelenting need for both academic and emotional support even in the last year of high school.

It is no secret that parents with resources who have a firm goal of college for their children often seek counseling outside the public school system, hiring private counselors that cost thousands of dollars to shepherd their children through the college application process, including preparation for taking college admissions tests.[10] Or these parents simply enroll their children in private high schools where the student-counselor ratio is much lower than that in the public schools. The overwhelming majority of Latino students, who are from immigrant and low-income homes, have parents with no knowledge of the higher education system (in fact they commonly have little knowledge of the K–12 school system). These students do not come to the attention of the few counselors in their school as "college material" because their test scores and academic performance do not compare well with those of their more advantaged peers, and issues of poverty and social advantage place inordinate hurdles in their paths to academic success. These are the students who most desperately need counseling and guidance, but they are the least likely to receive it. In California, as in other states, strained education budgets often result in the letting go of personnel who are "external to the classroom." And the anthem of harried administrators faced with inadequate resources is frequently "put the resources into the classroom." This ignores the critically important role of counselors and other ancillary personnel who are the only such resource for low-income students.

As we came to know many of the Puente counselors over the years, and observed them for countless hours in different contexts, it was evident that even with a reduced student-counselor ratio of fifty or a hundred to one, the job was a full-time, seven-day-a-week job. Counselors gave out their home phone numbers and students called them every evening and on weekends. They often held parent and student meetings into the late hours of the day, and planned field trips and college-access activities for weekends and after school. Counselors literally ran from one class, one student, one activity to another, collapsing at the end of a very long day to fill out forms, keep records, and do class scheduling activities. Their informal client rolls continued to expand as students who left school or went off to college continued to call on them for advice and support when no one else was available who could understand their predicaments. It was a burnout job. And yet it is clear that most of the students we studied would not have met with the successes they did without this person in their lives. We continue to wonder how things might have turned out differently for some of these students if only their counselor had had a somewhat smaller student-teacher ratio and could have found the time to counsel them to go straight to college, to borrow money if they had to, to find allies when they felt lonely and isolated, to reach higher because the rewards would accrue to their families as well as to themselves.

If there had been social workers in these students' schools to address some of the deep psychological and social service needs of the families, it might have made the job of the counselor easier. Or if there had been a nurse or psychologist readily available to answer concerns about drug abuse, diet and obesity, or the loss of a parent—all issues that students in our sample dealt with alone—it might have reduced some of the pressures on these students and allowed them to cope more effectively with a shorter list of issues. Such social services are rare in the public schools that serve Latino youth, and yet it is easy to imagine how these pupils' academic outcomes could have been enhanced with effective intervention.

Among those students who did go to college, many went feeling homesick and tentative about their decisions. The lack of social and academic support that some encountered at college undermined the work of the Puente program and resulted in declining grades and even a return home. Others, like Angela, who were fortunate to be placed in a special program to help them adapt to college, fared better. In the next two chapters we explore the factors associated with college persistence and the kinds of programs that hold promise for guiding more Latino students successfully through college.

CHAPTER SIX

Beating the Odds
and Going to College

Given the multiple barriers that most Latino students confront, it is hardly surprising that so few complete high school and go on to college. Even those who do attend college remain much less likely than other groups to complete a four-year degree or continue on to graduate or professional schools. Significantly, the pool of Latino students who graduate from high school prepared to attend competitive colleges and universities is extremely small. For example, only slightly more than 50 percent of Latino students graduated with their high school class in 2005, and only 54 percent of these graduates went directly to college, compared to 73 percent of white students.[1] Of the 54 percent who went on to college, most enrolled in a two-year institution. In the same year, only 7 percent of bachelor's degrees were awarded to Latinos.[2] But what are the characteristics of those who successfully navigate the path to and through college? What distinguishes them from their peers who are not as academically successful? And what can we learn from these success stories that can help pave the way for others?

Based on both quantitative and qualitative analyses, we find that a number of factors separate these high achievers from their peers, including social background, language use, aspirations, choice of friendship groups, adult support, extracurricular activities and the particular schools these students attend, and their self-concept as learners. The availability of financial aid as students make their way from high school to college appears to be critical as well. Our data do not show to what extent these factors separate college-goers from those who do not go to college. Nonetheless, it is clear that a host of factors do provide a context for achievement and engagement in school, and serve as the foundation for the motivation, persistence, and resilience of those Latino students who beat the odds and transition to higher education.

The analyses we report here rest on several data sources: (1) College Board data from 2004 on more than 1.5 million students (137,285 of whom were Latinos) who took the SAT and completed the accompanying Student Descriptive Questionnaire (SDQ), (2) a comparative study of approximately five hundred students of various ethnicities as they moved from ninth grade to twelfth grade in an urban and a rural high school, (3) a quantitative study of sixty Latino college-goers and their perceptions of their own abilities based on their SAT scores, (4) qualitative studies and interviews of high school and college students from West Coast schools and colleges, and (5) a national sample of over seventy individuals who made the journey from the barrio to the Ph.D., M.D., or J.D. degree.[3] These interviews and studies include Latinos who are or have been students during the 1970s, 1980s, 1990s, and 2000s. It is striking how consistent their stories are. The primary differences among them are not found in personal circumstances but in the opportunity structure of the time: individuals who went to college in the 1970s and 1980s place critical importance on government financial aid and college recruiters, while those from the 1990s and 2000s frequently credit an outreach or special college preparatory program as the key to their beating the odds.

This difference reflects the various policy environments in which they have lived. The 1970s to the mid-1980s was an era of more generous governmental assistance and affirmative-action policies whereby recruiters were used to locate and support Latino and other students of color. The 1990s and 2000s were characterized by an increasing shift from grants in aid by the government to a heavier reliance on subsidized and bank loans coupled with college-access programs (rather than recruiters).[4] Increasingly, as well, we are encountering the problem of high-achieving undocumented students struggling to get into, and stay in, college. Even if these students are allowed to pay in-state tuition, as is the case in some states, they do not qualify for federal financial aid and therefore usually cannot afford to attend.

We first look at overall trends in SAT scores because the SAT is a gatekeeper at many selective colleges and universities in the country (especially on the two coasts, where most of the Latino population groups are located and where many of the selective colleges are also found). In order to gain insight into how those Latino students who prepared themselves to enter selective colleges and universities differed from their peers who had more modest educational success, we then divided the College Board SDQ sample into quintiles and compared the top quintile of Latinos with all Latino students, and the top quintile of white students with all white students on a series of characteristics that are reported in the SDQ questionnaire.

There are limitations to these data that should be acknowledged. The SAT data are admittedly skewed toward the highest-achieving and most ambitious students in the nation, because normally only students who intend to apply to selective colleges and universities take the exam. As a result, socioeconomic status, as well as other related characteristics, are likely to be higher for these SAT takers than for a group that includes all students. Additionally, Latinos tend to be underrepresented among those who take the SAT because they generally perform less well than other groups in school and, when they go to college, they disproportionately choose nonselective colleges that do not require the test.[5] Moreover, those Latinos who take the SAT are more likely to come from the more advantaged subgroups— foreign-born Central and South Americans, and Cuban Americans. In 2004, while Latinos comprised approximately 13 percent of all high school graduates, they made up less than 10 percent of those taking the SAT.

SAT Profiles over Time

In Figure 6.1 we chart the average Math SAT performance for all Latinos and the two largest Latino subgroups, as well as whites and Asian students, from 1986 to 2006.

All Latino subgroups trailed both white and Asian students over the entire period. Notably, however, the gaps have grown over time.

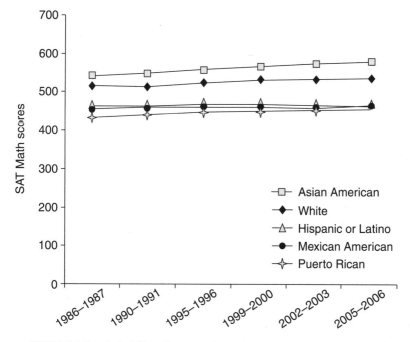

FIGURE 6.1 Trends in SAT performance in mathematics by race/ethnicity, select years, 1986–2006. (Data from U.S. Department of Education 2005, tables 126 and 14.1b.)

Asian students showed the greatest growth in scores over this period, from 541 to 578, a 37-point difference, followed by white students who rose from an average score of 514 to 536, a 26-point boost. Latinos, by contrast, only improved their scores by 10 points, from 455 to 465. Whereas the gap between Latinos and whites was 59 points, around one-half of a standard deviation in 1986, by 2006 it had grown to 79 points, or more than three-quarters of a standard deviation. Puerto Ricans almost closed the small gap between them and Mexican-origin students. The greatest gap, however, was between Latinos and Asians—113 points, or more than a full standard deviation.

Why are scores declining for some Latinos compared to others? We cannot say with certainty, but some possible explanations include that an increasing proportion of Latinos is taking the exam, and when the pool gets larger it also takes in more lower-performing students; that the Latino populations are also shifting, with a higher proportion of low-income, immigrant families entering the mix; and that the American economy is further polarizing, so that differences in incomes (and therefore resources to support children) are greater today than they were ten and twenty years ago.[6]

Whatever the reason for the increasing gap between Latinos and these other two groups, it inhibits their competitive eligibility for admission to selective colleges and universities at a time when the competition for admission to these institutions has increased substantially, and when the returns for a college degree versus a high school diploma have grown dramatically. In 1972, a male with a bachelor's degree could expect to earn 22 percent more than a male high school graduate. The difference for females was greater, over 40 percent. In 2003, however, the typical male college graduate earned 60 percent more than the typical male high school graduate, and for females the difference had risen to 69 percent. This change reflects not only that a college degree pays so much more, but also that the value of a high school diploma has declined.

College is increasingly critical to one's ability to enter the middle class, and stay there, and in the wake of a number of anti-affirmative action initiatives, it is increasingly difficult for Latinos (and other underrepresented students) to access a college education. A 2007 study of access to selective institutions, using data from the Integrated Postsecondary Education System (IPEDS), found that Latinos and blacks were proportionally less represented at selective institutions (the top 20 percent of institutions with respect to SAT score means) in 2004 than in 1994.[7] The stakes are high, indeed, for college admission, and so it makes sense to ask: what accounts for the very large differences in test scores among groups, scores that can make the difference between being admitted to a selective college (where the likelihood of actually completing a degree is much higher than elsewhere) or not?[8]

Socioeconomic Status and Success in School

A consistent finding in the literature is the strong relationship between social class and both test scores and grades. Other studies have demonstrated the strong relationship between social class and SAT scores.[9] It is important to note, however, that the same advantage of high socioeconomic status that accrues to students across racial and ethnic groups also occurs within racial and ethnic groups (see Table 6.1).

Significantly, Table 6.1 shows (1) the extremely strong relationship between income and test score means across all groups; that is, without exception, as income increases so do test scores; (2) for all groups, there is a larger standard deviation among the scores of high-income students than among those of low-income students— that is, except for whites, low income is more a determinant of test

Table 6.1   Mean SAT Math score by income and ethnicity, 2004

	<$35,000		$35,000–$60,000		$60,000–$100,000		>$100,000	
	Mean	Std. Dev.	Mean	Std. Dev.	Mean	Std. Dev.	Mean	Std. Dev.
Other Latino	434.47 (n=19,134)	94.36	467.92 (n=7,689)	98.01	497.26 (n=5,229)	100.18	540.79 (n=2,994)	107.57
Mexican American	433.25 (n=23,885)	90.22	465.71 (n=11,035)	91.76	484.84 (n=7,533)	95.38	520.82 (n=3,047)	101.77
Puerto Rican	419.68 (n=5,749)	92.21	454.58 (n=3,215)	95.56	477.23 (n=2,393)	96.69	516.95 (n=1,112)	100.97
White	492.67 (n=76,494)	100.70	507.64 (n=122,070)	97.41	524.67 (n=169,704)	98.145	562.76 (n=125,129)	101.10
Asian	541.80 (n=28,133)	126.81	554.19 (n=14,294)	118.23	573.81 (n=14,235)	116.77	620.39 (n=9,857)	112.99

Source: Data from College Board 2004.

scores than is wealth; (3) there is a relatively large standard deviation for the Asian group, indicating a greater variability in their scores
at each income level; and (4) low-income Asians score higher than
high-income Mexican Americans and nearly the same as high-income
"other Latinos." This last observation often leads to pointed comparisons between the groups. Without getting deeply into discussions
of the enormous diversity in background and socioeconomic status
among Asian subgroups in the United States, or the "myth of the
model minority," it is observable that Asians are less likely to fall into
the very-low-income category (42 percent versus 52 percent for Mexican Americans) and more likely to fall into the very highest income
group (15 percent versus 6 percent for Mexican Americans).[10] This
different distribution of income can result in varying levels of resources available in the communities that these students come from
and therefore a different infrastructure and support system for education. The sociologist Min Zhou writes about how higher-income
Asians set up supplemental schools and other educational support
programs that lower-income Asian students can also take advantage of.[11] By contrast, there is comparatively very little wealth in the
Mexican American community, and little of this educational infrastructure. Moreover, Asians in the SAT sample are more likely than
Mexican Americans to be first- or second-generation and to have parents who are "temporarily" low-income because of the adjustments
associated with recent immigration.[12]

For our analyses, we focused on the top quintile of test takers because these are generally the honors and Advanced Placement students most likely to attend selective colleges and actually complete
their degrees.[13] We acknowledge that the absolute SAT scores of students in the top quintile for their group vary substantially across
groups (see the Appendix, Table A.1), but our interest is in identifying the students who are doing well in their own context and who are
oriented toward college, rather those outliers who perform to stan-

dards of other groups that are more advantaged. Our analyses of parent education and income for students taking the 2004 SAT mirror the findings in the literature: as income and education increase for Latinos, so do test scores. Upper-quintile Latino students have mothers with significantly more education and higher incomes than the mothers of their lower-performing co-ethnic peers. White and Asian students, both the aggregate groups and those in the top quintile, have considerably higher parent education levels (bachelor's degree or greater) than all of the Latino subgroups. But among Latinos, Mexican Americans (approximately half of all the Latino test takers) look very different from the others. Mexican American high achievers are more likely than the others to have two parents who never graduated from high school than they are to have a parent with a bachelor's degree or graduate education. Thus, many Mexican American high achievers come from homes with relatively little educational capital compared to those of their peers.

Although top Latino achievers are more likely to have higher-income parents than all Latinos, more than one in four Mexican Americans and approximately one in five other Latinos comes from a low-income home. By contrast, only about one in twenty high-achieving white students comes from a similar background. This discrepancy is enormous and has potentially far-reaching implications for the competitiveness of these relatively high-achieving Latino students as they attempt to transition from high school to college. It also begs the question: what factors operate to ameliorate the effects of low-income status and low parent-education levels among high-performing Latino students?

Parental Encouragement and Literacy Support

Mexican immigrant parents come from a country in which the average formal educational attainment is much lower than in the United States and where students are not necessarily expected to complete

Table 6.2 Mother's education level of all and top-quintile SAT test takers, 2004 (percentages)

Ethnicity	Less than high school		High school		Some college/ Associate's degree		Bachelor's degree		Graduate degree	
	All	Top quintile	All	Top quintile	All	Top quintile	All	Top quintile	All	Top quintile
Mexican American	34.1	18.3	20.5	18.7	22.8	27.4	8.5	16.0	5.1	9.7
Puerto Rican	12.8	14.9	23.1	17.3	31.8	28.3	16.3	23.6	8.4	16.0
Other Latino	21.3	8.8	20.8	15.1	24.1	25.9	12.6	20.5	10.5	17.5
White	2.3	.7	19.8	9.8	29.2	20.9	24.4	33.5	13.6	22.8
Asian American	8.9	12.0	8.7	11.9	12.0	16.4	24.8	33.8	19.2	26.0

Source: Data from College Board 2004.

Table 6.3   Parent income levels of all and top-quintile SAT test takers, 2004 (percentages)

Ethnicity	<$35,000		$35,000–$60,000		$60,000–$100,000		>$100,000	
	All	Top quintile	All	Top quintile	All	Top quintile	All	Top quintile
Mexican American	43.1	25.7	18.6	20.1	12.5	18.2	4.9	11.2
Puerto Rican	37.0	18.1	18.8	19.6	13.9	18.6	6.2	14.0
Other Latino	41.3	22.9	15.5	15.5	10.3	15.4	5.9	13.0
White	11.0	5.9	17.2	11.5	23.4	21.1	17.2	25.9
Asian American	25.7	17.9	12.6	9.2	12.4	11.6	8.5	13.1

Source: Data from College Board 2004.

Note: A large percentage—48.3 percent of the Asian American students scoring in the top quintile, and 40.6 percent of the aggregate group—did not respond to the income question on the Student Data Questionnaire.

the equivalent of a high school diploma.[14] In Mexico, compulsory education only extends to the "secundaria" or roughly the equivalent of middle school in the United States, but this is hardly enforced, and many children leave earlier out of economic necessity or lack of access to schooling.[15] Thus in Mexico not having completed high school does not carry the same social stigma as in the United States. Still, Mexican immigrant parents almost always want more education for their own children and they have often left school themselves out of necessity rather than choice.[16] Immigrant "hopefulness"—the strong belief that with enough hard work anyone can attain the American Dream—is also a well-known characteristic of newcomers to the United States, and it tends to reinforce an emphasis on schooling for newcomer children. (Many third- and fourth-generation Latinos, by contrast, may have left school out of frustration and loss of hopefulness about their chances of realizing the American Dream.) In addition, we have found that many parents of high achievers who have low levels of formal education themselves nonetheless have very high levels of informal education and are able to assist their children's literacy and general education in relatively sophisticated ways.

A study by Patricia Gándara, in which she interviewed seventy Latinos of Mexican descent who had beaten the odds by anyone's definition, sheds some light on the characteristics of the homes that produce high achievers in spite of low socioeconomic status.[17] The subjects of this study came from homes in which the average parental education was at the elementary school level and in which neither parent held a position above semiskilled labor; most were factory workers and field hands. The majority of interviewees spoke Spanish at home because this was the language of their parents. The average number of siblings was five; hence they came from large families. These are all typical predictors of low academic performance. And yet all of these individuals excelled academically, attended highly selective colleges and universities, and acquired doctoral-level degrees. Certainly some of these individuals' extraordinary academic success was due to a fluke of circumstance or the gift of excellent genes, but there were many characteristics common to the group, and by their own accounts, many noted that they were not the smartest kids in their families or in their classes. Many siblings and classmates whom they considered much brighter than themselves had not been as successful academically or professionally. What, then, had led these students to beat the odds and succeed?

One strong theme that ran through the lives of almost all of these highly academically successful individuals was that they had mothers that dreamed out loud of extraordinary futures for their children. The mothers framed those dreams in stories about their families or their ancestors that conveyed to their children that their present socioeconomic state was anomalous, uncharacteristic of their family. It was something that could and must be overcome. A typical story was recounted by the son of a single mother who could barely make ends meet. The mother frequently told tales about

> how her grandfather was like a multimillionaire type. He was a genius in the mines. And none of that went down to her family because of wills and stuff like that. And they were always very proud

because her uncles owned a hotel [in Mexico]. . . . She would say,
"You know you can hold your head up high." And we never believed it. We always thought she was just making it up.[18]

The university professor who told this story also concluded that although he and his siblings doubted the stories, they were also shaped
by them. It was clear that their mother's expectations for them were
high. She had set the standard for success in life not by comparing their situation to that of other generally accomplished people,
but by recounting tales of prodigious success from their own family,
which suggested to the children that they were not only capable of
great achievements but practically owed it to the family legacy. Leo
Grebler and his colleagues found a similar phenomenon among Mexican immigrants whom they had interviewed several decades earlier.[19]
Many told stories of great wealth and prestige in their families back
home. The researchers concluded that it was simply impossible for so
many Mexican immigrants to have come from such illustrious families, but that the stories' veracity probably wasn't as important as the
messages of hope, pride, and ambition that they conveyed. These immigrants had benefited from a set of attitudes and beliefs that offered
the possibility of personal transformation.

Most of these individuals who succeeded beyond all expectations were also exposed to a great deal of reading and writing even
though their parents had very limited formal educations. Many parents scraped together the money to buy encyclopedias and other
books for their children, even in circumstances where the next meal
was not a certainty. Many parents were avid newspaper readers,
though they could not afford a newspaper subscription. Conversations about politics and labor issues were common in many of the
households, and many learned to read at home through daily read-
ings of the Bible. Most of the reading and conversation was conducted in Spanish. One young Chicana whose parents had no more

than an elementary school education, but who later became a linguistics professor, explained,

> My father was an exceptional man. Education was very important to him. . . . He would give us like statement problems, "What if I bought this." . . . We would sit there and try to figure it out . . . then when we started going to church everything was in Spanish and everybody was supposed to read chapters and report. So I had a great deal of instruction in the Spanish language without knowing it. Also it sort of set the stage for literature. By the time I went into literature, that kind of stuff was not difficult at all. I would simply write in a biblical style.[20]

Spanish, English, or Both?

Although much remains to be learned about how the language a student uses at home influences that student's test results, some research by the Educational Testing Service does show that it likely has an effect on the testing outcomes of Latino students, and therefore their likelihood of being among the top 20 percent of performers.[21] Table 6.4 shows that the highest-performing Latino students—those in the upper quintile—are more likely to be English-only speakers than either primarily Spanish speakers or students who "speak more than one language." Unfortunately the Student Descriptive Questionnaire attached to the SAT only allows for these three categories, so that students who list themselves as having more than one language may fall anywhere on a continuum from speaking very little Spanish to being fully bilingual and biliterate. Nonetheless, the general finding makes sense. Students who speak only English are more assimilated and less likely to have attended racially and linguistically isolated schools where poverty is the greatest and opportunity the most rationed. They also perform better on all tests because they un-

Table 6.4 Best language of all and top-quintile SAT test takers, 2004 (percentages)

	Other Latino		Puerto Rican		Mexican American		Asian		White	
	Top quintile	All	Top quintile	All	Top quintile	All	Top quintile	All	Top quintile	All
No response	1.0	1.5	1.1	1.5	.9	1.5	8.3	5.2	1.2	1.6
English only	59.9	48.7	76.2	66.6	74.2	58.7	52.0	57.7	95.5	95.6
English and another language	31.4	39.0	18.7	26.3	22.1	33.8	24.4	25.0	2.3	2.1
Another language	7.7	10.8	4.0	5.6	2.8	6.0	15.3	12.1	1.0	.8
Total N	11,876	53,677	3,360	18,368	12,228	65,240	26,670	119,893	150,247	755,207

Source: Data from College Board 2004.

derstand well the English instructions and test questions. Perhaps more surprising is that more than one out of five high-achieving Mexican Americans, and almost one-third of high-achieving "other Latinos," falls into the category of "more than one language" or putative bilinguals. This finding certainly belies the notion that bilingualism is necessarily a handicap to high achievement.

Certainly, lacking full proficiency in English presents challenges for students attempting to enroll and succeed in higher education, no matter how academically qualified and talented they are. Alex, for example, was in high school when his family immigrated from Mexico. His parents, who had been born in the United States but returned to Mexico to raise their family, were middle-class and Alex and his siblings had received a strong education in Mexico. The language barrier that Alex encountered upon arriving in the United States, however, was profound and almost fatal to his academic aspirations. Because American schools are so fundamentally monolingual, students with strong educational backgrounds but who are not English proficient cannot demonstrate what they know in the classroom, and so are assumed to have a weak educational background.

> Many people have put me down. They think that because I am not able to speak the language well that I am ignorant. I have struggled and proved so many people wrong. So many teachers back in Yakima told me that "you should go to community college because you do not have the language skills to do well in college."

Not only did Alex have to struggle with the language in class, but also there were no counselors in his school who could communicate in Spanish. He did not know what courses he needed to take to graduate and prepare for college until he came in contact with a Spanish-speaking college counselor.

One of the biggest challenges was in my senior year. There were so many requirements I had to meet to go to the university. Basically, I did two years of high school in the last year and the summer. Thanks to a [college] recruiter, I was able to finish the requirements. What happened was the first two years I had ESL classes and they did not want to accept these classes. And I took Latino literature and transitional English that in my high school counted, [but] it did not count for the university. So I ended up taking Sophomore, Junior and Senior English my last year. I was taking classes at 7 a.m. and one after school.

Holding socioeconomic status constant, using mother's education and parent income, we also analyzed the effects of language on both SAT scores and grade point average (GPA). Here we found interesting differences. While speaking another language was inversely related to SAT Math scores for Latinos (but not for Asians), taking the SAT out of the equation revealed that, for all ethnic groups, speaking English and another language was associated with a higher GPA (see the Appendix, Tables A.2 and A.3). It is not at all clear why bilingualism or speaking another language has such a differential effect on GPA and standardized test scores.

Richard Duran attributes the lower SAT scores among Latinos to four factors that may influence the SAT test performance of Spanish speakers: guessing, test anxiety, test duration (time limitation), and a lack of familiarity with the vocabulary contained in the exams.[22] And while we do see considerable differences in GPA between Latinos and whites across all income levels (Table A.4), speaking another language for Latinos had a positive effect on GPA, or performance in school. This fact, taken together with recent research by Saul Geiser and Veronica Santelices that shows GPA is a better predictor of college performance than test scores, argues for a much heavier reliance on GPA and perhaps even an eschewing of test scores for Latino students whose first language is not English.[23]

The Importance of GPA and High-Level Coursework

There has been a great deal of debate over the years about what exactly tests like the SAT measure. Is it "aptitude" or achievement?[24] Is it, as Anne Anastasi has described it, learning that has occurred in informal contexts versus learning in formal contexts like school?[25] Even the College Board, the organization that administers the test, appears to be unclear about this: they no longer indicate whether the "A" in SAT stands for "achievement," "aptitude," or something else. Whatever it is, it is apparently less dependent on classroom effort than are grades. Thus GPA is another important and quasi-independent measure of students' academic achievement. Moreover, while GPA reflects past and current school performance, it is also a predictor of future accomplishments—and opportunities. Students with high GPAs are generally considered more capable than those with low GPAs and are thus more likely to be selected for college preparatory classes and given access to rationed college counseling resources.[26]

But is the GPA as a measure of achievement objective and fair? Most teachers use implicit or explicit ranking systems or a curve to grade their students. The students who write the best essays or score the highest number of points on a test in the class get the A's, those with somewhat less stellar performance receive the B's, and so forth. Thus grades are contextual; they depend on who else is in the class, and what the teacher's experience has been with other students at the same grade level. It is well established that grading standards vary considerably by teacher, school, and other factors.[27] Grades also vary by racial and ethnic background (see the Appendix, Table A.4).

Some of the disparities in grades by ethnicity may be due to differences in motivation or informal learning, but some are almost certainly due to variations in the quality of prior educational experiences, and Latinos are less likely than white and Asian students to have access to high-quality teaching and rigorous coursework. An additional portion of the disparity is likely due to lower expectations for Latinos and other students of color that convert into students' lower expectations for themselves. Among SAT test takers, and at all income levels, white students outperform Latinos with respect to GPA by a substantial margin. High-income Latino students do not perform as well in the classroom for a host of reasons, but perhaps in part because they are less likely than high-income white students to have taken honors and Advanced Placement (AP) courses.

Analyses of the relationship between taking honors courses and students' scores on the SAT Math yielded a highly significant relationship for all groups, including Latinos. This is consistent with other studies that show that a rigorous curriculum leads to higher achievement levels and fosters a college-going culture among students.[28] Regardless of the type of honors course, having access to an honors curriculum in high school is positively related to SAT Math scores. That is, even courses like honors European history or an honors foreign classical language are associated with higher SAT Math scores (see the Appendix, Table A.6). We conjecture that this is because taking honors courses means that a student has been identified as highly able, an important signal to teachers to invest in their development, and because an honors student has been placed in the college preparatory track, which will confer additional benefits, such as attention from counselors and supportive peers and access to the most qualified teachers.

As discussed in Chapter 3, several studies have shown that the schools that Latinos attend are less likely to offer many AP and honors courses than those that are attended by white and Asian students, and since many schools augment the grade point average with extra points for honors and AP courses, students without access to them can be penalized on their GPA irrespective of their academic talents. Parent education is also a factor in whether students take AP and honors courses. Controlling for income, we found that, for both Latino and white students in the 2004 SAT sample, the mother's level of education was a significant predictor for whether a student would enroll in honors courses. Because Latino students' parents have such dramatically lower education levels than other groups, they are consequently also less likely to be admitted to or to take honors, AP, or other rigorous college preparatory classes. This in turn can result in a less competitive GPA and academic profile, critical factors in college admissions.

We heard about this diminished access to rigorous courses from students whom we interviewed. For example, Amalia, the Arizona-born daughter of a single mother of five, recounted how all of her siblings had dropped out of school by their sophomore year. But she fought to be placed in college preparatory classes even though it meant having to run to catch the bus to get home in the afternoon.

> The difference was I was in the AP classes. I demanded to be in the AP courses. In the ninth grade they put me in a cooking class. They told me that they put me in that class because "when you come out of class it will be closer to the bus stop. You don't want to miss the bus, do you?" I went to the counselor and demanded they take me out of that class.

As with all other students, Latinos can improve their chances of excelling in school and going on to college by being born into families with greater financial and educational resources, and in particular, by having a mother with a more extensive educational background. Of course this is not a choice that students can make. But luckily, informal educational resources are also critically important and can be present even when parents have completed relatively few years of formal schooling. And students, informed about the importance of taking particular courses by a teacher, counselor, or friend at school, can and do change their educational trajectories.

Participation in Extracurricular Activities

Students who perform well in school also tend to participate in more extracurricular activities. In part this is because they are more engaged in school, find it a more rewarding place to be, and have their friends there.[29] It is also no secret that ambitious students who are attempting to gain admission to a selective college need to show that they not only perform well on academic measures, but are "well-rounded" individuals, and so such students choose to participate in extracurricular activities in order to strengthen their college applications. Table 6.5 shows the participation levels in various extracurricular activities as reported by students on the SAT's Student Descriptive Questionnaire.

Two things are immediately notable in Table 6.5: (1) white students tend to participate in most extracurricular activities (except "ethnic activities") at higher rates than Latinos do, and (2) top quintile students in both groups participate in extracurricular activities at higher rates than all students. In fact, Latinos who take the SAT appear to participate at substantially higher rates than the norm for Latinos generally.[30] Margaret Gibson and her colleagues studied students in a high school in central California that was composed almost entirely of middle-income white students and low-income Mexican American students and found that in the ninth grade only 11 percent of Mexican-origin students were involved in a school-sponsored sport compared to 52 percent of their white classmates.[31] They also found that only 6 percent of the Mexican-origin students had joined a club compared to 22 percent of the whites. Students with more financial resources are better able to participate in extracurricular activities that require additional time, transportation, and often money to pur-

Table 6.5   Participation in extracurricular activities by Latinos and whites, by SAT score, 2004 (percentages)

Activity	Latino		White	
	Top quintile on SAT	All	Top quintile on SAT	All
Student government	15.2	10.7	14.8	11.1
ROTC	5.4	4.9	4.5	4.3
Religious activity	14.4	10.1	20.1	16
Instrument/music performance	15.5	10.7	18.3	12.2
Honors program	32.9	16.9	37.0	19.1
Fraternity/sorority social club	26.5	23.8	25.0	25.6
Ethnic activity	17.3	13.5	1.9	1.4
Drama/theater	13.6	12.2	13.8	12.9
Work or internship experience	25.7	18.3	22.9	19.1
Community service organization	30.1	24.2	30.6	23.8
Varsity sports	27.0	26.5	28.1	28.2
Intramural sports	25.9	17.6	36.7	28.1
Art	16.1	16.4	14.0	15.1

Source: Data from College Board 2004.

chase materials or equipment and pay related fees. But Gibson and her colleagues found that an important additional reason that the Mexican students participated less is that they felt they didn't fit in. One student explained,

> Most sports and clubs are made up of white people, and if you join you probably feel out of place. . . . We feel embarrassed or afraid as to what other people might think . . . and you feel intimidated because you are thinking the white people are better than you.[32]

It is important to note that the high-achieving Latino students looked on paper very much like their white counterparts, and tended to participate at similarly high rates in the same high-profile activities: student government, honors programs, community service, and varsity sports. The only two places in which they differed substantially were that white students tended to be more involved in religious activities and intramural sports, and Latinos tended to be somewhat more involved in work or internship programs. With the exception of Latinos' relative lack of involvement in religious activity, which may be somewhat counterintuitive, their relative avoidance of intramural sports and attraction to internships may also be related to socioeconomic status. Intramural sports often imply additional expenditures, whereas work and internships frequently pay a wage or some kind of stipend.

In addition to providing leadership opportunities and a chance to expand a college application portfolio, extracurricular activities can help students find out about college by expanding their peer network beyond the classroom. They also encourage students to become more engaged at school in ways that ultimately may foster positive educational outcomes.[33] In particular, for disadvantaged students who may have fewer academic achievements in high school, extracurricular activities have been found to contribute to a measurable and meaningful gain on SAT Verbal and Math scores.[34]

We examined the effect of participating in a host of different extracurricular activities to determine which were more likely to contribute to higher grade point averages and SAT scores for Latino and other students. Realizing that income and parent education may affect participation in clubs, we controlled for socioeconomic status.[35] Using participation in any organized club at school as a reference, we found that participation in a school honors program, instrumental music group (band or orchestra), intramural sports team, work or internship program, religious activity, ethnic activity (for Mexican Americans and Puerto Ricans), and student government (for Mexican Americans) were associated with higher SAT Math scores for Latinos (see the Appendix, Table A.7). A similar pattern emerged when we substituted GPA as the measure of academic achievement. Enrollment in a school honors program, instrumental music group, or intramural sports team; involvement in a community service organization; foreign study or study abroad; student government; and religious activity were the extracurricular activities associated with higher grade point averages for Latinos (see the Appendix, Table A.8). The same pattern emerged among white students.

Most of these activities make intuitive sense. Some, however, bear further discussion. For example, intramural sports as opposed to varsity sports appear to be associated with higher achievement for Latinos, as well as for whites. We speculate that intramural sports demand less time than team sports, and therefore compete less with academics while providing the same benefits that come from engagement in athletic activities, such as cross-cultural friendships, the development of collaborative skills, and deeper engagement in school. Although intramural sports do not confer the same social status as varsity sports, participation in student government, which is associated with higher achievement, can fill that role. Instrumental music probably has many of the same benefits as intramural sports, but with the addition of the discipline that is learned in having to practice an instrument. We are also reminded of the Latina professor, introduced in Chapter 3, who mentioned that it was in band that she was placed in a setting with high-achieving students and where she learned about the college preparatory curriculum. Students who dedicate themselves to the practice required to learn an instrument are probably more serious about learning for learning's sake, and provide an academically supportive culture for each other.

We also found curious the importance of study abroad in this context where socioeconomic status was controlled. Not many students have the opportunity to study abroad during high school, especially in the schools that educate many low-income Latinos; however, when such international study did occur, it did seem to distinguish those who did engage in this activity from their peers in important ways. We speculate, though, that some students may have thought the survey question meant any experience outside the country. In this case, many Latino students may have had the opportunity to experience life in another country (including Puerto Rico as "abroad"), and these experiences may have indeed added importantly to their world views and their motivation to excel.

Are some activities associated with higher academic performance than others? We conclude from these analyses that yes, several activities are in fact more positively associated with higher grade point averages and SAT Math scores.

School Quality and the College-Going Culture

Strong schools that send many students to college tend to have well-organized, compelling programs designed to involve students in the school in many different ways. Weak schools often have failing programs, a lack of organization, and faculty and administrators with limited experience, inadequate preparation, and a short tenure in the school.[36] When students talk about the special programs that helped them to get to college, these usually occurred in the context of a reasonably well-organized school that was attempting to create a college-going culture. Our interviews with students include many dramatic accounts of how they managed to get into schools that would provide opportunities that could lead to college. Liliana, for example, described the series of schooling decisions that led her to college. Although her family lived in Section 8 housing in a poor neighborhood with weak schools, her mother somehow knew that there were better schools in an adjacent neighborhood.

> My mom knew about the schools in [the other neighborhood] and we took the bus an hour to get over to the elementary school in [that neighborhood]. We did that until the sixth grade. So, when I went to middle school, I was tracked up because I was coming from a higher ranking school. . . . With my grades, I was at the top of my class, in honors in middle school. My history/English

teacher told me to apply to the [university charter school]. "You have to apply, you have to go," she said. Five in our class got in. It was way far, and there was no [school] bus. It took us two hours to get there. . . . Going to [this school] I was really exposed to the privilege that other people have. Why did I have to come here to get pushed to go to college?

Liliana had the opportunity to go to a school outside her neighborhood, a school whose reputation she knew was better than her local high school. So, unlike her brother and sister who chose to go to the neighborhood school, she took a bus every day to get to that school. According to Liliana, the consequences of their choices were not surprising. "Both my brother and sister dropped out in their sophomore year . . . they went to that other school and it wasn't very good. Everyone knew it."

An earlier generation of academically successful Latino students was faced with the same challenges, and they or their parents made similar choices to find the better schools, even when it meant significant hardships. A young man who became a Harvard-educated lawyer talked about the decisive point in his life when he had the choice of attending two high schools because his home was on the boundary between two districts. He chose the Anglo school.

When I graduated from junior high school the big question was which of the two high schools I was going to choose. And the reason why the choice was important was because Lincoln was predominantly, 95 percent, Mexican American and that's where most of the kids from my junior high were going. . . . Franklin, at that time, was 99 percent Anglo. And the choice was very critical at that point primarily because it was a choice of following the rest of the crowd. . . . I was involved in gangs when I was in junior high school. . . . Most of them had been arrested for one reason or another. . . . My decision was to go to Franklin. . . . I knew the only way to escape this was to disassociate myself from all of them by going to a high school where they weren't going.[37]

Sometimes Latino students whose parents do not know about the quality of the schools their children attend nonetheless figure it out for themselves. The brothers of one young Latino who was raised by a single mother with an elementary school education, for instance, shaped his educational choices, setting him up to eventually complete his Ph.D. He recounted how his two older brothers had decided they wouldn't go to the segregated school in the barrio where they lived:

They wanted to go to college . . . they didn't want to go to the schools there . . . they found a Catholic high school through a friend of theirs, and that's where the whole movement started. We used to . . . take the bus across town. . . . [They said the barrio school] "isn't good enough, look at all those guys, they're not going anywhere." They saw the writing on the wall. Pretty perceptive, actually.[38]

Educational Aspirations

Students with early, high, and consistent aspirations to go to college are more likely to go than those who do not have such aspirations or develop them late in high school. Studies consistently find that most Latino students have very high aspirations for going to college, though there is also consensus that they appear to have the lowest aspirations of all groups, and they certainly attend college at lower rates than other groups.[39] Grace Kao and Marta Tienda, in one analysis of the National Educational Longitudinal Study (NELS)—which was begun in 1988 with approximately fifteen thousand eighth-graders from across the country—found that educational aspirations are generally high among ethnic minority groups from eighth to twelfth grades, but that they vary by group.[40] Many Latinos and African Americans, for instance, do not make it to the twelfth grade. Another study of NELS 88 data found that 97.4 percent of the Latinos "hoped" to attend college "at some time," but only 57.6 percent enrolled in a form of postsecondary education right after high school.[41] A second study of the same data found that while 73 percent of Latinos said they aspired to postsecondary education right after high school graduation, only 55 percent were planning on getting a bachelor's degree.[42] Such research seems to raise the question of "whether educational aspirations hold the same significance for each ethnic group."[43] For instance, is there a difference in meaning for some students between "going to college" and getting a degree? Latinos in particular are more likely to pursue their postsecondary education in community colleges where four-year bachelor's degrees are not conferred.

The issue of what it means to "aspire" to go to college is indeed complex. Researchers have found that students' aspirations, and parents' aspirations for their children, vary greatly depending on how the question is asked.[44] It seems almost everyone wants to go to college if asked, "What do you want to do or hope to do when you finish high school?" But if the question is "What do you expect to do when you finish high school?" (or "What do you expect your child to do when he or she finishes high school?"), then the numbers of those likely to go to college fall considerably. It seems people do make distinctions between what they would like and what they think will probably occur. Nonetheless, much higher percentages of both students and parents still report that they expect they will go to college than actually do, and this is especially true for Latinos. So there remains a large gap between aspirations, however defined, and reality. Consequently, just convincing students that they should want to go to college, that it's a good idea with long-term advantages, may not go far enough to actually get students to attend.

To circumvent the problem of confusing desires with expectations, Patricia Gándara and her colleagues asked approximately five hundred students what they "planned" to do when they finished high school, as they moved through the four high school years.[45] The students were a diverse group of mostly low-income whites, Southeast Asians, blacks, and Latinos, all from an inner-city and a rural high school. Although in the ninth grade only half of the Latinos and 61 percent of all others reported planning on going to college, by tenth grade college aspirations had shot up to 81 percent for the non-Latino students—even as Latinos opting for college had only risen to 58 percent. At twelfth grade, 80 percent of Latinos and 85 percent of non-Latino students planned to go to college. We took this to mean that the non-Latino students were getting consistent and earlier encouragement from school personnel and others to go to college, while Latinos either were not hearing or being given the same encouragement. The delay in rising aspirations for Latinos may be an indicator of the time it takes for these students to acquire information in their weak social capital networks. In other words, if students have friends who know what it takes to go on to college, they are likely to be exposed often and informally to information about college preparation and how to apply. Without such friends, however, this information is likely to take much longer to filter into the social networks of most Latino students, if it ever does. Because so few Latino students actually attend college, we can conclude that the last-minute rise in aspirations is probably too late in many cases to "take hold" or to be converted into reality in many cases, and that it may, in fact, be a default answer when students actually are not sure what they will do after high school.

The Paradox of High "Aspirations" and Low School Effort

Latino students overall have much higher aspirations than their actual college-going rates show, and their grades are lower than those of most students who expect to attend college. In the words of Barbara Schneider and David Stevenson, Latinos (and black males) have particularly "misaligned" college ambitions—that is, they know little about what is required to be admitted to even the most modestly selective colleges.[46] For most Latinos and many other low-income students living in the inner city or rural areas, "going to college" means enrolling, often part-time, at the local community college. In our study of rural and urban low-income youth, we found that even as students' aspirations to go to college rose, their grades fell. That is, they appeared to be putting less effort into their studies even though they were increasingly committed to the idea of "going

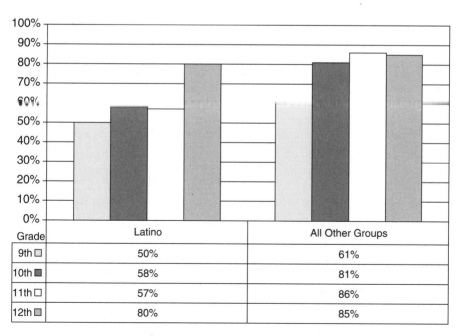

Grade	Latino	All Other Groups
9th ☐	50%	61%
10th ■	58%	81%
11th ☐	57%	86%
12th ▨	80%	85%

FIGURE 6.2 Percent of Latinos and others who aspire to go to college, by high school year. (Data from Gándara, O'Hara, and Gutiérrez 2004, p. 47.)

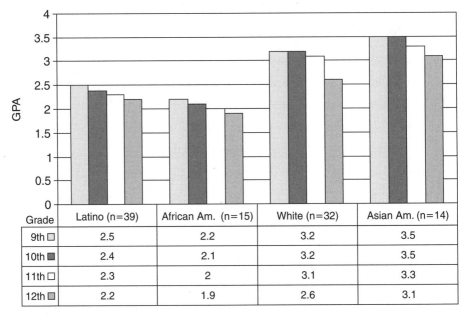

Grade	Latino (n=39)	African Am. (n=15)	White (n=32)	Asian Am. (n=14)
9th ☐	2.5	2.2	3.2	3.5
10th ◼	2.4	2.1	3.2	3.5
11th ☐	2.3	2	3.1	3.3
12th ▨	2.2	1.9	2.6	3.1

FIGURE 6.3 Grade point averages each year of high school, by race/ethnicity. (Data from Gándara, O'Hara, and Gutiérrez 2004, p. 48.)

to college." For purposes of comparison, we tracked the grades and records of a subsample of Latinos, whites, blacks, and Asians over the four years of school to follow their educational progress. The overall pattern was the same for all ethnic groups—downward, even though their actual grade point averages differed widely.

When queried in focus groups about this seeming paradox, students commonly replied that they realized they needed to put more effort into school and they were definitely going to do it "next year." But senior year arrived much more quickly than they had imagined and they had not made good on their promise. Community college for most of these students became a default choice when no better post–high school option seemed possible. In focus groups, Latino students talked about the difference between their ambitions and their probable reality. One Latino student noted, "Students say they are going to a four-year college because it sounds good. It's the ideal thing to do after you graduate." But, he went on, "they might get tired of school and end up dropping out, or they won't get the grades, or the money." Another student added, "A lot of times students don't really know what it takes to get there." There is considerable evidence in the literature that this final comment captures well the plight of many Latino students.[47]

In general, students who are high academic performers and who have taken the required courses for admission to a selective college typically apply to these selective institutions. Latinos are unlike most other students in this regard. While more than 16 percent of white students and almost 34 percent of Asian students who go on to college attend either highly selective or selective colleges and universities, only a little more than 9 percent of Latinos attend similarly selective institutions. Even among the most highly qualified upper quintile of students, 58 percent of Asians and 35 percent of whites attend selective colleges and universities, but only slightly more than 23 percent of similarly qualified Latinos do.[48] As a group, Latinos are inclined to enroll in colleges that are less selective than they qualify to attend. That is, Latinos who could go to selective four-year colleges and universities are more likely than others to opt for an open access, or less selective, college; and those who could qualify for a less selective four-year school are more likely to attend a community college.

Studies have consistently shown that the more selective the institution of higher education, the greater the likelihood of successfully completing a degree for all ethnic groups.[49] More than 60 percent of Latinos who go on to college begin their postsecondary careers in community college, however, and few of these students will ever get a degree. For example, in the cohort of students who began community college in 1995 in the United States, only 5.9 percent of Latinos had obtained a bachelor's degree six years later (compared to 12 per-

cent of whites and 7 percent of Asians in the same circumstance).[50]
The consequences, then, of "shooting low" in selecting a college are
significant and negative.

Why do Latino students consistently attend less selective colleges?
One explanation is that less selective institutions generally cost less,
and Latinos who aspire to go to college come from lower-income
families than other groups. But Latino students also have far less information about the differences among postsecondary institutions,
the differences in the likelihood of completing a degree at a two-year
versus a four-year college, and the ways in which it is possible to
finance a college education. In a multiyear study of the low application rates of Latino students conducted by the University of California, one primary finding was that students and their families were far
less familiar with how to prepare for and apply to college than any
other group of students.[51] Those students who make it into four-year
colleges usually encounter someone who guides them. Peers are one
source of that guidance for these successful college-goers.

The Influence of Friends on College-Going

Data from the SAT do little to illuminate the role of friends in the
choice to go to college, though many studies of adolescents and
schooling have found peers to be among the most important influences on young people's behavior.[52] Most students go to college
where their friends are planning to go. In part this happens because students don't want to make such a huge life transition all by
themselves, but it is also because they discuss options among themselves—if they talk about college at all—and so their information networks shape the choices they believe they have. If a student's friends
are interested in highly selective schools, they probably will be, too.
By contrast, if their friends are not interested in college at all, it will
be harder to make the decision to go. Patricia McDonough, in her
study of how students make choices about the colleges they will at-

tend, quoted a young woman who described the pervasiveness of college information available to her in her private school,

> There are people at Paloma [high school] who if they had been in a public school they wouldn't be going to college, there's just no way. . . . You find out so much just sitting around the senior lounge during one period. . . . Just word of mouth and sisters and brothers who have gone to college and we just all constantly were sharing the information about college and it was like the center of our minds.[53]

In contrast to this all-consuming preoccupation with getting ready to go to college, in our study of low-income students from an inner-city and rural high school, few Latinos, in particular, spent much time talking with friends about college. When asked why, one Chicana student replied,

> It's not an everyday thing you talk about. Sometimes you will talk about GPA, but you don't ask each other how you are doing academically. You want to spend time with friends, you don't want to talk about school. You spend most of the day in school, so you just want to relax and hang out.[54]

But if students do fall in with a crowd that is college bound—typically by being placed in college preparatory, honors, and Advanced Placement classes—they frequently report that their peers offer critical support in the form of both advice and encouragement. Alex described how he and his friends, now all at a major West Coast university, supported one another:

> I was going to go to [a college] near my home or a technical college. But my friends in my classes were all applying to [the univer-

sity] and encouraged me to apply with them. We filled out our applications together . . . helped each other . . . and got in. To this
day we are still very close.

Occasionally students from low-income backgrounds are so focused on going to college because of a teacher or some other individual who has inspired them that they change friendship groups to help
support this goal. More often, however, they do not reject a non-
college-bound group of friends, but simply "add" another friendship
group that they know can give the support and information they need
to get to college. Abel, a college sophomore, is a case in point. He explained:

> I went through two groups of friends in high school. The first
> group I thought were my friends weren't. They would make racial
> comments and put me down. I met them through sports, soccer,
> and basketball. And they were not as ambitious. The second group
> had already been my friends, but I started to hang out with them
> more. When I told them my goals, they would say things like, "I
> could see you doing that." If I ran for a ASB [office] they would
> help me campaign. When I was applying for college they would
> help me review my statement. They are all in college now too. The
> other group of friends were not on that path at all.

Abel consciously decided which friends would help him achieve his
goal to go to college and changed whom he associated with at a critical point during high school.

Many Latinos studied by Gándara who had made great educational leaps demonstrated this kind of behavior. For example, a young
man who rose from a very low-income family to become a high-level
federal policymaker described the two worlds in which he lived in
high school:

> In high school . . . I got involved in all the clubs. I was an officer. I
> got scholarships, I was in all the college prep classes. I was getting
> A's and B's. I was associating with the white kids, but only on a
> superficial level, as in those clubs. Once out of school, I became
> rowdy, a pachuco like the rest.[55]

Another Harvard-educated Latino who became a community orga-
nizer and media mogul talked to Gándara about how he maintained
two different peer groups—one that supported academic aspirations
and the other that supported his identity as a Mexican:

> I hung out in high school with smart, good kids . . . studious,
> mostly girls, white girls. . . . The smart ones, you know, were active
> and ran the clubs and I was part of that. . . . So I had two sets of
> friends, Mexican friends and my white friends. Outside of school
> . . . [we] formed our own band. [An all-]Mexican band.[56]

To get a sense of the likely influence of students' friends' attitudes
toward school and going to college, we asked all respondents in our
study of five hundred high school students to rate how important it
was to their friends to get good grades (a behavior linked to college-
going).[57] Only about a fourth of all of these low-income students reported that their friends believed it was "very important" to get good
grades, and Latinas did not differ significantly from all others in this
regard. But Latino males were significantly different from this group:
only 3 to 6 percent of urban Latinos thought their friends believed
that getting good grades was very important and less than 10 percent
of rural Latinos in our study felt similarly. Not only do Latino students, in general, have friends with much less social capital to share,
but many of their friends are "turned off" from school and actually
help to sustain an anti-college culture. Large percentages of Latino
males in our high school study said they never did homework and

more than a fourth said their friends "did not care about school at all." While Latinas were more likely than their male counterparts to report that they wanted to be viewed as "smart" or "a good student" in our surveys, they didn't think their friends shared this view. Overwhelmingly they thought their friends preferred to be seen as "nice" or "fun to be around." This was the same for the Latino males.

There is no doubt that peer pressure reinforces the tendency of many students with low educational aspirations to reject school and its demands, and that it can dampen the aspirations of others whose goals may be more tenuous and partially formed. But some students who have achieved an academic focus and know they want to go to college find ways to "manage" the attitudes and aspirations of their friends. One young woman talked to Gándara about how her high school friends who were not planning to go to college nonetheless were supportive of her ambitions. This attitude seemed to be linked to her acceptance of them and the fact that she did not flout her academic prowess, but used it to their advantage as well.

> We were about six, seven girls . . . like a clique. But none of them went to college. They got married after high school . . . worked in factories . . . [but] then I was very popular because I helped them with their work and with school. And actually a lot of people say that bright kids were made fun of and all that, but in my case, it wasn't the case. It was the opposite. They would look up . . . and say, "She's smart," and "She's a brain," and like that. But in a nice way, you know.[58]

The Importance of Adults in Students' Lives

Peers can be critically important for linking students to information networks that help them understand the role that college might play in their lives, and for providing support for the decision to go to college. But if there is any common denominator among virtually all Latino students whom we have known to beat the odds, it is that some adult steps forward in their lives to encourage them—tell them they are smart and "can do it"—and provides guidance for how that might happen. Sometimes it is a teacher or counselor, sometimes a clergyperson or family friend; often it is someone associated with a special program who takes them under their wing. Parents are usually encouraging and supportive, but because Latino parents generally do not have the social capital to guide the way, they often cannot play the role that middle-class parents do for their children. Some of the more successful parenting techniques may be evidenced in a study conducted using 1988 NELS data to assess the academic performance of Asian Americans compared to their white peers. In that study, Grace Kao found that Asian parents differed from whites in that they were more likely to use resources at home to encourage their children to study, to restrict the number of hours that children watched television, and to have rules about maintaining grades (74 percent versus 68 percent of whites). Asian parents were also more likely to use their financial resources to enroll their children in art, music, ethnic history, and computer classes.[59] While the study did not include a comparison to Latinos or groups other than whites and the Asian subgroups, it provides a good overview of the practices and use of home resources that may not be readily available in those Latino households in which parents have less education and less disposable income. Beating the odds requires that someone who does have social capital take over that role.

One young Chicano who later became a professor in a prestigious university shared his memories of "the most important person in [his] whole educational experience":

> A teacher I had in fifth and sixth grade. . . . She was a wonderful
> woman, an Anglo woman, who was from the Midwest. . . . I re-

member very clearly that she bought the World Book encyclopedia for the class. . . . Up until then I could hardly write my
name. . . . I could hardly read. . . . She took me . . . and she took
this one Anglo boy who was a migrant worker . . . he used to wear
rags to school. . . . I started doing a lot of book reports and stuff
from the World Book encyclopedia. She introduced me to libraries and to reading and that's when I really started picking up because once I discovered reading it just opened up a whole new
world. . . . In those two years I learned how to learn.[60]

Because completion rates for Latinos who go on to community college are so low, being diverted from applying only to community college to instead seeking admission at a four-year college or university
can make the critical difference between getting a degree and not.
Raquel, a Mexican American student, recounted how that essential
diversion occurred in her life:

There was a counselor in my senior year that really changed my
mind about college. She was a Chicana and she had contacts to
help me get in. One day she stopped me and asked me where I decided to attend college . . . and I responded, [the local community
college]. Then she said to come and visit her and she would ar-
range for me to meet her colleague. I met her colleague, another
Latina, and she took me on a campus tour and showed me around
and explained how to apply. . . . She walked me through the process. And that is how I ended up at [a four-year institution] instead
of community college.

Since most Latinos will go to community colleges if they go to
college at all, it is also critical to encounter someone who can help
students transfer. One Chicana who received intensive mentoring

from a community-college history teacher described how it changed her life:

> She just supported me in every way she could. . . . In fact, she is the one who got me into UCLA. I had never heard of UCLA. . . . She's the one who helped me get the scholarship. She really pushed me. It was like, "You can do it!" She always used to say that she knew I was going to make it big. Where she got it from, I don't know . . . she became a very close friend of our family. [She] was also a sort of a mentor to . . . a lot of Chicanos who came from East LA.[61]

Sometimes the critical adult does not provide specific academic support or guidance on how to get to college, but plays a pivotal role in helping students to believe in themselves and consider loftier goals than they might otherwise have chosen. Leticia, a twenty-three-year-old Mexican immigrant, remembered the person she believes made the biggest difference in her life—a dance teacher whom she met in her ballet folklórico class:

> My folklórico teacher. . . . I started dancing when I was twelve. . . . She is the woman I admire most, she's very kind, everyone respects her, a woman of her word. She would always tell us, you are going to college, you are *all* going to college! She taught us the importance of discipline . . . responsibility, and education. *Todos sus estudiantes van a la universidad.* [All of her students go to college.]

Many of the students with whom we have spoken have never seen or heard of a college recruiter, a key player in helping bring more minority students into colleges and universities during eras that were more accepting of affirmative action. But most students were beneficiaries of one of the growing number of college-access programs that have proliferated on high school campuses, in part as a response to the demise of affirmative action and the increased pressure on high schools to have their students of color more "college ready" and better informed about the process of applying to college. Leticia, one of two daughters of a single mother on disability, was placed into the AVID (Advancement via Individual Determination) program at her high school, which helped her prepare for college and acquire the funds necessary to attend.[62] Leticia noted how "in AVID we would work on scholarships . . . they made us apply, and I got $10,000."

An additional benefit of the program was the peers with whom she was surrounded. They were so motivated by the program to study that, according to Leticia, "They were always asking me, 'Are you going to study?' It put me in a study mode."

Perceptions of Ability

Many factors contribute to making students feel competent and able to undertake demanding academic work, or incompetent and out of place in school. On the SAT student survey, students are asked to rate their ability in select subject areas (writing, math, and science) on a four-point Likert scale. Latino students were less likely than their white peers to place themselves in the highest tenth percentile or above average in ability in any of the three areas. Even those Latino students who scored in the top twentieth percentile appeared to be less confident than their white peers in their writing, science, and math abilities. In fact, Latinos were more likely than whites to mark "average" in all ability areas. And those Latinos in the top twentieth percentile were more likely to mark "above average" rather than "in the highest tenth percentile" (see the Appendix, Table A.9).

Confidence levels appear to be slightly higher in math compared to the writing and science subjects that we reviewed. Writing in particular was an area that had the lowest self-perception ratings by the Latino subgroups. Yet even though greater percentages of Latino students rated themselves in the "above average" category on math than on writing, a large percentage of Latino students still rate themselves only "average" on both categories. These self-ratings, however, may reflect a reasonably accurate assessment of their situation. Latino students overall, as well as those who score in the top quintile on the SAT, do indeed score lower than their white peers, by about three-fourths of a standard deviation for math and verbal scores, and for Mexican American students in particular, by more than a full standard deviation in writing (see the Appendix, Table A.10).

Gándara and López explored the extent to which the SAT scores themselves may influence students' self-perceptions of ability. They asked a sample of sixty high-achieving Latino high school graduates to rate their ability in a variety of subject areas, then compared these ratings with their SAT scores in those same subjects. Holding grades constant, the students with the lower SAT scores rated themselves as less able than those with higher scores, even though their grades in the subjects were not significantly different. They also interviewed students about their SAT scores, focusing especially on how the lower-scoring students explained their scores when they had been such excellent students. Some students were clearly shaken by their scores and were concerned about whether they could really make it in college, but most brushed off the scores and said that standardized tests were simply a poor measure of their abilities. Nonetheless, these same students tended to rate themselves lower in ability than their peers who had scored higher.[63]

Proven links between students' belief in their own abilities and their likelihood of succeeding academically make these findings especially important. Doubts about one's ability, especially in intensely competitive colleges, can lead a student to underperform on critical academic assessments, and it can also lead to extreme psychological pressure that can reduce a student's motivation to even try to achieve. Liliana, the young woman who was accepted into the university charter high school where "everyone went to college," recounted the difficulties she encountered when she went to a highly competitive university.

> I didn't know what to do when I first came here. I felt like dropping out and going back to the community college because I am not good enough. This is too hard for me. I thought maybe I should just go get married or something! It wasn't just academic, it was socially, finding my niche. . . . People here are more research oriented, but we didn't do that till senior year. . . . I care more about learning than being competitive. I wasn't trying my hardest, but I was learning a lot. I didn't have the competitive mindset, but everyone here is SO competitive!

Liliana continued, reflecting on reading one of the papers of a white friend from one of her classes and feeling inadequate by comparison,

> Maybe she was taught how to do that, how to think better. It's not that they're smarter, we just weren't given the resources to think analytically, How do I go about this? . . . You have to seek out those resources.

As we will show in Chapter 7, even excellent programs in good high schools have difficulty making up for the years of weak education offered to many Latino students in their under-performing elementary and middle schools. Students in this situation may have to work much harder than others just to keep up. In order to strive for academic success, most students will need to believe that they are capable of achieving it and that studying hard will help them attain that goal.[64] So how do Latino students who may encounter very few models of academic success come to see themselves as capable students? Certainly parents play an important role in encouraging their children and making them feel competent. The psychological literature is replete with studies that demonstrate the importance of parental encouragement. But those studies are also almost always conducted on middle-class, "middle-America" families. And certainly some innate ability to do well in school factors into these perceptions. But by their own admission, many of the people we interviewed conceded they were not the smartest people in their classes nor in their families.

Researchers have found that student self-perceptions are related to teacher perceptions and are better predictors of academic performance than some other measures of ability.[65] One recent study that included a largely Latino population sought to understand how support provided by teachers, parents, and classmates helps explain student competence in math and science at the middle school level. The researchers found that appraisals of adults predicted the students' own self-perceived competence and academic performance in their math and science courses. They also found, importantly, that Latino students reported lower mean levels of competence in these courses compared to their white peers.[66] Raquel, a student at a large West Coast university, described how in middle school her teacher's assessment made her believe that she was not an honors-level student. A particular incident stuck in her mind for years, shaping her aspirations for her future:

> In junior high, I was doing very well. But in my last math class I
> got a B; I clearly remember my teacher checked off honors and
> then she crossed it off. I remember crying that I was not put in

honors. [And] in high school, I would not consider myself to be at the top of my class. I did not really think I was preparing for college either.

Another study that focused on minority students in the fields of science, technology, engineering, and math found that the higher a student rated his or her own ability, the greater the likelihood that the student would succeed in academic tasks. This study also found that certain teaching practices—in particular, hands-on learning experiences, collaborative learning experiences, continuous specific feedback, and teacher clarity—could have a greater effect on student achievement and self-perceptions for women and minorities majoring in those fields than other contextual factors like school climate and socioeconomic status, and in fact predicted performance better than SAT scores. These researchers concluded that faculty members had a significant influence on minority students' self-perceptions of ability, and perhaps more important, whether they would complete an engineering degree.[67]

In terms of first choice of major, Latinos in the SAT sample subgroups are comparable to their white peers. But how can we ensure that those students interested in science, technology, engineering, and math are prepared to succeed in such fields? Approximately 29 percent of the Latino subgroups and 28 percent of whites in the SAT sample selected a science or related major as their first choice (see the Appendix, Table A.11, which also shows that Asian American students stand out as heavily concentrated in these science- and math-oriented fields; 40 percent of these students intend to pursue one of the science- or math-related majors). Unfortunately, however, Latinos are less likely to obtain degrees in math and science, but not because they lack interest or even persistence in these fields. One recent study utilizing the Beginning Postsecondary Students Longitudinal Study of the National Center for Education Statistics found that in the 1995–1996 entering cohort of college freshmen, Latinos were more likely than whites or African Americans to major, or express an interest in majoring, in a science, technology, engineering, or math field. Six years later, however, only about two-thirds who had begun in these fields received a degree in one, compared to about 87 percent of whites and 95 percent of Asians. They did not, for the most part, change majors; they simply struggled to finish their degrees. It seemed that they had been less well prepared by their high schools, where they had taken fewer rigorous AP classes; they had spent more time working because they were from lower-income circumstances; and they had lacked specific guidance about college. The researchers concluded that Latinos (and African Americans) do not need to be encouraged to enter these fields; rather they need to be supported to complete their degrees.[68]

In sum, Latino students do indeed score lower than their white counterparts on all kinds of measures of academic achievement, and this fact can, in turn, reduce their self-confidence in applying to competitive colleges, choosing a major, and excelling in their chosen field. The role of the teacher or counselor in helping Latino students interpret test scores and other achievement data in the context of the students' own situations, and assuring them of their competence, appears to be critical in mediating what can otherwise be debilitating news. A support network seems essential for helping to sustain the motivation of Latino students who may be doing everything right but who may still not be able to overcome these challenges by themselves.

Financial Aid

Talent, ability, high grades and test scores, and powerful ambition are still not enough to ensure college attendance if students cannot find a way to pay for their education. While the American Dream conveys the idea that anyone can make it in this country if he or she is willing to work hard, even hard work isn't always sufficient to pay the tuition bills. Research on who goes to college shows without a doubt that money matters—a lot. For example, one major study using national data found that high-ability low-income students were less likely to go to college than those with low ability but high family income.[69] Lack of funds is an especially high barrier to attending selective colleges and universities, which are more expensive than community colleges or other lower-cost alternatives, but where students are actually more likely to complete a degree.[70] Latino families have an average median income that is only 69 percent that of white families and 59 percent that of Asian families.[71] The far more limited income that Latino students and their families have to allocate for higher education is probably one important reason why approximately 60 percent of Latinos choose to attend a two-year rather than a four-year college.

We noted earlier that since the mid-1970s there has actually been a decline in the percentage of Latinos who go on to college. There is reason to believe that the cost of college is a factor in this decline. According to the National Center for Public Policy and Higher Education, the proportion of income necessary to pay for college has increased for most families in the United States. While the median income level has grown 127 percent since 1982, the average cost of college has increased 375 percent.[72] In 1980 the lowest-income families had to devote 6 percent of their income to pay tuition for a two-year college, but in 2000, such tuition required 12 percent of their income. Likewise, in 1980, attendance at a public four-year college cost 13 percent of the lowest-income family's resources, but in 2000, that proportion had increased to 25 percent.[73] Such a large percentage makes college seem out of reach for most low-income families that are considering tuition for one child, let alone two or more. Hence figuring out how to pay for college becomes a critical piece of the college-going puzzle.

Both all Latino students and those Latinos in the top quintile were more likely to plan to get a part-time job than their white or Asian peers. Specifically, 74 percent of the Mexican American students who took the SAT in our 2004 sample planned to work part-time in college, while only 55 percent of their Asian American and 63 percent of their white peers planned to work part-time (see Table 6.6). More than 77 percent of the Mexican American SAT test takers in the top quintile and 80 percent of all Mexican Americans planned to apply for financial aid. Their white counterparts in both categories were less likely than all the Latino subgroups to have plans to apply for financial aid.

Among the reasons that Latinos give when explaining why they plan to seek financial aid in greater proportions than their white counterparts is that they have many fewer resources to support their education and they have much less information about other means for financing it.

The students who report that they will apply for financial aid are in some ways the lucky ones; at least they are aware that there are

Table 6.6   Plans to apply for financial aid by Latinos and whites taking the SAT, 2004 (percentages)

	Other Latino		Puerto Rican		Mexican American		White	
	Top quintile	All test takers	Top quintile	All test takers	Top quintile	All test takers	Top quintile	All test takers
No response	9.1	7.2	7.6	5.9	7.8	6.2	10.4	8.9
Yes	69.7	75.8	75.6	80.5	77.1	80.0	59.3	63.5
No	5.5	3.6	3.3	2.3	3.1	2.4	9.4	7.5
Don't know	15.6	13.5	13.5	11.3	12.1	11.4	20.8	20.1

Source: Data from College Board 2004.

sources of financial support available. A recent survey by the Tomás Rivera Policy Institute found that Latinos have less knowledge of financial aid options than any other group and that three-quarters of those students surveyed who had not gone to college reported they would have been more likely to attend if they had known about financial aid. A very small percentage of Latinos even considered that they might receive a scholarship.[74]

In 2003–2004, Latinos received the lowest average financial aid award of any racial/ethnic group ($6,250); the average total award was $6,890. Asian Americans had the highest level of aid ($7,260).[75] The reasons for these disparities are related to the types of institutions that students attend. Because Latinos disproportionately attend low-cost and two-year institutions, their aid awards are lower than those for students who, as a group, tend to enroll in higher-cost institutions (notwithstanding disparities in income).

There is also a growing proportion of Latino students who receive no financial aid because they are undocumented. It is not uncommon for such students to have entered the United States many years earlier, when they were toddlers or young children with no understanding of their citizenship status. Upon applying to college, they are informed that they are not citizens and therefore do not qualify for any financial aid. This news can be heartbreaking for a student who has worked hard throughout school to go to college, only to find out that this goal is out of reach financially. The federal Dream Act, now stalled in Congress for several years, would address this problem and provide access to financial aid for students who have been in the country for several years, graduated from a U.S. high school, and qualified for college admission. Without such legislation, an increasing number of students who had no role in choosing to come to the United States, and who have never really known any other country, will find themselves unable to contribute to society and the economy. A recent *Time* article put this problem into sharp focus:

Fernanda had been in the U.S. since eighth grade and graduated last year from Beardstown Middle/High School. . . . Fernanda had dreams of going to college to study Nursing, and Beardstown badly needs bilingual nurses. But she is illegal, and after the deportation of her parents, she had to support the entire family. So she's looking for work at local hog farms, a manual labor job that does not make the most of her talents. . . . The reality is that Fernanda is here to stay. She is not going back to Mexico. Amnesty would offer . . . her a fighting chance at self-sufficiency and social mobility.[76]

Latinos who were fortunate enough to go through college at a time when college cost considerably less, no matter where one went, and who were able to get financial aid, commented on what a huge difference it had made in their lives. A young Latino who went first to Harvard College and then to Harvard Law School described his situation compared to that of his older brother:

It was . . . the first or second year that financial assistance was available. Had that not presented itself, I probably would have gone to city college. That's what my brother did; it took him eight years to get a B.A. from the state university. Availability of financial aid was really, really important. What I got from Harvard was more than my dad earned all year.[77]

Another young Latina, the daughter of cannery workers who became a physician, mused,

It was a good time to come along in the educational system. . . . There were opportunities and I either reached for them or stumbled on them. . . . I don't know. I was lucky. If there weren't the opportunities, I don't know if I'd be a doctor.[78]

Unfortunately, today is not as good a time to be a Latino student in the U.S. educational system. Proportionately fewer Latinos are going to college today than in the mid-1970s when college was less costly, financial aid was more available, and social policies were in place that encouraged more students of color to pursue higher education. What is clear from the lives of so many of these Latino students is that even the brightest, most talented students who come from low-income backgrounds with little social capital and few safety nets can be derailed by the same factors associated with low-achieving students. Their academic futures are fragile, hanging by a thin thread of hope that nothing goes wrong in their families, or in school, and that appropriate mentors and resources will appear when needed. The stars must all be aligned to ensure that these promising, hard-working students are in fact able to beat the odds.

Who Makes It to College?

Latino students who defy expectations and make it to a four-year college equipped to complete a degree differ in many ways from their Latino peers who are not as educationally successful. On average, they come from homes with more resources and their parents are better educated, although many of these college-goers still come from low-income and immigrant households in which parents have less than a high school education. More than one in five of these high achievers (and more than one in four Mexican American students) comes from such a home, compared to only one in twenty for white students. Most Latino college students are the first in their families to go to college. The students who beat the odds, though, are typically, though not exclusively, English-only speakers, because the United States has a particularly poor system of education to support learning in any language other than English. These high-achieving Latino students have higher grade point averages and have taken more honors and Advanced Placement courses than their lower-achieving Latino classmates, and have participated in extracurricular activities at rates similar to their white peers. Both adults and peers support their schooling and they are likely to have been exposed to early literacy in the home even if their parents lacked much formal education. They are also more likely to have been exposed to intervention efforts either at school or in the community.

Despite all these positive attributes, high-achieving Latino students tend to have less confidence in themselves as students and see themselves as less capable than their white or Asian peers. They also have significant financial aid needs that may not be met under current policies, and they lack basic information about how to finance their educations, so they are more likely to work while going to school, which slows their progress toward completing a degree and can place college graduation at risk altogether.[79] Finally, the students who beat the odds often possess a passion for helping their families and others in their community, based on the inequities or overt discrimination they have experienced in their own lives or witnessed with their parents. And these high achievers are likely to participate in community-service-oriented extracurricular activities in addition to traditional school activities like sports or social clubs.

Preparing students for college and preparing them for admission to college are two separate, though related, tasks. Preparing for success in college requires that students take rigorous courses, learn good study habits, and have an academic focus. But preparing to gain admission to college involves helping students make the best decisions about what will contribute to a strong admissions profile, especially if their grades and test scores are not as competitive as others. Today, when affirmative action is under attack in many parts of the country, and is no longer used in a number of states, Latino students are more likely to be scrutinized for "race neutral" attributes such as their involvement in extracurricular activities. Consequently, it is important that they choose these activities wisely. Our analyses suggest that some activities may be especially important to consider. The first, enrollment in an honors program, was consistently the strongest predictor of high grade point average and high scores on the SAT Math exam. Playing an instrument in a band or orchestra is consistently associated with higher achievement, as are participation in intramural sports, involvement in a religious activity, and internships or work experience opportunities (that do not take away too much time from schoolwork). Participation in student government also plays a positive role in student achievement, as do foreign study and study abroad programs. Finally, involvement in a community service organization is positively correlated with grade point average.

Because of the significance of these extracurricular activities to students' futures, it is important that schools devote the resources to make such opportunities available to Latino students, who may lack the knowledge or money to pursue these on their own. Teachers or counselors may also play a valuable role by encouraging students to engage in such activities while simultaneously working toward or enrolling in an honors curriculum. Significantly, all of these extracurricular activities give Latino students the chance to be exposed to peers who can support college-going behaviors beyond the classroom—and who may have valuable information to share about the college application process.

Because Latino students are often less able to participate in critically important extracurricular activities because of constraints on time or resources, or a lack of information or a sense of belonging, schools probably need to consider removing the "extra" from extracurricular. The challenge is to help more Latino students meet the profile of the high achievers while also providing a firmer foundation on which to launch their postsecondary careers. One way that schools attempt to accomplish this dual goal is through intervention programs based at the school's site. Another approach involves community-based programs that provide a broad range of services to support these students' healthy development overall. In the next chapter we examine these efforts and attempt to determine the cost of providing Latino students with a real chance to go to and succeed in college.

CHAPTER SEVEN

The Costs and Effectiveness
of Intervention

Recent widespread public service announcements, using the theme "going to college begins in kindergarten," have aimed to motivate parents to start thinking early about their children's future and what it will take to get there. In reality, though, going to college begins long before kindergarten; perhaps before conception. The economic situation of parents, their schooling history, the neighborhoods into which children are born and raised—all have powerful effects on children's aspirations and preparation for schooling before they ever step inside a classroom.

By kindergarten, as we have shown, large gaps in school readiness already exist between poor children and middle-class children, as well as between white and Asian children and their black and Latino peers. By third grade it is alarmingly easy to predict who will go to college and who will not based on reading scores. That's not to say that some students won't beat the odds, but with each year of typical American public schooling, it becomes increasingly difficult to close the achievement gaps. Thus intervention to increase a child's odds of going to college must begin at the earliest stages of the child's life.

Given the enormity of the challenge, we argue that public schools cannot, and probably never will be able to, meet this challenge alone. Schools are still responsible for doing everything they possibly can to equalize opportunity and help ensure that every student successfully graduates from high school. But they will need help.

Since the inception of the No Child Left Behind Act in 2001, the nation's schools have been pushed in unprecedented ways to have all students in every school proficient in core academic subjects by 2014. The strategy that the federal government invoked was test-based accountability and reform led by the stick rather than the carrot. This approach has meant relentless testing and pressure on schools to bring the lowest-performing students, year by year, closer to proficiency, but with little evidence that achievement gaps among racial and ethnic groups have narrowed at all; in fact, they may have increased.[1]

Even the law's critics concede that pointing the spotlight of public attention on the achievement of the nation's poorest and most overlooked students has been important. But the pressure to bring all students up to a level of proficiency in core subjects, a goal that is virtually impossible with present (or possibly any) resources, has frustrated and demoralized many educators.[2] No one would argue against providing the opportunity for all students to become academically proficient, but it can engender a sense of hopelessness to work with students with very high needs in schools and communities that simply do not have the resources to accomplish the task. This sense of hopelessness can then turn into paralysis, and a belief that there is little point in trying anything at all if the inevitable outcome is punishment for not having achieved an impossible goal.[3] Under No Child Left Behind, schools can ultimately be dismantled if they do not meet the act's unrealistic goals, and all along the way to 2014 many are being scapegoated for not doing enough to meet every benchmark. In this chapter we point to interventions that have the potential to make a difference even as the research and commitment to school reform catch up to these often overwhelming demands.

Public schools in the United States are, with few exceptions, underfunded for the job they are given to do. In a country with such weak social policy, at least as it pertains to the poor, schools are asked to educate children whose basic health needs are not met for lack of health insurance, who cannot see the board in front of the classroom or the print on the pages of their books for lack of vision care and glasses, who come to school hungry and cold due to lack of food and a winter coat—for even when both parents work full-time, some simply cannot earn enough on minimum wage to adequately support a family. Schools are asked to educate students who do not speak English, although they have few or no teachers with the necessary training or language skills, and to motivate youngsters to go to college although their parents have no idea what a college is. They are held accountable for test scores for children whose minds are more on the shooting they witnessed last night than the math problem before them. Compared with other developed nations, U.S. per-pupil expenditures do not always look inadequate (consider, for example, the unusually high $12,000 per pupil spent by Washington, D.C.). But no other developed nation—with the possible exception of Great Britain—expects so much from its schools, with so little support from the larger society.

To date the major federal investment in schooling of low-income and minority youth, limited though it is, has been at the preschool (Head Start) and elementary levels, with relatively little attention paid to the acute needs of secondary schools, where students have little time left to prepare for graduation or college. The GEAR UP and TRIO programs are the major federal investment in secondary school students, serving a small percentage of those who need the services, which limits the programs' impact and reach. Total federal expenditures for education average less than 10 percent of state education budgets. Thus addressing the serious and chronic underachievement of Latino students often requires schools to seek outside partners— other state or federally funded programs, philanthropic efforts, community-based organizations, or colleges and universities—to provide special intervention programs that target "disadvantaged youth."

Such programs extend from preschool into college, although the greatest proliferation of programs appears to be in the high schools. Interventions there attempt to address the dramatic dropout rate of minority students, and to increase access to college for those who survive high school. Sometimes it is difficult to tell the difference between dropout prevention programs and college-access programs; their stated goal is often simply to improve the achievement and postsecondary options for groups who are underrepresented in the usual college-going cohort. Nonetheless, there is a significant focus on adolescence as the target age, and high schools as the target site. This may be because the problems of the non-college-bound students become so much more evident or acute at this age, because disaffected teenagers appear to be more threatening to society than disaffected third-graders, or because it becomes undeniable that there is little time left to change course once students are in high school. Whatever the reason, there are thousands of such programs in the United States and most high schools across the nation have at least one, if not several.[4]

In spite of this focus, Clifford Adelman of the U.S. Department of Education has estimated that no more than about 5 percent of Latino students who could benefit from such programs actually come into contact with one.[5] Moreover, little is known about those few students who do. We do not know if they have extensive or little contact with the programs—if they sign up one day never to be heard from again, or if they receive services for several years. Few programs actually collect longitudinal data on these students, which is not surprising given that such research, especially on nongovernmental programs, is so poorly funded.[6] And very little effort has gone into determining if these programs are even effective, and if so, if they are more effective than any other strategy that might be implemented at a similar or lesser cost.[7] The few rigorous studies conducted of programs such as Head Start and TRIO have delivered mixed results, hardly a resounding affirmation of their effectiveness. Yet despite such weak evaluation outcomes, program designs have not been greatly affected. The same observation can be made of programs funded by private foundations—funders are loathe to admit that their programs may not be particularly effective at their stated goals, especially after they have developed such a strong constituency. But good public policy is not made based on ignorance.

Moreover, there is no coordinated policy about how to best provide services for disadvantaged youth. Although the single largest provider of educational intervention programs is the federal government, with a combined budget in the hundreds of millions of dollars, for programs ranging from Head Start for preschool youngsters to GEAR UP and TRIO for college-bound high school students, there are many other providers, and together they no doubt affect more students than federal government programs do. The rather ad hoc system for providing services means that there has been no overarching thought given to when or how to effectively reach the students.

Sometimes programs are exceptionally effective at things they did not intend to do. For example, some college-access programs have ended up keeping a lot of students from dropping out of school, even if they do not go immediately on to college, and there are preschool programs that have had little effect on immediate school achievement but have, over the long run, kept young people out of trouble with the law and increased their employment prospects. The case can easily be made to fund such programs, but it's important to know what they do well, and what they do not do well—and whom they serve most effectively. Determining how to spend limited dollars in the best way possible is always challenging. For this reason, this chapter presents an overview of different types of intervention programs, their distinctive features, and their costs. Specifically, we discuss the characteristics of private nonprofit programs, K–16 partnerships, government-sponsored programs, community-based programs, and K–12 programs and what is known about their effectiveness in increasing student engagement and raising school achievement. We also discuss what is known about their effectiveness with Latino students in particular. Some programs that appear to show great promise, such as First Things First, but whose effects on Latino students are nevertheless as yet unknown, are not included in this discussion. Finally, we attempt to draw conclusions about the cost-effectiveness of such interventions in meeting the challenges we have raised. We also borrow from Scott Swail's admonition to attend to the critical issues of cost analysis while also being cognizant that "not everything that can be counted counts, and not everything that counts can be counted."[8] Our aim is to provide a means for policy-makers to understand both the challenges of raising the achievement of Latino students and the resource commitments that will be necessary to do so.[9]

Preschool Intervention

Efforts that target preschool-age children can be divided into two groups: one provides intensive medical, social service, and educational resources to parents to help them to create enriched and supportive early environments for their children from birth to about three years of age. These programs are usually targeted to exceptionally high-risk children—those from the most impoverished settings. The second usually begins with children at age three or four and attempts to socialize them to schooling and provide a firm foundation for school-based learning. Such programs are motivated by research on early brain development and on the critical role of the first few years in setting the course for later development. The Abecedarian Project and Head Start are well-researched examples of these two types of preschool intervention programs.

Abecedarian Project

The Carolina Abecedarian Project is probably the best researched of these early childhood intervention strategies.[10] More an experiment than a program, it was expensive, labor-intensive, and evidently quite effective at raising the intellectual capacity of children from low socioeconomic backgrounds and impoverished environments. The Abecedarian Project was a controlled study that began in 1972 with fifty-seven infants from low-income families who were randomly assigned to receive high-quality early intervention services through the age of five. Each child received an individualized prescription of educational games and activities that emphasized language and "addressed the social, emotional and cognitive development needs of each student."[11]

The project also included a follow-on component in which mothers and families of children participating in the project were assigned during the first three years of public school a homeschool teacher who would provide parents with home curriculum activities designed for each child.[12] In addition to the curriculum support for parents, homeschool resource teachers served as a liaison between the home and the school, advocating for the child both within the family and between the family and school.[13] The homeschool teacher also assisted families with issues such as medical attention, housing, employment, childcare, or adult education—any potential obstacle to the child's healthy development.[14]

Fifty-four students were in a nontreated control group, closely matched with respect to mean levels of maternal education, age, and IQ.[15] The results of this intervention at different stages in the students' lives included significantly higher test scores on reading and math from primary school to the age of twenty-one. The researchers also found that program participants experienced lower levels of grade retention and enrollment in special education.[16] In addition, participants were twice as likely to attend an institution of higher education (40 percent compared to only 20 percent of the control group). By 2002, 35 percent of participants had earned a bachelor's degree or were attending a four-year college, compared to only 14 percent of the control group.

These promising results, however, were costly. One study of the project published in 2002 found that the per-participant expense was approximately $13,900 (in 2002 dollars) annually for the duration of the experiment.[17] This represents twice the average per-pupil amount spent for Head Start participants.[18] Yet the researchers also calculated that school districts could expect a savings of over $11,000 per pupil over the course of their K–12 school years, or approximately $1,000 per year, due to lower special education and remediation expenditures as a result of participating in the Abecedarian Project. Table 7.1 shows the total per-student cost of the Abecedarian Project in 2008 dollars.

In addition to the savings to the school system with respect to remediation and special education, the individual benefits that participants achieved are noteworthy. The researchers projected that participants would earn approximately $143,000 more over their life-

Table 7.1   Estimated program costs for the Abecedarian Project, 2008

Program cost elements	Amount
Total program budget (5 years)	$8,856,813
Number of students served	111
Approximate cost per student	$16,023
Evaluation costs	Not specified

Source: Masse and Barnett 2002.

Note: Data are presented in 2008 dollars according to the Consumer Price Index (http://www.bls.gov/cpi) and were modified from the 2002 data noted in the program's own evaluation.

times compared to those who needed but did not participate in the program and that the mothers of children enrolled in the experiment could also expect approximately $133,000 in greater earnings over their lifetimes, presumably due to increased social support and connection to the labor market.

Program evaluators concluded that the Abecedarian Project was indeed cost-effective over the long term. As with other preschool interventions, however, it can take many years to realize the full benefits to program participants and reclaim the costs of the program. Policymakers, unfortunately, are often reluctant to invest funds that will not see a return during their tenure in office. Moreover, such expensive prevention-oriented programs frequently have trouble competing financially with programs that address more immediate and painfully visible needs.

Head Start

Head Start is perhaps the best known preschool program in the United States that provides early education for pre-K children as well as family support. Founded in 1965, Head Start is a national comprehensive school-readiness program that serves the needs of low-income preschool children and their families. Since 2000 the program has experienced almost no growth, generally serving a little more than 900,000 children annually.[19] In 2006, Head Start served approximately 310,000 Latino students, or 34 percent of all students who participated. Once viewed as targeting mostly black students, this program now serves more low-income white (39.8 percent) and Latino students (34 percent) than blacks (30.7 percent).[20]

Head Start programs are designed to support the healthy early development of low-income children. The programs, which can vary considerably from site to site—both by design so that they can best serve distinct communities, and by default because each program is locally run—have the primary goal of preparing children to make a successful transition to school. To do so, the programs are supposed to focus on health education and services, pre-academic skills, and parent and community involvement in children's healthy development. Because Head Start is a funding agency, and not a particular program, the quality of programs as well as their specific features depend on the skills and resources of the local program providers. Attempts to determine if Head Start as an entity is "effective" have met with controversy for this reason. Nonetheless, a number of evaluations of Head Start have been conducted to justify the government's spending billions of dollars on it.

The results of the first year of the most recent Head Start effectiveness study showed small to moderately positive effects on pre-writing, vocabulary, and (parent-reported) child literacy skills for three- and four-year-old children.[21] Access to health care also increased, but there was not a noticeable effect on the overall health status of children. Finally, the researchers reported that parents used educational activities more frequently and used less physical discipline with their Head Start children.[22] These early findings are largely consistent with other studies of Head Start and Head Start–type programs. Researchers generally find moderate effects on pre-academic skills, greater parental awareness of the needs of their children and increased skills in meeting those needs, and provision of health and nutrition services and information. Some studies have even found marginal increases in cognitive scores, including IQ.[23] A common finding, however, is that those cognitive effects are quickly lost after children begin school, usually by the end of first grade.[24] The argument has been made that the reason Head Start children lose the early cognitive advantages is that the weak public schools that low-income children attend fail to sustain the gains made by the program. There is some evidence, however, that gains may in fact be sustained for white children and for Latinos as well.[25]

Perhaps the most well-known study of Head Start–type programs was conducted beginning in the 1970s. Known as the Perry Preschool Project evaluation, it used the High Scope curriculum model developed at Eastern Michigan University to evaluate the effectiveness of one such program—and later would provide a rationale for expanding the use of Head Start nationwide. The Perry Preschool Project evaluation found that children who had been enrolled in the program were less likely to repeat grades and to be placed in special education, and ultimately had higher rates of employment, lower rates of welfare reliance, fewer contacts with the criminal justice system, and more stable marriages. These findings provided an important answer to the critics who had claimed Head Start was ineffective because early cognitive gains were not sustained into elementary school. Reduction in grade retention and special education placement could be shown to pay for the program in reduced costs to the education system, and declines in the use of social welfare services later had a long-term positive effect on society and on public coffers. Head Start was deemed to be a grand success. Indeed, Clive Belfield, Hank Levin, and their colleagues have recently extrapolated the potential impact of the Perry Preschool Project, or others like it, and claim that the nation could add an additional nineteen high school graduates for every one hundred students if such programs were implemented nationwide.[26] According to these researchers' calculations, each of those additional high school graduates would produce an extra $209,200 in earnings, and consequently a boost in tax revenue for the federal government that would more than offset the cost of the program.[27]

But the Perry Preschool Project was not a Head Start project, and it had many services that extended beyond the typical Head Start program. It was located near a major university and benefited from a curriculum and service delivery system supervised by well-known researchers in the field who hand-picked highly qualified teachers and staff. It included home visits and ongoing contact with students. It was a "Cadillac" program, unique then and now. Consequently, it is not possible to claim that all Head Start programs are capable of realizing this potential. Nonetheless, even the researchers who call into question inflated claims of academic success for specific preschool programs generally concede that preschool, when well implemented, represents an important early asset for children's social and academic development.[28]

Well-designed and well-implemented preschool programs require considerable resources. The annual per-student cost of the Head Start Program in 2008 dollars is shown in Table 7.2.

By comparison, it costs approximately 17 percent less to support each Head Start student in a half-day program than the average state pays for full-day schooling and all the attendant services provided by the public schools.[29] Moreover, a recent study conducted by the RAND Corporation put the estimated per-child cost of universal preschool in California (notoriously among the states with the highest cost of living) to be about $5,700, considerably less than the per-pupil costs of the Head Start program. The researchers do not attempt to reconcile this disparity, but they do conclude that the long-term benefits to the California taxpayer would be $2.62 for each dollar invested in preschool.[30] Researchers make the argument that if a government-supported preschool is of high quality, society can recoup its costs and more over the lifetime of the program recipient. A somewhat different argument for supporting intensive preschool in-

Table 7.2   Estimated program costs for Head Start, fiscal year 2008

Program cost elements	Amount
Total program budget	$7,177,744,000
Number of students served	909,201
Approximate cost per student	$7,894
Evaluation costs	$20,959,000

Source: http://www.acf.hhs.gov/programs/hsb/about/fy2007.html.

Note: Data are presented in 2008 dollars according to the Consumer Price Index (http://www.bls.gov/cpi) and were modified from the 2006 data noted in the program's own 2007 evaluation. This estimate does not take into account potential budget cuts at the federal level.

tervention has been made by researchers with the Federal Reserve Bank. They assert that the investment in early education can help grow the economy more efficiently than other forms of economic investment.

> Investments prior to kindergarten—especially for children considered at-risk because of poverty, abuse, neglect, parent chemical dependency, among other factors—can have a substantial impact on the sorts of students, workers, and citizens the children eventually become. This is the most efficient means to boost the productivity of the workforce fifteen or twenty years down the road.[31]

K–8 Programs

The majority of programs in the elementary years focus on raising reading, language, and math achievement levels through schoolwide reform efforts, but rarely explicitly attempt to create a cadre of young scholars ready for college admission. There are some exceptions, such as Kids to College (which is geared toward sixth-graders), that specifically target early awareness and knowledge of college.[32] Unfortunately these programs tend to be shorter-term, informational interventions and there is generally little evidence of their long-term effectiveness for increasing achievement or successfully preparing students for postsecondary education. A few exceptions are discussed here.

Success for All

Success for All, founded in 1987 by Robert Slavin at Johns Hopkins University, operates in forty-eight states and several other countries. It is one of the few programs that focuses on the earlier grades and targets individual achievement as well as whole-school reform and that has evaluated its effects specifically on Spanish-speaking students. Success for All provides programs designed to enhance literacy skills, as well as develop mathematical, scientific, listening, and social skills, from an early age.[33] Reading is at the core of the program, and the lessons are highly structured. Teachers at each grade level begin the instructional period by reading literature to students and engaging them in story discussion to enhance comprehension, listening and speaking vocabulary, and knowledge of story structure. In kindergarten and first grade, teachers emphasize the development of reading and language skills by using storybooks and instruction on phonemic awareness, auditory discrimination, and sound blending. For most of the day, students in grades one through six are assigned to heterogeneous, age-grouped classes comprising approximately twenty-five students. The main component of the Success for All program, however, occurs during a regular ninety-minute reading period, when they are regrouped into reading classes of fifteen to twenty students who all perform at the same reading level. Regrouping allows teachers to teach without having to break the class into reading groups. The science curriculum is designed to prepare students for success in high school science through hands-on activities, observation, simulations, and a host of cooperative learning techniques.

The program also has a whole-school reform effort for grades pre-K–6. The elementary program has a school-climate component that strengthens the social and problem-solving skills of children, and coordinates family, community, and school resources to raise the culture of achievement among students and their families. Importantly, Success for All has researched the comparative value of its Spanish/English bilingual curriculum and its English-only curriculum—finding additional achievement advantages for those students in the Success for All bilingual program.[34] Perhaps one of the most unique features of Success for All is that it works with the school as a partner, rather than as an outside disconnected entity. By engaging parents, students, school staff, and teachers, Success for All takes a holistic approach to school reform in an attempt to raise achievement levels. In particular, the program provides professional development opportunities and resources for teachers to assist them in raising the achievement levels of their underperforming students. Consistent with the development of the bilingual literacy curriculum, the program has also invested in the development of skills of bilingual teachers.[35]

Success for All has conducted numerous evaluations of the program over time, but of particular interest are two independent studies.[36] The first, published in 2002, found that Success for All students scored higher on reading and math standardized exams, and needed fewer remediation services in school over the long term.[37] The second, published in 2007, was a randomized field trial in which the investigators examined the schoolwide effects of Success for All as well as a longitudinal sample of K–2 students.[38] They found significant schoolwide effects for early literacy skills (letter and word identification, word attack, and passage comprehension), as well as individual improvements as great as one-third of a standard deviation for word attack skills. Success for All has received a nod from the U.S. Department of Education's What Works Clearinghouse, which evaluates the evidence for programs' claims of effectiveness. The clearinghouse cites one recent study that met their strict criteria, "with reservations."[39] Table 7.3 illustrates the average costs to implement the Success for All program.

Table 7.3   Estimated program costs for Success for All, 2008

Program cost elements	Amount
Total program budget (annual estimate for 5 schools)	$1,810,464
Number of students served (5 schools)	1,572
Approximate cost per student	$958
Evaluation costs	Not specified

Source: Borman and Hewes 2002.

Note: Data are presented in 2008 dollars according to the Consumer Price Index (http://www.bls.gov/cpi) and were modified from the 2001 data noted in the program's own evaluation.

Project GRAD

Project GRAD is a comprehensive nonprofit education reform program founded in 1993 in the Houston Independent School District to reduce the achievement gap by improving the schools' institutional culture and effectiveness in dealing with at-risk students. By the year 2000, Project GRAD had expanded from Houston, to Atlanta, Columbus, Los Angeles, and Newark. It is presently being implemented in twelve school districts, and is reaching over 135,000 students in 217 of the most disadvantaged schools in the country. While the program focuses on whole-school reform, it tracks students longitudinally and offers specific services for particular students. In Los Angeles, it is also focusing on Latino students and English learners.

Recognizing that high school was too late to change the path of many at-risk youth toward graduation and college, the Houston district, together with a retired Fortune 500 CEO and several agencies and businesses, set out to rethink education from the time these students first enter the educational system. Project GRAD's philosophy is that educational failure is avoidable through a strong curriculum that builds students' self-discipline and confidence while stimulating a love for learning. Unique to Project GRAD is its systemic approach; the program follows students from their first days of school to high school. Even if students change schools, for example, as long as they remain in the same cluster of high school feeder schools, they continue to be monitored through the program. The program also attends to the development in students of those habits of learning and self-discipline that it considers vital for success.

The project targets four areas for reform: math, reading, instructional environment, and parent involvement. MOVE IT Math and the University of Chicago School Math Program address mathematics instruction from the first years of elementary school through high school; Success for All as well as Cooperative Integrated Reading and

Composition focus on reading and writing development from kindergarten or first grade through middle school; Consistency Management and Cooperative Discipline, a classroom management and self-discipline program, is implemented throughout all grades to address the learning environment in the classroom and school; and the Communities in Schools program provides for the social service needs of pupils and their families by organizing parent-involvement activities. Finally the scholarship program is designed to make it financially possible for students to go to college.

The first evaluation results of Project GRAD in Houston showed higher achievement for students who stayed in the program over the long term.[40] The Comprehensive Assessment of School Environments (CASE) instrument was used to measure and monitor those factors either negatively or positively affecting student achievement. Students in the Houston high school graduated at double the pre-program rates, and college-going was quadrupled over pre-program intervention numbers. But two more recent evaluations of the program, by MDRC, had more modest findings.[41] MDRC found that the flagship high school in Houston continued to have greater success than control schools in graduating students on time and preparing them to pass the core academic curriculum; two newer Project GRAD schools in the Houston area that were included in the study showed no statistically significant improvement; and two high schools in Columbus and Atlanta showed promising early results for increasing attendance and promoting more ninth-graders to the tenth grade. MDRC included in its evaluation fifty-two schools in four districts (Houston, Atlanta, Columbus, and Newark) and concluded that while two districts (Houston and Atlanta) were able to show better achievement for Project GRAD schools than for controls on national achievement tests (though not on state tests), the other two districts (Newark and Columbus) did not show any significant improvement on either test. It also found that because Project GRAD does not provide any curricular reform in the high schools or professional development of teachers and staff, it is highly dependent on the existing resources of the schools, which are often weak.

The researchers make several important points about their study of Project GRAD. The program is predicated on working with students from the time they enter school through high school with the bulk of the academic intervention occurring in elementary school, so the effectiveness of the program is dependent on students' staying in the same group of schools. But students are highly mobile and so the assumption that high school students would have had the Project GRAD experience in elementary school frequently did not prove to be true. High schools often "inherited" program students with no prior exposure to the program. Researchers also found that all districts did not implement the program faithfully or well, so what was tested at some sites was not the Project GRAD model, but whatever the schools were doing instead of the model, which turned out to be not very effective. Third, Project GRAD is comprehensive, ambitious, and multilayered, which means it is complex to implement and depends on many pieces falling together in just the right way, and in the real world this does not always happen. Finally, because the model is longitudinal, encompassing the thirteen years of students' public schooling, long-term data are not yet available for most sites. The researchers applauded the program coordinators for their commitment to ongoing candid evaluation and for learning from their mistakes. In an area in which so many people are ready to say they have the answer, but in which solutions are neither easy nor certain, the researchers' comments were high praise for the program. Project GRAD has an evaluation under way by American Institutes for Research to help identify ways to strengthen the program.

The comprehensive nature of Project GRAD, particularly across multiple cities and sites, requires consistent support and monitoring as well as stable investment, both of which are difficult to ensure.

Table 7.4   Estimated program costs for Project GRAD, 2008

Program cost elements	Amount
Total program budget	$32,781,000
Number of students served	144,000
Approximate cost per student	$633
Evaluation costs	Not specified

Source: Project Grad Data Pack, 2005. http://www.projectgradusa.org.

Note: Data are presented in 2008 dollars according to the Consumer Price Index (http://www.bls.gov/cpi) and were modified from the 2004 data noted in the program's own evaluation.

The model, however, takes the long view on students' needs and attempts to monitor them across school transitions. It appears that the developers may have relied too much on the belief that high schools did not need fundamental reform or infusions of new resources, but the systemic nature of the model, and the fact that it is working in schools with high concentrations of Latino students, makes it unique and worthy of attention. Because Project GRAD utilizes a great deal of existing resources and infrastructure within the schools, the full cost of program implementation is likely to be greater than the stated costs. Table 7.4 illustrates the estimated costs for implementing Project GRAD.

Project GRAD, like many of the school reform and intervention programs discussed here, utilizes school resources and staff in a partnership effort to raise achievement levels, and these costs usually do not show up in the overall organizational budgets. This program has secured several sources of private funding from national and regional corporations, foundations, and government agencies to sustain the effort.

Achievement for Latinos through Academic Success

The program called Achievement for Latinos through Academic Success (ALAS, which means "wings" in Spanish) was developed in 1990 to provide a comprehensive approach to meet the "whole child" needs of Latinos at the middle school level. While it was not specifically geared to get students to college, it represented the first step along that pathway—holding students in high school to graduation. It focused on "comprehensively at-risk" Latino youth living in an urban area with high poverty rates.[42] That is, the ALAS students were deemed at high risk for dropping out of school before ever reaching high school because of the presence of certain social-psychological stressors in their lives. A key feature of the program was comprehensive support for both students and their families provided by a social worker. This individual's job was to be a problem solver for the student and family and to advocate for the student vis-à-vis the school. Intervention strategies ranged from intense instruction in problem-solving techniques, bonding activities to increase self-esteem and self-perception, monitoring of attendance patterns closely and intervening with parents when problems arose, and relaying ongoing feedback from the teacher to both the parents and the student. Another important strategy that ALAS implemented involved working with parents to improve their school participation as well as their effectiveness in dealing with their preteen or teenage youngsters. The program linked families with community resources, but it did more in this area than refer parents to services such as psychiatric and mental health assistance, alcohol and drug counseling, or gang intervention programs; it directly assisted families with appointments, transportation, and navigating the various social service systems.[43]

Evaluation of the ALAS program found that it was successful at its primary goal—keeping very high-risk students in school. In the ninth grade, ALAS was able to retain 97 percent of its students compared to a control group that had just 86 percent retention; by tenth grade, the differences were even more dramatic—82 percent of ALAS students versus 69 percent of the controls were still in school. Because ALAS services ended after the ninth grade, the high rate of retention declined after that year: only 32 percent of ALAS students graduated with their class compared to 27 percent of the control students. Table 7.5 shows the costs for ALAS.

ALAS served a relatively small number of students, just 107 over its three-year life (the program was ended in 1996 due to lack of funding), and it served these students at a relatively high cost, around $1,000 per student. But the social costs of dropping out of school are high. A recent study found that each dropout would cost state and federal governments $392,000 in lost tax income over the student's lifetime and in social services that would have to be provided.[44] By contrast, the researchers found that the state and federal governments gained three dollars for every dollar invested in a dropout prevention program. If ALAS had been able to extend its success rate into high school, the per-student cost would have been minuscule in comparison to the cost savings it represented.

At first blush, the K–8 programs reviewed here would seem to have had a very modest impact on student outcomes—small gains in academic achievement, delays if not significant reductions in dropout rates—even though they are based on well-researched strategies and most have enjoyed quite substantial investment. But the lessons of these programs are important. Students seldom make giant leaps, but small academic gains can be built on over time and dispositions toward achievement acquired by students can last a lifetime. The factors that impede greater success—student and staff mobility, lack of

Table 7.5   Estimated program costs for ALAS, 2008

Program cost elements	Amount
Total budget for ALAS	$111,609
Number of students served	107
Approximate cost per student	$1,043
Evaluation costs	Not specified

Source: ALAS data for 1997, as reported in Gándara 1998.

Note: Data are presented in 2008 dollars according to the Consumer Price Index (http://www.bls.gov/cpi) and were modified from 1997 estimates.

adequate infrastructure in the schools, unstable investments in programs—continue to challenge efforts to increase student achievement by even the best of programs. The limitations of these programs must be viewed through the prism of the schools and the society in which they are embedded.

College-Access Secondary School Programs

Like the pre-K and K–8 programs already discussed, the impetus for college-access programs comes from a variety of sources. Patricia Gándara and Deborah Bial conducted a comprehensive review of college-access programs across the country in an effort to identify successful strategies for underserved students.[45] Arguing that the funding source often drove key characteristics of programs, they grouped them in five categories: private nonprofit; higher-education sponsored ("K–16 partnerships"); community-based (CBO-sponsored); K–12 sponsored; or state and federally funded. Government-sponsored programs usually have more generous budgets, and cover larger numbers of students, both per site and at a larger number of sites. But sometimes the kinds of access to resources that both K–12 schools and higher education institutions can offer "in kind" are even more valuable. Funding does not always generate the kinds of relationships with community that community-based organizations can offer and that can help sustain programs over the long run. Thus each kind of funding source or sponsorship is linked to a unique set of resources and tends to result in a different combination of strategies.

Private Nonprofit Programs

Private nonprofit programs originate from foundations, agencies, or even corporate entities with goals related to better preparing students for college. These programs tend to grow out of a belief that the focused attention of a benefactor "outside the system" can bring to light effective new ideas that may later be picked up and integrated into the educational system. In cases where a corporation sponsors such an initiative, the program activity is typically conducted under the auspices of a nonprofit subsidiary or foundation set up for this purpose. Or it may be sponsored out of the community-relations department of the company. Foundations will frequently fund such programs for a limited demonstration period with the idea that if they are successful they will attract support from other sources.

I Have a Dream. Sometimes these programs incorporate themselves and become permanent features on the educational landscape. I Have a Dream (IHAD) is such a program. It began with the good intentions of one person to inspire one classroom of students in New York City. Today, it has expanded to a nationwide nonprofit program at more than 140 sites across the country, and its components have grown—from the single-minded notion of inspiring students to go to college by providing guaranteed scholarships, to ensuring that the students in the program receive a host of supplemental services. Nonetheless, each program site must attract its own benefactor who provides support for the program. Benefactors of IHAD may be individuals, communities, agencies, corporations, or foundations. The impetus for the program, though, revolves around a belief that people outside the public schools can influence students and that their status as outsiders is of particular value in this effort.

IHAD focuses on individual students in a selected class, and the interventions that each student receives can vary considerably. Joseph Kahne and Kim Bailey conducted a careful study of two IHAD programs in the Chicago area during the 1990s.[46] For two-and-a-half years, they studied two classes composed of nearly all African American or Latino students. The two sites were selected for study because they were "models" of good implementation. Unlike all other sites in the Chicago area, these two had maintained the same staff throughout their program period and they had extensive additional resources in the form of Americorps and Princeton Project 55 volunteers. High school graduation rates were double those of their comparison schools, and the percentages of students going to college appeared to be about three times more than their comparison schools, although these data were not as carefully collected. In sum, the programs appeared to be extremely successful with respect to increasing high school graduation and college-going in very at-risk environments.

An important key to the success of the program—and one that complicates our understanding of how to replicate the outcomes—was that more than half of the program participants had been removed from their local public schools and placed in parochial (Catholic) schools. It is thus difficult to separate the effects of IHAD interventions from those of the parochial schools in which the students were enrolled. The evaluators did note, however, that students who attended parochial schools were four times as likely as the students who remained in the public schools to go on to four-year colleges versus two-year colleges. Summarizing the most important aspects of the program, Kahne and Bailey cited the critical role of the program coordinator, who built a strong relationship with each participant and carefully monitored both their school and personal lives. In fact, the evaluators noted that the program coordinator was effectively on call twenty-four hours a day, often dealing with participants' personal crises in the middle of the night. As a result, it was very difficult to hold people in these positions for more than two years: they burned out.

Because there is so much variation in program offerings and funding from site to site, and there is no overall budget, the cost of the program appeared to range from about $1,395 to $3,641 per student per year in 2008 dollars, based on various center reports. Costs varied according to the extent to which students were rerouted into private or parochial schools, and both parents and the private schools also made substantial additional contributions to the costs of schooling.

In-kind contributions of many volunteers were also not counted in the costs of the program—it would be difficult to account for, or to replicate, the large numbers of young volunteers who contributed time through the Americorps and Princeton programs. It is clear, however, that some part of the program's effectiveness stemmed from personal relationships that were established, which require time— and thus can be costly. Those costs do not appear to be accurately represented in the information we were able to garner.

Posse. The Posse Foundation program operates on the assumption that there are many low-income urban students whose talents are obscured by colleges' over-reliance on traditional measures of ability for admission, and that these students could not just survive but thrive if they went in small groups (posses) to college so that they had a built-in support system. The Posse Foundation is a nonprofit program developed in New York City that selects a multicultural group of urban high school students (most are Latino or black) who under normal circumstances would not have been chosen to attend highly selective colleges and universities because of mediocre test scores—but show leadership potential through what staff members call a "dynamic assessment process." These students are placed in "posses" before beginning study at one of the Posse Foundation's twenty-six selective partnership institutions of higher education. Students are provided an intensive leadership training program for eight months to prepare them for college and the Posse Foundation follows them, providing occasional meetings and activities to ensure that the students remain in contact and supportive of each other while in college. The foundation monitors both students' progress and success. Posse has served over 1,850 students since its inception.

An external evaluation found the Posse scholars to be relatively high-achieving students in their high schools.[47] Their overall grade point average in high school was 3.53.[48] Compared to their peers at the partner colleges and universities, however, their SAT scores were lower, with 81 percent of the Posse scholars having scored below the middle range of the combined average SAT scores of their peers at respective institutions.[49] As for enrolling in a rigorous high school curriculum, Posse students were likely to have been enrolled in Advanced Placement classes and therefore were not typical of most Latino students.

One of the most notable outcomes reported in the Conservation Company (now the TCC Group) evaluation was that 70 percent of the 174 scholars completing the survey had started an organization or academically related program on their campus. Posse appears to be very effective in its leadership training, or at least in identifying students with leadership potential. In addition, over 90 percent of the Posse scholars persisted and graduated from college, and over half of the Posse scholars had grade point averages greater than a 3.0—with an additional 40 percent earning grade point averages between 2.5 and 3.0.[50] Less clear from evaluation findings were the longer-term outcomes for the scholars with respect to performance beyond the bachelor's degree, such as enrollment in graduate school or their professional employment path. One component missing from the evaluation was a control group to see how Posse students compared to their peers in comparable high school classes with respect to going to college, performance while there, graduation from college, and post-bachelor's-degree pathways.

What we can glean from the Posse Foundation's efforts as well as the external evaluation is that college admission test scores may be poor predictors of the contributions that some students of color can make to their communities, and that evidence of leadership is a characteristic that should be of interest to colleges, both as a possible predictor of college outcomes and as a trait that should be valued and nurtured. It is difficult to know to what extent participation in leadership activities was a factor in the students' college success, or simply a by-product of that success. As discussed earlier, even the most academically talented low-income Latino students can become derailed. Consequently, it seems that a program like Posse could be a critically important support network, both before and after college enrollment.

Because it is a partnership program offering a full scholarship to a selective institution, it is difficult to assess the costs of Posse. The value of such a scholarship is, of course, enormous both in dollar terms as well as in the incentive it offers students to enroll in postsecondary education. As seen in Table 7.6, the programmatic costs for Posse are considerably different depending on whether tuition is included or not, and tuition varies greatly depending on whether the university is a public or private institution. It would be a mistake to overlook the important role that paid tuition plays in the influence of the program. It is also noteworthy that Posse is not embedded in a particular college, university, or government agency, so its perstudent programmatic costs are closer to "actual" costs, unlike the expenses of many of the other programs cited here that rely on others for much of their infrastructure.

Table 7.6   Estimated program costs for Posse Foundation, 2008

Program cost elements	Amount
Total program budget: with tuition	$4,688,349
Total program budget: without tuition	$788,761
Number of students served	220
Approximate cost per student: with tuition	$21,310
Approximate cost per student: without tuition	$3,585
Evaluation costs	Not specified

Source: Posse Foundation 2006 budget data, in authors' possession.

Notes: Data are presented in 2008 dollars according to the Consumer Price Index (http://www.bls.gov/cpi) and were modified from the program's 2006 data. Under the "Management and General Budget" category, the likely line item to have included evaluation costs, the total was $31,318 in 2006.

Higher-Education-Sponsored Programs or K–16 Partnerships

A 1994 survey by the U.S. Department of Education showed that about one-third of all colleges and universities offered at least one program designed to increase access for educationally and/or economically disadvantaged precollegiate students.[51] Since that time, it is likely that such programs have proliferated; in California, for example, programs expanded and new ones came online almost daily in the late 1990s in response to the ban on affirmative action. Colleges and universities had to find new ways to channel academically competitive minority students onto their campuses. But the reasons that universities become involved in these efforts are diverse. At one level, universities see themselves as consumers of the products of public schools—high school graduates. And to the extent that these students are arriving at the university underprepared for the rigors of college-level work, leaders of these institutions believe it to be in their self-interest to help strengthen the public schools. At another level, the involvement of public colleges and universities stems in part from a growing perception by taxpayers that the university holds some responsibility for the state of American education, and that some of its resources should be put to the task of improving public schooling. And at still another level, faculty in education and related fields have sometimes relished the opportunity to test out their own theories in model interventions.

These programs can focus on partnerships between colleges and schools, usually high schools, in an effort to share resources, strengthen the public schools, and establish connections among the various educational communities. Clearly, when universities are lending to a program their efforts—as well as possibly administrative staff, faculty, student participants, and outreach personnel—there are many unaccounted-for costs. Even when dollars do not change hands, the exchange of "in kind" contributions from higher education is critical to these programs' survival.

Puente: A Community-Based Program

While currently supported by university, state, and some foundation funds, Puente had its impetus as a community-based program. Community-based programs originate from members of a community who see a need among their own youth and develop a program to address it, or emerge through an existing community-based organization that identifies a challenge it wants to take on. They often focus on supporting students outside the school environment. Strategies used by community-based programs are frequently similar to those in school-based programs, but they can also incorporate elements specific to a particular community, including cultural experiences that help students to develop a healthy self-concept. These programs typically draw from resources within their own community, such as mentors who represent backgrounds similar to those of the children whom they serve.

The Puente program was designed to facilitate the "bridge" from one segment of education to another.[52] The program started at a community college in 1981 as a response to the low transfer rates among Latino students and is now located in approximately forty community colleges in California. In 1993, Puente began a spinoff high school program to increase the number of Latino students who graduate from high school and go on to college. The two primary goals of high school Puente are to increase the number of Latinos going to college, and to reform a variety of practices in the schools where the program is located.[53]

Puente aims to prepare the large population of underachieving Latino students in California for a college education. To reach this goal, it incorporates literature from the students' own community into a rigorous two-year college-preparatory English curriculum, focuses on developing sophisticated writing skills, and provides both mentors and counselors from the Latino community who can communicate in Spanish with parents and serve as inspirational models of educational accomplishment. An important aspect of the two-year English course is that students form supportive cohorts that are encouraged through various program activities to "stick together" over the course of high school. A significant portion of the Puente budget is devoted to the professional development of teachers, counselors, and mentors. In addition to supporting students as they prepare for and transition to college, Puente thus develops experienced and well-trained school staff members who stay on after the cohorts of students graduate.

The Puente program relies on school personnel to deliver much of the program, reducing its costs substantially. But these personnel must be provided with professional development and they must be at least partially subsidized for their participation in the training and in the program. Puente budgets include partial subsidies but they do not include the cost of training personnel—which are borne as in-kind contributions from some of the funding sources. Moreover, there can be considerable variability in some costs depending on how the school tailors the program to its own needs, and on the manner and intensity of the staff development provided by the program. Table 7.7 shows the basic budget for Puente, which is used to determine the estimated cost of $639 per participant.

Table 7.7   Estimated program costs for Puente, 2008

Program cost elements	Amount
Total program budget (one high school)	$76,658
Number of students served	120
Approximate cost per student	$639
Evaluation costs	$317,750

Source: Puente budget for 2004, as reported in Gándara 1998.

Note: Data are presented in 2008 dollars according to the Consumer Price Index (http://www.bls.gov/cpi) and were modified from the program's own 2004 data.

The most comprehensive evaluation of the Puente program found that participants had lower dropout rates, believed they were better prepared for college, and enrolled in some kind of college at double the rate of the control students.[54] Puente students also had a significantly higher desire to be "good students" and to be known as such. Although there appeared to be no effect of the program on grade point average (consistent with almost all other college-access programs), Puente students applied to and attended four-year colleges at nearly double the rate of non-Puente students (43 percent versus 24 percent).[55]

Government-Sponsored Programs

There are two major kinds of government-sponsored programs: state and federal. A number of states have taken on statewide initiatives to stimulate students to go to college. The impetus for these large-scale programs is often economic—the state is not preparing enough highly qualified college graduates to fuel its economy, and it may be losing population as a result (Indiana is one such example). Or demographic trends in the state may threaten to create social problems if higher education is not made more accessible to the increasing portion of the state's population that is low-income and nonwhite.

Federal initiatives tend to stem from an evolving philosophy about the role of the federal government in education. While educating American youth is a state responsibility, the role of the federal government has largely been one of equalizing opportunity across the states, and more recently of applying the stick rather than the carrot in holding them accountable for student achievement. The federal government has also become involved in helping to provide financial support for low-income (and increasingly, middle-income) students to attend college. While the states tend to see the value of increasing the education level of their citizens in more economic terms, the federal government has considered its responsibility to be to increase equity across jurisdictions while challenging the states to meet higher standards.

The federal government's TRIO programs are a prime example of how the federal government has stepped in to provide comprehensive ancillary services from middle school to college in order to increase the likelihood that low-income and underrepresented students will gain access to postsecondary opportunities. Upward Bound is the largest of these TRIO programs.

Upward Bound. Upward Bound, perhaps the best known and most visible of the early intervention programs funded by the U.S. Department of Education, served 61,339 students in 2006. It targets high school students with an array of supplemental services, including college counseling as well as summer residential programs at local colleges and universities, where students receive intensive academic instruction and preview college life.[56] The summer residency is the single most expensive intervention offered by Upward Bound, and most but not all program sites offer it. Where it is not offered, cost is generally the reason.

Upward Bound was first established in 1965 with the goal of helping disadvantaged students prepare to enter and succeed in college. It was an integral part of the War on Poverty and a partner program to Head Start, which concentrated on much younger children. Upward Bound students submit an application to participate, and most applicants who are eligible can be enrolled within the resource constraints of the program. Upward Bound provides a wide range of services to low-income and underrepresented youth including residential summer "academies"; school-year instructional programs in core academic areas such as English, math, and science; and counseling and tutoring for participants. Each Upward Bound site operates independently, so particular features of the program may vary, but the core academic components must be present in order for a program to receive funding.

The most recent evaluation of Upward Bound was published in 2004.[57] That study, like the ones preceding it that were conducted by the same organization, assessed the high school outcomes and postsecondary enrollments and progress of students participating in the program. The 2004 evaluation included a sample of sixty-seven Upward Bound sites across the country with approximately 1,500 students compared to 1,200 randomly selected control students. The results from the Third Follow Up Data Collection in 2004 were comparable to those of an earlier 1999 study, including "limited to no effects on high school credits or grades" and "no effect on the overall enrollment or total credits earned in postsecondary institutions."[58] The study showed that Upward Bound students were more likely to take certain college preparatory courses, but that the program had no significant influence on high school grade point average, high school graduation, or college-going. Upward Bound did have a significant effect on the number of math credits earned in high school, however; one in five students participating in Upward Bound completed additional math courses "over and above what they would have completed in the absence of the program."[59] The researchers also found that students with lower educational expectations did earn more high school credits and the program did have "large effects on enrolling students with initially lower educational expectations at four-year institutions."[60] Both the 1999 and 2004 evaluations found that students who stayed in the program longer had better outcomes; for example, they earned more postsecondary credits, and were more likely to enroll in four-year institutions.

One of the more interesting and perhaps confusing study findings was that Upward Bound increased the number of honors and Advanced Placement courses taken by high school students in the "lower expectation" group, that is, those students having lower expectations than their peers.[61] Yet the effect of Upward Bound on high school graduation and grade point average was found to be not statistically significant for this group.[62]

The 1999 study in particular was criticized for lumping together very successful programs with less successful ones, which made it easy to overlook the very large gains that some programs had achieved. This is a common—and valid—critique of large-scale national evaluations of programs that are implemented differently across sites. Nonetheless, because of Upward Bound's estimated annual cost of almost $5,000 per participant in 2008 dollars (another statistic that continues to be debated), its cost-effectiveness has been questioned. What is needed is a study of the separate elements of the program that may be more and less effective so that funds can be allocated to those elements that increase college-going the most. It is not at all clear that the Bush administration's rationale for cutting the current program—that it should focus more on higher-risk students—is valid or reasonable. This was a recommendation of the 1999 evaluation, but the researchers did not provide evidence that it was workable. If the program were redeveloped to include higher ratios of very high-risk students, critical personnel time would need to be increased for these needier students, and there would be fewer students with college savvy and higher aspirations to support and inspire others in the group. Such a shift in the students targeted for intervention could at least theoretically reduce the resources available to participants and actually lower the yield of the program.

Both the 1999 and 2004 evaluations showed that Upward Bound generally provides a rich and challenging academic program in which students take a number of rigorous nondevelopmental classes geared toward bolstering their academic skills. This strategy is consistent with the research on increasing student achievement.[63] Yet Upward Bound did not measurably raise students' academic achievement. It did, however, appear to increase college-going for certain groups—

males, Latino and white students, and those who persisted in the program until graduation—and raise aspirations for those students who initially demonstrated weak academic performance.

According to the U.S. Department of Education, approximately 56,430 students in the United States participate in regular Upward Bound (see Table 7.8).[64]

While Upward Bound may spend less time engaged with students on a day-to-day basis than some other programs, a significant portion of Upward Bound's cost is related to the expense of providing a residential summer program, which normally lasts four to six weeks and involves full-time supervision and intensive coursework on a college campus. While expensive, there is evidence that such summer precollege programs, when well designed and well run, can have powerful, positive effects on first-generation college students.[65]

K–12 Sponsored Programs

Many programs that purport to help students get to college are spearheaded by U.S. public school systems. It is somewhat ironic, then, that many of these programs focus on individual students rather than attempt to solve the problems of the schools that these students at-

Table 7.8 Estimated program costs for Upward Bound, 2008

Program cost elements	Amount
Total program cost	$282,399,000
Number of awards	761
Number of participants	56,430
Average site award	$396,460
Average number of participants	74
Approximate cost per participant	$5,004
Evaluation costs	Not specified

Source: Upward Bound, 2006 data. http://www.ed.gov/programs/trioupbound/funding.html.
Notes: The fiscal-year 2006 funding for regular Upward Bound included $24,012,812 for 255 Upward Bound Initiative supplemental grants. Data are presented in 2008 dollars according to the Consumer Price Index (http://www.bls.gov/cpi) and were modified from the program's own 2006 data.

tend. Some programs begin as early as grammar school, while most are initiated by high schools. Superintendents of public schools or individual principals may begin programs that they feel can help their students both succeed in school and better prepare them for college.

The impetus for the public schools to develop strong intervention efforts for their students is clear. The public is increasingly demanding that all students complete high school with the option to go to college, and the public schools have been criticized heavily over the past two decades for failing at this mission, especially with low-income and nonwhite children. In addition to the natural desire of all teachers to successfully teach their students, K–12 public schools have been under the microscope and such programs are an important way for schools to demonstrate their commitment to improving outcomes for all students.

Programs that simply attempt to increase student achievement can have a powerful, albeit indirect, effect on the chances that students will enroll in postsecondary education. Such programs, however, are too numerous to mention or catalogue, and typically lack strong evidence of their effectiveness. Thus to understand the direct effects of K–12 sponsored programs on college-going, it is necessary to look specifically at those programs that hold this as a program goal, and for which reasonably rigorous evaluation data exist.

AVID. The program AVID (Advancement via Individual Determination—a misnomer if there ever was one) is an example of one that attempts to increase college-going by opening up a rigorous college-preparatory curriculum to students who would not otherwise be selected to take such courses. It was initiated by a high school English teacher who had become frustrated with her school's academic tracking system. She decided in 1980 that she would put a group of mostly low-income minority students who showed academic promise into college preparatory English and provide them with the support to succeed. From this bold experiment grew a program whose focus has been "untracking" students and providing them with the academic support and encouragement to go on to college. In the 2007–2008 school year, AVID served nearly 300,000 students in over 3,500 elementary and secondary schools in forty-five states, the District of Columbia, and across fifteen countries.[66]

The AVID program selects students who are deemed underachievers by the discrepancy between their grade point averages and their test scores. Eligible students, who are generally doing C-level work in the classroom, must demonstrate with reading-test scores the capability to do grade-level or higher work. The students' problem, as AVID identifies it, is largely lack of motivation and specific study skills, which leads to their being placed in courses that are below their actual ability. Once selected for the program, AVID students take daily a one-period class in which they learn specific study skills, receive information about how to prepare for college, are counseled into taking college preparatory courses, go on field trips and hear motivational talks to stimulate their desire for college, and form a supportive college-bound peer group. The AVID teacher also functions as an additional counseling support for students.

One of the most impressive outcomes of AVID's success is the increase in the rate of program participants' attending four-year colleges. In 2006, for example, 75 percent of the AVID high school graduates were reported to have been accepted to a four-year college. Because AVID does not normally track or report on attrition from the program—that is, how many students who begin the program are actually still in it during twelfth grade—it is hard to know what portion of those students who have ever been in AVID go on to four-year colleges. Previous research on AVID found that the program had a positive effect on high school graduation, college enrollment, and academic performance in college.[67] A 1998 study found that 43 percent of Latino AVID students who participated for three years enrolled in four-year colleges, compared to 20 percent of other Latino students in the school district, and "the longer these students participate in the program, the better their college enrollment record."[68] Another noteworthy finding from this evaluation was that the AVID students from the lowest income strata enrolled in higher education at equal to or higher proportions than students from the higher income strata.[69]

Table 7.9 illustrates the costs of operating AVID in a California high school (as reported by AVID staff and adjusted to 2008 dollars). The AVID central administration estimates the costs to be at least two dollars more per student per day for operating the program out of state.[70] This is in part because the program must bear more of its own costs when implemented outside California.

AVID contends that these costs are reduced substantially in subsequent years, to less than $1.50 per day per student.[71] But this is difficult to reconcile with ongoing costs for teachers' tutoring and advising, the housing of AVID coordinators, and the training of teachers and others. A seemingly more accurate estimate was provided by a previous evaluation of AVID that estimated the per-student cost to be $625 per student in 1997 dollars, or $831 in 2008 dollars.[72]

Table 7.9   Estimated program costs for AVID, 2008

Program cost elements	Amount
Total program budget	$14,076,000
Program costs per site (in California)	$18,202
Number of students served	105,000
Approximate cost per student	$606
Evaluation costs	Not specified

Source: AVID, IRS 990 form for 2004, available from the authors.

Notes: Data are presented in 2008 dollars according to the Consumer Price Index (http://www.bls.gov/cpi). Be advised that AVID's central administrators provided all budget numbers, which do not easily reconcile. Program administrators contend that it costs $3 per student to provide the program in the first year and thereafter only about $1.50 per student. But their formula for reaching these numbers is unclear, and costs and services provided by others seem not to be included. We have attempted here to provide some middle ground by estimating costs based on an evaluator's assessment.

Charting the Effects of College-Access Programs

It is first important to be clear about what we mean by "effective" programs. None of the programs reviewed here, or that we have reviewed for other purposes, appears to make any significant difference in raising the grade point average or test scores of its participants on average. At the lower grades, grade point average is not normally tracked, and at the upper grades (secondary school), there appears to be a consensus that it is probably too late to significantly change the grade point averages of groups of students (that is, some individual students may show gains, but the group as a whole does not), except perhaps by adding honors and Advanced Placement points to their averages. There is also very little evidence that such programs raise test scores, except possibly by encouraging and providing test-prep courses for students.[73] This point is important because college admission is largely dependent on students' high school grades and test scores. What effective college-access programs do seem to do is raise students' motivation to apply to and go to college and help them prepare with the right courses and knowledge of procedures—with the result that the number of students who actually go on to some kind of college increases substantially or even doubles. Bridge programs, such as those offered by Posse or Upward Bound, also ease the transition from high school to college. For students who initially had low expectations for going to any college, the colleges they attend are not normally very selective and are often two-year institutions, but they do begin the journey to a possible four-year degree.

Counseling

Most programs that have been proven to be effective incorporate a counseling component.[74] The lack of adequate college counseling has been identified as a major obstacle to college-going for underrepresented students.[75] In addition, it is well documented that many

Latino students are reluctant to visit counselors because the counselors are perceived to be ill-informed about minority student issues or have a reputation for counseling these students into low-level classes.[76] Thus for intervention programs that incorporate counseling features to be successful, they must provide enough qualified counseling help to meet students' needs and build trust with this population among both students and families.

The goal of effective counseling efforts is the same for most successful programs: to provide students with access to the information necessary for preparing for and applying to college. Programs employ a number of strategies to disseminate "college knowledge" and provide advice. Some offer individual consultations with students to help them better understand the college search and application process. Others employ peer, staff, or college-representative speakers in a workshop or classroom setting. These individuals may speak with groups of students about college opportunities and campus life. Sometimes programs offer assistance with financial aid forms and college applications. For many students, these forms, which may seem overwhelming, can become a significant barrier to attending college. In some cases, programs that target special disciplinary areas—such as MESA (math, engineering, and science achievement)—counsel their student participants to enter particular fields.

Academic Enrichment

Most college-access programs that are able to demonstrate success also include an academic enrichment component. Academic enrichment addresses the problem of underpreparation for college, and attempts to strengthen students' college eligibility and later success. In a post-affirmative-action era, when underrepresented students are required to compete with more advantaged students for limited slots in selective institutions, academic enrichment plays a very important role in college eligibility and later success. To strengthen students' academic preparation, some programs (like AVID) provide tutoring or extensive supplemental courses to augment the schools' curriculum (Upward Bound is a good example); alternatively, they may focus on changing the curriculum and method of delivery (like Project GRAD does). Some also offer before-school, after-school, and/or Saturday programs, while others form partnerships with local colleges and universities so that students can take college-level courses—sometimes for credit. All of these strategies have been proven helpful. Tutoring has been shown to be an effective way of strengthening students' core academic skills, and providing additional skilled, targeted instruction has also has been shown to increase achievement.[77]

A key strategy for many programs is to help students gain access to Advanced Placement or honors courses, which can confer extra grade points for college admission and/or provide college credit, which can reduce the time (and therefore, costs) required for college graduation. Additionally, some programs allow students to experience college life prior to matriculation or provide them with a head start on their college requirements by offering college classes, seminars, or workshops to help students improve their reading, writing, math, and analytic skills. These may occur as an adjunct to the regular academic year program, or may be offered in a summer bridge format. Bridge programs take advantage of the time before students begin college to help prepare them academically, socially, and psychologically for the rigors of a competitive curriculum. The objective of these programs is to help ensure that students make a smooth transition into college and that they experience early social and academic success. For underrepresented students, the normal challenges of college are often accompanied by feelings of isolation, so making friends and meeting faculty before starting the academic year can reduce the students' anxiety and enhance their feelings of belonging.

The summer Challenge Program sponsored by Georgia Institute of Technology ("Georgia Tech") is one of the more thoughtful.[78] It began as a retention program for underrepresented students and took place on campus. It was based on a theory that if students felt connected to the campus, and to faculty and peers, they would be more inclined to complete their degrees. But program directors noted that it had taken on a remedial orientation that stigmatized the participants, and was inadvertently sending the message that "getting by" academically was sufficient for these students. Given this general perception, high-achieving students avoided it. In the early 1990s, in response to such internal evaluations, the program shifted focus and began to emphasize socializing students to faculty norms (giving students a preview of what faculty would expect), preparing students for a rigorous curriculum, and helping to ensure that the first semester would be academically successful. The program has no real curriculum. Regular faculty teach in the program and are instructed to provide an in-depth overview of the first semester's curriculum in calculus and chemistry. Students are exposed to enough of the course that they will have a head start at the beginning of the year, but not so much that they become overly confident and neglect studying in the fall. Students are also given the option of taking first-semester psychology during the summer. This allows them to lighten their academic loads in the fall and provides more time to adjust to demands of the college. Most participants score relatively high on early exams because they have already been exposed to this part of the curriculum, and this both increases their self-confidence and provides a leg up on their grade point averages. As a result, students come to see themselves as capable of performing at high levels and are more likely to make this their goal.

Personal and Cultural Support

Beyond offering college counseling, particularly effective programs tend to see students as whole individuals with interests and concerns that reach beyond the academic. These programs also tend to recognize that students' lives can be complicated and that the ability to perform well in school often depends on the extent to which other aspects of their lives are functioning at least moderately well. Toward this end, many of these programs are at least cognizant that a healthy peer group can be a critical source of support both socially and academically. Hugh Mehan writes about the essential importance of a peer group that helps students to feel confident about their academic achievement and the role that peers play in navigating their different worlds of community and school.[79] Mehan describes how the AVID program focuses on developing a supportive peer group through the AVID class and activities, and how it raises students' awareness about the critical function that shared goals can play in helping students to counter social structures that can work against them. Puente also creates opportunities for students to bond through activities like college visitation trips and club outings. Cultural support can come in a variety of forms. Many times program directors or staff come from the same communities and backgrounds of the participants and are therefore able to provide supportive counseling and advice based on common experiences.

Mentoring

The term "mentoring" is used in research literature and common discourse in ways often related to academic support, inspiration, and fostering personal achievement. Some people refer to college-access programs in general as "mentoring programs"—a particularly ill-defined use of the term. Most, however, define mentoring as the monitoring of an individual student participant by a concerned and connected adult. Nothing appears to be more important for helping underrepresented students navigate successfully through high school and into college than the formation of a strong relationship with a caring adult who truly knows the student. Mentoring, defined in this way, is the single most common characteristic of all of the successful intervention programs we assessed, and it seems crucial to each program's success. Perhaps surprisingly, there is very little evidence in the literature to support the notion that mentoring in the technical sense—meeting at unspecified periods with a student to impart guidance—improves academic performance. Only a couple of studies have shown even modest increases in grades and these could be explained by a Hawthorne effect (that students who are selected for any kind of program tend to show some effects from simply being treated specially).[80] Other studies have shown that mentoring can ameliorate particular negative student behaviors—for example, it can reduce student truancy or drug and alcohol use.[81] One difficulty with this research is the problem of measuring the nature of mentoring relationships across large groups of students and finding appropriate comparison groups of students against which to test the effectiveness of the program, since nonprogram students can identify mentors through informal means. Nonetheless, when defined as a caring, monitoring relationship that is not episodic, but ongoing, mentoring of students is clearly key. But it is also probably the most expensive of all the options—and limiting in the sense that many trained individuals are required to make the program succeed.

Scholarships

To put it simply, money matters. A critical reason why many low-income and underrepresented students do not attend college is because they believe—rightly or not—that they cannot afford to go. Many believe that college is for "rich kids," not kids like them, and that no matter how well they do in school, it will not be a realistic possibility. Many low-income students are reluctant to place the burden of financial support on their parents, and even feel torn about the idea of not entering the workforce directly after high school to help the family financially. Lack of money shapes students' thinking about what is possible and limits their ambitions and the choices they make, and not without cause. Over the decade from the early 1990s to the early 2000s, inflation-adjusted tuition for public and private four-year colleges rose 40 percent, while income for a typical family of four only rose by 8 percent.[82] In 2004, it required almost 40 percent of the average income of a low-income family to pay the annual tuition and room and board costs at a public four-year college for just one child.[83] The percent of tuition at a four-year public college covered by a federal Pell grant dropped from 98 percent in 1986 to a little more than 50 percent in 2000.[84] Recent legislation has raised the amount of Pell grants, but it still covers only between one-third and one-half of the costs of a typical four-year college. It is no surprise, then, that high-achieving low-income students are less likely to go to college than low-achieving high-income students. Opportunities for higher education in the United States are rationed by family income, creating a vicious cycle of undereducation from one generation to the next.

While many college-access programs focus on preparing students for college, they are often woefully ignorant about the extent to which students are simultaneously ruling out choices based on their belief that they cannot afford to attend a four-year college. If a student believes that only community college would be an option in the best of cases, it is more difficult to convince him or her to work for the highest possible grades. Students know that they can enter community college without even getting a diploma and "make up the grades later." Thus scholarships can both make college more possible in a financial sense, and help students to raise their ambitions.

Parent Involvement

While a growing literature touts the advantages of parent involvement for students' academic achievement, this research has sometimes been misconstrued to suggest that involvement in students' schools is a causal factor. Some have been quick to equate parents' attendance at PTA meetings or willingness to volunteer at school with parents' interest or influence on their children's schooling. In fact, it is the parents' involvement in their children's education—wherever that occurs—that is the more critical factor in achievement.[85] It is very difficult to measure this level of involvement, especially for language-minority parents and others who have not themselves had extensive experience with the American schooling system. Many of these parents feel uncomfortable in the schools and will not go to parent meetings. This reluctance seldom means that they are uninterested in their children's education or their schooling, but it does make it more difficult to communicate important information to them. Thus a major challenge for some intervention programs is to find ways to communicate with parents about the goals of the program and how parents can help support those goals.

Some programs, like Puente, require that parents sign a contract to support their child's participation in the program and attend parent information meetings (although this is not strictly monitored). At a minimum, programs that have a parent involvement component provide informational sessions on college requirements, financial aid, and other related topics. A number of programs also offer training for parents on helping students to excel in school. These training sessions may cover monitoring homework, maintaining communication and discipline with adolescents, issues in adolescent development, and other related topics. In order to attract parents to these sessions, some programs conduct them in the families' primary language and add other cultural elements to the activities. Even though parent involvement has been shown to be correlated with higher academic achievement in students, schools are notoriously ineffective at connecting with parents, especially in communities of color and where a language other than English is spoken.[86] Our research shows that this is one of the areas in which teachers feel they have the fewest skills.[87]

Parent Institute for Quality Education

Founded in 1987, Parent Institute for Quality Education (PIQE) offers a program that claims to bring parents together with schools in support of children's achievement. The nonprofit community-based organization works with Latino and immigrant parents to help them strengthen particular academic skills and behaviors in their children. The program consists of an eight- or nine-week course for parents and four months of follow-up "coaching" calls afterward. The classes are taught by instructors who reflect the parents' community. Parents are taught how to establish and maintain supportive home learning environments; communicate and collaborate with teachers, counselors, and principals; navigate the school system and access its resources; encourage college attendance; identify and avoid obstacles to school success; and support children's emotional and social development. Founded in San Diego more than fifteen years ago, PIQE has served nearly 180,000 participants and operates in several states.

One group of researchers from the University of California at Santa Barbara conducted an evaluation of the program that used innovative techniques and multiple measures to determine its effects on parent participants months after the program had ended.[88] This study included ninety-five pre-post questionnaires on behaviors that the program had targeted, such as reading to children and monitoring homework. Parents reported increased reading with their children as a result of participating in the program. But to get around the problem that what people report doing on a survey and what they actually do often differ considerably, the researchers corroborated the survey findings with other techniques such as phone interviews six to nine months later to see how often parents engaged in these behaviors and if they retained the earlier reported increases. The researchers found that as a result of participating in the program, parents did read more to their children. Similarly, the researchers found through parent surveys and monthly phone calls home that specific behavioral changes did occur. In sum, self-reported data are always suspect because people are known to bias responses in favor of what they perceive to be the "right" answer. The researchers in this study, however, attempted to triangulate their data in ways that lend confidence to their conclusion that the program influenced parent behaviors. We suspect that it did.

In 2004, PIQE served approximately 31,000 parents at nine locations. A look at the program budget in Table 7.10 illustrates a very lean operation. It is important to note, however, that there are hidden costs and in-kind supports that are not likely to be accurately accounted for in the final budget presentation of any given nonprofit organization. Table 7.10 shows a modest per-parent cost in 2008 dollars, for example, but the program relies on a great deal of volunteer help—hours that are not counted as an expense, but that do add value to the program.

The majority of PIQE's annual contributions come from public support, with approximately $2.5 million (82 percent) of its revenue in 2003 coming from public sources and only 18 percent stemming from private funders such as foundations and corporate grants. This heavy reliance on public monies in an era of cyclical budget cuts means that PIQE may be vulnerable financially. If the organization can find stable support outside the public social-services sector, it has

Table 7.10   Estimated program costs for PIQE, 2008

Program cost elements	Amount
Total program budget	$3,926,680
Number of parents served	31,000
Approximate cost per parent	$109
Evaluation costs	Not specified

Source: PIQE, http://www.piqe.org.

Note: Data are presented in 2008 dollars according to the Consumer Price Index (http://www.bls.gov/cpi) and were modified from the program's own 2003 data.

a better chance of staying alive when the inevitable federal, state, and local budget cuts hit.

A Caveat about Costs

In this chapter, we have provided an overview of typical or representative programs for low-income Latino students and discussed what is known about their effectiveness and approximate costs. There are many other programs that we might have included in such a list, but these had reasonably comprehensive published evaluations that allowed us to draw at least tentative conclusions about their effectiveness. Our information about costs was provided by either public or private sources. In most cases, however, these program costs were seriously underestimated. Most nongovernmental programs do not include in their cost estimates items such as building space and maintenance, communications, personnel training, and often even the personnel themselves when they are "on loan" from another governmental entity. Thus, per-student costs for many of these programs are only realistic if the programs are embedded in schools and partially supported by partnership institutions. In other words, one should not conclude that it would be possible to create freestanding programs for the costs described here. Additionally, many nongovernmental programs rely extensively on corporate and foundation funding, which can be fickle and is often offered as "start-up" money, with the idea that programs will eventually go out and find other ways to support themselves. Unfortunately, as the ALAS program administrators found, there are not a lot of other ways to support these comprehensive programs.

It is also important to note what we have not attempted to do in this chapter. We have not attempted to tackle the issue of school reform and the kinds of deep changes that might be necessary for schools to better educate Latino students (with the possible exception of our overviews of Project GRAD and Success for All, which make specific programmatic interventions in schools but do not try to reinvent them). We do think such reforms are necessary, even critical, but the research on school reform is much less clear about what works under what circumstances, especially for Latino students, than is the research on programmatic interventions. We believe, however, that school reform efforts can be informed by what has been learned from these programs. Schools are massively complex institutions with many moving parts and many things they cannot control. The kinds of schools that serve most Latino students are overcrowded, under-resourced, with high rates of mobility for students, teachers, and staff. In such settings it is very hard to know "what works" for which students because neither the reforms nor the students are consistent enough to assess over time. Most intervention programs, by contrast, provide the opportunity to look closely at a smaller number of students engaged in well-defined activities over time. At least this is what happens when they are carefully evaluated. For this reason, we have attempted also to call attention to the amount of funding dedicated to the study, or evaluation, of these programs. Unfortunately, with the exception of large federal programs, information on the amount of funding dedicated to evaluating these programs is often very difficult to obtain—and when available, is often woefully inadequate.

Although we have argued throughout the book that neither the society at large nor the public schools in particular have dedicated the kinds of basic resources to poor students, and Latinos specifically, to support healthy development, we have not yet addressed the issue of how much more it will cost to have sufficient numbers of well-trained and experienced teachers, counselors, librarians, nurses, psychologists, and other medical personnel available to fill this need. We have sidelined this issue as one of fundamental school reform, and have instead described other programmatic responses that employ social workers to link students and families to existing social welfare and health services in the community, or counselors to provide guidance and support for students in the context of schools. We fully acknowledge the limitations of our analyses given this approach. But our topic is not school reform per se; rather we seek to illuminate the broader contexts in which Latino youth grow and develop.

A consistent finding of the intervention research is that students need sustained support across the critical transitions of schooling and development, and that the longer students are in supportive programs, the greater their positive effects. Short-term interventions generally provide short-term benefits; when the program ends, the gains begin to erode. Several of the studies we have discussed have demonstrated this phenomenon at different points on the developmental continuum. Moreover, each program profiled contributes only an incremental difference to overall achievement. None has been shown to create huge leaps in achievement, but if used in sequence, these programs could provide a threshold of continuous services that could be expected to give Latino students a better start in school and help sustain the early gains through middle school. We believe that together, these services would improve the general health and welfare of Latino students and help low-income parents better understand how to work with the schools on behalf of their children. High school–level programs would then theoretically be in a much better position to help students prepare for and get to college with services built around college access.

Table 7.11 presents an overview of the interventions and costs that could occur across the span of student development. We include intensive intervention at ages one to three years because there is evidence that this can be a powerful stimulus to improved developmental outcomes, but we assume that only a small percentage of Latino—

Table 7.11   Interventions and estimated costs on a developmental continuum

Ages 1–3	Preschool 3–5	K–8	High school	College transition	College support
Intensive child/family intervention: $15,000	Social services for student & family: $1,000	Social services for student & family: $1,000	Social services for student & family: $1,000	Summer Bridge/Upward Bound/Posse-type program: $3,300–$5,200	Full cost of public four-year college on a sliding scale according to income (including cost of living)
	Quality preschool with 10:1 student-staff ratio, bilingual personnel Half day: $5,700–$7,700 Full day: $7,700–$9,900	Specific school-based program intervention: $600 Parent program: $100	College-access program: $600 Parent involvement: $100	Parent program: $100	
Total cost: $15,000	Total cost: $6,700–$10,900	Total cost $1,700	Total cost: $1,700	Total cost $3,400–$5,300	Total cost: $10,000–$30,000

Source: Authors' calculations based on data provided throughout Chapter 7.

or other—students would need this intensive early intervention.[89] We do assume, however, that all low-income Latino students, as well as many middle-income Latino students who are the first in their generation to go to college, will need all or most of the other interventions.

The average cost for intervening in the personal and educational development of Latino students in the most effective ways that we have been able to glean from the research, then, appears to range from $15,000 annually for the most at-risk toddlers, to a more modest $7,000 to $11,000 for social services and a high-quality half- or full-day preschool. This amounts to a little less than $3,000 additional dollars beyond the per-student investment by the public schools, an added boost of $3,400 to $5,300 at the transition to college to help ensure access and success, and support for the full cost of college (that is, an extension of the historical tradition of supporting public education to K–16). We also attempt to provide an estimate of the costs associated with better integrating and involving Latino parents in these programmatic efforts, to keep them informed and actively engaged in the educational experiences of their children. We recommend that these efforts and researched practices be systematically connected into the everyday life of schools, where resources can be maximally shared and cost burdens fairly distributed. As we have noted, the figures presented here are rough and based on estimates usually provided by program directors that, in our view, probably underestimate actual costs by ignoring the valuable contributions of partner organizations and volunteers. But in a wealthy nation such as ours, these investments are not too much to sustain. For example, many nations in Europe that compete with the United States economically have already established free public education, starting with full-day preschool and extending through higher education. We do not argue in favor of an ongoing, ad hoc set of interventions that simply append themselves to schools in nonintegrated ways, but we must move forward now with the best research and cost estimates that we have at hand to implement the most effective strategies available. If we do not start intervening in the lives of today's Latino students, a generation of talent and potential contributions will be lost.

CHAPTER EIGHT

Rescatando Sueños—
Rescuing Dreams

As a group, Latino students today perform academically at levels that will consign them to live as members of a permanent underclass in American society. Moreover, their situation is projected to worsen over time. But as alarming as this is for Latinos, it is equally so for the U.S. population as a whole; neither the economy nor the social fabric can afford to relegate so many young people to the margins of society. If their situation is not reversed, the very democracy is at peril. In earlier chapters, we described the enormous disparities in both academic opportunity and educational achievement between Latinos and others in the United States. We have also shown how Latinos struggle with poverty, isolation, and lack of social supports, challenges that are clearly linked to the abysmal statistics on the educational achievement. Weak social policy is as much to blame for this state of affairs as are educational policies that fail to support these students' aspirations. Both must be addressed if we are to narrow achievement and opportunity gaps for the Latino population.

In 2006, Latinos constituted about 19 percent of the national school-age population; in 2025 one in four students in the United

States will be Latino. Already in California 48 percent of all students and the majority of the incoming kindergartners are Latino. Thus as the National Center for Public Policy and Higher Education warns in a 2005 bulletin, the racial group that is least educated is also the fastest growing, and the "income of [the] U.S. workforce [is] projected to decline if education doesn't improve."[1] Because California has the largest Latino population, it will take the biggest and earliest hit. For example, if there is no change in the rate at which Latinos are receiving college degrees, the per capita annual income in that state will drop 11 percent by 2020, from $22,728 to $20,252. To place this in context, the California per capita income has grown over the last two decades by 30 percent, so the standard of living that Californians have become accustomed to has been based on a rapid increase in income. Moving backward would mean a substantial drop in the tax base and therefore the state's ability to fund all kinds of public services, including education, public health, roads, and transportation— many of the things that residents take for granted and that are critical for continuing economic development. But other states should not feel complacent: fourteen other states have at least half a million Latinos, and in twenty-two states Latinos are the largest ethnic minority. To quote the humorist Richard Armor: "What California is today, the rest will be tomorrow."

We see no particular initiative that has been instituted to head off this looming social and economic disaster. Recent state and national policies, as well as the court decisions we described in Chapter 1, have if anything exacerbated the situation. Students who are beginning school today will graduate after 2020, meaning that they would need to change course and perform at much higher levels than they are now to avoid these projected outcomes. Yet there is no indication of a greater commitment to the public schools or to developing more humane policies affecting poor and minority students. Certainly some communities have initiated major school reform efforts, but the outcomes have varied. Improving the culture of schools is slow, hard work, especially if the actors are constantly changing, and the resources are inadequate, as is chronically the case in poor schools. And poverty is not abating; rather the gap between the wealthy and poor is widening, with the wealthiest households accounting for the largest gains in aggregate household net wealth.[2] More than 30 percent of very young Latinos still live in poverty and its effects on intellectual and academic development can be pernicious.

The challenge is enormous, with very high stakes and potentially serious negative consequences if we fail. This can engender a sense of hopelessness—"paralysis by analysis." But it would be a mistake to allow this paralysis to take hold. Although it is unrealistic to think that we can make all the needed changes immediately and completely, there are things that can be done now, and others that can be accomplished in a slightly longer time frame. This is a crisis with solutions. If we can make significant inroads in the immediate future, we may be able to reduce the need for more massive social intervention in the longer term.

Throwing money at educational problems does not necessarily eliminate the gaps in performance, but putting resources to work can. Michael Martinez, a psychologist with the University of California, reminds us that "the plasticity of intelligence is not a mere theoretical possibility, but is an established fact."[3] In a careful synthesis of the research on the development of intelligence in individuals and across populations, he points out how formal and informal education have been shown to directly increase the intellectual ability of humans. We take Martinez's discussion of intelligence and "IQ" to mean developed abilities and not just the skills that are measured or "mismeasured" by intelligence tests. As we noted earlier, a mother's education has perhaps the most potent effect on her children's measured ability or achievement. Psychologists have explained this connection by pointing to the kinds of educative experiences that well-educated mothers engage in with their children.[4] For example, college-educated mothers spend more time with their children on activities that advance cognitive development, such as reading, fostering exploration of the environment, and asking children to explain things. This difference in childrearing practices presents a certain chicken-and-egg dilemma. Intelligence "predicts educational attainment, but educational attainment predicts subsequent IQ even more."[5] Unfortunately, we cannot confer college degrees, or the skills and abilities that those degrees represent, on a generation of Latina mothers in order to improve their children's achievement. But a partnership of equals between home and school can. Patricia Greenfield, a cultural psychologist who has spent her career trying to understand the factors that contribute to intelligent behavior in different cultures, concludes that increases in (measured) intelligence are the product of four interlocking factors in modern society: technology, urbanization, formal education, and nutrition.[6]

Ironically, the same urbanization that on a global scale has brought populations in contact with an array of goods and experiences and fostered intellectual growth has also created certain types of privation that impede intellectual development. Urbanization is a double-edged sword. But there can be no argument that access to technology (from simple pencils and blackboards to internet access and cutting-edge hand-held technology), formal education, and adequate nutrition (and health care) are powerful contributors to the kind of intelligence that is required to succeed in American schools. To the extent that there are differences in these factors in the lives of children, they will be reflected in different levels of achievement. We believe that the research on education and achievement yields seven areas in which public policy that acknowledges the interlocking nature of schools and communities can change the course of academic achievement for Latino students, and all of these are within our grasp. A description of these seven follows.

Early and Continuing Cognitive Enrichment

School-based programs alone, especially those that start late, do not appear to raise measured achievement significantly; their primary function appears to be increasing motivation and helping students to exploit the talents they have already developed. But we have also seen that early intervention, if sustained over time, can change the intellectual development of children. The evidence suggests that this early intervention needs to extend beyond the classroom involving the homes of preschool children, helping parents to understand the demands of school and how practices in the home can work hand in hand with the goals of schooling. Most important of all are literacy practices in the home—reading to and with children, but also talking to them about ideas, about how things work, about the skilled activities that parents engage in. These activities are referred to by researchers as the "funds of knowledge" that parents have and can share with their children. Norma González and Luis Moll described these kinds of activities with examples of the ways that skilled seamstresses design and measure clothing, create patterns, and match shapes and forms, or the way that skilled carpenters use sophisticated, albeit intuitive, geometry to determine how to build a structure, and estimate and measure the various parts.[7]

Many low-income Latino parents have been led to believe that they cannot help their children learn academic tasks either because they have not experienced much formal education themselves, or because they do not speak English and consequently their skills and abilities have been overlooked by their children's schools. In their eagerness for their children to learn English, many Latino parents forgo teaching their children to read in Spanish, thinking this will hinder their English learning. But the research has demonstrated otherwise. Learning to read, even just being read to, in Spanish is an important precursor to achievement in English. Developing a strong vocabulary in Spanish will help students to develop a strong vocabulary in English. There is much that Latino parents, of all educational and economic levels, can do to support their children's schooling, if they are encouraged and helped to do so. Teachers need to be prepared to invite and facilitate this home support.

Similarly, a preschool that prepares Latino children for formal schooling needs to incorporate and build on the learning that occurs in the home. A critical area of learning that can be extended in preschool is language. Building young children's vocabulary in the language they use at home provides a strong basis for cognitive development. It allows children to quickly expand what they already know, for two well-established reasons: learning is most efficient when it builds on prior learning, and knowledge acquired in one language is transferred to other languages once the corresponding vocabulary and linguistic structures have been learned. Thus, teaching a child to read in a language in which the child already knows the sounds (phonemic awareness) and some word meanings (vocabulary) is more efficient than attempting to teach that child to read in a language with which she has little meaningful experience. In short, once an individual has learned to read, this task never has to be learned again. Basic decoding skills can be applied to any language; when the languages share the same alphabet and similar sounds, the task is even more parallel. Moreover, teaching the child at least part of the time in the home language provides a bridge to parents' literacy teaching in the home. If everything that happens in school occurs in a language that the parents do not know, it is difficult for them to partner with the school and support their children's learning.

If using a young child's home language in school enhances learning, the opposite is also true. Policies that begin English immersion in preschool can hamper rather than accelerate children's learning. Likewise, preschools (and K–12 schools) that ask parents to "speak to your child in English" when parents do not have a good command of

English can undermine parents' ability to be an essential teaching resource for their children. Over time, this interference often also undermines parents' authority within the family as children come to see their parents as deficient and less knowledgeable because of their lack of English skills. Lily Wong Fillmore has written about the disruption that this process can cause in family relationships and the disciplinary problems that can ensue, jeopardizing students' personal and academic development.[8] Bruce Fuller concurs, arguing passionately that children's psychological and academic development is best served by preschools that fit the cultures of families rather than preschools where children and families are forced to adapt to the culture of the school.[9]

This is not to say that children should not be exposed at young ages to other languages. Preschool children offered a rich bilingual curriculum can benefit both linguistically and academically. In the many other countries where this approach is followed, children not only achieve grade-level academic proficiency but also become multilingual. A recent randomized study of preschool programs that use English immersion versus two-way bilingual instruction found that in high-quality programs, the children made the same significant advances in language, literacy, and mathematics (tested in English), and the Spanish-speaking children in the dual-language program experienced significant gains in Spanish vocabulary as well.[10]

Children who live in poor communities and suffer the kinds of privations we discussed earlier perform, on average, at lower levels academically regardless of the language they speak. Contrary to stereotypes and oversimplifications, speaking Spanish is not fundamentally what holds Latino students back academically; experiencing inadequate opportunities for learning is a far more important factor. Poor children of English-speaking backgrounds also perform significantly below their middle-class English-speaking peers, and this is especially true for African American children for whom English is their only language. When language is added to socioeconomic status and race, an already challenging situation simply becomes more complicated.

Latino children who arrive at school already behind their peers in kindergarten need additional instructional time, and those who must also acquire a new language probably require even more time. They also need more consistent and extensive exposure to English spoken by people who have a good knowledge and command of the language. And they have to have many opportunities during each day to use the new language they are learning, in formal classroom contexts as well as in informal conversation with peers and others. Studies we have conducted show that even in very good school systems, English learners are often given little more than a few minutes a day to actually speak in class.[11] Increasing racial and linguistic isolation of English-learner students means that many of these students will not attend schools with many other native English speakers. But even when they do, intensive segregation of students within the school itself results in few opportunities to interact with those English-speaking students.[12] The answer is to provide extended opportunities for both exploratory and language learning. Recent research suggests that full-day preschool, with well-prepared bilingual teachers who can enrich students' learning in both languages, should be part of any serious plan to narrow achievement gaps.[13]

Preschool, however, is just the beginning. A consistently rigorous curriculum must be provided for these students once they enter elementary school and additional time must be allotted to allow these students to attain both language and academic skills that are commensurate with their non-Latino peers. In a recent study conducted by Patricia Gándara and Russell Rumberger that looked at the resource needs for educating English learners, virtually all respondents from a series of case study schools noted that extra instructional time was key to closing achievement gaps, but that resources were not normally available to provide this time.[14] As another recent study notes, attaining high proficiency in academic English involves doing double the work.[15] At the secondary level, respondents in the case study schools also noted that computer technology was key to helping students work at their own pace and, for those who were behind, catch up on learning outside the confines of the regular classroom.

Importantly, to actually close achievement gaps requires strategies that target the entire spectrum of achievement, not just low performance. As we have noted, even at the highest levels of achievement, there are significant gaps between the average performance of Latinos and that of white or Asian students. It would take enormous gains in the achievement of the lower-performing students to bring up the average for all Latinos if those students at the upper end of the achievement distribution were not given a similar boost. Moreover, it would be a strategic mistake to overlook the needs of these relatively high achievers because they are among the intellectual leaders of a new generation. These are the students who are most poised to assume leadership roles in society and the economy, but they will not receive the preparation they need if they are not given the same opportunities and challenges as their white and Asian peers.

Achievement gaps will not be narrowed until Latino students are given the same access to highly rigorous gifted and talented programs; Advanced Placement, International Baccalaureate, and honors courses; as well as other academic enrichment opportunities. Unfortunately, if Latino students are viewed as less capable—on the basis of early test scores, language difference, or other indicators of academic preparation—they are not likely to be assigned to the classes and activities that can catapult them into higher achievement, setting up a vicious cycle from which it is difficult to emerge.

Housing Policies that Promote Integration and Stability

Ethnic, linguistic, and socioeconomic segregation of Latinos by neighborhood results in segregation in the lowest-performing, most under-resourced schools. In the West, Latinos are now the most segregated ethnic group in the schools, and English-learner Latinos are often similarly segregated into schools where most students do not speak English as a native language.[16] Without the opportunity to be exposed consistently to strong English role models in the community or in school, it is difficult to learn the language, especially the language of the classroom. Such isolation also results in a peer and community context that lacks critical social capital—in particular, information about how to prepare for and apply to college. When non-native speakers are isolated from mainstream experience, they have less knowledge and fewer critical social contacts to share.

It has been argued that housing is the fulcrum of opportunity, linked to many factors critical to the success of both adults and children in American society: access to good schools as well as "wealth, healthy and safe environments, positive peer groups for children, good local health care, convenient access to areas of greatest job growth, high quality public services, networks to jobs and college, and many other forms of opportunity."[17] As Gary Orfield and Nancy McArdle have asserted, inequities in housing are the "vicious cycle" that traps families into intergenerational inequality because housing is so closely connected to quality of schools and quality of schooling is so closely connected to future economic opportunity. Students in neighborhoods that are segregated by race and socioeconomic status are not likely to attend schools that prepare them for college and are much less likely therefore to complete a college degree—the primary means of social mobility for members of the lower and working classes. So their children become victims of the same inequality that they have experienced. An unending cycle of limited opportunities occurs.

Unfortunately, even increased income does not protect Latino families from this syndrome. As McArdle writes, "Poor blacks and Latinos are more than twice as likely to live in high poverty neighborhoods as poor whites. Indeed, a substantial share of poor whites reside in largely middle-class suburban neighborhoods. . . . Incredibly even black and Latino households with incomes over $50,000 per year are twice as likely to live in high poverty neighborhoods than whites with incomes less than $20,000."[18]

Latino students must be assigned to schools that will give them the chance to break the vicious cycle of poor schooling and limited opportunity. But given the increasing legal impediments to desegregation of schools, educators must consider innovative ways to redistribute students across schools to achieve less ethnic, socioeconomic, and linguistic isolation. Changing school boundaries, providing magnet schools that are balanced racially and by socioeconomic status, and offering opportunities for students to transfer into two-way language programs are among the many options that schools can employ.

The most powerful remedy, however, is to desegregate housing. Although it is not a simple challenge, policies do exist and can be implemented. For example, in 2004, after years of intense debate, Sacramento County, California, adopted a policy requiring all new residential developments to reserve 15 percent of the housing for owners or tenants who are low-income, very low-income, and extremely low-income (below about $18,000 annually for a family of three). Protections were also put into place to prevent developers from concentrating the low-income housing in specific geographical areas.[19] In new developments, schools can also be sited in areas that encourage integrated attendance, and can offer the enticements of magnet programs with high-quality facilities to draw middle-class and white families into otherwise segregated neighborhoods.

The challenges are often greater in urban centers that have experienced white flight; there, few middle-class white or Asian families are present. But increasing gentrification of urban centers across the country is beginning to attract middle- and upper-middle-class people back to the inner cities. Mayors should seize on these opportunities to create schools that will strengthen the attractiveness of their cities to all families with children.

A couple of innovative experiments have tested the effects of moving low-income families, who are generally of color, out of segregated inner-city neighborhoods and into desegregated suburban communities. The Gauteaux housing experiment in Chicago between 1976 and 1998 provided vouchers for randomly selected poor black families to move to subsidized housing in white suburbs and tested the effects on both families and children. Although the study sample was relatively small, students reported being happier in the suburban schools and their dropout rates decreased significantly.[20] An experiment that has generated a great deal of research is the Moving to Opportunity program undertaken by the U.S. Department of Housing and Urban Development during the mid-1990s. Researchers found positive effects on schooling and behavioral outcomes for females; for example, they stayed in school longer, and were less likely to engage in risky behaviors. The same findings were not found for males, which raises interesting questions about the differences in responses to neighborhood factors by gender.[21] Perhaps the boys didn't respond as well because not all families were provided with the opportunity to move to significantly better communities than those they left, and few additional supports were provided in the schools for the newcomers. The weakness of the intervention and the failure to meet many of the social and psychological needs of the boys (who may need more counseling and social support than girls to make positive academic and behavioral changes) may have made the difference. Nonetheless, study outcomes suggest that improved neighborhood conditions can change students' educational outcomes for the better. An added long-term benefit was that families who moved experienced a greater sense of tranquility living in less chaotic neighborhoods.[22]

Because residential mobility has such negative effects on students' academic achievement, some schools have become involved in the affordable housing movement, partnering with landlords and public housing authorities to allow families that would otherwise have to vacate because of inability to pay the rent to stay through the school year.[23] Creating more stable housing and consequently school situations for low-income children must become a priority for both schools and local government.

Given that housing is so intimately tied to schooling and schooling is so critical for students' life chances, it is incumbent on all who seek better educational outcomes for Latino (and other minority) students to consider the ways in which housing policy can be implemented to provide safer and more stable neighborhoods and stronger schools for these students.

Integrated Social Services

As we write in 2008, President Bush has vetoed a bill that would have increased by five million the number of poor children who are provided health insurance coverage (including dental and mental health services) under the State Children's Health Insurance Program, or SCHIP. In the current political environment, many poor Latino children (and especially those who through no fault of their own are undocumented) are not likely to be able to access health care through federal programs.

A number of attempts have been made at the state and regional levels, however, to provide integrated health services for low-income students through cooperative arrangements between schools and county and regional health agencies. (Unfortunately, many of these also rely on some federal funds to make ends meet.) Such efforts have experienced challenges. But there is evidence that when implemented well, they can have substantially positive effects on children's physical and mental well-being, which can be at least indirectly related to schooling outcomes. Some studies have also shown that they can reduce student mobility, a critically important benefit of the programs.[24]

School-based health centers were operating in at least 1,400 locations in forty-five states in 2001.[25] In 1992 California passed a state law establishing Healthy Start centers, in what eventually became more than 1,200 schools. These centers were provided funding for three years to develop integrated, collaborative services that would draw on both school and community resources. These services included family support, basic social services, medical and preventive care, tutoring, employment training, and youth development activities such as sports and service learning projects. Each program varied in its configuration of partners, but these included schools, community agencies, hospitals, and mental and physical health clinics.[26] Evaluations of the program reported two findings that were consistent with other studies of school-based health services: (1) weak effects on academic achievement, and (2) problems in coordinating efforts among agencies that had no experience working together.[27] There is, of course, no basis in the research to assume that providing social or health services to students and families will result in increased test scores in math over a single year (which is the normal evaluation period). Schooling effects are necessarily cumulative and complex. Supporting a child's physical and emotional health may make the child more attentive at school, but it takes time to make up for lost ground, and many other aspects of the school and home have effects on achievement as well. Moreover, it is hardly surprising that agencies that often compete with each other for scarce public resources would not know how to cooperate. Unfortunately, with only three years to work out the coordination and logistics, and under pressure to demonstrate that they had made a measurable difference in outcomes that were largely out of their control (like test scores), many of these programs faltered and could not find substitute funding after the fixed start-up funds offered by the state ran out. In fact, "start-up" funding models for programs that offer core services in distressed communities seldom work. They are based on the false premise that costs can be absorbed by these programs when the start-up money dries up or that there are a plethora of funders willing to step in and support these programs. Neither premise is true.

Social service agencies can learn to collaborate if they are given the tools and the models to do so and provided with stable funding. Stable funding is critically important because, apart from removing the fear of an uncertain future that can stymie an organization, it is difficult, if not impossible, for programs to maintain continuity in services when employees must worry about the security of their own employment. Talented people will move into more secure jobs. Another essential factor for a program's success involves realistic measures of outcomes for children and families, such as decreased absenteeism, reduced residential mobility, better nutrition, or fewer behavioral problems—all of which programs can affect directly. Students may also show increased academic achievement, but this is more likely to be demonstrated over many years, and as the result of a comprehensive set of interventions in the school, home, and community. The idea that significant and sustained improvements for children can be expected from short-term investments is politically convenient but naive. If children of any background are to flourish, they must be provided with basic health care and nutrition and their families must be provided with the means and opportunity to support their basic physical, intellectual, and emotional needs over the entire period of their development. Both state and federal resources must be committed to the goal that every child, regardless of social or income status, be provided with the resources to achieve healthy development through adolescence. Coordinating services for children at or near their schools offers the opportunity to achieve this goal in a cost-effective and accessible manner, and should be at the core of a comprehensive child welfare policy.

Recruiting and Preparing Extraordinary Teachers

We have argued that the single most critical resource in any school is the teacher. We have also shown that well-prepared and experienced teachers for Latino students are in short supply in the schools that they attend, and that this is especially true if the students do not speak English. All of the programs we discussed in Chapter 7 took for granted well-prepared teachers, and the best programs spent considerable resources developing teacher capacity to work with Latino and other students from disadvantaged communities. Without strong teachers, it is not possible to address the challenges that Latino students face. And without teachers who both understand and can communicate with these students and their families, it is not likely that their needs can be accurately assessed and met. School districts often despair of finding teachers with the skills and aptitude to work in low-income communities, and with children who require individualized attention, and when they are able to recruit them they commonly find that they leave for other schools and other jobs that are less demanding and pay more.[28]

There are solutions to the problem of teacher quality and stability for Latino students, and they involve more than just increased salaries. First, teachers must be recruited from the students' own communities. These would-be teachers already have a unique knowledge of and sensitivity to the culture and language of this group; training them as teachers is the easier task.[29] Teachers from these communities are also much more likely to remain in those communities as teachers.[30] One problem is that because so few Latinos successfully make it through the college pipeline, the pool of such potential teachers is small; further, those individuals who complete college degrees often have many professional options. But many Latino students (like other students from low-income backgrounds) are eager to make a difference in their communities and can be enticed into teaching with targeted incentives such as scholarships, housing allowances or mortgage loans, signing bonuses, and the like. To retain these teachers, the research suggests that school administrators should improve the teachers' working conditions by assigning them smaller classes, providing assistants in the classroom, allowing time for planning and collaboration with colleagues, and making school campuses safe, clean, and attractive.[31]

Beyond these measures, teachers must be given the specialized tools to be successful with the Latino population, and contrary to the oft-heard mantra that good schools are good schools for all children, some additional supports must be present in the schools that serve this population. Teachers must have the skills and means for communicating with parents and enlisting them as allies; they must be able to communicate with and motivate their students; they must understand the circumstances of the students' lives and histories. Critically, teachers must know how to provide deep, rich, and intellectually challenging instruction that pushes students to excel. In the words of Michael Martinez, they must be able to cultivate intelligence, not just the acquisition of knowledge.[32] They must be able to help children learn to think deeply and creatively about problems and they must be able to build on the foundations of learning that students bring with them to the school. True school reform will require that teachers are prepared in this way to teach and that they are rewarded for attaining these skills.

Even as we wait for such reforms to occur, however, we must begin the important job of recruiting more teachers from the students' communities. One way to find and recruit college-educated Latino teacher candidates, as discussed, is to provide substantial incentives for talented people from the students' communities to prepare for teaching. These incentives should include tuition-free college and teacher preparation for those who will later serve the public schools—one year of tuition reimbursement for each year of successful teaching. Teachers from these communities should also be helped to purchase a home through low-interest, low-down-payment home ownership programs. The incentives we have proposed to attract and retain these teachers are inexpensive in comparison to the taxpayer investment lost when teachers leave the field prematurely to find better-paying and less stressful jobs. A recent study puts the cost of teacher turnover nationally at $7 billion per year.[33]

Exploiting the Latino Advantage

Although in American schools speaking a language other than English is generally considered an impediment to learning, a defect to be corrected, and a characteristic with little relevance to other students, other developed nations typically view the command of multiple languages as essential to a well-rounded and economically productive education. Given that many of these nations are now overtaking the United States in average years of education per person, the United States might consider taking a page from some of their educational policies.[34] The popularity of English as a world language may free Americans from the necessity of speaking other languages in many contexts. But it does not obviate the advantage that accrues to individuals who can speak directly and in a culturally appropriate way to colleagues, clients, and business partners in other parts of the world, or to individuals within our own borders who speak another language and who increasingly represent a vast market opportunity. Nor does it address the need to speak heritage languages that are rich with family and community culture and history and tie children to their ancestors and extended families. An English-only outlook also fails to capitalize on the human resources and cognitive advantages that are conveyed by having full literacy in another language—not just for students who speak another primary language, but also for those who would choose to become multiliterate.

If the United States is not to be left further behind in a globalizing economy, the ability of its people to work and interact across cultural and linguistic borders must become a greater priority. The notion that speaking a language other than English is an educational liability must be turned on its head. Languages must be seen as resources, as invaluable human capital, and as doorways to enhanced cognitive skills. This is the one area in which many Latino students arrive at school with an advantage over their non-Hispanic peers. We should be making the most of this advantage, for the educational benefit of not only the Latino students, but also their fellow students.

Multilingual programs have come a long way in recent years, despite a general lack of governmental support for them. For example, today there are hundreds of two-way immersion programs (those that combine students from both target languages and in which both groups learn in two languages simultaneously) identified by the Center for Applied Linguistics.[35] Some of these have developed as a result of restrictive language policies in states, but there is a tendency for such programs to spring up in very highly educated communities (often in close proximity to university campuses) where parents—especially English speakers—are eager to have their children learn a second language. It is easily argued that the students who participate in such programs are neither "typical" English speakers nor "typical" speakers of other languages, since their parents tend to be highly motivated to provide opportunities for their children to be multilingual. Hardly the American way. Nonetheless, in numerous studies of the academic and linguistic achievement of students in such programs compared with similar students who are in English-only programs, there is a consistent finding that the two-way immersion students either perform as well as those students in the English-only program (in addition to being similarly skilled in a second language) or they outperform the English-only students, across all academic areas.[36] Moreover, students in two-way or dual-immersion programs tend to have more positive attitudes toward non-English languages and cultures and demonstrate better intercultural relations with students who speak other languages. That is, these programs appear to prepare students to live and work in the global village.[37]

Two-way or dual-immersion programs, however, are not a panacea for all the challenges of English learners.[38] An important critique of the two-way programs is that they often ignore—or even reinforce—preexisting disparities in social status between those students and parents who speak the non-English language (and who are usually low-income) and those from the dominant language and economic group. Anecdotes abound of the ways in which schools and teachers privilege the curricular needs of English speakers to the disadvantage of Spanish speakers. Because the English-speaking parents often initiate such programs, and the presence of their children is critical for the programs' political viability, their concerns often take precedence. For example, Guadalupe Valdés describes a common situation in which the Spanish used in the classroom is modified to be more accessible for the English speakers, but then results in the Spanish speakers' receiving less challenging lessons in their own language.[39] The outcome, of course, is that highly sophisticated, cognitively stimulating Spanish is omitted from the curriculum. English speakers are not hurt measurably by this change, because the language that ultimately counts for achievement tests is English. The Spanish speakers, however, fail to develop high levels of skill in their primary language—the one that will be critical for their early cognitive growth. Inequities like these are a serious concern, and need to be constantly guarded against. Nonetheless, the research appears to converge on the conclusion drawn by Kathryn Lindholm-Leary and Graciela Borsato that "the educational outcomes of bilingually educated students, especially in late-exit and two-way programs, were at least comparable to and usually higher than their comparison peers."[40]

Importantly, researchers also find that there are no achievement disadvantages for English speakers who are educated in two-way programs. They generally do as well and often better than their English-only peers, in addition to acquiring a second language. The English-speaking students in these programs tend to come from particularly well-educated homes in which parents foster many learning opportunities for their children, however, so it is not always clear what constitutes a reasonable comparison group for these students.

If the benefits appear to be so great for all students in such programs, why are they not virtually universal? Language attitudes and ideologies, the fear of parents that their children will be harmed educationally by undertaking the additional burden of learning in two languages, and the perception that it is more costly to teach second languages no doubt all play a role in decisions by parents, school administrators, and policymakers to not initiate more two-way or bilingual programs. The biggest impediment to more widespread adoption of such programs, however, is almost certainly the lack of qualified teachers to teach in them. Strong programs require teachers who are themselves fully bilingual and who have expertise in developing innovative programs. We could have many such teachers, given that in states like Texas and California as many as 40 percent of the college-age students come from second-language backgrounds. But developing and recruiting this talent has never been a priority of state or federal government. We argue that it should be. By capturing more of these potential teacher candidates in the college pipeline through tuition supports and helping them to succeed in college, we can begin to build the capacity to break the cycle of Latino underachievement and language loss.

College Preparation and Support Programs

We have argued that college-access or college preparation programs are seriously limited in their ability to increase college-going among Latino students because they generally begin too late and affect too few students directly. We have also advocated that effective strategies from such programs be embedded in the routines of schooling rather than simply existing in add-on programs. But, just as with school reform, we cannot wait until the day that public schools have the resources to adopt all of the effective practices of college-access programs; instead we must reinforce what is now in place to help as many students as possible. Certainly, a critical feature of such programs must be to connect the K–12 schools with colleges and universities. Those programs that have demonstrated their effectiveness should be implemented in schools as early as possible and should be linked to effective college support programs.

We have noted that summer bridge programs, while expensive, when carefully implemented also appear to confer considerable benefits—social, psychological, and academic. They help students build networks of support and give them the confidence that they can perform at the college level. But the support cannot stop at the door to college. Latino students who are the first in their families to go to college need sensitive counselors and friends who can give them the support and encouragement they need not just to survive, but to excel. There are models of these kinds of programs that support high achievement, and we have discussed these in depth elsewhere.[41] The most important features of such programs, however, include recruiting a critical mass of Latino students; creating supportive peer study and social groups; placing the best teachers in freshman classes; extending program components beyond the freshman year; acknowledging that skill development is cumulative and that some students may require more time to excel; and providing meaningful financial aid. All of these features were present in the most effective college support programs we have seen and need to be replicated widely.

College Financial Aid

Even in the most generous states, a four-year college education is now outside the reach of most low-income students. This is reflected in the data showing that four-year colleges and universities are admitting fewer low-income students, who opt instead for lower-cost two-year colleges.[42] Most Latino students go to two-year colleges where they are much less likely to receive any financial aid at all.[43] And for most of these low-income students, the cost of tuition, which is about all that can be covered with most financial aid packages, is only part of the economic burden. Even if they live at home and commute to college, they must consider very seriously the problem of forgone income. Latino adolescents often feel that they don't have the luxury of not working. Studies of Latino students show that lack of financial aid—whether it is due to lack of knowledge of how to obtain it, or actual lack of available funds—is a key impediment to their going to college. Because the states have so much to gain from increased college-going and college completion, especially for this very large sector of underrepresented and underserved youth, they would benefit by ensuring a cost-free four-year education for all qualified low-income students, with stipends and/or interest-free loans for living expenses. This could be accomplished, in part, by better aligning federal and state financial aid programs, and easing the family income threshold for financial aid eligibility so that those students eligible for any federal program like TRIO or Gear Up, as well as those on free and reduced-price lunch programs, would be included.[44] Given the severe fiscal consequences to the states and the nation of not helping much larger percentages of Latino students attend college, these policies simply make good economic sense.

For those Latino students who are undocumented, but who have completed significant portions of their K–12 education in the United States, the passage of federal—as well as several state-level—Dream Act bills is critical to their motivation and ability to go to college. These bills, now stalled at the federal level and working their way through various states, allow undocumented students with U.S. educations and no criminal record to have provisional legal status, to access student aid, and eventually to apply for citizenship under specific conditions. (The state bills, of course, do not focus on citizenship, but rather on access to state financial aid resources.) Without the promise of some kind of legalization of status, it is very difficult for these highly educated students to acquire a job. And if they are unable to get a job in the legal labor market, there are few incentives to pursue a college education, especially because doing so requires such enormous economic sacrifice. But many of these students are trapped—they have lived most of their lives in this country, do not have ties or supports elsewhere, and want to continue to live and work in the United States. Immigrant optimism has spurred many students to do well in school and look forward to a future of making major contributions to U.S. society, but without legal status they are currently precluded from doing so. In fact, they are being channeled back into the underclass where most of their parents have been stuck. This is a true squandering of important human resources. Undocumented students who have established a life in this country, as the result of decisions made by their parents, must be given access to higher education and the means to pay for it.

Costs and Benefits of Fully Educating Latino Students

A few years ago, Georges Vernez and Lee Mizell of the RAND Corporation were commissioned by the Hispanic Scholarship Fund to conduct a study looking at the costs and benefits of doubling the college completion rate of Latino students in the United States—a goal that the fund had set out to achieve.[45] The Vernez-Mizell study contained a number of critically important findings, including that the Hispanic (Latino) population is the only U.S. ethnic minority group that was projected to increase its share of high school dropouts—by 15 percent—between 2000 and 2010. This prediction was closely related to a second, that 45 percent of Latino youth would be living in economically poor homes by 2010. The extent to which demographic projections for Latinos are heading in the wrong direction—toward more poverty and more undereducation—is alarming, especially given their growing percentage of the school-age population. Vernez and Mizell asserted that the only way to break this cycle of poverty and undereducation in the Latino population is to intervene strategically and significantly in the promotion of education through the post-secondary level. They argued that three types of intervention are necessary: (1) support at the middle and high school levels to prepare students academically for college, (2) support at the transition from high school to college, and (3) programs to retain students in college through graduation. Vernez and Mizell then ran various simulations of costs for providing this level of support, as well as analyzed the benefits that would accrue to the society, and to the individuals, if this goal were achieved.

These researchers noted two major investments necessary to achieve the goal of doubling the college completion rate of Latino students: first, investment in the high school and higher education infrastructure to support increased numbers of students; and second, direct investments in these students. They calculated the infrastructure investment at $6.5 billion in 2000 dollars, but argued that this was only half the value of the benefits that would accrue to society—$13 billion—from both increased tax collection on enhanced earnings and decreased social service costs. They were less certain about the direct costs for students, citing anywhere from $300 to $6,000 per student. At the highest level of per-student expenditures ($6,000), they continued to argue that the economic benefits to society outweigh the costs. Of course, their assumption was that additional expenditures would only be made for enough students to double the numbers of current Latino college completers. But we cannot entertain this as viable social policy. How would we know in whom to invest? How could we justify only investing in some and not others?

We agree that an articulated approach that extends across different levels of schooling all the way to college completion is critically important. But we believe that starting in middle school is too late, especially if there are few supports in the social environment to help Latino students develop in mentally, physically, and socially healthy ways.

We have estimated the costs for supporting students across the span of development and we conclude that a constant investment of public funds is necessary to keep students on a successful pathway toward college completion. Intervention among the youngest children (and this would be with relatively few children from birth to age three) and at the other end of the spectrum, at the level of a four-year college, are the most expensive and can easily double the $6,000 (in 2000 dollars) per student that Vernez and Mizell estimated as the upper parameter of costs. Yet expenditures during the K–12 years would be considerably less per child (though these costs could rise substantially if schools were actually funded at levels that would allow them to meet the real academic and social needs of their students). Moreover, no matter what we do, all students will not go on to college, and all of those who do will not stay four years to complete a college degree. Consequently, expenditures at the college level will be lower when averaged over all students.

But crunching numbers is only part of the larger equation, for Latino students and for our country as a whole. A true understanding of the costs and benefits of boosting the numbers of Latino college completers will require a different kind of analysis, one that includes broader social and economic benefits. For reversing the undereducation of Latino students will lead not only to increased tax revenues and decreased social service expenditures, but also to an economy that will continue to grow rather than stagnate or decline, and to the healthier social conditions fostered by a society that can gainfully employ its youth rather than leaving them to the streets to find less productive ways to sustain themselves. Moreover, it will prepare Latino youth to participate fully in American democracy, and increase the likelihood that they will vote and make meaningful contributions to their communities.[46] Subsequent generations of all Americans stand to reap enormous benefits from these steps toward a healthier society and more robust economy.

Rescuing the American Dream

America is still the land of hope. Presidents win elections by invoking the hopefulness of this country, and more than a million people come here each year, hoping to make the American Dream their dream. This fundamental lack of cynicism in the American people is perhaps this country's greatest asset. And it is why immigrants are so good for this country. They remind us of what we stand for, and what the rest of the world wants to share in. We can harness that hopefulness to create the more equitable society that we, as a people, believe in. And we can start immediately with a few steps that can put us on the road to a larger vision for ourselves and our children.

A policy agenda for the nation that could immediately begin to address the inequitable status of Latinos would include the following:

1. Better health care and access to social services. Many states are currently trying to provide universal health coverage for all poor children. Massachusetts is an example of a state that has been successful in this goal. The federal government could lend a hand to the states by expanding the SCHIP program, and by providing incentives for states to expand their own programs to include the full gamut of basic

health and social services for these children and their families right at their schools. If all Latino children could rely on having accessible health and social services, it would take a large burden off the schools for meeting the needs of students whose learning is jeopardized by a lack of basic health care.

2. Subsidized preschool programs. Most of the states are also trying to find ways to provide universal preschool, at least for all of their low-income children. With a little added incentive from the federal government, this could become a reality across the nation and program quality could be enhanced. The federal role could be especially important for helping to subsidize salaries for highly qualified teachers at these sites, so that they can be paid for their skills while still keeping program costs reasonable. It could provide research funding to develop an intellectually rigorous curriculum that is sensitive to the language and cultural needs of Latino students and help to disseminate it across communities.

3. Housing desegregation and stabilization initiatives. The federal government can stimulate housing desegregation through programs aimed at moving "welfare" families into suburban areas where their children can attend a good school and enter mainstream society. The states, working with their cities and counties, can provide both carrots (tax subsidies) and sticks (legislation) to require developers to build and subsidize more low-income housing in suburban areas. Cities can also work with their school districts to provide world-class schools, so that gentrifying inner cities will draw middle- and upper-income families and desegregation of schools can occur naturally. Moreover, these partnerships can foster policies to help stabilize the school attendance of low-income youth, helping parents to stay in housing when money runs short, and helping students to stay in the same schools even if parents move.

4. Target recruitment and better preparation for teachers. Excellent, well-prepared, and caring teachers are the most important so-

cial resource for Latino students, but they are in terribly short supply. By reinstituting the Title VII graduate fellowships, the federal government could help to train more bilingual, bicultural faculty, who can then prepare a cadre of highly qualified teachers for Latino students. And by providing college tuition free (one year's worth of tuition loan paybacks and living expenses for each year of service) to those students who want to serve in the public schools as teachers and ancillary personnel (counselors, psychologists, nurses, and social workers), the states can draw teachers and other professionals from Latino students' own communities. States will recoup their expenditures quickly, because community-based teachers are more likely to stay longer in their jobs, using their valuable experience to create more successful students.

5. Immigration policy reform. Policymakers need to break the logjam over immigration policy and pass Dream Acts, at both the federal and state levels, so that hard-working, high-achieving immigrant students who find themselves in the United States through no choice of their own can take part in the American Dream for their own benefit—and enrich the nation as a whole.

6. Support for dual-language education. Through small subsidies the federal and state governments can support the development of dual-language programs that provide the opportunity for Latinos to develop a natural asset and non-Latinos to acquire one by becoming fully educated bilingual, biliterate individuals. This would be a progressive move that would not only benefit the nation in human capital, but send a message that we have joined the rest of the developed world in subscribing to the idea that nurturing linguistic resources serves all citizens well.

7. Dropout prevention and college-access programs that support the connection between home and school. School districts can institute, at relatively little cost, programs that take teachers into students' homes so that teachers and parents can partner in supporting

students' learning. In addition, they can implement programs that track students who are at risk of dropping out so that intensive intervention can occur. Because these programs, in reality, often serve the dual purpose of holding students in school and preparing them for postsecondary education, a relatively modest investment by the federal government to evaluate these programs could help point to the most effective intervention strategies for achieving both goals.

These recommendations are a starting point, not an end point. They provide us with a direction to do something now at a cost that would not be prohibitive, to begin to reclaim the American Dream for all our people, especially those Latinos whose futures are so at risk. They may also stave off a social and economic disaster, but that is not primarily why we should do this. We should do this because we have a moral imperative to match our actions to our rhetoric, and because it will ultimately be good for the soul of America.

ACKNOWLEDGMENTS

This work would not have been possible without support from the philanthropic organizations that have sustained our work and believed in this project. We would like to thank the Rockefeller Foundation for selecting us as scholars in residence at the Bellagio Center in June 2005. This was a true turning point in conceptualizing the book. We would also like to thank Pilar Palacia of the Bellagio Center for her support and good counsel during our time there. Special thanks go to Rafael Magallan and Jim Montoya of the College Board for providing us with access to individual-level College Board data sets on Latino students. Gratitude also goes to the staff of the Puente project—Felix, Pat, Mary K., Liz, Frank, and the teachers and counselors who taught us so much about advocating for Latino students.

We are grateful to our colleagues Elena Erosheva, Lisa Chavez, Juan Sanchez, Rashmita Mistry, Russell Rumberger, and Gary Orfield, who have provided us with editorial comments and suggestions as we shaped and edited this manuscript. And we offer a special thank you to Gabriel Baca, a Ph.D. student at UCLA, both for his literature review and editorial efforts during the final stretch of writing, and for adhering to tight deadlines and demands.

Finally, we would like to thank the editorial staff for Harvard University Press, especially Elizabeth Knoll and Julie Carlson, for ongoing suggestions and outstanding editorial help.

Table A.1 Mean SAT Math scores by top quintile, select groups, 2004

	SAT Math	
	Mean	Std. dev.
Other Latino	611.59	62.32
	(N=10,521)	
Mexican American	588.08	52.10
	(N=13,780)	
Puerto Rican	590.28	53.42
	(N=3,807)	
White	664.52	47.11
	(N=173,512)	
Asian	731.69	39.24
	(N=26,670)	

Source: Data from College Board 2004.

Table A.2   Relationship between best language and SAT Math score, after controlling for socioeconomic status, select ethnic groups, 2004

	Asian American		Mexican American		Puerto Rican		Other Latino		White	
	B	SE	B	SE	B	SE	B	SE	B	SE
Independent variables										
Mother's education	.922***	.021	.523***	.022	.554***	.043	.787***	.023	1.097***	.007
Parent income	.404***	.014	.553***	.014	.689***	.025	.681***	.016	.461***	.005
Best Language										
English only (Ref)										
English and another language	1.265***	.044	−1.108***	.101	−2.091***	.198	−1.070***	.114	.956*	.101
Another language	5.128***	.134	−1.844***	.202	−4.278***	.374	−2.140***	.188	3.589*	.172
N	63,026		44,248		12,247		34,030		487,179	
R^2	.076		.103		.130		.151		.094	
Adjusted R^2	.076		.103		.130		.151		.094	
F	1,298.00***		1,275.58***		457.30***		1,518.61***		12,645.52***	

Source: Data from College Board 2004.

Notes: B (the regression coefficient) and SE (std. error) represent the unstandardized coefficients; *p<.05; **p<.01; and ***P<.001.

Table A.3 Relationship between best language and grade point average, after controlling for socioeconomic status, select ethnic groups, 2004

	Asian American		Mexican American		Puerto Rican		Other Latino		White	
	B	SE	B	SE	B	SE	B	SE	B	SE
Independent variables										
Mother's education	.035***	.001	.024***	.001	.046***	.003	.032***	.002	.040***	.000
Parent income	.011***	.001	.009***	.001	.020***	.002	.018***	.001	.004***	.000
Best Language										
English only (Ref)										
English and another language	.030***	.005	.051***	.006	.149***	.013	.032***	.007	.029***	.006
Another language	.052***	.005	.072***	.012	.416***	.025	.137***	.012	.069***	.010
N	63,823		48,689		13,135		36,846		501,213	
R^2	.030		.013		.074		.035		.021	
Adjusted R^2	.030		.013		.074		.035		.021	
F	501.35***		165.05***		262.05***		334.09***		2,674.25***	

Source: Data from College Board 2004.

Notes: B (the regression coefficient) and SE (std. error) represent the unstandardized coefficients; °p<.05; °°p<.01; °°°P<.001.

Table A.4   Mean grade point average of Latino and white students taking the SAT, by income, 2004

	<$35,000		$35,000–$60,000		$60,000–$100,000		>$100,000	
	Latino	White	Latino	White	Latino	White	Latino	White
All	3.10	3.28	3.18	3.33	3.23	3.35	3.29	3.40
Top quintile on SAT	3.53	3.75	3.56	3.76	3.58	3.77	3.56	3.72

Source: Data from College Board 2004.

Table A.5   Correlation between parents' combined household income and cumulative grade point average on a four-point scale, 2004

	Pearson correlation	N
Latino	.075°°	131,039
White	.005°°	728,000

Source: Data from College Board 2004.
Note: The Pearson correlation is significant at the 0.01 level (two-tailed).

Table A.6 Relationship between select honors courses and SAT Math score, after controlling for socioeconomic status, select ethnic groups, 2004

	Asian American		Mexican American		Puerto Rican		Other Latino		White	
	B	SE	B	SE	B	SE	B	SE	B	SE
Mother's education	.724	.019	.459	.019	.250	.038	.610	.020	.770	.006
Parent income	.133	.012	.494	.012	.618	.022	.571	.013	.318	.004
Courses										
Natural science (Ref)										
Honors psychology	−.075	.213	.596*	.255	−.686	.499	.407	.255	−.466***	.063
Honors geography	−1.146***	.236	−1.549***	.188	−1.405**	.519	−1.117***	.258	−1.251***	.066
Honors economics	.869***	.187	−.090	.193	−.180	.444	−.641**	.217	−.101	.056
Honors anthropology	−.599	.861	−.094	1.213	−2.856	1.811	−1.478	1.066	−1.195***	.268
Honors world history	−.849***	.165	−.448**	.160	−.591	.367	−.649**	.190	−.993***	.047
Honors European history	1.704***	.192	2.021***	.243	.739	.459	1.446***	.249	1.156***	.055
Honors government/civics	−1.795***	.173	−.179	.182	.197	.398	−.636**	.207	−.606***	.048
Honors U.S. history	−.759***	.169	.148	.156	.263	.355	−.112	.189	.163**	.047
Honors physics	2.187***	.163	1.397	.166	2.281***	.374	2.026***	.192	2.202***	.048
Honors chemistry	1.025***	.165	.379*	.161	.330	.369	.992***	.192	.632***	.048
Honors biology	−.224	.159	.267	.152	.889	.348	.192	.188	.083	.045
Honors calculus	5.195***	.160	4.493***	.163	4.864***	.413	5.277***	.208	4.870***	.048

	Asian American		Mexican American		Puerto Rican		Other Latino		White	
	B	SE	B	SE	B	SE	B	SE	B	SE
Honors precalculus	.628***	.172	.871***	.171	1.622***	.389	.942***	.205	.619***	.051
Honors trigonometry	.579**	.169	1.146***	.190	.357	.393	1.121***	.215	.517***	.050
Honors geometry	.397*	.197	-.062	.191	-.523	.448	.043	.226	.176**	.059
Honors algebra	.223	.190	.254	.185	.355	.428	.311	.218	-.114*	.057
Honors other language	-2.081***	.545	1.839	1.171	-.808	2.193	-1.981*	.876	-1.166***	.274
Honors Spanish	-1.230***	.186	-.019	.151	-.365	.303	.145	.158	-.201***	.052
Honors social science and history	-.001	.167	.924***	.151	1.267***	.314	1.055***	.176	1.038***	.044
Honors mathematics	5.081***	.150	4.385***	.147	4.755***	.317	4.532***	.175	5.066***	.043
Honors foreign classical language	2.070***	.165	1.025***	.154	1.410***	.317	1.071***	.164	1.104***	.046
Honors English	-1.517***	.139	1.392***	.118	1.152***	.248	.827***	.144	1.062***	.035
Honors arts and music	.709***	.174	.575**	.187	.116	.352	.602**	.201	-.075	.047
N	63,026		44,248		12,247		34,005		487,179	
R^2	.209		.301		.298		.338		.328	
Adjusted R^2	.208		.301		.297		.338		.328	
F	664.77***		761.88***		207.88***		695.76***		9,517.38***	

Source: Data from College Board 2004.
Notes: B (the regression coefficient) and SE (std. error) represent the unstandardized coefficients; *$p < .05$; **$p < .01$; ***$p < .001$.

Table A.7 Relationship between extracurricular activities and SAT Math score, after controlling for socioeconomic status, select ethnic groups, 2004

	Asian American		Mexican American		Puerto Rican		Other Latino		White	
	B	SE	B	SE	B	SE	B	SE	B	SE
Independent variables										
Parent income	.258***	.013	.554***	.013	.703***	.024	.650***	.014	.421***	.004
Mother's education	.733***	.020	.460***	.021	.303***	.041	.657***	.022	.862***	.007
Ref.: Departmental Org./Club										
Student government	.624***	.143	.387**	.142	.266	.271	-.057	.163	.162***	.043
ROTC	-3.097***	.221	-.073	.197	-.793***	.315	-.357	.221	.195**	.061
Religious activity	-.979***	.137	1.054***	.131	.840**	.274	.606***	.169	.652***	.036
Vocal music performance	-.667***	.160	-.660***	.167	-.908	.262	-.862***	.183	-.816***	.047
Instrumental music performance	4.279***	.125	1.825***	.132	2.184***	.261	1.893***	.160	2.573***	.040
Journalism/literary activity	-.110	.150	-.124	.147	.467	.274	.379*	.167	-.318***	.041
Honors program/academic honor society	4.933***	.111	4.994***	.115	5.380***	.232	5.034***	.131	6.425***	.035
Fraternity, sorority, or social club	-2.238***	.121	-.007	.097	.639**	.197	.098	.118	-.715***	.030
Foreign study/study abroad	1.765***	.119	1.450***	.121	1.647***	.249	1.406***	.136	2.062***	.037
Ethnic activity	-1.107***	.123	1.075***	.121	.301	.239	.909***	.151	-.493***	.108
Environment/ecological activity	1.621***	.166	.653***	.184	.818*	.371	.656**	.206	.065	.053

	Asian American		Mexican American		Puerto Rican		Other Latino		White	
	B	SE	B	SE	B	SE	B	SE	B	SE
Drama/theater	−.040	.159	.145	.141	.108	.237	−.100	.155	.030	.042
Debate/public speaking	2.198***	.153	.345°	.154	.532	.290	.636***	.173	.967***	.047
Dance	−2.732***	.143	−2.569***	.121	−2.267***	.227	−2.814***	.135	−2.060***	.048
Cooperative work/internship program	.672***	.115	1.260***	.113	1.114***	.205	1.030***	.131	−.087°	.034
Community service organization	.487***	.111	.002	.102	.430°	.215	.173	.124	.108°°	.033
Varsity sports	−.967***	.114	−.782***	.096	−.452°	.186	−.317°°	.112	−.307***	.029
Intramural sports	1.679***	.117	1.886***	.110	1.556***	.212	2.029***	.130	1.858***	.029
Art	−1.563***	.119	−.366°	.115	−.394	.225	−.334°	.134	−.839***	.037
N	63,026		44,248		12,247		34,030		487,179	
R²	.150		.190		.207		.232		.203	
Adjusted R²	.150		.190		.206		.231		.203	
F	530.43***		495.07***		152.34***		488.87***		5,921.17***	

Source: Data from College Board 2004.
Notes: B (the regression coefficient) and SE (std. error) represent the unstandardized coefficients; °p<.05; °°p<.01; °°°p<.001.

Table A.8 Relationship between extracurricular activities and grade point average, after controlling for socioeconomic status, select ethnic groups, 2004

	Asian American		Mexican American		Puerto Rican		Other Latino		White	
	B	SE	B	SE	B	SE	B	SE	B	SE
Independent variables										
Parent income	.006***	.001	.005***	.001	.011***	.002	.011***	.001	.003***	.000
Mother's education	.027***	.001	.016***	.001	.046***	.003	.026***	.001	.024***	.000
Ref.: Departmental Org./Club										
Student government	.071***	.007	.073***	.009	.036	.019	.059***	.011	.073***	.003
ROTC	-.090***	.011	-.092***	.012	-.076***	.021	-.065***	.014	-.097***	.004
Religious activity	.031***	.007	.107***	.008	.127***	.019	.113***	.011	.146***	.002
Vocal music performance	-.021*	.008	-.023*	.011	.010	.018	-.002	.012	.004	.003
Instrumental music performance	.068***	.007	.027**	.008	.044*	.018	.038***	.010	.059***	.002
Journalism/literary activity	.005	.008	-.006	.009	-.0000138	.019	.002	.011	.003	.003
Honors program/academic honor society	.392***	.006	.414***	.007	.508***	.016	.446***	.009	.465***	.002
Fraternity, sorority, or social club	-.063***	.006	-.040***	.006	-.038**	.014	-.036***	.008	-.033***	.002
Foreign study/study abroad	.071***	.006	.065***	.008	.125***	.017	.091***	.009	.104***	.002
Ethnic activity	.024***	.006	.023**	.008	-.022	.017	.020*	.010	-.071***	.007
Environment/ecological activity	.015	.009	.010	.012	.087**	.026	.020	.013	-.011***	.003

	Asian American		Mexican American		Puerto Rican		Other Latino		White	
	B	SE	B	SE	B	SE	B	SE	B	SE
Drama/theater	−.059***	.008	−.006	.009	−.013	.016	−.034**	.010	−.016***	.003
Debate/public speaking	.031***	.008	−.055***	.010	−.046*	.020	−.018	.011	−.032***	.003
Dance	−.023**	.007	−.007	.008	.008	.015	−.013	.009	.030***	.003
Cooperative work/internship program	.016**	.006	.032***	.007	−.038**	.014	−.024**	.009	−.023***	.002
Community service organization	.101***	.006	.087***	.007	.076***	.015	.101***	.008	.082***	.002
Varsity sports	−.071***	.006	−.050***	.006	−.051***	.013	−.046***	.007	−.026***	.002
Intramural sports	.030***	.006	.038***	.007	.037*	.015	.027*	.008	.052***	.002
Art	−.042***	.006	−.055***	.007	−.017	.015	−.046***	.009	−.071***	.002
N	63,823		46,689		13,135		36,846		501,213	
R^2	.148		.114		.154		.139		.168	
Adjusted R^2	.147		.113		.152		.139		.168	
F	526.44***		297.43***		113.53***		283.49***		4,816.72***	

Source: Data from College Board 2004.
Notes: B (the regression coefficient) and SE (std. error) represent the unstandardized coefficients; *p<.05; **p<.01; ***p<.001.

Table A.9   Self-perception of math ability compared to peers, by SAT test takers, 2004 (percentages)

	Highest 10%		Above average		Average		Below average	
	All	Top 20% on SAT	All	Top 20% on SAT	All	Top 20% on SAT	All	Top 20% on SAT
Ethnicity								
Latino	10.9	32.7	27.9	42.5	45.2	13.1	5.3	.4
White	18.4	52.6	33.4	31.3	32.1	3.4	3.5	.1

Source: Data from College Board 2004.

Table A.10   SAT scores by ethnicity, 2004 (mean)

Ethnicity	Math	Std. dev.	Verbal	Std. dev.	SAT II Writing	Std. dev.
American Indian/ Alaskan	487.8 (N=8,219)	107.3	483.4 (n=8,219)	107.7	577.2 (n=889)	103.3
Asian, Asian American, or Pacific Islander	576.8 (N=112,542)	123.0	506.72 (N=112,542)	121.4	581.3 (N=37,751)	115.8
African American or black	427.3 (N=137,953)	98.6	30.35 (N=137,953)	99.0	540.6 (N=9,400)	101.7
Mexican or Mexican American	458.01 (N=57,739)	97.8	450.6 (N=57,739)	99.5	506.8 (N=10,956)	96.0
Puerto Rican	452.4 (N=16,449)	102.0	457.3 (N=16,449)	101.9	560.8 (N=1,387)	97.2
Other Latino	465.0 (N=48,192)	105.1	461.3 (N=48,192)	105.1	544.5 (N=6,778)	107.2
White	530.8 (N=719,753)	102.0	527.8 (N=719,753)	100.4	626.0 (N=97,313)	94.7

Source: Data from College Board 2004.
Note: As of March 2006, the SAT has been modified to include a writing portion; there is no longer an SAT II exam.

Table A.11 Choice of select college majors by ethnic groups, 2004 (percentages)

Major	Other Latino	Puerto Rican	Mexican American	Asian	White
Biological/life sciences	4.6	4.6	4.4	8.7	5.4
Physical sciences	.9	1.1	1.1	1.7	1.8
Computer & information sciences/ Engineering technologies	5.2	5.2	4.3	6.9	4.4
Health professions & allied services	17.7	17.7	19.7	21.2	15.6
Mathematics	.7	.5	.8	1.5	.9
Business & commerce	16.5	13.5	13.1	16.3	12.3
Education	5.6	7.1	8.2	3.0	10.1
Social sciences & history, general	10.4	10.7	10.1	6.5	9.4
N	53,677	18,368	65,240	119,893	755,207

Source: Data from College Board 2004.

Introduction

1. The National Commission on Educational Excellence was formed by U.S. Secretary of Education Terrence Bell and chaired by the president-elect of the University of California, David Gardner. It presented this report in April of 1983 and immediately drew wide media attention.
2. Rumbaut 1995, p. 52.
3. See, for example, Kao and Tienda 1995; Suárez-Orozco and Suárez-Orozco 1995.
4. Rumberger and Larson 1998b.
5. Pew Hispanic Center, based on 2005 American Community Survey data.
6. Philip Kasinitz et al. (2008) look at the second generation of five different ethnic groups in New York City, including Latinos, and find that they are making progress in English acquisition and occupational achievement very similar to former generations. Their findings counter the notion that immigrants are not incorporating into American culture as rapidly as prior generations.
7. Livingston and Kahn 2002.
8. Perlmann 2005.
9. Ibid., p. 122.
10. James Smith (2003) argues that intergenerational mobility among Mexican immigrants is far greater than most studies have shown because those studies have examined the issue cross-sectionally, by looking at the education levels of first-, second-, and third-generation group means in the same time period. He asserts that it is necessary to look backward, charting grandparents', parents', and children's mean education levels to get a sense of the mobility that has occurred over time. While this argument makes some sense, it is also flawed in that social and educational conditions have changed radically over time and mobility in a prior time may be neither sufficient to keep pace with current labor market demands nor replicated in the contemporary context. Nonetheless, we agree that some progress does occur across the generations.
11. These projections are based on recent work by Patrick Kelly of the National Center for Higher Education Management Systems (NCHEMS), Boulder, Colo.
12. The series of reports for ten states and the nation as a whole can be found at http://www.highereducation.org/reports/pa_decline/index.shtml.
13. No Child Left Behind (NCLB) was the newest incarnation of Elementary and Secondary Education Act (ESEA) legislation, which funds federal education programs for the nation's schools.
14. See, for example, Parrish et al. (2006) and Rolstand, Mahoney, and Glass (2005) for analyses of the impact of these restrictive language policies in Cali-

fornia and Arizona. Neither state has produced any research showing that the policies have reduced achievement gaps for these students.

15. At a macro level this "expectations" argument is represented in the standards movement, which is based on the assumption that if standards are raised, students will meet them. The intentions of standards-based reform were best captured in the slogan "high standards for all students." See, for example, McLaughlin and Shepard (1995).

16. According to 2006 Census data, Central Americans represent 7.6 percent and South Americans 5.5 percent of all Latinos.

17. All preceding data are from the 2006 Census, available at http://factfinder.census.gov/servlet/ACSSAFFPeople?_submenuId=people_10&_sse=on.

18. See, for example, Tienda (1989) for a discussion of the reasons that Puerto Ricans, in spite of having U.S. citizenship, have experienced disproportionately high unemployment, and are characterized by low socioeconomic status comparable to and sometimes worse than that of the Mexican-origin population. In Tienda and Mitchell (2006), the editors report that child poverty rates for Dominicans and Puerto Ricans are between 33 and 35 percent, somewhat higher than for Mexicans, with a 28 percent child poverty rate.

19. Poll reported by L. Roug in the *Los Angeles Times*, December 6, 2007.

20. Samuel Huntington, a noted Harvard professor of foreign affairs, notoriously argued in the journal *Foreign Affairs* in 2004, "The persistent inflow of Hispanic immigrants threatens to divide the United States into two peoples, two cultures, and two languages. Unlike past immigrant groups, Mexicans and other Latinos have not assimilated into mainstream U.S. culture, forming instead their own political and linguistic enclaves—from Los Angeles to Miami—and rejecting the Anglo-Protestant values that built the American dream. The United States ignores this challenge at its peril." The article caused a firestorm of rebuttal within the Latino academic community.

21. Hakimzadeh and Cohen 2007.

22. Tienda and Mitchell (2006) cite one multigenerational study in Los Angeles in the mid-1970s that found only 25 percent of women by the third generation were even considered bilingual; 84 percent spoke only English in the home. And Rubén Martínez, a professor of English at Loyola Marymount University, writing in the *Los Angeles Times* (December 29, 2007) on the topic of how to improve education in Los Angeles's failing schools, notes, "We should view the knowledge that immigrant students have of their native language as one of our greatest strengths" but instead, "we turn out immigrant kids today with shaky English and a withering native language."

23. Fortuny, Capps, and Passel 2007. Almost 80 percent of unauthorized immigrants are Latino in origin. http://pewhispanic.org/files/reports/61.pdf.

24. Batalova 2008.

25. Fortuny, Capps, and Passel 2007. The authors find that nationwide, 66 percent of children of immigrants are born in this country, with 76 percent of immigrants in Los Angeles (the metro with the largest number of undocumented residents, and a more "settled" community) born here.

26. *Plyler v. Doe*, 457 U.S. 202 (1982).

27. Fix and Passel 1994; Goldman, Smith, and Sood 2006.

28. See, for example, Borjas 1995, 2003; and Card 2001. Even Borjas (1995), a famous skeptic on the economic benefits of low-skilled immigration, concedes

that the net tax contributions of immigrants are greater than the cost of services provided to them.

29. See Myers 2007.
30. "Consequences of the Mexican Diaspora," presentation at University of California, Los Angeles, January 27, 2008. The basis for Minister González Gutiérrez's comments can be found in population projections from El Consejo Nacional de Población (http://www.conapo.gob.mx/00cifras/5.htm).
31. Massey, Durand, and Malone 2002.
32. Suárez-Orozco and Páez 2002, pp. 5, 6, 7, and 9.

1. The Crisis and the Context

1. Dowell Myers (2007) reports that fully half of Mexican immigrants to the United States are homeowners twenty to twenty-nine years after arriving, suggesting a strong motivation to integrate into American society.
2. U.S. Department of Commerce, Census Bureau 2007b.
3. Perlmann 1987.
4. Smith 2003; Grogger and Trejo 2002.
5. West, Denton, and Germino-Hausken 2000.
6. Gándara 2006.
7. Borman, Stringfield, and Rachuba 2000.
8. Ibid., p. 79.
9. Gándara 2006.
10. Oakes 1986; Valenzuela 1999; Kao and Tienda 1998; Gándara, O'Hara, and Gutiérrez 2004.
11. Laird et al. 2007.
12. Lavan and Uriarte 2008.
13. Orfield et al. 2004.
14. Fry 2002.
15. De Los Santos, Jr., and De Los Santos 2003.
16. Fry 2002.
17. Coley 2001.
18. Shulock 2006.
19. Coley 2001.
20. Orfield et al. 2004.
21. Ibid.
22. LoGerfo, Nichols, and Chaplin 2007.
23. Ibid.
24. Coley 2001; Barton 2003.
25. See, for example, Sommers 2000; Epstein et al. 1998.
26. Ibid.
27. Mortenson 1999.
28. Coley 2001.
29. Coleman et al. 1966; Jencks et al. 1972; and Bowles, Gintis, and Groves 2005.
30. On cultural capital, see Bourdieu 1973; DiMaggio 1982. On social capital, see Coleman 1987a and 1987b; Lareau 1989, 2003.
31. Brooks-Gunn, Denner, and Klebanov 1995; Jarret 1997; Leventhal and Brooks-Counn 2004.
32. Kao and Tienda 1998; Gándara, O'Hara, and Gutiérrez 2004.

33. Ream 2005.
34. Rumberger 2003; Ream 2004.
35. Horn and Chen 1998.
36. Gándara, Gutiérrez, and O'Hara 2001; Teranishi, Allen, and Solórzano 2004.
37. Geiser and Santelices 2006, in Gándara, Orfield, and Horn 2006; Oakes 1986.
38. Lucas 1999.
39. Rumberger and Gándara 2004; Betts, Reuben, and Dannenberg 2000; UCLA IDEA/UCACCORD 2007.
40. Orfield and Yun 1999.
41. U.S. Census Bureau, *Current Population Survey* 2008.
42. *Lau v. Nichols*, 414, U.S. 563 (1974).
43. Greene 2002; Slavin and Cheung 2005; Rolstad, Mahoney, and Glass 2005; Zehler et al. 2003.
44. Rumberger and Tran 2008.
45. *Plyler v. Doe*, 1982 (457 U.S. 202).
46. Olsen 2000.
47. The Dream Act, also known as the Development, Relief, and Education for Alien Minors Act of 2005, S.2075, was introduced in the Senate by Senator Richard Durbin, but has been stalled in the Congress ever since. It had been attached to immigration legislation when it appeared that immigration reform might be on a fast track, but when negotiations on immigration reform collapsed in 2007, it was sent to the floor for a vote on its own, where on October 24, 2007, Democrats were unable to overcome a filibuster and it once again was moved off the national legislative agenda.
48. The U.S. Constitution online, http://www.usconstitution.net.dream.html (accessed April 20, 2008).
49. Connerly 2000; D'Souza 1995; Heilman, Block, and Lucas 1992; Nacoste 1990.
50. Steele 1999.
51. Chavez 1991.
52. Alon and Tienda 2003.
53. Lyndon B. Johnson's commencement address at Howard University, June 4, 1965. http://www.lbjlib.utexas.edu/johnson/archives.hom/speeches.hom/650604.asp.
54. For a thorough and fascinating account of the campaign for Proposition 209, see Chavez 1998.
55. P. Gándara and J. Maxwell-Jolly conducted this unpublished analysis of print articles and opinion pieces using LexusNexus as the primary search tool.
56. *Chronicle of Higher Education,* April 1996, p. 2.
57. Gable 1995.
58. Thernstrom and Thernstrom 2002.
59. Alon and Tienda 2005. These researchers investigated what they call the "mismatch hypothesis," which predicts lower graduation rates for minority students who attend selective postsecondary institutions compared with those who attend colleges and universities where their academic credentials are better matched to the institutional average. These investigators came to the same conclusion as Bowen and Bok (1998): that is, controlling for grade point average and test scores, students or color graduated at higher rates from more selective institutions.

60. Ronald Unz, personal communication with the authors, April 16, 1999.
61. Parrish et al. 2006.
62. Gándara and Maxwell-Jolly 2005.
63. See Merickel et al. 2003.
64. *California Teachers Association v. State Board of Education* 2000.
65. Yettick 2006.
66. See Mahoney, MacSwan, and Thompson 2005; Rolstad, Mahoney, and Glass 2005.
67. See, for example, statement by Reg Weaver, President of the National Education Association on April 23, 2008, "NEA President Labels Proposed Changes to Federal Education Law 'Too Little and Too Late.'" http://www.nea.org/newsreleases/2008/nr080423.html (accessed April 23, 2008).
68. Krueger 2005; Isaacs 2008.
69. Borjas 2005; Grogger and Trejo 2002.
70. See, for example, Oakes and Wells (1998), in which the authors describe the strong efforts made by middle-class parents against a "detracking" reform that would have allowed any student who wanted to take more rigorous college preparatory courses to have access to them. The parents argued that this would reduce the rigor of the courses for their children, and their protest effectively ended the reform.

2. On Being Latino or Latina in America

1. Analyses of Early Educational Longitudinal Study (ECLS) data, Gándara 2006.
2. Quotations from these three students (names used are pseudonyms) come from informal interviews with students known to the authors over a period of months during the winter of 2007–2008. All were students at West Coast universities who volunteered to discuss their backgrounds and academic trajectories.
3. See Rideout, Roberts, and Foehr (2005), which presents survey data on eight- to eighteen-year-olds' media habits, including the finding that on average eight- to eighteen-year-olds watch almost four hours a day of television, including video programming. Mark Fetler (1984) draws from survey data of California school-age children to find that low-income children watch more television programming than middle-class students, up to an average of six hours a day. Fetler also finds that there is a significant correlation between high levels of viewing and low achievement.
4. Shirley Brice Heath, in her 1983 ethnography *Ways with Words,* demonstrates the differences in language socialization between urban children of color and middle-class white children.
5. Bellah et al. 1985; Rainwater and Smeeding 2003. Several state and local initiatives over the last several years have sought to deny public services to undocumented immigrants (in 1994, for example, California passed Proposition 187, barring most public services to undocumented immigrants, although the state courts have since overturned most of its provisions). In 2004, Proposition 200, which denies most public services to undocumented immigrants, passed in Arizona with 55.6 percent of the vote and so far has survived legal challenges. Typical of the sentiment in that state is a quote from Rep. Russell Pearce (R), who led the Proposition 200 drive: "[Illegal immigrants] can't come to America and get free stuff. It's just wrong. You've got to take

their benefits away" (August 31, 2005, Stateline.org; http://www.stateline.org). Dowell Myers (2007) reports, too, that polling data from Gallup and the Public Policy Institute of California show large percentages of Americans believe that "immigrants cost taxpayers too much by using government services rather than eventually becoming productive citizens and paying their fair share of taxes" (p. 6).

6. Hochschild and Scovronick 2003.
7. Jeannie Oakes makes this argument skillfully in her 1990 RAND study *Multiplying Inequalities*. There she argues that school systems like to portray themselves as value-neutral institutions so as to redirect the blame for educational failure away from the schools and toward the students and their communities—in essence, they engage in "blaming the victim."
8. Hochschild 1995; Hochschild and Scovronick 2003.
9. Philips 2003.
10. Rainwater and Smeeding 2003.
11. Ibid., p. 22.
12. According to federal poverty guidelines, a family of four would fall below the poverty threshold with an income below $20,650 in 2007. For each additional family member, the federal government adds $3,480. For comparison purposes the threshold in 2004 was $19,307 for a family of four and $22,831 for a family of five in 2004. Guidelines are available at http://www.census.gov/hhes/www/poverty/thrshld.
13. Nord, Andrews, and Carlson 2004.
14. Institute of Education Sciences 2006.
15. Capps et al. 2004.
16. Reliable data are not kept on how many students and their families cross back and forth between Mexico and the United States. Data are collected on apprehensions of individuals crossing the border into the United States, but not the other way. And it is unknown how many apprehensions are of individuals who have crossed before. It is estimated, however, that about 3 to 3.5 million people per decade will continue to flow across the Mexican border until at least 2030 (see Simcox 2002). The social and economic forces that drive border crossing are relatively resistant to minor policy changes and increased enforcement. As Suárez-Orozco and Suárez-Orozco (1995) have pointed out, migration is a historical and global phenomenon that reflects the basic human drive for survival.
17. Capps et al. 2004.
18. Wilson 1996.
19. Rothstein 2004.
20. See M. Martinez (2000), pp. 140–144, for descriptions of several studies showing the effects of vitamin and dietary supplementation on academic performance.
21. Berliner 2006; Gillespie 2001.
22. Rothstein 2004.
23. Ibid.
24. Berliner 2006.
25. Fraser 2005.
26. Ibid.
27. Rainwater and Smeeding 2003.

28. DeNavas-Walt, Proctor, and Lee 2006.
29. Tienda and Mitchell 2006.
30. Zill et al. 1995.
31. Gándara 2006.
32. U.S. Department of Commerce, Census Bureau 2007a.
33. For extensive discussion of the intertwining of poverty with stress and depression see, for example, Jencks 1993; Wilson 1996.
34. Haro, Rodríguez, and Gonzales 1994; Delgado-Gaitán 1990; Steinberg 1996.
35. Lareau 1989; Steinberg 1996.
36. Robinson et al. 1998.
37. Lareau 1989.
38. Useem 1992.
39. Miller 1995; Patillo-McCoy 1999.
40. Baumrind 1989; Steinberg 1996.
41. Gándara 1995; Clark 1984.
42. Clark 1984; Gándara 1995.
43. Steinberg, Dornbusch, and Brown 1992.
44. South, Crowder, and Trent 1998; Crowley 2003.
45. Entwisle, Alexander, and Olson 1997.
46. Rumberger and Larson 1998a; Rumberger, 2003.
47. Ream and Stanton-Salazar 2006, p. 7.
48. Fine 1991.
49. Ream 2005.
50. National Fair Housing Alliance 2006.
51. Brooks-Gunn, Denner, and Klebanov 1995.
52. Jarret 1997.
53. Darling and Steinberg 1997.
54. Coulton et al. 1995; Tienda and Mitchell 2006. In 2003, Latina adolescents ages fifteen to nineteen had 82.2 births per 1,000, compared to 41.7 for all females of this age group (black adolescent girls had 64.8 births, and white adolescent girls, 27.5 births per 1,000).
55. National Research Council, Panel on High Risk Youth 1993.
56. Steinberg 1996; Ong and Terriquez 2008.
57. Ong and Terriquez 2008.
58. Martin 2006.
59. Iceland and Weinberg 2002.
60. McArdle 2004; Martinez 2006
61. Gifford and Valdés 2006, p. 147.
62. Henderson 1997.
63. Stanton-Salazar 1997.
64. Steinberg 1996; Kao and Tienda 1998.
65. Epstein and Karweit 1983; Rumberger and Rodriguez 2002.
66. In our surveys of adolescents, as well as observations on campus, we have consistently found what is commonly reported in the literature (e.g., Peshkin 1991; Tatum 1997): most students form their closest relationships with others of the same ethnicity.
67. Steinberg 1996.
68. Matute-Bianchi 1986.
69. Tatum 1997.

70. Gándara, O'Hara, and Gutiérrez 2004. This study of approximately five hundred adolescents moving from ninth to twelfth grade through a large urban and relatively large rural (1200) high school were analyzed by ethnic background.
71. Hurd 2004.
72. Ibid., p 76.
73. Mexican origin and Puerto Rican families are significantly less likely to fall into this income category, however, than are other Latino subgroups.
74. U.S. Department of Commerce, Census Bureau 2006.
75. Sean Reardon of Stanford University reported that the average Hispanic household making $45,000 lives in a neighborhood with the same median income ($40,000) as the average white family making $10,000, based on Census tract data. See the School and Neighborhood Segregation conference sponsored by the Charles Hamilton Houston Center of Harvard Law School in San Francisco, January 17, 2008.
76. Telles and Ortiz 2008; Grebler, Moore, and Guzman 1970.
77. Suárez-Orozco and Suárez-Orozco 1995; Written testimony of Mr. John Trasviña, Interim President and General Counsel, MALDEF, July 26, 2006, in Tucker 2007.
78. Forsbach and Pierce 1999.
79. Delgado et al. 2006.
80. Hayes-Bautista 2004.
81. Ibid., p. 163.
82. Ibid., p. 163.
83. Phinney 1989.
84. Steele 1997.
85. See, for example, Good, Aronson, and Inzlicht 2003; Schmader and Johns 2003; and Salinas and Aronson 1998.
86. Gándara, O'Hara, and Gutiérrez 2004. In a survey of attitudes toward school conducted of approximately five hundred students in a rural and urban high school in 2002, we found that 27 percent of the rural Latinos claimed their friends "did not care about school at all." This was the highest percentage for any ethnic or gender group in the study. Survey results were matched by exceptionally low grades for these Latino males.
87. Hurd 2004.
88. Ibid., p. 80.
89. Census data show that the average Hispanic female has 2.8 children compared to 2.0 for white females, resulting in Latino family sizes that are about 30 percent larger than those of whites. See Martin et al. 2005.
90. Pew Hispanic Center 2006.
91. Johnson 2006.
92. See Mary Patillo-McCoy (1999) for an extended discussion of the drain that low-income family members can be on emerging middle-class families of color.
93. See Noguera and Wing (2006) for a discussion of the lowered expectations of urban youth, and Valenzuela (1999) for a discussion of the negative interactions between some white teachers and their Latino students.
94. The concern that schools alone cannot resolve the problems of unequal

schooling outcomes is not new. The report by Coleman (1966) has been strongly criticized for its conclusion that most of the effects on student achievement occur outside the schools and therefore schools are limited in their ability to equalize educational outcomes. The report was widely viewed as an apology for schools that had failed particular communities and a way of blaming the victims, that is, the students who were poorly served by those schools. But Coleman's findings that schools were not contributing greatly to narrowing achievement gaps or equalizing opportunity are not in conflict with the idea that schools in fact could do more in this regard. In the well-known book *Fifteen Thousand Hours: Secondary Schools and Their Effects on Children* (1979), Michael Rutter and his colleagues discussed the challenges of equalizing educational outcomes for poor children when schooling constitutes such a relatively small portion of their lives.

95. Gándara 2006.

3. American Schools and the Latino Student Experience

1. Capps et al. 2005.
2. Grogger and Trejo (2002) discuss that while there is considerable intergenerational mobility with respect to increased educational attainment for Mexican Americans, there is little mobility at the level of higher education. That is, Mexican Americans are not making significant gains in college-degree completion compared to other groups, and the expected third- and fourth-generation movement up the higher education ladder has not occurred.
3. McDonough 1997.
4. Gándara and Maxwell-Jolly 2000.
5. All data come from California Department of Education, Fast Facts 2008. California has recently improved its staffing ratios significantly. Traditionally, the student/staff ratios in California have been even more extreme than depicted in the 2007 data. For example, throughout the 1990s and until 2005, the student/counselor ratio averaged about 1,000 to 1 (compared to 815:1 in 2007) and the student/psychologist ratio averaged between 1,700 and nearly 2,000 to 1 (compared to 1383: 1 in 2007). (See Fast Facts 2008, 1995–1996 through 2006–2007, available at www.cde.ca.gov/fastfacts, accessed May 5, 2008).
6. Hart and Risley 1995.
7. Bates, Thala, Finlay, and Clancy 2003.
8. M. Martinez 2000.
9. U.S. Department of Education, National Center for Education Statistics 2007.
10. Zigler and Styfco 1993; Karoly et al. 1998; Garcia and Gonzalez 2006.
11. Children's Defense Fund 2000.
12. Fuller et al. 1996.
13. Zill et al. 1995.
14. Barr and Dreeben 1983; Entwisle, Alexander, and Olsen 1997; Gamoran 1992.
15. Entwisle, Alexander, and Olsen 1997.
16. Oakes, Mendoza, and Silver 2004.

17. The 163-day calendar is largely a phenomenon of the Los Angeles schools, which have been ordered to curtail this practice over the next several years, yet because Los Angeles is the nation's second-largest district, with a majority population of Latino students, it has affected many thousands of Latino schoolchildren.
18. National Education Association 2006.
19. Unmuth 2007.
20. Arizona Education Association 2008 [Arizona Education Association website]. The History of Flores v Arizona. http://www.arizonaea.org/politics.php?page= 186 (accessed May 5, 2008).
21. See http://www.decentschools.org for the court documents and the final settlement in the Williams case.
22. Earthman 2002.
23. Karcher 2002; Darling-Hammond 2002.
24. Hanushek, Kain, and Rivkin 2001; Loeb and Page 2001.
25. Gándara et al. 2003; Rumberger and Gándara 2004.
26. U.S. Department of Education 2005.
27. Fairlie et al. 2006.
28. Sweet et al. 2004.
29. Wilhelm, Carmen, and Reynolds 2002.
30. Ibid.
31. Jones, in preparation.
32. Fairlie et al. 2006.
33. Beltran et al., in Fairlie 2006.
34. Barr and Dreeben 1983; Gamoran 1992.
35. There is now a massive amount of research on the topic of tracking, including both quantitative studies (e.g., Alexander, Cook, and McDill 1978; Gamoran 1989, 1992; Lucas 1999) and qualitative studies (e.g., Useem 1992; Lareau 1989; Valenzuela 1999) of the mechanisms and outcomes of curriculum assignment and class and race inequities.
36. Roslyn Mickelson (2001) conducted a study in which she found that black students were significantly less likely to be placed in gifted programs than white students with the same grades and test scores; the Education Trust has data that show how low-income students are much less likely to be placed on a college-bound track than high-income kids even when test scores are controlled; Lucas (1999) also explores the influence of prior curriculum placement on the likelihood of later being placed in a college-bound track.
37. Betts, Rueben, and Danenberg 2000, p. 72.
38. Solorzano and Ornelas 2004.
39. Adelman 1999.
40. The Office for Civil Rights has not collected or published data on minorities in gifted programs since 1997–1998. The latest figures published by the National Academy of Sciences (Donovan and Cross 2002) were based on 1998 data.
41. This interpretation is based on analyses we conducted of the NELS 88 dataset.
42. Crosnoe 2006b, pp. 38–39.
43. See Laosa 1978. Laosa refers to Mexican American mothers in this study as "Chicanas," and we use the term interchangeably with "Mexican Americans."
44. Peske and Haycock 2006. These attributes for teachers were holding a degree from a competitive college, having less than four years of experience, having

an emergency or provisional credential, failing the basic skills tests on the first attempt, and average ACT scores.

45. Goldhaber and Brewer (1996), in an analysis of NELS 88 data, showed a positive relationship between teachers' degrees in technical areas (math and science) and students' achievement. As mentioned in Chapter 4, Sanders and Rivers (1996) were able to demonstrate, using data from the Tennessee Value Added Study, that three consecutive years of poorly qualified teachers could make it impossible for a student to ever catch up. See also Carbonaro and Gamoran 2002; Darling-Hammond 2004; Oakes and Saunders 2004.

46. A highly influential 1968 study by Robert Rosenthal and Lenore Jacobson entitled *Pygmalion in the Classroom* asserted that simply assigning a label to a student—in this case researchers told teachers that some students were "late bloomers" and would be showing significant academic growth—could result in a self-fulfilling prophecy whereby students would live up to their label because teachers' expectations would influence their achievement. Reanalyses of the original experiment called into question whether such direct and dramatic achievement gains were possible by simply labeling students as bright or not bright. But continuing research does show that teachers can influence student achievement by either placing students into learning groups, based on their perceptions of students' ability, or by favoring some students and providing them with more time and attention (see Good and Brophy 1994).

47. Alexander, Entwisle, and Thompson 1987.

48. Brophy and Good 1974.

49. U.S. Commission on Civil Rights 1974; Valenzuela 1999; Foley 1990.

50. Roderick 2003; Swanson 2004.

51. Garcia and Guerra 2004.

52. Ream 2005.

53. Weinstein 1989.

54. Rist 1970; Cummins 2001.

55. Valenzuela 1999, p. 61.

56. Hurd 2004, p. 68.

57. Prince 2002.

58. Ibid., p. 15.

59. Waters and Marzano 2006.

60. Elmore 2005; Blasé and Blasé 2001.

61. Elmore 2005; Garcia 1996; Haberman 1996.

62. Scheckner et al. 2002.

63. U.S. Department of Education, National Center for Education Statistics 2005.

64. Laub and Lauritsen 1998.

65. See Elliott et al. 2006.

66. Vigil 2004.

67. Ringwalt, Ennett, and Johnson 2003; Beauvais et al. 1996.

68. Vigil 2004, p. 90.

69. Reported by Gándara (1999), in the final evaluation submitted to the Puente Program, Office of the President of the University of California.

70. Gibson et al. 2004.

71. Gándara and Gibson 2004.

72. Orfield and Lee 2006.

73. U.S. Department of Education, National Center for Education Statistics 2007.

74. Orfield and Eaton 1996; Mickelson 2001.
75. Orfield and Yun 1999; Orfield and Lee 2006.
76. Orfield and Eaton 1996, p. 67.
77. Orfield and Lee 2006.
78. Orfield and Lee 2005.
79. Linquanti 2006.
80. Zehler et al. 2003.
81. Rumberger, Gándara, and Merino 2006.
82. Gándara et al. 2003; Rumberger and Tran 2006.
83. Brown and Theobald 1998.
84. Rumberger and Rodriguez 2002.
85. See, for example, Gándara, O'Hara, and Gutiérrez 2004 and Gibson et al. 2004 for data and discussion of Latino students who feel that they don't "belong" in school because of experiences of marginalization.
86. Gándara and Gibson 2004.
87. Coleman et al. 1966; Frazier 1993; Orfield and Lee 2005.
88. Kao and Tienda 1998; Gándara, O'Hara, and Gutiérrez 2004.
89. Gándara, O'Hara, and Gutiérrez 2004.
90. Zarate and Pachón 2006.
91. Lareau 1989.
92. Gándara 1995, p. 102.
93. Ibid., p. 74.
94. In California's 2006–2007 budget, $548 million was earmarked for services and $2 million for the state's department of education for administrative purposes.
95. Kane 2004.
96. Ibid.
97. Huang et al. 2000.
98. Halpern 2002.
99. Gándara and Bial 2001; Adelman 2001.
100. Gándara et al. 2003.
101. Moreno 2002.
102. See, for example, Kazis, Vargas, and Hoffman 2004.
103. Robinson et al. 1998; Gándara 1995, 2006.
104. Werner and Smith 2001.
105. Benard 1996; Horn and Chen 1998.

4. Is Language the Problem?

1. See Delgado-Bernal 1999. Gary Orfield (1978) cites W. Henry Cooke, who described the situation in California in 1948 this way: "Schools for 'Mexicans' and schools for 'Americans' have been the custom in many a Southern California city . . . it has been the custom that they be segregated, at least until they could use English well enough to keep up with English-speaking children. . . . Since the Spring of 1947 . . . it is not now legal . . . and yet the practice still continues in many cities" (p. 199).
2. There is tremendous diversity in how states and districts identify English learners and, especially, how they decide who is no longer an English learner. In fact, the same student in different locales can be classified differently, rais-

ing questions about the accuracy of aggregate numbers of English learners in research studies.

3. Pew Hispanic Center/Kaiser Family Foundation 2004.

4. Carter 1970.

5. Schmidt 2000.

6. For political reasons, the primary sponsor of the Bilingual Education Act, Senator Ralph Yarborough of Texas, was purposely vague on the issue of the act's intent. He told his fellow lawmakers, "It is not the purpose of the bill to create pockets of different language throughout the country . . . not to stamp out the mother tongue, and not to make the mother tongue the dominant language, but just to try to make those children fully literate in English" (Crawford 2004, p. 107). Thus the "bilingual" bill did not actually encourage bilingualism in its original language. Bilingual education was inextricably associated with War on Poverty legislation and was, from the beginning, a compensatory program to remediate the language deficits of limited English speakers.

7. Gary Orfield (1978) notes that Bambi Cárdenas, one of the Department of Health, Education and Welfare's leading consultants on the education on Hispanic students, mentioned to him in an interview in September of 1974 that the department was especially pleased with an educational plan that she helped to draft for the El Paso schools because "they [the department] were willing to do anything so long as they did not have to desegregate" (p. 303).

8. There are no reliable national data on the percent of Latino students who are English learners, in part because this is an ever changing number. In California 46 percent of Latino students in 2006 were English learners, but California also has the largest number of immigrant Latinos. The National Council of La Raza computes the figure at 45 percent in 2002–2003 based on data from the National Clearinghouse for English Language Acquisition and Language Instruction Educational Programs and U.S. Census Bureau, *Current Population Survey* (October 2003). Thus we estimate that nationally between 40 percent and 45 percent of Latino K–12 students could be classified as English learners.

9. Harklau, Losey, and Siuegal 1999; Valdés 2001; Wong-Fillmore 1985.

10. Wong-Fillmore and Snow 2000.

11. See the California Department of Education website, http://dq.cde.ca.gov/dataquest (accessed April 25, 2008).

12. Zehr 2007a, 2007b.

13. Maxwell-Jolly, Gándara, and Méndez-Benavídez 2006.

14. In 1994, Title VII of ESEA, newly named Improving America's School Act (IASA), was reauthorized and for a brief time "maintenance" bilingual education enjoyed a new respectability. The act specifically recognized maintenance programs once again; however, this was relatively short lived, as the next authorization in 2001 completely removed any reference to bilingual education at all. Even the office of bilingual education disappeared and was renamed the Office of English Language Acquisition, Language Enhancement, and Academic Achievement for Limited English Proficient Students.

15. For evidence on the positive outcomes of busing for African American (and white) students, see Orfield and Eaton 1996.

16. Danoff et al. 1978.

17. Ramírez et al. 1991.
18. Because most bilingual teachers are primary English speakers, English more often predominates over Spanish in bilingual classrooms. See ibid.
19. Ream 2004; Rumberger 2003.
20. Genesee et al. 2006.
21. Ibid. Bilingual is defined as a program in which English learners are taught through two languages, and two-way is a program in which English learners and English speakers are taught through two languages together. ELL is the acronym for English language learner, a common variation of English learner, which we prefer; SEI is the acronym for structured English immersion, an English-only curriculum with structured adaptation to the needs of English learners; ESL is the acronym for English as second language instruction; and EO refers to English only.
22. See Valdés 1997 for discussion of power imbalances and unintended consequences.
23. Baker and de Kanter 1981.
24. Willig 1985; Greene 1998; Rolstad, Mahoney, and Glass 2005.
25. August and Hakuta 1997.
26. Ibid., p. 28.
27. Snow, Burns, and Griffin 1998, p. 325.
28. August and Shanahan 2006.
29. Preamble to California Proposition 227 of 1998. http://www.primary98.sos .ca.gov/VoterGuide/Propositions/227text.htm (accessed May 10, 2008).
30. Carpenter-Huffman and Samulon 1981; Chambers and Parrish 1992.
31. Proponents of this position included prominently Baker and De Kanter 1983; Rossell and Baker 1996; and Gersten 1985.
32. National Research Council 1993.
33. Ibid., p. 397.
34. Cummins 1981.
35. Cummins 1984.
36. Snow 1992; August and Hakuta 1997.
37. See, for example, Hurd (2004) for an ethnographic description of limited-English adolescents having to contend with peer ridicule because of their accented and grammatically incorrect English.
38. Suárez-Orozco and Suárez-Orozco 1995; Rumbaut 1995.
39. See, for example, Portes and Zhou 1993.
40. Genesee and Gándara 1999.
41. Reynolds 1991; Bialystok et al. 2004; August and Hakuta 1997.
42. Suárez-Orozco and Suárez-Orozco 1996; Portes and Rumbaut 1990, 2001; Grogger and Trejo 2002.
43. Hakuta, Butler, and Witt 2000.
44. August and Hakuta 1997.
45. Flores-Solano 2008 discusses the many variables to be considered in assessing progress of EL students.
46. Thomas and Collier 1997; Hakuta, Butler, and Witt 2000; Parrish et al. 2006.
47. Snow and Hofnagle-Hohle 1978. See also Hakuta 1986.
48. See Bialystok and Hakuta 1994.
49. Parrish et al. 2006.
50. Ibid.
51. See, for example, Unz 1997.

52. See Gándara et al. 2003, for examination of these trends.
53. Sunderman and Orfield 2006.
54. 20 USCS, Sec. 6311 of No Child Left Behind. See http://www.ed.gov/policy/elsec/leg/esea02/index.html.
55. Zehr 2007a, 2007b; Parrish et al. 2006.
56. Abedi et al. 2000; Rivera et al. 2000.
57. Maynard 2007.
58. Schlesinger 1991.
59. Schmidt 1998.
60. For example, a poll by the Pew Hispanic Center/Kaiser Family Foundation (2004) found that 92 percent of Latino parents say it is "very important" for the public schools to teach immigrant children English; 88 percent say they think it is important, as well, for the schools to help students "maintain their native tongue."
61. On August 20, 2000, Jacques Steinberg of the *New York Times* famously printed a front-page story with the opening lines, "Two years after Californians voted to end bilingual education and force a million Spanish-speaking students to immerse themselves in English as if it were a cold bath, those students are improving in reading and other subjects at often striking rates." Steinberg's assertions were based on a fax from Ron Unz; he never checked their legitimacy. If he had, he would have learned that Unz's assertions were unfounded.
62. See *Bye Bye Bilingual.*
63. McQuillan and Tse 1996.
64. Crawford 2004.
65. Escamilla et al. 2003.
66. Ibid., p. 366.
67. Rumberger and Gándara 2004.
68. Gándara et al. 2003.
69. Sanders and Rivers 1996.
70. Ibid.
71. Gándara et al. 2003; Zehler et al. 2003.
72. Gándara, Maxwell-Jolly, and Driscoll 2004.
73. Woolfolk, Rosoff, and Hoy 1990. Goddard and Goddard 2001.
74. Esch et al. 2005.
75. Zehler et al. 2003.
76. Ibid.
77. See, for example, Farber 1991.
78. Hanushek and Rivkin 2006; Murnane et al. 1991; Nye, Konstantopoulos, and Hedges 2004.
79. Zehler et al. 2003; National Center for Education Statistics 2003–2004.
80. Trostel 2008.
81. Ruiz 1984.
82. Cziko (1992) argues that political rather than pedagogical considerations have kept dual-language education from taking hold in the United States.

5. Inside the Lives of Puente Students

1. Affirmative action and targeting of students on the basis of race for special programs was banned in California in 1996. As a result the Puente program was threatened with lawsuits for its focus on Latino students. It resolved the

issue by opening up the program to any student who wished to enroll. Since the program emphasized Latino literature and cultural experiences, few non-Latino students opted to join.

2. See Hakuta, Butler, and Witt (2000) for a discussion of the time it takes to learn academic English.
3. See, for example, Vasquez Garcia et al. 2000.
4. See Levine (1997) for a discussion of clock time versus event time.
5. See, for example, Tinto (1993) for a discussion of how the inability to become socially integrated and make friends affects a student's decisions to leave college prior to attaining a degree. Students who do not go directly to college are less likely to go at all or to get a degree (p. 11).
6. Cooper et al. 1995.
7. Villaruel 1998.
8. Christopher, Johnson, and Roosa 1993.
9. Data we have collected on other samples of high school students suggest that it is not uncommon for them to mention school as a significant pressure in their lives, although Latino students tend to mention it less than others. It is uncommon, however, for this pressure to be as pervasive as it evidently was for these Puente students. This suggests that the program, while obviously effective in many ways, may have added some stress to the lives of many of these students. Whether this was ultimately a good thing is not known.
10. See McDonough, Korn, and Yamasaki (1997) for a discussion of the use of private counselors and their role in college admissions for upper-income students.

6. Beating the Odds and Going to College

1. U.S. Department of Education, National Center for Education Statistics 2007.
2. U.S. Department of Education, National Center for Education Statistics 2006.
3. This set of more than seventy interviews was previously published in Gándara (1995). All quotations in this chapter are from this study unless otherwise identified.
4. According to the National Center for Public Policy and Higher Education (2002), in 1981 loans accounted for 45 percent and grants for 52 percent of federal student financial aid. In 2000, loans represented 58 percent and grants were only 41 percent of aid.
5. Fry 2004.
6. See, for example, McCarty, Poole, and Rosenthal 2006; Phillips 1991.
7. Saenz, Oseguera, and Hurtado 2007.
8. Baum and Payea 2005.
9. See, for example, Crouse and Trusheim 1988 and 1991.
10. For more on the "myth of the model minority," see Lee 1996.
11. Zhou and Kim 2006.
12. Although the SAT does not ask students about their immigrant status, we infer from the SAT data that immigrant Asians are a larger portion of the pool because they have the highest percentage (12.8) of students who mark a language other than English as being their "best language." This is double the percentage for Mexican Americans, and is only comparable to "other Latinos," which is the category into which foreign-born Latinos would also fall.

13. Bridgman and Wendler (2005) show a very high correlation between taking rigorous courses and AP courses and scoring high on the SAT.
14. According to INEGI (Instituto Nacional de Estadistica Geografia e Informática), the average education level of individuals fifteen years old and older in Mexico in 2005 was 8.1 years, with about a four-month advantage for males over females.
15. Data cited in the newspaper *La Reforma,* August 24, 2007.
16. See, for example, Pew Hispanic Center/Kaiser Family Foundation 2004; Tornatzky, Cutler, and Lee 2002.
17. Gándara 1995.
18. Ibid., p. 52.
19. Grebler, Moore, and Guzman 1970.
20. Gándara 1995, p. 42.
21. See Durán, Enright, and Rock 1985; Durán, 1983; Pennock-Roman 1988.
22. Durán 1983. p. 67; see also Steele 1997.
23. Geiser and Santelices 2007.
24. For extensive discussion of this topic, see Lemann 1999.
25. Anastasi 1996.
26. Lucas 1999; McDonough 1997.
27. See, for example, Strenta and Elliott 1987.
28. See Perna 2007.
29. Brown and Theobald 1998.
30. Studies that have included data for Latino students tend to find that they participate in extracurricular activities at much lower rates than white students. See, for example, Brown and Theobald (1998) as well as Gibson et al. (2004), n. 46.
31. Gibson, Bejínez, Hidalgo, and Rolón 2004.
32. Ibid., p. 139.
33. Marsh and Kleitman 2002.
34. Everson and Millsap 2005.
35. Parent income and mother's education level were used as the socioeconomic status control variables.
36. There has been a plethora of research done in the last two decades on failing schools and the students who attend them. Latino and African American students are many times more likely to be assigned to segregated, failing schools than are Asians or white students. See, for example, Oakes, Mendoza, and Silver 2004.
37. Gándara 1995, p. 65.
38. Ibid.
39. Somers, Cofer, and Vanderputten 2002; Kao and Tienda 1998; Schneider and Stevenson 1999; Gándara, O'Hara, and Gutiérrez 2004; Swail, Cabrera, and Lee 2004; Adelman 2001.
40. Kao and Tienda 1998. The researchers also added focus groups to their quantitative analyses to tease out the meaning of their survey data.
41. Adelman 2001.
42. Swail, Cabrera, and Lee 2004, p. 14.
43. Kao and Tienda 1998, p. 375.
44. Mickelson 1990; Schneider and Stevenson 1999.
45. Gándara, O'Hara, and Gutiérrez 2004.

46. Schneider and Stevenson 1999.
47. Kao and Tienda 1998; Schneider and Stevenson 1999; Fry 2004.
48. Fry 2004.
49. Bowen and Bok 1998; Carnevale and Rose 2003; Golden 2006.
50. Hoachlander et al. 2003; Asian Americans tend to be "bimodal" in the sense that some Asian groups, such as Chinese, Japanese, and Korean, tend to do very well on all measures of academic achievement and to attend college at much higher rates than whites, but others, such as Southeast Asians, Hmong, Mien, and Cambodians, tend to score no better than Latinos on most measures of school achievement. Moreover, those groups that excel tend to eschew the community colleges, while the lower-performing Asian groups, like Latinos, are channeled into or "choose" to go to community colleges. See Lee (1996) for further discussion of this issue.
51. University of California Latino Eligibility Study 1997.
52. Coleman (1988) studied the way in which high school peer clusters influence members' behavior by establishing behavior norms; in his 1966 study, Coleman and his colleagues found that the most critical resource in schools that contributed to academic outcomes was the peers with whom students associated. Many other studies since that time have confirmed the important role of peers on a myriad of adolescent behaviors that ultimately affect college readiness and attitudes toward school and college. See, for example, Epstein and Karweit 1983; Steinberg 1996; Mehanet al. 1996.
53. McDonough 1997; quote on p. 137.
54. Gándara, O'Hara, and Gutiérrez 2004, p. 52.
55. Gándara 1995, pp. 76–77.
56. Ibid., p. 77.
57. Gándara, O'Hara, and Gutiérrez 2004.
58. Gándara 1995, p. 75.
59. Kao 1995.
60. Gándara 1995, p. 68.
61. Ibid., pp. 65–66.
62. AVID, Advancement via Individual Determination (oddly named, given that a core strategy of the program is to create supportive peer groups), was begun in the 1980s in San Diego, California, and has spread across the country and even abroad. It provides students with study skills, academic tutoring and support, and information about preparing for and applying to college in a self-contained high school class. Hugh Mehan and his colleagues have written extensively about the AVID program; see, for example, Mehan at al. 1996.
63. Gándara and López 1998.
64. Bandura 1997; Seligman 1990; Seligman et al. 1995.
65. Hackett et al. 1992; Pajares 1992; Miller 1995.
66. Bouchey and Harter 2005.
67. Colbeck, Cabrera, and Terenzini 2001, p. 176.
68. Anderson and Kim 2006.
69. Terenzini, Cabrera, and Bernal 2001; Horn and Chen 1998.
70. Golden 2006.
71. DeNavas-Walt, Proctor, and Lee 2006. From 2003 to 2005, the average income level for Latino households was $35,467, compared to $50,677 for whites and $59,877 for Asian Americans. Family sizes, however, differ consid-

erably, with Latinos having larger families and therefore more demands on family income.

72. See National Center for Public Policy and Higher Education 2006.
73. National Center for Public Policy and Higher Education 2002.
74. Zarate and Pachón 2006b.
75. Excelencia in Education and the Institute for Higher Education Policy 2005.
76. Thornburgh 2007, p. 42.
77. Gándara 1995, p. 115.
78. Ibid.
79. See National Center for Public Policy and Higher Education 2002.

7. The Costs and Effectiveness of Intervention

1. Fuller et al. 2007.
2. See Wiley and Wright 2004.
3. Mintrop 2004; Ladd 2001.
4. Gándara and Bial 2001.
5. Adelman 2001.
6. Swail 2004.
7. Ibid.
8. Ibid., p. 18.
9. While we obtained detailed budget data from many of the programs we discuss, we decided to only provide an overall cost estimate and per-student cost because every organization describes their costs differently and includes and excludes different cost elements. (There is no standard reporting form for program budgets.) In addition, many actual costs are not reported. For example, many programs rely on outside university or government organizations to provide large portions of their infrastructure costs, such as buildings and maintenance, that are not included in their budgets. Consequently, the per-student costs shown here, provided by the programs themselves, are most useful for broad comparison with other similar types of programs. The reader must be cognizant of the limitations of these estimates, and that in most cases, they represent "stand-alone" versions of the programs that would likely cost much more to implement than the estimates here might suggest.
10. Ramey and Campbell 1984, 1991; Campbell and Ramey 1995.
11. For the quote, and details on the Abecedarian project, see http://www.fpg.unc.edu/~abc.
12. Ibid.
13. Campbell and Ramey 1995.
14. Ibid.
15. Campbell and Ramey 1995, p. 748.
16. Ibid.
17. Masse and Barnett 2002.
18. Ibid.
19. See, for example, Irish, Schumacher, and Lombardi 2004.
20. Office of Head Start 2007.
21. Puma et al. 2005. The congressionally mandated study is being conducted across eighty-four nationally representative grantee agencies. Approximately five thousand three- and four-year-old children applying for Head Start were

randomly assigned to either a Head Start group with access to Head Start services or a non–Head Start group that could enroll in the available community (non–Head Start) services that the agency or organization provides. Data collection began in 2002 and continued through 2006. Cognitive and social-emotional development, health, and parenting practices were the primary areas measured in this study. The first-year results showed a marginally significant effect on the domains of parenting practices, health, and cognitive development.

22. Ibid., p. 3.
23. See, for example, Karoly and Bigelow 2005; Karoly et al. 1998; Rumberger and Tran 2006.
24. See Currie and Thomas 1995; Rumberger and Tran 2006.
25. Currie and Thomas 1995.
26. Levin et al. 2007.
27. Ibid., p. 189.
28. See, for example, Fuller 2007. The book criticizes the standardization of preschool experiences and the bureaucratization of early childhood programs, but nonetheless argues for supporting culturally sensitive child development "programs." Garcia and Gonzalez 2006.
29. Per-student public education expenditures are notoriously difficult to compute because of differences of opinion about what should be included and excluded in such cost estimates. Both the National Center for Education Statistics (http://www.nces.ed.gov) and the National Education Association (http://www.nea.org), however, report average per-pupil expenditures in the United States in 2006 at just below $9,000.
30. Karoly and Bigelow 2005.
31. Rolnick and Grunewald, 2008 p. 4.
32. Established with funding from the Sallie Mae Fund as part of their $1 million statewide education initiative, Kids to College is an early outreach program designed to bring early awareness of the importance of higher education by introducing sixth-graders to college opportunities. Sixth grade classrooms are paired with a local college or university to participate in a six-session curriculum that combines hands-on activities with information on careers, college life, and a range of options for education beyond high school. The program culminates with a visit to the partner college for students and parents or guardians.
33. For details on the program, see http://www.successforall.net.
34. See Slavin and Cheung (2004) for results of the bilingual versus English-only Success for All curriculum study (first- and second-grade students were evaluated).
35. Calderón 2006.
36. See, for example, Slavin and Fashola (1998) for a summary review of earlier evaluations, and Slavin and Cheung (2004) for a more recent review of Success for All program evaluations.
37. Borman and Hewes (2002) conducted a quasi-experimental study focusing on a cost-benefit analysis of 1,388 Success students from five Success for All schools and compared it to 1,848 students from a control group of schools. The researchers found significant differences in reading and reduced special education placements in favor of the Success for All students.

38. Borman et al. 2007.
39. Chambers et al. 2004
40. Opuni 1999.
41. See Snipes, Holton, and Doolittle 2006; and Snipes et al. 2006. These evaluations were commissioned by the Ford Foundation and included five district sites.
42. Gándara et al. 1998, p. 7.
43. Ibid., p. 11.
44. See Belfield and Levin 2007.
45. Gándara and Bial 2001.
46. Kahne and Bailey 1999.
47. TCC Group 2004.
48. Ibid., p. 4.
49. Ibid.
50. Ibid., pp. 27, 30.
51. Perna and Swail 1998; Chaney, Lewis, and Farris 1995.
52. Gándara et al. 1998.
53. Ibid., p. 31.
54. Gándara et al. (2001) annually surveyed about two thousand students (half Puente, half non-Puente) about attitudes toward school, college, peer influences, and family support; 144 students were followed annually (half Puente, half controls) from entry into high school to graduation four years later to track test scores, GPA, course completions, and college enrollments; and 28 high school students participated in an in-depth case study of Puente from three school sites and were interviewed and observed several times a year over four years. Several of those students were followed up at two and four years after high school graduation.
55. Ibid.
56. See Upward Bound website: http://www.ed.gov/programs/trioupbound/ubgrantees2006.pdf.
57. Meyers et al. 2004.
58. Ibid., p. xviii.
59. Ibid., p. 25.
60. Ibid., p. xviii.
61. Meyers et al. 2004, p. 25.
62. Ibid. The researchers acknowledge, for example, that the evaluation design sought to understand the "value added" of Upward Bound because "many of the students assigned to both the treatment and control groups participate in pre-college services other than regular Upward Bound." Thus students in both the control and the treatment groups are likely to have already been engaged in a college-going culture within their high school.
63. See, for example, Adelman 1999.
64. See http://www.ed.gov/programs/trioupbound/funding.html.
65. Gándara and Bial (2001) reviewed the research on college-access programs and which features appeared to have the greatest effects. They found considerable support in the literature for pre-college summer bridge programs.
66. For more information, see the AVID website: http://www.avidonline.org/info.
67. Gándara et al. 1998; Guthrie and Guthrie 2000.
68. Gándara et al. 1998, p. 22.

69. Another study, Guthrie and Guthrie (2000), assessed 1,029 AVID middle school and high school students, finding that AVID "positions students well for life after high school," with the vast majority of the sample assessed enrolled in a college or university. While the researchers did not disaggregate the sample and findings by race and ethnicity, their evaluation also found that over 80 percent of AVID graduates enrolled right after high school and approximately 85 percent of the first cohort and 70 percent of the second cohort were on track to graduate from college within five years.

70. Conversation with Judy Riffle, vice president for finance, and Corey Suarez, contracts manager, AVID Center, April 2007, San Diego.

71. Avid Center 2007, http://www.avidonline.org (accessed May 1, 2008).

72. For the publication *Capturing Latino Students in the Academic Pipeline,* the evaluator was asked to provide cost estimates based on his knowledge of the program components. He estimated $625, noting that a significant amount of the actual cost was still not included because schools provided a lot of support that did not appear on the AVID ledgers.

73. We have seen no college-access studies that track pre-post SAT or ACT scores based on test prep before or after test preparation support, so this comment is speculative.

74. Gándara and Bial 2001.

75. Oakes 1995; Romo and Falbo 1996; McDonough 1997.

76. Atkinson, Jennings, and Livingston 1990; McDonough 1997.

77. Slavin and Karweit 1985; Walberg 1993; Carroll 1963.

78. See Gándara and Maxwell-Jolly 1999 for extensive discussion of this program and its evaluation.

79. Mehan et al. 1996.

80. Grossman and Tierney 1998; Rumberger and Brenner 2002.

81. Rogers and Taylor 1997; Grossman and Garry 1997.

82. Redd 2003.

83. College Board 2008.

84. National Center for Public Policy and Higher Education 2002.

85. Moles 1982, pp. 44–47; Vaden-Kiernan and McManus 2005.

86. See, for example, Henderson and Berla 1994.

87. Gándara, Maxwell-Jolly, and Driscoll 2005.

88. See Chrispeels, Wang, and Rivero 2000.

89. Belfield and Levin 2007. Levin, Belfield, Muenning, and Rouse 2007a.

8. *Rescatando Sueños*—Rescuing Dreams

1. National Center for Public Policy and Higher Education 2005, quotation on p. 1.

2. Di 2007.

3. Martinez 2000, p. 87.

4. See also Grissmer, Flanagan, and Williamson 1998.

5. Martinez 2000, p. 127

6. See Greenfield 1998.

7. González and Moll 2002.

8. Wong-Fillmore 1991.

9. See Fuller 2007.

10. Barnett et al. 2007.

11. Gándara, Maxwell-Jolly, and Driscoll (2005) conducted a year-long commissioned study of a Northern California district's program for English learners. This unpublished study yielded surprising findings, including the minuscule amount of time that English learners were afforded opportunities to speak or write in English (even though all of the district's teachers were "highly qualified" and many had sophisticated understandings of the needs and appropriate strategies for educating English learners). One of the study's conclusions was that even in a very successful school district, the challenges of teaching English-learner students place very large burdens on teachers, especially when teachers must address the needs of students at various skill levels in more than one language.

12. See Gándara, Gutiérrez, and O'Hara (2001), in which English learners were segregated into a separate part of the campus and clustered together in the "free lunch" cafeteria area during lunch break, so that they seldom had contact with the English speakers in their school. English learners noted that other Latinos who spoke English were as hostile to them, or more so, than the white students on campus.

13. Robin, Frede, and Barnett 2006. This study, while relatively small (about 340 children were included), tested the outcomes for eight-hour versus two-and-a-half- to three-hour preschool programs on low-income, largely Latino students. The children were randomly assigned to the programs through a lottery, which added to the strength of the findings. Those children in the extended-day preschool significantly outperformed the shorter-day-preschool students in vocabulary, math, and literacy skills, and approached national norms. Moreover, with a somewhat extended kindergarten program (two additional hours daily more than the controls), they were able to maintain a significant advantage in these academic areas through the last testing at first grade.

14. See Gándara and Rumberger 2008.

15. See Short 2007.

16. See Rumberger, Gándara, and Merino 2000.

17. Orfield and McArdle 2006.

18. McArdle 2003.

19. "Why Retreat on Affordable Housing Ordinance?" Editorial, *Sacramento Bee,* August 5, 2007, p. E6. The editorial urges the county supervisors to resist efforts by the building industry to undermine the ordinance (the industry wanted to cluster low-income housing or shift the burden of actually constructing the housing to the county). Bold policies like Sacramento's are always vulnerable to political influence.

20. See the discussion of the Gautreaux experiment in Rosenbaum et al. (2005); and Orfield and Eaton (1996), pp. 325–326.

21. See Kling and Liebman 2004.

22. Ibid.

23. Fowler-Finn 2001.

24. Whalen 2002; Hayle 1997.

25. Geierstanger and Amaral 2005.

26. California Department of Education 1997.

27. See Rumualdi 2000.

28. Research on teacher turnover, or loss from the teaching field, shows that half of new teachers leave the field within five years (see Darling-Hammond 2004). Because many new teachers are young women beginning families of their own, some eventually return to teaching, but the schools that serve most Latino children will attract those with the least experience and seniority. Moreover, teachers who have school-age children of their own are more inclined to teach near where they live so they can be accessible to their own families, and most teachers do not live in segregated black and Latino neighborhoods. See Murnane et al. 1991.

29. See, for example, Gándara and Maxwell-Jolly 2005.

30. Murnane et al. 1991.

31. Darling-Hammond, L., and G. Sykes 2003.

32. Martinez 2000.

33. National Commission on Teaching and America's Future 2007. The study, which estimates teacher turnover as high as 20 percent annually in urban districts, considered the costs of recruiting, hiring, and training teachers in arriving at its estimates. http://www.nctaf.org.

34. Data from the Organisation for Economic Cooperation and Development (OECD) for 2005, published in 2007, show that almost half of the member nations outperform the United States with respect to percent of population completing college degrees. See Education at a Glance at http://www .oecd .org.

35. The Center for Applied Linguistics maintains a database of two-way immersion programs. But programs contribute information about themselves on a voluntary basis; many programs are known to exist that have not listed themselves with the center. It is thus impossible to know how many programs exist across the country. The list, however, can be accessed at http://www.cal.org, under "Resources."

36. See a discussion of this topic in Genesee et al. (2006), esp. pp. 200–205.

37. See Genesee and Gándara (1999) for a discussion of the issue of intercultural relations and attitudes toward other language speakers.

38. Sometimes dual-immersion programs are distinguished as those programs that teach two languages but do not necessarily incorporate the speakers of both languages in the same classroom.

39. Valdés 1997.

40. Here "late exit" refers to programs in which students are taught in their primary language through the upper elementary grades, with the goal of achieving true biliteracy. See Lindholm-Leary and Borsato 2006, p. 201.

41. See Gándara and Maxwell-Jolly 1999.

42. Fischer 2008. Fischer reports an overall 7 percent decline in enrollment of Pell grant students in four-year institutions between 2004 and 2005 and 2006 and 2007, and an average 1 to 2 percentage point decline even at the wealthiest colleges that can afford to subsidize poor students.

43. Heller 2005.

44. See Fitzgerald and Kane (2006, pp. 53–73) for a thoughtful discussion of ways to address the financial impediments to going to college for low-income students.

45. See Vernez and Mizell 2001.

46. Baum and Ma 2007.

REFERENCES

Abedi, J., M. Courtney, and S. Leon. 2003. *Effectiveness and Validity of Accommodations for English Language Learners in Large-Scale Assessments* (CSE technical report 608). Los Angeles: University of California, National Center for Research on Evaluation, Standards, and Student Testing.

Abedi, J., C. Lord, C. Hofstetter, and E. Baker. 2000. "Impact of Accommodation Strategies on English Language Learners' Test Performance." *Educational Measurement: Issues and Practice* 19, no. 3: 16–26.

Adelman, C. 1999. *Answers in the Tool Box: Academic Intensity, Attendance Patterns, and Bachelor's Degree Attainment.* Washington, D.C.: U.S. Department of Education, Office of Educational Research and Improvement.

———. 2001. "Putting on the Glitz: How Tales from a Few Elite Institutions Form America's Impressions about Higher Education." *Connection: New England's Journal of Higher Education and Economic Development* 15, no. 3: 24–30.

Alexander, K. L., M. A. Cook, and E. L. McDill. 1978. "Curriculum Tracking and Educational Stratification." *American Sociological Review* 43: 47–66.

Alexander, K. L., D. Entwisle, and M. Thompson. 1987. "School Performance, Status Relations, and the Structure of Sentiment: Bringing the Teacher Back In." *American Sociological Review* 52: 665–682.

Alon, S., and M. Tienda. 2003. "Hispanics and the 'Misfit' Hypothesis: Differentials in College Graduation Rates by Institutional Selectivity." Paper presented at the Color Lines conference, Boston, organized by the Civil Rights Project of Harvard University, September 1.

———. 2005. "Assessing the Mismatch Hypothesis: Differentials in College Graduation Rates by Institutional Selectivity." *Sociology of Education* 78, no. 4: 294–315.

Anastasi, A. 1996. *Psychological Testing,* 7th ed. New York: Macmillan.

Anderson, E., and D. Kim. 2006. *Increasing the Success of Minority Students in Science and Technology.* Washington, D.C.: American Council on Education.

Atkinson, D., R. Jennings, and L. Livingston. 1990. "Minority Students' Reasons for Not Seeking Counseling and Suggestions for Improvement." *Journal of College Student Development* 1: 42–50.

Attewell, P., and J. Battle. 1999. "Home Computers and School Performance." *The Information Society* 15: 1–10.

August, D., and K. Hakuta. 1997. *Improving Schooling for Language Minority Children: A Research Agenda.* Washington, D.C.: National Research Council, Institute of Medicine.

August, D., and T. Shanahan, eds. 2006. *Developing Literacy in Second-Language Learners: Report of the National Literacy Panel on Language-Minority Children and Youth.* Mahwah, N.J.: Lawrence Erlbaum. http://www.erlbaum.com/august.

Baker, K., and A. de Kanter. 1981. *Effectiveness of Bilingual Education: A Review of the Literature.* Washington, D.C.: U.S. Department of Education, Office of Planning, Budget, and Evaluation.

―――. 1983. "Federal Policy and the Effectiveness of Bilingual Education," In Baker and de Kanter, eds., *Bilingual Education: A Reappraisal of Federal Policy.* Lexington, Mass.: Lexington Books, pp. 33–86.

Bakke v. Regents of the University of California. 1978. 438 U.S. 265.

Bandura, A. 1997. *Self-Efficacy: The Exercise of Control.* New York: W. H. Freeman.

Barnett, W. S., J. T. Hustedt, K. B. Robin, and K. L. Schulman. 2005. *The State of Preschool: 2005 State Preschool Yearbook.* New Brunswick, N.J.: National Institute for Early Education Research, 2005. http://nieer.org/yearbook.

Barnett, W. S., D. J. Yarosz, J. Thomas, K. Jung, and D. Blanco. 2007. "Two-Way and Monolingual English Immersion in Preschool Education: An Experimental Comparison." *Early Childhood Research Quarterly* 22: 277–293.

Baron, R. M., D. Y. H. Tom, and H. M. Cooper. 1985. "Social Class, Race, and Teacher Expectations." In J. B. Dusek, ed., *Teacher Expectancies,* pp. 251–269. Hillsdale, N.J.: Lawrence Erlbaum.

Barr, R., and R. Dreeben. 1983. *How Schools Work.* Chicago: University of Chicago Press.

Bartolome, L. 1994. "Teaching Strategies: Their Possibilities and Limitations." In B. McLeod, ed., *Language Learning: Educating Linguistically Diverse Students.* Albany, N.Y.: State University of New York Press.

Barton, P. 2003. *Hispanics in Science and Engineering: A Matter of Assistance and Persistence.* Princeton, N.J.: Educational Testing Service.

Batalova, J., 2008. "Mexican Immigrants in the United States." Washington D.C.: Migration Policy Institute. http://www.migrationinformation.org/USfocus/display .cfm?id=679 (accessed April 23, 2008).

Bates, E., D. Thala, B. Finlay, and B. Clancy. 2003. "Early Language Development and Its Neural Correlates." In S. J. Segalowitz and I. Rapin, eds., *Handbook of Neuropsychology,* 2d ed., pt. 2: 2–42. Amsterdam: Elsevier Science.

Baum, S., and J. Ma. 2007. *Education Pays, 2007: The Benefits of Higher Education for Individuals and Society.* New York: College Board.

Baum, S., and K. Payea. 2005. "Trends in College Pricing 2005." *College Board Trends in Higher Education Series.* New York: College Board. http://www.collegeboard .com/trends.

Baumrind, D. 1989. "Rearing Competent Children." In W. Damon, ed., *Child Development Today and Tomorrow,* pp. 349–378. San Francisco: Jossey-Bass.

Beauvais, F., E. Chavez, E. Oetting, J. Deffenbacher, and G. Cornell. 1996. "Drug Use, Violence, and Victimization among White American, Mexican American, and American Indian Dropouts, Students with Academic Problems, and Students in Good Academic Standing." *Journal of Counseling Psychology* 43: 292–299.

Belfield, C., and H. Levin. 2007a. *The Price We Pay.* Washington, D.C.: Brookings Institution Press.

―――. 2007b. *The Return on Investment for Improving California's High School Graduation Rate.* Santa Barbara, Calif.: California Dropout Research Project. http:// www.lmri.ucsb.edu/dropouts/pubs.htm.

Bellah, R., R. Madsen, W. Sullivan, A. Swidler, and S. Tipton. 1985. *Habits of the Heart: Individualism and Commitment in American Life.* Berkeley: University of California Press.

Benard, B. 1996. "Fostering Resilience in Urban Schools." In B. Williams, ed.,

Closing the Achievement Gap: A Vision for Changing Beliefs and Practices, pp. 25–33. Baltimore: Association for Supervision and Curriculum Development.

Berliner, D. 2006. "Our Impoverished View of Educational Reform." *Teachers College Record* 108: 949–995.

Betts, J., K. Rueben, and A. Danenberg. 2000. *Equal Resources, Equal Outcomes? The Distribution of School Resources and Student Achievement in California.* San Francisco: Public Policy Institute of California. http://www.ppic.org/main/home.asp.

Bialystok, E., F. I. M. Craik, R. Klein, and M. Viswanathan. 2004. "Bilingualism, Aging, and Cognitive Control: Evidence from the Simon Task." *Psychology and Aging* 19: 290–303.

Bialystok, E., and K. Hakuta. 1994. *In Other Words: The Science and Psychology of Second Language Acquisition.* New York: Basic Books.

Blasé, J., and J. Blasé. 2001. *Empowering Teachers: What Successful Principals Do,* 2d ed. Thousand Oaks, Calif.: Corwin Press.

Borjas, G. J. 1995. "The Economic Benefits from Immigration." *Journal of Economic Perspectives* 9, no. 2: 3–22.

———. 2003. "The Labor Demand Curve Is Downward Sloping: Reexamining the Impacts of Immigration on the Labor Market." *Quarterly Journal of Economics* 118: 1335–1374.

———. 2005. *Labor Economics,* 3d ed. New York: McGraw-Hill.

Borman, G. D., and G. M. Hewes. 2002. "The Long-Term Effects and Cost-Effectiveness of Success for All." *Educational Evaluation and Policy Analysis* 24, no. 4: 243–266.

Borman, G. D., R. Slavin, A. Cheung, A. Chamberlain, N. Madden, and B. Chambers. 2005. "The National Randomized Field Trial of Success for All: Second-Year Outcomes." *American Education Research Journal* 42, no. 4: 673–696.

———. 2005. "Success for All: First-Year Results from the National Randomized Field Trial." *Educational Evaluation and Policy Analysis* 27, no. 1: 1–22.

———. 2007. "Final Reading Outcomes of the National Randomized Field Trial of Success for All." *American Educational Research Association* 44, no. 3: 701–731.

Borman, G. D., S. Stringheld, and L. Rachuba. 2000. *Advancing Minority High Achievement: National Trends and Promising Programs and Practices.* New York: College Board.

Bouchey, H. A., and S. Harter. 2005. "Reflected Appraisals, Academic Self-Perceptions, and Math/Science Performance during Early Adolescence." *Journal of Educational Psychology* 97, no. 4: 673–686.

Bourdieu, P. 1973. "Cultural Reproduction and Social Reproduction." In R. Brown, ed., *Knowledge, Education and Cultural Change: Papers in the Sociology of Education,* pp. 71–112. London: Tavistock.

Bowen, W. G., and D. Bok. 1998. *The Shape of the River: Long-Term Consequences of Considering Race in College and University Admissions.* Princeton, N.J.: Princeton University Press.

Bowles, S., H. Gintis, and M. O. Groves, eds. 2005. *Unequal Chances: Family Background and Economic Success.* Princeton, N.J.: Princeton University Press.

Bridgeland, J., J. Dilulio Jr., and K. Morison. 2006. *The Silent Epidemic: Perspectives of High-School Dropouts.* A report by Civic Enterprises in conjunction with Peter D. Hart Research Associates for the Bill and Melinda Gates Foundation. http://www.civicenterprisess.net/pdfs/thesilentepidemic3-06.pdf.

Bridgman, B., and C. Wendler. 2005. *Characteristics of Minority Students Who Excel on the SAT and in the Classroom.* Princeton, N.J.: Educational Testing Service.

Brisk, M. 1998. *Bilingual Education: From Compensatory to Quality Schooling.* Mahwah, N.J.: Lawrence Erlbaum.

Brooks-Gunn, J., J. Denner, and P. Klebanov. 1995. "Families and Neighborhoods as Contexts for Education." In E. Flaxman and A. Passow, eds., *Changing Populations, Changing Schools: Ninety-fourth Yearbook for the National Society for the Study of Education,* pt. 2. Chicago: National Society for the Study of Education.

Brophy, J. E., and T. L. Good. 1974. *Teacher-Student Relationships: Causes and Consequences.* New York: Holt, Rinehart & Winston.

Brown, B., and W. Theobald. 1998. "Learning Context beyond the Classroom: Extracurricular Activities, Community Organizations, and Peer Groups." In K. Borman and B. Schneider, eds., *The Adolescent Years: Social Influences and Educational Challenges* (Ninety-seventh Yearbook of the National Society of the Study of Education), pp. 109–141. Chicago: University of Chicago Press.

Bye Bye Bilingual. 2000. Film. Available in both video stream and transcript at http://www.hoover.org/multimedia/uk/3412956.html.

Calderón, M. 2006. "Quality Instruction in Reading for English Language Learners." In K. Tellez and H. Waxman, eds., *Preparing Quality Educators for English Language Learners: Research, Policies, and Practices,* pp. 121–144. Mahwah, N.J.: Lawrence Erlbaum.

California Department of Education. 1997. "Healthy Start Works." *Quarterly Newsletter for Healthy Start and Friends.* http://hsfo.ucdavis.edu/Download/HS-Works_1997March.pdf.

———. 2005. *R-30 Language Census, 2005.* http://data1.cde.ca.gov/dataquest (accessed September 25, 2006).

———. 2006. *STAR Program Results.* http://www.cde.ca.gov/nr/ne/yr06/yr06rel89.asp.

———. 2007. *Fast Facts 2007.* http://www.cde.ca.gov.

California Department of Finance. 2007. *Population Projections, 2007.* http://www.dof.ca.gov/html/demograp/reportspapers/projections/p3/p3.php.

California Teachers Association v. State Board of Education. 2000. Opinion of the Court of Appeals of the Ninth Circuit, Argued and Submitted October 10. Pasadena, Calif.

Campbell, F., and C. Ramey. 1995. "Cognitive and School Outcomes for High-Risk African-American Students at Middle Adolescence: Positive Effects of Early Intervention." *American Educational Research Journal* 32, no. 4: 743–772.

Campbell, F., C. Ramey, E. Pungello, J. Sparling, and S. Miller-Johnson. 2002. "Early Childhood Education: Young Adult Outcomes from the Abecedarian Project." *Applied Developmental Science* 6, no. 1: 42–57.

Capps, R., M. Fix, J. Murray, J. Ost, J. S. Passel, and S. Herwantoro. 2005. *The New Demography of America's Schools: Immigration and the No Child Left Behind Act.* Washington, D.C.: Urban Institute. http://www.fcd-us.org/usr_doc/HealthandWellbeingofYoungChildrenbrief.pdf.

Capps, R., M. Fix, J. Ost, J. Reardon-Anderson, and J. S. Passel. 2004. *The Health and Well-Being of Young Children of Immigrants.* Washington, D.C.: Urban Institute. http://www.urban.org/UploadedPDF/311139_ChildrenImmigrants.pdf.

Carbonaro, W. J., and A. Gamoran. 2002. "The Production of Achievement Inequality in High School English." *American Educational Research Journal* 39: 801–827.

Card, D. 2001. "Immigrant Inflows, Native Outflows, and the Local Labor Market Impacts of Higher Immigration." *Journal of Labor Economics* 19, no. 1: 22–64.

Carnevale, A. P., and S. J. Rose. 2003. *Socioeconomic Status, Race/Ethnicity and Selective College Admissions.* New York: The Century Foundation. http://www.tcf.org/Publications/Education/carnevale_rose.pdf.

Carpenter-Huffman, P., and M. Samulon. 1981. *Case Studies of Delivery of Bilingual Education.* Santa Monica: RAND Corporation.

Carroll, J. 1963. "A Model for School Learning." *Teachers College Record* 64: 723–733.

Carter, T. 1970. *Mexican Americans in the Southwest: A History of Educational Neglect.* New York: College Board.

Chambers, B., R. E. Slavin, N. A. Madden, A. Cheung, and R, Gifford. 2004. *Effects of Success for All with Embedded Video on the Beginning Reading Achievement of Hispanic Children.* Baltimore: Johns Hopkins University, Center for Research on the Education of Students Placed at Risk.

Chambers, J., and T. Parrish. 1992. *Meeting the Challenge of Diversity: An Evaluation of Programs for Pupils with Limited Proficiency in English,* vol. 4: *Cost of Programs and Services for LEP Students.* Berkeley, Calif.: BW Associates.

Chaney, B., L. Lewis, and E. Farris. 1995. *Programs at Higher Education Institutions for Disadvantaged Pre-College Students.* NCES-96-230. Washington, D.C.: U.S. Government Printing Office.

Chavez, L. 1991. *Out of the Barrio: Toward a New Politics of Hispanic Assimilation.* New York: Basic Books.

———. 1998. *The Color Bind: California's Battle to End Affirmative Action.* Berkeley: University of California Press.

Children's Defense Fund. 2000. *Fact Sheet on Head Start.* Washington, D.C.: Children's Defense Fund. http://www.childrensdefense.org.

Chrispeels, J., and E. Rivero. 2000. *Engaging Latino Families for Student Success: Understanding the Process and Impact of Providing Training to Parents.* Paper presented at the annual meeting of the American Educational Research Association, New Orleans.

Chrispeels, J., J. Wang, and E. Rivero. 2000. *Evaluation Summary of the Impact of the Parent Institute for Quality Education on Parents' Engagement with Their Children's Schooling.* Report submitted to PIQE Foundation. http://www.piqe.org/Assets/Home/ChrispeelEvaluation.htm.

Christopher, F. S., D. C. Johnson, and M. W. Roosa. 1993. "Family, Individual, and Social Correlates of Early Hispanic Adolescent Sexual Expression." *Journal of Sex Research* 30: 54–61.

Chunn, E. W. 1989. "Sorting Black Students for Success and Failure: The Inequity of Ability Grouping and Tracking." *Urban League Review* 2: 93–106.

Clark, R. 1984. *Family Life and School Achievement: Why Poor Black Children Succeed or Fail.* Chicago: University of Chicago Press.

Colbeck, C., A. Cabrera, and P. Terenzini. 2001. "Learning Professional Confidence: Linking Teachers Practices, Students' Self Perceptions, and Gender." *Review of Higher Education* 24, no. 2: 173–191.

Coleman, J. S., E. Campbell, C. Hobson, J. McPartland, A. Mood, F. Weinfeld, and R. York. 1966. *Equality and Educational Opportunity.* Washington, D.C.: U.S. Government Printing Office.

———. 1987a. "Families and Schools." *Educational Researcher* 16, no. 6: 32–38.

————. 1987b. "Social Capital and the Development of Youth." *Momentum* 18: 6–8.

————. 1988. "Social Capital in the Creation of Human Capital." *American Journal of Sociology* 94: 95–120.

Coley, R. 2001. *Differences in the Gender Gap: Comparisons across Racial/Ethnic Groups in Education and Work.* Princeton, N.J.: Educational Testing Service.

College Board. 2004. *SAT Student Descriptive Questionnaire.* New York: College Board.

————. 2008. *Trends in College Pricing, 2007.* New York: College Board.

Connerly, W. 2000. *Creating Equal: My Fight against Race Preferences.* New York: Encounter Books.

Contreras, F. 2005. "The Reconstruction of Merit Post Proposition 209." *Educational Policy.* Thousand Oaks, Calif.: SAGE Publications.

Contreras, F., and P. Gándara. 2006. "Latinas/os in the Ph.D. Pipeline: A Case of Historical and Contemporary Exclusion." In J. Castellanos and A. Gloria, eds., *Journey to a Ph.D.: The Latina/o Experience in Higher Education.* Sterling, Va.: Stylus Publishing.

Cooper, C. R., J. F. Jackson, M. Azmitia, E. M. Lopez, and N. Dunbar. 1995. "Bridging Students' Multiple Worlds: African American and Latino Youth in Academic Outreach Programs." In R. F. Macías and R. G. García Ramos, eds., *Changing Schools for Changing Students: An Anthology of Research on Language Minorities,* pp. 211–234. Santa Barbara: University of California Linguistic Minority Research Institute.

Coulton, C. J., J. E. Korbin, M. Su, and J. Chow. 1995. "Community Level Factors and Child Maltreatment Rates." *Child Development* 66: 1262–1276.

Crawford, J. 2004. *Educating English Learners: Language Diversity in the Classroom.* 5th ed. Los Angeles: Bilingual Educational Services.

Crosnoe, R. 2006a. "Health and the Education of Children from Race/Ethnic Minority and Immigrant Families." *Journal of Health and Social Behavior* 47: 77–79.

————. 2006b. *Mexican Roots, American Schools.* Stanford, Calif.: Stanford University Press.

Crouse, J., and D. Trusheim. 1988. *The Case against the SAT.* Chicago: University of Chicago Press.

————. 1991. "How Colleges Can Correctly Determine Selection Benefits from the SAT." *Harvard Educational Review* 61: 125–147.

Crowley, S. 2003. "The Affordable Housing Crisis: Residential Mobility of Poor Families and School Mobility of Poor Children." *Journal of Negro Education* 72: 22–38. http://www.ets.org/Media/Research/pdf/PICGENDER.pdf.

Cummins, J. 1981. "The Role of Primary Language Development in Promoting Educational Success for Language Minority Students." In *Schooling and Language Minority Students: A Theoretical Framework.* Los Angeles: California State University Evaluation, Dissemination, and Assessment Center.

————. 1984. *Bilingualism and Special Education: Issues in Assessment and Pedagogy.* Clevedon, Eng.: Multilingual Matters.

————. 2001. "Empowering Minority Students: A Framework for Intervention." *Harvard Educational Review* 71, no. 4: 649–675.

Currie, J., and D. Thomas. 1995. "Does Head Start Make a Difference?" *American Economic Review* 85, no. 3: 341–364. http://citeseer.ist.psu.edu/currie95does.html.

Cziko, G. 1992. "The Evaluation of Bilingual Education: From Necessity and Probability to Possibility." *Educational Researcher* 21: 10–15.

Danoff, M., B. Arias, G. Coles, and B. Everett. 1978. *Evaluation of the Impact of ESEA Title VII Spanish/English Bilingual Education Program.* Palo Alto, Calif.: American Institutes of Research.

Darling-Hammond, L. 2002. *Redesigning Schools: What Matters and What Works.* Stanford, Calif.: School Redesign Network at Stanford University.

———. 2004. "Inequality and the Right to Learn: Access to Qualified Teachers in California's Public Schools." *Teachers College Record* 106, no. 10: 1936–1966.

Darling, N., and L. Steinberg. 1997. "Community Influences on Adolescent Achievement and Deviance." In J. Brooks-Gunn, G. Duncan, and L. Aber, eds., *Neighborhood Poverty,* vol. 2: *Policy Implications in Studying Neighborhoods.* New York: Russell Sage Foundation.

Darling-Hammond, L., and G. Sykes. 2003. "Wanted: A National Teacher Supply Policy for Education. The Right Way to Meet the 'Highly Qualified Teacher' Challenge." *Educational Policy Analysis Archives* 11, no. 3. http://epaa.asu.edu/epaa/v11n33.

Davis-Kean, P. E. 2005. "The Influence of Parent Education and Family Income on Child Achievement: The Indirect Role of Parental Expectations and the Home Environment." *Journal of Family Psychology* 19, no. 2: 294–304.

DeBell, M., and C. Chapman. 2006. *Computer and Internet Use by Students in 2003.* Report prepared by the U.S. Department of Education Institute of Education Sciences. http://www.wfaa.com/sharedcontent/dws/img/09-06/0906ncesreport.pdf.

DeFreitas, G. 1995. *Immigration, Inequality, and Policy Alternatives.* New York: Russell Sage Foundation.

Delgado-Bernal, D. 1999. "Chicana/o Education from the Civil Rights Era to the Present." In J. Moreno, ed., *The Elusive Quest for Equality,* pp. 77–108. Cambridge: Harvard Education Press.

Delgado-Gaitán, C. 1990. *Literacy for Empowerment: The Role of Parents in Children's Education.* London: Falmer Press.

De Los Santos, A. G., Jr., and Gerardo E. De Los Santos. 2003. "Hispanic-Serving Institutions in the Twenty-first Century: Overview, Challenges, and Opportunities." *Journal of Hispanic Higher Education* 10, no. 2: 377–391.

DeNavas-Walt, C., B. D. Proctor, and C. H. Lee. 2006. *Income, Poverty, and Health Insurance Coverage in the United States: 2005.* Current Population Report, U.S. Census Bureau. http://www.census.gov/prod/2006pubs/p60-231.pdf.

Di, Zhu Xiao. 2007. *Growing Wealth, Inequality, and Housing in the United States.* Publication of the Joint Center for Housing Studies, Harvard University, W07-1. http://www.jchs.harvard.edu/publications/markets/w07-1.pdf.

DiMaggio, P. 1982. "Cultural Capital and School Success: The Impact of Status Culture Participation on the Grades of U.S. High School Students." *American Sociological Review* 47: 189–201.

Donovan, M., and C. Cross, eds. 2002. *Minority Students in Special and Gifted Education: Committee on Minority Representation in Special Education.* Washington, D.C.: National Academy Press.

D'Souza, D. 1995. *The End of Racism: Principles for a Multicultural Society.* New York: Free Press.

Durán, R. P. 1983. *Hispanics' Education and Background: Predictors of College Achievement.* New York: College Entrance Examination Board.

Durán, R. P., K. Enright, and D. Rock. 1985. *Language Factors and Hispanic Freshmen's Student Profile.* New York: College Entrance Examination Board.

Earthman, Glen I. 2002. *School Facility Conditions and Student Academic Achievement.* Los Angeles: UCLA's Institute for Democracy, Education, and Access (IDEA). http://www.idea.gseis.ucla.edu/publications/williams/reports/pdfs/wws08-Earthman.pdf.

Elliott, S. D., S. Menard, B. Rankin, A. Elliott, D. Huizinga, and W. J. Wilson. 2006. *Good Kids from Bad Neighborhoods: Successful Development in Social Context.* Cambridge, Eng.: Cambridge University Press.

Elmore, R. 2005. *School Reform from the Inside Out: Policy, Practice and Performance.* Cambridge: Harvard Education Press.

Entwisle, D., K. Alexander, and L. S. Olson. 1997. *Children, Schools and Inequality.* Boulder, Colo.: Westview.

———. 2001. "Keep the Faucet Flowing: Summer Learning and Home Environment." *American Educator* 25: 10–15, 47.

Epstein, D., J. Elwood, V. Hey, and J. Maw, eds. 1998. *Failing Boys? Issues in Gender and Achievement.* New York: Taylor & Francis.

Epstein, J., and N. Karweit, eds. 1983. *Friends in School: Patterns of Selection and Influence in Secondary Schools.* New York: Academic Press.

Escamilla, K., S. Shannon, S. Carlos, and J. Garcia. 2003. "Breaking the Code: Colorado's Defeat of the Anti-Bilingual Education Initiative (Amendment 31)." *Bilingual Research Journal* 27: 357–382.

Esch, C. E., C. M. Chang-Ross, R. Guha, D. C. Humphrey, P. M. Shields, J. D. Tiffany-Morales, M. E. Wechsler, and K. R. Woodworth. 2005. *The Status of the Teaching Profession, 2005.* Santa Cruz, Calif.: Center for the Future of Teaching and Learning.

Everson, H., and R. Millsap. 2005. *Everyone Gains: Extracurricular Activities in High School and Higher SAT Scores.* New York: College Board.

Excelencia in Education and the Institute for Higher Education Policy. 2005. *How Latino Students Pay for College: Patterns of Financial Aid in 2003–2004.* Washington, D.C.: Excelencia in Education and the Institute for Higher Education Policy. http://www.edexcelencia.org/research/how_latinos_pay.asp.

Fairlie, R. W. 2004. "Race and the Digital Divide." *Contributions to Economic Analysis and Policy* 3, no. 1, article 15. http://www.bepress.com/bejeap/contributions/vol3/iss1/art15.

———. 2005. "The Effects of Home Computers on School Enrollment." *Economics of Education Review* 24: 553–547.

Fairlie, R., R. London, R. Rosner, and M. Pastor. 2006. "Crossing the Divide: Immigrant Youth and Digital Disparity in California." Santa Cruz: Center for Justice, Tolerance and Community, University of California, Santa Cruz.

Farber, B. 1991. *Crisis in Education: Stress and Burnout of the American Teacher.* San Francisco: Jossey-Bass.

Ferriss, S. 2007. "Reports Decry Hate in Debate on Immigrants." *Sacramento Bee,* November 18, 2007. http://www.sacbee.com/101/v-print/story/500515.html (accessed March 29, 2008).

Fetler, M. 1984. "Television Viewing and School Achievement." *Journal of Communication* 34, no. 2: 104–118.

Fine, M. 1991. *Framing Dropouts: Notes on the Politics of an Urban Public High School.* Albany: State University of New York Press.

Fischer, K. 2008. "Top Colleges Admit Fewer Low-Income Students." *Chronicle of Higher Education,* May 2, 2008, pp. A1, A19–20.

Fitzgerald, B. K., and T. J. Kane. 2006. "Lowering Barriers to College Access: Opportunities for More Effective Coordination of State and Federal Student Aid Policies." In P. C. Gándara, G. Orfield, and C. L. Horn, eds., *Expanding Opportunity in Higher Education: Leveraging Promise*. Albany: State University of New York Press.

Fix, M., and J. Passel. 1994. *Immigration and Immigrants: Setting the Record Straight*. Washington, D.C.: Urban Institute. http://www.urban.org/UploadedPDF/305184 _immigration_immigrants.pdf.

Flores v. State of Arizona. 1999. 48 F. Supp 2d 937.

Flores-Solano, G. 2008. "Who Is Given Tests in What Language by Whom, When, and Where? The Need for Probabilistic Views of Language in the Testing of English Language Learners." *Educational Researcher* 37, no. 4: 189–199.

Foley, D. 1990. *Learning in a Capitalist Culture: Deep in the Heart of Tejas*. Philadelphia: University of Pennsylvania Press.

Forsbach, T., and N. Pierce. 1999. *Factors Related to the Identification of Minority Gifted Students*. Paper presented as a poster session at the annual American Educational Research Association conference, Montreal.

Fortuny, K., R. Capps, and J. S. Passel. 2007. *The Characteristics of Unauthorized Immigrants in California, Los Angeles County, and the United States*. Washington, D.C.: Urban Institute. http://www.urban.org/UploadedPDF/ 411425_Characteristics_Immigrants.pdf.

Fowler-Finn, T. 2001. "Student Stability vs. Mobility." *School Administrator* 58, no. 7: 36.

Frances A., C. Campbell, T. Ramey, E. Pungello, J. Sparling, and S. Miller-Johnson. 2002. "Early Childhood Education: Young Adult Outcomes from the Abecedarian Project." *Applied Developmental Science* 6, no. 1: 42–57.

Fraser, D. 2005. "Diabetes and Hispanic Americans: More Than Just Genetics." *NaturalNews.Com*. http://www.naturalnews.com/008951.htm.

Frazier, L. 1993. *Deteriorating School Facilities and Student Learning*. ERIC Digest 82. Washington, D.C.: U.S. Department of Education.

Freedle, R. 2003. "Correcting the SAT's Ethnic and Social-Class Bias: A Method for Reestimating SAT Scores." *Harvard Educational Review* 73, no. 1: 1–43.

Fritzberg, G. J. 2001. "Less Than Equal: A Former Urban Schoolteacher Examines the Causes of Educational Disadvantagement." *Urban Review* 33: 107–129.

Fry, R. 2002. "Latinos in Higher Education: Many Enroll, Too Few Graduate." Washington, D.C.: Pew Hispanic Center. http://pewhispanic.org/reports/ archive.

———. 2004. *Latino Youth Finishing College: The Role of Selective Pathways*. Washington, D.C.: Pew Hispanic Center. http://pewhispanic.org/reports/report .php?ReportID=3.

Fuligini, A. 1997. "The Academic Achievement of Adolescents from Immigrant Families: The Roles of Family Background, Attitudes, and Behavior." *Child Development* 68, no. 2: 351–363.

Fuller, B. 2007. *Standardized Childhood: The Political and Cultural Struggle over Early Education*. Stanford, Calif.: Stanford University Press.

Fuller, B., C. Eggers-Piérola, X. Liang, and S. Holloway. 1996. "Rich Culture, Poor Markets: Why Do Latino Parents Forgo Preschooling?" *Teachers College Record* 97: 400–418.

Fuller, B., J. Wright, K. Gesicki, and E. Kang. 2007. "Gauging Growth: How to Judge No Child Left Behind?" *Educational Researcher* 36: 268–278.

Gable, M. 1995. "Not Fair." *UCLA Magazine* (Spring): 24–28.

Gamoran, A. 1989. "Rank, Performance, and Mobility in Elementary School Grouping." *Sociological Quarterly* 30: 109–123.

———. 1992. "Access to Excellence: Assignment to Honors English Classes in the Transition from Middle to High School." *Educational Evaluation and Policy Analysis* 14: 185–204.

Gándara, P. 1995. *Over the Ivy Walls: The Educational Mobility of Low-Income Chicanos.* Albany: State University of New York Press.

———. 1998. *Final Report of the Evaluation of High School Puente, 1994–1998.* Davis: University of California, Davis.

———. 2002. "Learning English in California: Guideposts for the Nation." In M. Suárez-Orozco and M. Páez, eds., *Latinos Remaking America,* pp. 339–348. Berkeley: University of California Press.

———. 2006. *Fragile Futures: Risk and Vulnerability among Latino High Achievers.* Princeton, N.J.: Educational Testing Service. Policy information available at http://www.ets.org/Media/Research/pdf/picfragfut.pdf.

Gándara, P., and D. Bial. 2001. *Paving the Way to Postsecondary Education, K–12 Interventions for Underrepresented Youth.* Washington, D.C.: National Center for Education Statistics.

Gándara, P., and M. Gibson. 2004. "Peers and School Performance: Implications for Research, Policy, and Practice." In G. Gibson, P. Gándara, and J. Koyama, eds., *School Connections: U.S. Mexican Youth, Peers, and School Achievement,* pp. 39–62. New York: Teachers College Press.

Gándara, P., D. Gutiérrez, and S. O'Hara. 2001. "Planning for the Future in Rural and Urban High Schools." *Journal of Education for Students Placed at Risk (JESPAR)* 6: 73–93.

Gándara, P., and E. López. 1998. "Latino Students and College Entrance Exams: How Much Do They *Really* Matter?" *Hispanic Journal of Behavioral Sciences* 20: 17–38.

Gándara, P., and J. Maxwell Jolly. 1999. *Priming the Pump: Strategies for Increasing the Achievement of Underrepresented Minority Undergraduates.* New York: College Board. http:// www.williams.edu/biology/hhmi/downloads/gandara-1999.pdf.

———. 2000. *The Initial Impact of Proposition 227 on the Instruction of English Learners.* Davis, Calif.: University of California Linguistic Minority Research Institute, Education Policy Center.

———. 2005. "Critical Issues in the Development of the Teacher Corps for English Learners." In H. Waxman and K. Tellez, eds., *Preparing Quality Teachers for English Language Learners.* Mahweh, N.J.: Lawrence Erlbaum.

Gándara, P., J. Maxwell-Jolly, and A. Driscoll. 2005. *Listening to Teachers of English Learners.* Santa Cruz, Calif.: Center for the Future of Teaching and Learning.

Gándara, P., H. Mehan, K. Larson, and R. Rumberger. 1998. *Capturing Latino Students in the Academic Pipeline.* Berkeley, Calif.: Institute for the Study of Social Change, Chicano Latino Policy Project.

Gándara, P., S. O'Hara, and D. Gutiérrez. 2004. "The Changing Shape of Aspirations: Peer Influence on Achievement Behavior," In G. Gibson, P. Gándara, and J. Koyama, eds., *School Connections: U.S. Mexican Youth, Peers, and School Achievement*, pp. 39–62. New York: Teachers College Press.

Gándara, P., G. Orfield, and C. H. Horn, eds. 2006. *Expanding Opportunity in Higher Education: Leveraging Promise.* Albany: State University of New York Press.

Gándara, P., and R. Rumberger. 2007. *Resource Needs for English Learners.* Stanford, Calif.: Stanford University, Getting Down to Facts Project. http://www.lmri .ucsb.edu.

————. 2008. "Defining the Resource Needs for English Learners." *Education Finance and Policy* 3: 130–148.

Gándara, P., R. Rumberger, J. Maxwell-Jolly, and R. Callahan. 2003. "English Learners in California Schools: Unequal Resources; Unequal Outcomes." *Educational Policy Analysis Archives.* http://epaa.asu.edu/epaa/v11n36.

Garcia, E. 1996. "Preparing Instructional Professionals for Linguistically and Culturally Diverse Students." In J. Sikula, ed., *Handbook of Research on Teacher Education.* New York: Simon & Schuster, pp. 802–813.

Garcia, E., and D. Gonzales. 2006. *Pre-K and Latinos: The Foundation for America's Future.* Washington, D.C.: Pre-K Now.

Garcia, S. B., and P. L. Guerra. 2004. "Deconstructing Deficit Thinking: Working with Educators to Promote More Equitable Learning Environments." *Education and Urban Society* 36: 150–168.

Geierstanger, S., and G. Amaral. 2005. "School-based Heath Centers and Academic Performance: What Is the Intersection?" In *Proceedings of the National Assembly on School-based Health Care, April 2004.* Washington, D.C.: National Assembly on School-based Health Care.

Geiser, S., and V. Santelices. 2006. "The Role of Advanced Placement and Honors Courses in College Admissions." In P. Gándara, G. Orfield, and C. Horn, eds., *Expanding Opportunity in Higher Education: Leveraging Promise*, pp. 75–114. Albany: State University of New York Press.

————. 2007. "Validity of High-School Grades in Predicting Student Success beyond the Freshman Year: High-School Record vs. Standardized Tests as Indicators of Four-Year College Outcomes." Research and Occasional Paper Series CSHE.6.07, University of California, Berkeley. http://cshe.berkeley.edu.

Genesee, F., and P. Gándara. 1999. "Bilingual Education Programs: A Cross-National Perspective." *Journal of Social Issues* 55: 665–685.

Genesee, F., K. Lindholm-Leary, W. Saunders, and D. Christian. 2006. *Educating English Language Learners: A Synthesis of Research Evidence.* New York: Cambridge University Press.

Gersten, R. 1985. "Structured Immersion for Language Minority Students: Results of a Longitudinal Evaluation." *Educational Evaluation and Policy Analysis* 7: 187–196.

Gibson, M., L. Bejínez, N. Hidalgo, and C. Rolón. 2004. "Belonging and School Participation: Lessons from a Migrant Student Club." In M. Gibson, P. Gándara, and J. Koyama, eds., *School Connections: U.S. Mexican Youth, Peers, and School Achievement*, pp. 129–149. New York: Teachers College Press.

Gifford, B. R., and G. Valdés. 2006. "The Linguistic Isolation of Hispanic Students in California's Public Schools: The Challenge of Reintegration." *Annual Yearbook of the National Society for the Study of Education* 5, no. 2: 125–154. http:// www.citeulike.org/article/892348.

Gillespie, K. 2001. "How Vision Impacts Literacy: An Educational Problem That Can Be Solved." *Harvard Graduate School of Education News,* vol. 17. http:// www.gse.harvard.edu/news/features/vision04172001.html.

Ginorio, A., and M. Huston. 2001. *Si Se Puede,* pp. 1–88. Washington, D.C.: American Association of University Women Foundation.

Giovanni, P. 2007. "How Immigrants Affect California Employment and Wages." *California Counts: Population Trends and Profiles* 8, no. 3. http://www.ppic.org/ content/pubs/cacounts/CC_207GPCC.pdf.

Goddard, R. D., and Y. L. Goddard. 2001. "A Multilevel Analysis of the Relationship between Teacher and Collective Efficacy in Urban Schools." *Teacher and Teacher Education* 17: 807–818. http://www.coe.ohio-state.edu/ahoy/Goddard%20&%20 Godard .pdf.

Golden, D. 2006. *The Price of Admission: How America's Ruling Class Buys Its Way into Elite Colleges and Who Gets Left outside the Gates.* New York: Crown.

Goldhaber, D. D., and D. J. Brewer. 1996. *Evaluating the Effect of Teacher Degree Level on Educational Performance.* Washington, D.C.: National Center for Education Statistics. http://nces.ed.gov/pubs97/975351.pdf.

Goldman, D., J. Smith, and N. Sood. 2006. "Immigrants and the Cost of Medical Care." *Health Affairs* 25: 1700–1711.

González, N., and L. Moll. 2002. "*Cruzando el Puente*/Bridging to Funds of Knowledge." *Educational Policy* 16: 623–641.

Good, C., J. Aronson, and M. Inzlicht. 2003. "Improving Adolescents' Standardized Test Performance: An Intervention to Reduce the Effects of Stereotype Threat." *Applied Development Psychology* 24: 645–662. http://www.nber.org/~sewp/ events/2005.01.14/Bios+Links/Good-rec1-Good_Aronson_&_Inzlicht.pdf.

Good, T., and J. Brophy. 1994. *Looking in Classrooms,* 6th ed. New York: Harper Collins.

Gould, S. J. 1995. "Mismeasure by Any Measure." In R. Jacoby and N. Glauberman, eds., *The Bell Curve Debate,* pp. 3–13. New York: Random House/Times Books.

Grebler, L., J. W. Moore, and R. Guzman. 1970. *The Mexican American People: The Nation's Second Largest Minority.* New York: Free Press.

Greene, J. P. 1998. *A Meta-Analysis of the Effectiveness of Bilingual Education.* Claremont, Calif.: Thomas Rivera Policy Institute.

————. 2002. *High School Graduation Rates in the United States.* New York: Manhattan Institute, Center for Civic Innovation.

Greenfield, P. M. 1998. "The Cultural Evolution of IQ." In U. Neisser, ed., *The Rising Curve: Long-term Gains in IQ and Related Measures,* pp. 81–123. Washington, D.C.: American Psychological Association.

Grissmer, D., A. Flanagan, and S. Williamson. 1998. "Why Did the Black-White Score Gap Narrow in the 1970s and 1980s?" In C. Jencks and M. Phillips, eds., *The Black-White Test Score Gap.* Washington, D.C.: Brookings Institution Press.

Grogger, J., and S. Trejo. 2002. *Falling Behind or Moving Up? The Intergenerational Progress of Mexican Americans.* San Francisco: Public Policy Institute of California.

Grossman, J. B., and E. M. Garry. 1997. *Mentoring: A Proven Delinquency Prevention Strategy.* Washington, D.C.: U.S. Department of Justice, Office of Juvenile Justice and Delinquency Prevention.

Grossman, J. B., and J. P. Tierney. 1998. "Does Mentoring Work? An Impact Study of the Big Brothers/Big Sisters Program." *Evaluation Review* 22: 403–426.

Guthrie, L., and G. Guthrie. 2000. *Longitudinal Research on AVID, 1999–2000: Results from the Third Follow-up Data Collection.* Los Angeles: Center for Research, Evaluation and Training in Education. http:// www.avidonline.org/content/pdf/418.pdf.

Haberman, M. 1996. "Selecting and Preparing Culturally Competent Teachers for Urban Schools." In J. Sikula, ed., *Handbook of Research on Teacher Education,* pp. 747–760. New York: Simon & Schuster.

Hack, M., N. Klein, and H. G. Taylor. 1995. "Long-Term Developmental Outcomes of Low Birth Weight Infants." *The Future of Children* 5: 176–196.

Hackett, G., N. E. Betz, J. M. Casa, and I. A. Rocha-Sing. 1992. "Gender, Ethnicity, and Social Cognitive Factors Predicting the Academic Achievement of Students in Engineering." *Journal of Counseling Psychology* 39: 527–538.

Hakimzadeh, S., and D. Cohen. 2007. *English Usage among Hispanics in the United States.* Washington, D.C.: Pew Hispanic Center. http://pewhispanic.org/files/reports/82.pdf.

Hakuta, K. 1986. *Mirror of Language: The Debate on Bilingualism.* New York: Basic Books.

Hakuta, K., G. Y. Butler, and D. Witt. 2000. "How Long Does It Take English Learners to Attain Proficiency?" Policy Report, 2000–2001. Santa Barbara: University of California Linguistic Minority Research Institute.

Halpern, R. 2002. "The History of After School Programs for Low Income Children," *Teachers College Record* 104, no. 2: 178–211.

Hanushek, E., J. F. Kain, and S. G. Rivkin. 2001. *Why Public Schools Lose Teachers.* NBER Working Paper 8599. Cambridge: National Bureau of Economic Research.

Hanushek, E., and S. Rivkin. 2006. "Teacher Quality." In E. Hanushek and F. Welch, eds., *Handbook of the Economics of Education,* vol. 2. Amsterdam: Elsevier.

Harklau, L., K. Losey, and M. Siuegal. 1999. *Generation 1.5 Meets College Composition.* Mahwah, N.J.: Lawrence Erlbaum.

Haro, R., G. Rodríguez, and J. Gonzales. 1994. *Latino Persistence in Higher Education: A 1994 Survey of University of California and California State University Chicano/Latino Students.* San Francisco: Latino Issues Forum.

Harris, D. 2006. *Lost Learning, Forgotten Promises: A National Analysis of School Racial Segregation, Student Achievement, and Controlled Choice.* Center for American Progress. http://www.americanprogress.org/issues/2006/11/lostlearning.html.

Hart, B., and R. Risley. 1995. *Meaningful Differences in the Everyday Experiences of Young American Children.* New York: Brookes.

Hayes-Bautista, D. 2004. *La Nueva California: Latinos in the Golden State.* Berkeley: University of California Press.

Hayle, L. 1997. *Healthy Start Helps: Evaluation of Its First Three Years Shows Gains for Kids and Families.* Action Alliance for Children. http://www.4children.org (accessed December 16, 2006).

Heath, S. B. 1983. *Ways with Words.* Cambridge, Eng.: Cambridge University Press.

Heilman, M. E., C. J. Block, and J. A. Lucas. 1992. "Presumed Incompetent? Stigmatization and Affirmative Action Efforts." *Journal of Applied Psychology* 77: 536–544.

Heller, D. E. 2005. "Public Subsidies for Higher Education in California: An Exploratory Analysis of Who Pays and Who Benefits." *Educational Policy* 19, no. 2: 349–370.

Henderson, A., and N. Berla. 1994. *A New Generation of Evidence: The Family Is Critical to Student Achievement.* Washington, D.C.: National Committee for Citizens in Education.

Henderson, R. 1997. "Educational and Occupational Aspirations and Expectations among Parents of Middle School Students of Mexican Descent: Family Resources for Academic Development and Mathematics Learning." In R. Taylor and M. Wang, eds., *Social and Emotional Adjustment and Family Relations in Ethnic Minority Families.* Mahwah, N.J.: Lawrence Erlbaum.

Hochschild, J. L. 1995. *Facing Up to the American Dream: Race, Class, and the Soul of the Nation.* Princeton, N.J.: Princeton University Press.

Hochschild, J. L., and N. Scovronick. 2003. *The American Dream and the Public Schools.* New York: Oxford University Press.

Horn, L., and X. Chen. 1998. *Toward Resiliency: At-Risk Students Who Make It to College.* Washington, D.C.: U.S. Department of Education, Office of Educational Research and Improvement. http://www.ed.gov/PDFDocs/resiliency.pdf.

Huang, D., B. Gribbons, K. Kim, C. Lee, and E. Baker. 2000. *A Decade of Results: The Impact of LA's Best After School Enrichment Program on Subsequent Student Achievement and Performance.* Los Angeles: UCLA Center for the Study of Evaluation.

Hunter, M. 2006. *Public School Facilities: Providing Environments That Sustain Learning.* New York: National Access Network, Teachers College, Columbia University. http://www.schoolfunding.info/resource_center/issuebriefs/facilities.pdf.

Huntington, S. P. 2004. "The Hispanic Challenge." *Foreign Policy* (March/April): 30–45.

Hurd, C. 2004. "Acting Out and Being a Schoolboy: Performance in an ELD Classroom." In M. Gibson, P. Gándara, and J. Koyama, eds., *School Connections: U.S. Mexican Youth, Peers, and School Achievement,* pp. 63–86. New York: Teachers College Press.

Iceland, J., and D. Weinberg. 2002. *Racial and Ethnic Segregation in the United States, 1980–2000.* Washington, D.C.: U.S. Census Bureau. http://www.censusbureau.biz/hhes/www/housing/housing_patterns/papertoc.html (accessed May 1, 2008).

Institute of Education Sciences. 2006. *The Condition of Education; Indicator 6: Concentration of Enrollment by Race/Ethnicity and Poverty.* Washington, D.C.: U.S. Department of Education.

Irish, K., R. Schumacher, and J. Lombardi. 2004. *Head Start Comprehensive Services: A Key Support for Early Learning for Poor Children.* Washington, D.C.: Center for Law and Social Policy. http://www.clasp.org/DMS/Documents/1075300806.3/HS_brf_4.pdf.

Isaacs, J. 2008. "International Comparisons of Economic Mobility." In R. Haskins, J. Isaacs, and I. Sawhill, *Getting Ahead or Losing Ground: Economic Mobility in America.* Washington, D.C.: Brookings Institution, pp. 37–44.

Jarret, R. 1997. "Bringing Families Back In: Neighborhood Effects on Child Development." In J. Brooks-Gunn, G. Duncan, and L. Aber, eds., *Neighborhood Poverty,* vol. 2: *Policy Implications in Studying Neighborhoods.* New York: Russell Sage Foundation.

Jencks, C. 1993. *Rethinking Social Policy: Race, Poverty, and the Underclass.* Cambridge: Harvard University Press.

Jencks, C., M. Smith, H. Acland, J. M. Bane, D. Cohen, H. Gintis, B. Heynes, and R. Mickelson. 1972. *Inequality.* New York: Harper & Row.

Johnson, H. B. 2006. "The Wealth Gap and the American Dream." In Johnson, *The American Dream and the Power of Wealth: Choosing Schools and Inheriting Inequality in the Land of Opportunity.* New York: Routledge.

Jones, M. In preparation. "Educational Advantages: Race, Class, and Teacher-Student Relationships." Ph.D. diss., Department of Sociology, University of California, Davis.

Kahne, J., and K. Bailey. 1999. "The Role of Social Capital in Youth Development: The Case of 'I Have a Dream' Programs." *Educational Evaluation and Policy Analysis* 21, no. 3: 321–343.

Kane, T. 2004. "The Impact of After School Programs: Interpreting the Results of Four Recent Evaluations." Working paper. New York: William T. Grant Foundation.

Kao, G. 1995. "Asian Americans as Model Minorities? A Look at Their Academic Performance." *American Journal of Education* 103, no. 2: 121–159.

Kao, G., and M. Tienda. 1995. "Optimism and Achievement: The Educational Performance of Immigrant Youth." *Social Science Quarterly* 76: 1–19.

———. 1998. "Educational Aspirations of Minority Youth," *American Journal of Education* 106, no. 3: 349–384.

Karcher, M. 2002. "The Cycle of Violence and Disconnection among Rural Middle School Students: Teacher Disconnection as a Consequence of Violence." *Journal of School Violence* 1: 35–51.

Karoly, L., and J. Bigelow. 2005. *The Economics of Investing in Universal Preschool Education in California.* Santa Monica, Calif.: RAND Labor and Population Program.

Karoly, L., P. Greenwood, S. Everingham, J. Hoube, R. Kilburn, C. P. Rydell, M. Sanders, and J. Chiesa. 1998. *Investing in Our Children: What We Know and Don't Know about the Costs and Benefits of Early Childhood Interventions.* Santa Monica, Calif.: RAND.

Kasinitz, P., J. H. Mollenkopf, M. C. Waters, and J. Holdaway. 2008. *Inheriting the City: The Children of Immigrants Come of Age.* Cambridge: Harvard University Press.

Kaufman, P. 2001. *The National Dropout Data Collection System: Assessing Consistency.* Cambridge: Harvard Civil Rights Project.

Kazis, R., J. Vargas, and N. Hoffman, eds. 2004. *Double the Numbers: Increasing Postsecondary Credentials for Underrepresented Youth.* Cambridge: Harvard Education Press.

Kenneth, R., E. Frede, and W. S. Barnett. 2006. *Is More Better? The Effects of Full-Day vs. Half-Day Preschool on Early School Achievement.* New Brunswick, N.J.: National Institute for Early Education Research. http://nieer.org/resources/research/IsMoreBetter.pdf.

Kindler, A. L. 2002. *Survey of the States' Limited English Proficient Students and Available Educational Programs and Services: 2000–2001 Summary Report.* Washington, D.C.: National Clearinghouse for English Language Acquisition and Language Instruction Educational Programs.

Kling, J. R., and J. B. Liebman. 2004. *Experimental Analysis of Neighborhood Effects on Youth,* IRS Working Paper 483. Princeton, N.J.: Princeton University.

Krueger, A. 2005. "Inequality, Too Much of a Good Thing." In J. Heckman and A. Krueger, eds., *Inequality in America: What Role for Human Capital Policies?* Cambridge, Mass.: MIT Press, pp. 1–76.

Ladd, H. 2001. "School-Based Educational Accountability Systems: The Promise and the Pitfalls." *National Tax Journal* 54, no. 2: 385–400. http://ntanet.org.

Laird, J., G. Kienzl, M. DeBell, and C. Chapman. 2007. *Dropout Rates in the United States, 2005.* Washington, D.C.: U.S. Department of Education, National Center for Education Statistics.

Landsberg, M. 2006. "LA Mayor Sees Dropout Rate as 'a Civil Rights Issue.'" *Los Angeles Times*, March 2.

Laosa, L. 1978. "Maternal Teaching Strategies in Chicano Families of Varied Educational and Socioeconomic Levels." *Child Development* 49: 1129–1135.

Lara-Cinisomo, S., A. Pebley, M. Vaiana, and E. Maggio. 2004. *Are LA's Children Ready for School?* Santa Monica, Calif.: RAND Labor and Population Report.

Lareau, A. 1989. *Home Advantage: Social Class and Parental Intervention in Elementary Education.* London: Falmer Press.

———. 2003. *Unequal Childhoods: Class, Race, and Family Life.* Berkeley: University of California Press.

Lau v. Nichols. 1974. 414 U.S. 563.

Laub, J. H., and J. Lauritsen. 1998. "The Interdependence of School Violence with Neighborhood and Family Conditions." In D. S. Elliott, B. Hamburg, and K. R. Williams, eds., *Violence in American Schools*, pp. 127–155. New York: Cambridge University Press.

Lavan, N., and M. Uriarte. 2008. "The Lost Children of Unz: Characteristics, Program Participation, and MCAS Outcomes of Latino Dropouts from Programs for English Language Learners and Regular Programs in the Boston Public Schools." Paper commissioned for the Conference on Restrictive Language Policies, University of California, Los Angeles, April 10–11, 2008. Boston: Mauricio Gaston Institute for Latino Community Development and Public Policy.

Lee, S. J. 1996. *Unraveling the "Model Minority" Stereotype: Listening to Asian American Children.* New York: Teachers College Press.

Leithwood, K., and C. Riehl. 2003. "What Do We Already Know about Successful School Leadership?" Paper presented at the annual American Education Research Association Conference, Chicago.

Lemann, N. 1999. *The Big Test: The Secret History of the American Meritocracy.* New York: Farrar, Straus, and Giroux.

Leventhal, T., and J. Brooks-Gunn. 2004. "A Randomized Study of Neighborhood Effects on Low-Income Children's Educational Outcomes." *Developmental Psychology* 40, no. 4: 448–507.

Levin, H. M., C. R. Belfield, P. Muennig, and C. E. Rouse. 2007. *The Costs and Benefits of an Excellent Education for America's Children.* Working Paper. New York: Teachers College, Columbia University.

Levine, R. V. 1997. *The Geography of Time.* New York: Basic Books.

Lindholm-Leary, K., and G. Borsato. 2006. "Academic Achievement." In F. Genesee, K. Lindholm-Leary, W. Saunders, and D. Christian, eds., *Educating English Language Learners: A Synthesis of Research Evidence.* New York: Cambridge University Press.

Linquanti, R. 2006. "What Do We Know about Improving the Teacher Quality for English Learners?" Presentation at the Grantmakers Forum in Education, San Francisco, Calif., November 7. Based on 1999 U.S. Census Data.

Linton, A. 2007. "Dual-Language Education in the Wake of California Proposition 227: Five Cases." *Intercultural Education* 18, no. 2: 111–128.

Livingston, G., and J. Kahn. 2002. "An American Dream Unfulfilled: The Limited Mobility of Mexican Americans." *Social Science Quarterly* 83: 1003–1012.

Loeb, S., and M. E. Page. 2001. "Examining the Link between Teacher Wages and Student Outcomes: The Importance of Alternative Labor Market Opportunities and Non-Pecuniary Variation." *Review of Economics and Statistics* 82, no. 3: 393–408. http://www.stanford.edu/~sloeb/Papers/loebpage.pdf.

LoGerfo, L., A. Nichols, and D. Chaplin. 2007. *Gender Gaps in Math and Reading Gains during Elementary and High School by Race and Ethnicity.* Washington, D.C.: Urban Institute. http://www.urban.org/url.cfm?ID=411428.

Lucas, S. R. 1999. *Tracking Inequality: Stratification and Mobility in American High Schools.* New York: Teachers College Press.

Luxembourg Income Study. 2004. http://www.lisproject.org.

Magnuson, K., and A. Waldfogel. 2005. "Early Childhood Care and Education: Effects of Ethnic and Racial Gaps in School Readiness." *The Future of Children: School Readiness, Closing Racial and Ethnic Gaps* 15, no 1.

Mahoney, K., J. MacSwan, and M. Thompson. 2005. *The Condition of Education of Arizona's English Learners.* Tempe: Arizona State University, Education Policy Laboratory. http://epsl.asu.edu/aepi/Report/EPSL-0509-110-AEPI.pdf.

Marsh, H., and S. Kleitman. 2002. "Extracurricular Activities: The Good, the Bad, and the Nonlinear." *Harvard Educational Review* 72, no. 4: 464–511.

Martin, J. A., B. E. Hamilton, P. D. Sutton, S. J. Ventura, F. Menacker, and M. L. Munson. 2005. "Births: Final Data for 2003." *National Vital Statistics Reports* 54, no. 2. http://www.cdc.gov/nchs/data/nvsr/nvsr54/nvsr54_02.pdf.

Martin, M. 2006. *Residential Segregation Patterns of Latinos in the United States, 1990–2000: Testing the Ethnic Enclave and Inequality Theories.* New York: Routledge.

Martinez, M. 2000. *Education as the Cultivation of Intelligence.* Mahwah, N.J.: Lawrence Erlbaum.

Martinez, R. 2007. "How to Leave No Child Left Behind: What Do L.A. Kids Need to Thrive?" *Los Angeles Times*, p. A27. http://www.latimes.com/news/opinion/la-op-bigfix-kids29dec29,0,4076217,full.story (accessed March 29, 2008).

Marzano, R., T. Waters, and B. Mcnulty. 2005. *School Leadership That Works.* Alexandria, Va.: Association for Supervision and Curriculum Development.

Masse, L. N., and W. S. Barnett. 2002. *A Benefit Cost Analysis of the Abecedarian Early Childhood Intervention.* New Brunswick, N.J.: National Institute for Early Education Research.

Massey, D S., J. Durand, and N. J. Malone. 2002. *Beyond Smoke and Mirrors: Mexican Immigration in an Era of Economic Integration.* New York: Russell Sage Foundation.

Matute-Bianchi, M. E. 1986. "Ethnic Identities and Patterns of School Success and Failure among Mexican-Descent and Japanese American Students in a California High School." *American Journal of Education* 95: 233–255.

Maxwell-Jolly, J., P. Gándara, and L. Méndez-Benavídez. 2006. *Promoting Academic Literacy among Secondary English Language Learners.* Davis: University of California, Davis, and University of California Linguistic Minority Research Institute.

Maynard, M. 2007. "Immigration Conflagration," *Minnesota Magazine,* November–December. http://www.alumni.umn.edu/Immigration_Conflagration.html.

McArdle, N. 2003. *Beyond Poverty: Race and Concentrated Poverty Neighborhoods in Metro Boston.* Cambridge: Civil Rights Project at Harvard University. http://www.civilrightsproject.ucla.edu/research/metro/McArdleBostonPoverty.pdf.

———. 2004. *Racial Equity and Opportunity in Metro Boston Job Markets.* Cambridge: Civil Rights Project at Harvard University.

McCarty, N., K. T. Poole, and H. Rosenthal. 2006. *Polarized America: The Dance of Ideology and Unequal Riches.* Cambridge: MIT Press.

McDonough, P. 1997. *Choosing Colleges: How Social Class and Schools Structure Opportunity.* Albany: State University of New York Press.

———. 2004. *The School-to-College Transition: Challenges and Prospects.* Report prepared for the American Council on Education, Center for Policy Analysis, Washington, D.C.

McDonough, P., J. Korn, and E. Yamasaki. 1997. "Admissions Advantage for Sale: Private College Counselors and Students Who Use Them." *Review of Higher Education* 20: 297–317.

McFarland v. Jefferson County Public Schools. 2007. 416 F. 3d 513.

McLaughlin, W. M., and L. A. Shepard. 1995. *Improving Education through Standards-Based Reform.* Report by the National Academy of Education Panel on Standards-Based Education Reform. Stanford, Calif.: National Academy on Education.

McQuillan, J., and L. Tse. 1996. "Does Research Matter? An Analysis of Media Opinion on Bilingual Education, 1984–1994." *Bilingual Research Journal* 20: 1–27.

Mehan, H., I. Villanueva, L. Hubbard, and A. Lintz. 1996. *Constructing School Success: The Consequences of Untracking Low-Achieving Students.* New York: Cambridge University Press.

Meissner, D. 2006. *Immigration and America's Future: A New Chapter: Report of the Independent Task Force on Immigration and America's Future.* Washington, D.C.: Migration Policy Institute. http://www.migrationpolicy.org/task_force/new_chapter_summary.pdf.

Merickel, A., R. Linquanti, T. B. Parrish, M. Pérez, M. Eaton, and P. Esra. 2003. *Effects of the Implementation of Proposition 227 on the Education of English Learners, K–12 Year 3 Report.* Palo Alto, Calif.: American Institutes for Research and WestEd. http://www.air.org/publications/documents/Yr%203%20FinalRpt.pdf.

Meyers, D., R. Olsen, N. Seftor, J. Young, and C. Tuttle. 2004. *The Impacts of Regular Upward Bound: Results from the Third Follow-Up Data Collection.* Washington, D.C.: U.S. Department of Education. http://www.ed.gov/rschstat/eval/highered/upward/upward-3rd-report.pdf.

Meyers, D., and A. Schirm. 1999. *The Short-Term Impact of Upward Bound: Final Report on Phase I of the National Evaluation.* Report submitted to the U.S. Department of Education. Washington, D.C.: Mathematics Policy Research.

Mickelson, R. A. 1990. "The Attitude-Achievement Paradox among Black Adolescents." *Sociology of Education* 63: 44–61.

———. 2001. "Subverting *Swann:* First and Second Generation Segregation in the Charlotte-Mecklenburg Schools. *American Education Research Journal* 38, no. 2: 215–252.

Miller, L. S. 1995. *An American Imperative: Accelerating Minority Educational Advancement.* New Haven: Yale University Press.

Minicucci, C., and L. Olsen. 1992. *Meeting the Challenge of Language Diversity: An Evaluation of Programs for Pupils with Limited Proficiency in English,* vol. 5: *An Exploratory Study of Secondary LEP Programs.* Berkeley, Calif.: BW Associates.

Mintrop, H. 2004. *Schools on Probation: How Accountability Works (and Doesn't Work)*. New York: Teachers College Press.

Moles, O. 1982. "Synthesis of Research on Parent Participation in Children's Education." *Educational Leadership* 40: 44–47.

Moore, C., and N. Shulock. 2006. *State of Decline? Gaps in College Access and Achievement Call for Renewed Commitment to Educating Californians*. Sacramento: Institute for Higher Education Leadership and Policy.

Moreno, J. 2002. "The Long-Term Outcomes of Puente," *Educational Policy* 16: 572–587.

Mortenson, T. G. 1999. *Fewer Men on Campus: A Puzzle for Liberal Arts Colleges and Universities*. Part of the online conference The Changing Gender Balance: An Overview, sponsored by Goucher College. http://www.postsecondary.org/archives/Reports/goucher111599.pdf.

Muller, P., F. Stage, and J. Kinzie. 2001. "Science Achievement Growth Trajectories: Understanding Factors Related to Gender and Racial-Ethnic Differences in Precollege Science Achievement." *American Educational Research Journal* 38, no. 4: 981–1012.

Murnane, R. J., J. D. Singer, J. B. Willett, J. J. Kemple, and R. J. Olsen. 1991. *Who Will Teach? Policies That Matter*. Cambridge: Harvard University Press.

Myers, D. 2007. *Immigrants and Boomers: Forging a New Social Contract for the Future of America*. New York: Russell Sage Foundation.

Nacoste, R. W. 1990. Sources of Stigma: Analyzing the Psychology of Affirmative Action. *Law and Policy* 12: 175–195.

National Center for Public Policy and Higher Education. 2002. *Losing Ground: A National Status Report on the Affordability of Higher Education*. San Jose, Calif.: National Center for Public Policy and Higher Education.

———. 2005. *Income of U.S. Workforce Projected to Decline If Education Doesn't Improve*. Higher Education Policy alert. http://www.highereducation.org/reports/pa_decline/pa_decline.pdf.

———. 2006. *Measuring Up, 2006: The National Report Card on Higher Education*. http://measuringup.highereducation.org/_docs/2006/NationalReport_2006.pdf.

National Clearinghouse for English Language Acquisition and Language Instruction Educational Programs and U.S. Census Bureau. 2004. *Current Population Survey, October 2003*. http://www.ncela.gwu.edu/policy/states/reports/statedata/2002LEP/Growing_LEP0203.pdf.

National Education Association. 2005. *Rankings and Estimates: Rankings of the States 2004 and Estimates of School Statistics*. Washington, D.C.: NEA. http://www.nea.org/edstats/images/05rankings.pdf.

———. 2007. *Rankings and Estimates: Rankings of the States 2006 and Estimates of School Statistics*. Washington, D.C.: NEA. http://www.nea.org/edstats/images/07rankings.pdf.

National Fair Housing Alliance. 2006. *Unequal Opportunity—Perpetuating Housing Segregation in America*. Washington, D.C.: NFHA. http://www.myfairhousing.com/pdfs/2006%20Fair%20Housing%20Trends%20Report.pdf.

National Research Council, Panel on High Risk Youth. 1993. *Losing Generation: Adolescents in High-Risk Settings*. Washington, D.C.: National Academy Press.

National Telecommunications and Information Administration and the Economics and Statistics Administration. *A Nation Online: How Americans Are Expanding Their Use of the Internet*. 2002. Washington, D.C.: U.S. Department of Commerce.

Noguera, P. 2001. "Racial Politics and the Elusive Quest for Equity in Education." *Education and Urban Society* 34, no. 1: 18–41.

Noguera, P., and J. Wing. 2006. *Unfinished Business: Closing the Racial Achievement Gap in Our Schools.* San Francisco: Jossey-Bass.

Nord, M., M. Andrews, and S. Carlson. 2004. *Household Food Security in the United States, 2003.* Food Assistance and Nutrition Research Report, no. 42. Washington, D.C.: U.S. Department of Agriculture, Economic Research Service.

Nye, B., S. Konstantopoulos, and L. Hedges. 2004. "How Large Are Teacher Effects?" *Educational Evaluation and Policy Analysis* 26: 237–257.

Oakes, J. 1986. *Keeping Track: How Schools Structure Inequality.* New Haven: Yale University Press.

———. 1990. *Multiplying Inequalities.* Santa Monica, Calif.: RAND Corporation.

———. 1995. "Two Cities' Tracking and Within-School Segregation." *Teachers College Record* 96, no. 4: 681–690.

———. 2003. *Critical Conditions for Equity and Diversity in College Access: Informing Policy and Monitoring Results.* Los Angeles: UC/ACCORD. http://ucaccord.gseis.ucla.edu/indicators/pdfs/criticalconditions.pdf.

Oakes, J., J. Mendoza, and D. Silver. 2004. *California Opportunity Indicators: Informing and Monitoring California's Progress toward Equitable College Access.* http://www.ucaccord.gseis.ucla.edu/publications/pubs/Indicators2004.pdf (accessed March 29, 2004).

Oakes, J., and M. Saunders. 2004. "Education's Most Basic Tools: Access to Textbooks and Instructional Materials in California's Public Schools." *Teachers College Record* 106, no. 10: 1967–1988.

Oakes, J., and A. S. Wells. 1998. "Detracking for High Student Achievement." In L. Abbeduto, ed., *Taking Sides: Clashing Views in Educational Psychology,* 4th ed., pp. 23–27. Dubuque, Iowa: McGraw-Hill/Dushkin.

Office of Head Start. 2007. *Head Start Program Fact Sheet.* Washington, D.C.: Administration for Children and Families. http://www.acf.hhs.gov/programs/hsb/about/fy2007.html.

Olsen, L. 2000. *Made in America: Immigrant Students in American Schools.* New York: Free Press.

Olsen, L., and A. Jaramillo. 2000. "When Time Is on Our Side: Redesigning Schools for Immigrant Students." In P. Gándara, ed., *The Dimensions of Time and the Challenge of School Reform,* pp. 225–250. Albany: State University of New York Press.

Ong, P., and V. Terriquez. 2008. "Can Multiple Pathways Offset Inequalities in the Urban Spatial Structure?" In J. Oakes and M. Saunders, eds., *Beyond Tracking: Can Multiple High School Pathways Prepare All Students for College, Career and Civic Participation?* Cambridge: Harvard Education Press.

Opuni, K. 1999. *Graduation Really Achieves Dreams.* Project GRAD Program Evaluation Report, 1998–1999. Houston: Project GRAD. http:// eric.ed.gov/ERICDocs/data/ericdocs2sql/content_storage_01/0000019b/80/16/5b/30.pdf.

Orfield, G. 1978. *Must We Bus? Segregated Schools and National Policy.* Washington, D.C.: Brookings Institution.

———, ed. 2004. *Dropouts in America.* Cambridge: Harvard Education Press.

Orfield, G., and S. Eaton, eds. 1996. *Dismantling Desegregation: The Quiet Reversal of "Brown v. Board of Education."* New York: New Press.

Orfield, G., and C. Lee. 2005. *Why Segregation Matters: Poverty and Educational*

Inequality. Cambridge: Civil Rights Project at Harvard University. http://www .civilrightsproject.ucla.edu/research/deseg/Why_Segreg_Matters.pdf.

———. 2006. *Racial Transformation and the Changing Nature of Segregation.* Cambridge: Civil Rights Project at Harvard University. http://www.civilrightsproject .ucla.edu/research/deseg/Racial_Transformation.pdf.

Orfield, G., D. Losen, J. Wald, and C. Swanson. 2004. *Losing Our Future: How Minority Youth Are Being Left Behind by the Graduation Rate Crisis.* Joint publication of The Civil Rights Project at Harvard University, Cambridge, The Urban Institute Advocates for Children of New York, and The Civil Society Institute, Newton, Mass.

Orfield, G., and N. McArdle. 2006. *The Vicious Cycle: Segregated Housing, Schools, and Intergenerational Inequality.* Cambridge: Joint Center for Housing Studies, Harvard University. http://content.knowledgeplex.org/kp2/cache/documents/ 2086/208618.pdf.

Orfield, G., and J. Yun. 1999. *Resegregation in American Schools.* Cambridge: Civil Rights Project at Harvard University. http://www.civilrightsproject.ucla.edu/ research/deseg/Resegregation_American_Schools99.pdf.

Ovando, C., and V. Collier. 1998. *Bilingual and ESL Classroom: Teaching in Multicultural Contexts.* Boston: McGraw-Hill.

Pajares, M. F. 1992. "Teachers' Beliefs and Educational Research: Cleaning Up a Messy Construct." *Review of Educational Research* 62: 307–332.

Pajares, M. F., and M. D. Miller. 1994. "Role of Self-Efficacy and Self-Concept Beliefs in Mathematical Problem Solving: A Path Analysis." *Journal of Educational Psychology* 86, no. 2: 193–203.

Parents Involved in Community Schools v. Seattle School District 1. 2007. 149 Wash. 2d 660.

Parrish, T. B., A. Merickel, M. Perez, R. Linquanti, M. Socias, A. Spain, C. Speroni, P. Esra, L. Brock, and D. Delancey. 2006. *Effects of the Implementation of Proposition 227 on the Education of English Learners, K–12: Findings from a Five-Year Evaluation.* Palo Alto, Calif.: American Institutes for Research and WestEd. http:// www.air.org/news/documents/227Report.pdf.

Pattillo-McCoy, M. 1999. *Black Picket Fences: Privilege and Peril among the Black Middle Class.* Chicago: University of Chicago Press.

Pennock-Roman, M. 1988. *The Status of Research on the Scholastic Aptitude Test and Hispanic Students in Postsecondary Education.* Princeton, N.J.: Educational Testing Service.

Perie, M., W. S. Grigg, and G. S. Dion. 2005. *The Nation's Report Card: Mathematics, 2005.* NCES 2006-453. U.S. Department of Education, Institute of Education Sciences, National Center for Education Statistics. Washington, D.C.: U.S. Government Printing Office.

Perie, M., W. S. Grigg, and P. L. Donahue. 2005. *The Nation's Report Card: Reading, 2005.* NCES 2006-451. U.S. Department of Education, Institute of Education Sciences, National Center for Education Statistics. Washington, D.C.: U.S. Government Printing Office.

Perlmann, J. 1987. "A Piece of the Pie: Reflections and New Evidence on Black and Immigrant Schooling since 1880." *Sociology of Education* 60, no. 1: 54–61.

———. 2005. *Italians Then, Mexicans Now: Immigrant Origins and Second Generation Progress, 1890–2000.* New York: Russell Sage.

Perna, L. 2007. *Improving the Transition from High School to College in Minnesota:*

Recommendations Based on a Review of Effective Programs. http://gj.production
.urbanplanet.com/sites/2d9abd3a-10a9-47bf-ba1a-fe315d55be04/uploads/HS_to_
College.pdf.

Perna, L., and W. S. Swail. 1998. *Early Intervention Programs: How Effective Are
They at Increasing Access to College?* Paper presented at the annual meeting of
the Association for the Study of Higher Education, Miami.

Peshkin, A. 1991. *The Color of Strangers, the Color of Friends.* Chicago: University
of Chicago Press.

Peske, H., and K. Haycock. 2006. *Teacher Inequality: How Poor and Minority Kids
Are Shortchanged on Teacher Quality.* Washington, D.C.: Education Trust.

Pew Hispanic Center. 2006. *Latino Labor Report 2006: Strong Gains in Employment.* Available at http://pewhispanic.org/reports/report.php?ReportID=70.

Pew Hispanic Center/Kaiser Family Foundation. 2004. *National Survey of Latinos:
Education.* Washington, D.C.: Pew Hispanic Center. http://pewhispanic.org/files/
factsheets/7.pdf.

Phillips, K. 1991. *The Politics of Rich and Poor: Wealth and the American Electorate
in the Reagan Aftermath.* New York: Random House.

———. 2003. *Wealth and Democracy: A Political History of the American Rich.*
New York: Broadway Books.

Phinney, J. 1989. "Stages of Ethnic Identity Development in Minority Group Adolescents." *Journal of Early Adolescence* 9: 34–49.

Plyler v. Doe. 1982. 457 U.S. 202.

Portes, A., and R. G. Rumbaut. 1990. *Immigrant America: A Portrait.* Berkeley: University of California Press.

———. 2001. *Legacies: The Story of the Immigrant Second Generation.* Berkeley:
University of California Press.

Portes A., and M. Zhou. 1993. "The New Second Generation: Segmented Assimilation and Its Variants." *Annals of the American Academy of Political and Social Science* 530, no. 1: 74–96.

Preamble to California Proposition 227. 1998. Codified as sec. 1, chap. 3, art. 1 of the
California Education Code. http://primary98.sos.ca.gov/VoterGuide/Propositions/
227text.htm.

Prince, C. 2002. *The Challenge of Attracting Good Teachers and Principals to Struggling Schools.* Paper prepared for the American Association of School Administrators, Arlington, Va.

Puma, M., S. Bell, R. Cook, C. Heid, and M. Lopez. 2005. *Head Start Impact Study:
First Year Findings.* Washington, D.C.: U.S. Department of Health and Human
Services, Administration for Children and Families.

Puma, M., N. Karweit, C. Price, A. Ricciuti, W. Thompson, and M. Vaden-Kiernan.
1997. *Prospects: Final Report on Student Outcomes.* Washington, D.C.: U.S. Department of Education, Office of the Under Secretary.

Rainwater, L., and T. Smeeding. 2003. *Poor Kids in a Rich Country.* New York: Russell Sage Foundation.

Ramey, C. T., and F. A. Campbell. 1984. "Preventive Education for High-Risk
Children: Cognitive Consequences of the Carolina Abecedarian Project." *American Journal of Mental Deficiency* 88: 515–523.

———. 1991. "Poverty, Early Childhood Education, and Academic Competence:
The Abecedarian Experiment." In A. C. Huston, ed., *Children in Poverty: Child
Development and Public Policy,* pp. 190–221. Cambridge, Eng.: Cambridge Uni-
versity Press.

Ramírez, J., S. Yuen, D. Ramey, and D. Pasta. 1991. *Final Report: Longitudinal Study of Structured English Immersion Strategy, Early-Exit and Late-Exit Bilingual Education Programs for Language-Minority Children.* Paper 300-87-0156 prepared for U.S. Department of Education. San Mateo, Calif.: Aguirre International.

Ready, D., L. LoGerfo, D. Burkham, and V. Lee. 2005. "Explaining Girls' Advantage in Kindergarten Literacy Learning: Do Classroom Behaviors Make a Difference?" *Elementary School Journal* 106, no. 1: 21–38.

Ream, R. 2004. *Uprooting Children: Mobility, Social Capital, and Mexican American Underachievement.* New York: LFB Scholarly Publishing.

———. 2005. "Toward Understanding How Social Capital Mediates the Impact of Mobility on Mexican American Achievement." *Social Forces* 84, no. 1: 201–224.

Ream, R., and R. Stanton-Salazar. 2006. "The Uprooted: Student Mobility and Academic Underachievement among Mexican Americans." *Policy Matters* 1: 1–15.

Redd, K. 2003. "Invited Commentary: The Gap between College Costs and Student Resources." *Education Statistics Quarterly* 5, no. 2. http://nces.ed.gov/programs/quarterly/vol_5/5_2/q2_4.asp#H5 (accessed April 29, 2008).

Reynolds, A. G. 1991. "The Cognitive Consequences of Bilingualism." In A. G. Reynolds, ed., *Bilingualism, Multiculturalism, and Second Language Learning.* Hillsdale, N.J.: Lawrence Erlbaum.

Rideout, V., D. Roberts, and U. Foehr. 2005. *Generation M: Media in the Lives of 8–18 Year Olds.* Menlo Park, Calif.: Kaiser Family Foundation.

Ringwalt, C. L., S. Ennett, and R. Johnson. 2003. "Factors Associated with Fidelity to Substance Use Prevention Curriculum Guides in the Nation's Middle Schools." *Health Education and Behavior* 30: 375–391.

Rist, R. 1970. "Student Social Class and Teacher Expectations: The Self-Fulfilling Prophecy in Ghetto Education." *Harvard Educational Review* 40, no. 3: 411–451.

Rivera, C., C. W. Stansfield, L. Scialdone, and M. Sharkey. 2000. *An Analysis of State Policies for the Inclusion and Accommodation of English Language Learners in State Assessment Programs during 1998–1999: Final Report.* ERIC Report #ED445037. Washington, D.C.: U.S. Department of Education.

Rivers, C., and R. Barnett. 2006. "The Myth of 'The Boy Crisis.'" *Washington Post,* Sunday, April 9, B1.

Rivkin, S. G., E. A. Hanushek, and J. F. Kain. 2001. *Teachers, Schools, and Academic Achievement.* Cambridge: National Bureau of Economic Research.

Robin, K., E. Frede, and W. S. Barnett. 2006. *Is More Better? The Effects of Full-Day vs. Half-Day Preschool on Early School Achievement.* Working paper. New Brunswick, N.J.: National Institute for Early Education Research.

Robinson, N., R. G. Lanzi, R. Weinberg, S. L. Ramey, and C. T. Ramey. 2002. "Family Factors Associated with High Academic Competence in Former Head Start Children at Third Grade." *Gifted Child Quarterly* 46: 278–290.

Robinson, N., R. Weinberg, D. Redden, S. Ramey, and C. Ramey. 1998. "Family Factors Associated with High Academic Competence among Former Head Start Children," *Gifted Child Quarterly* 42: 148–156.

Roderick, M. 2003. "What's Happening to the Boys? Early High School Experiences among African American Male Adolescents in Chicago." *Urban Education* 38: 538–607.

Rogers, A., and A. Taylor. 1997. "Intergenerational Mentoring: A Viable Strategy for Meeting the Needs of Vulnerable Youth." *Journal of Gerontological Social Work* 28: 125–140.

Rolnick, A., and R. Grunewald. 2008. "Early Education's Big Dividends: The Better Public Investment." *Communities and Banking* 19: 3–5.

Rolstad, K., K. Mahoney, and G. V. Glass. 2005. "The Big Picture: A Meta-Analysis of Program Effectiveness Research on English Language Learners." *Educational Policy*, 19: 572–594. http://www.public.asu.edu/~krolstad/big_picture.pdf.

Romo, H. D., and T. Falbo. 1996. *Latino High School Graduation: Defying the Odds.* Austin: University of Texas Press.

Romualdi, V. 2000. "Shared Dream: A Case Study of the Implementation of Healthy Start." Ph.D. diss., University of California, Davis. *Dissertation Abstracts International* 61(09), UMI no. 9315947.

Rose, H., and J. Betts. 2001. *Math Matters: The Links between High School Curriculum, College Graduation, and Earnings in College Readiness.* San Francisco: Public Policy Institute of California.

Rosenbaum, J., S. DeLuca, and T. Tuck. 2005. "New Capabilities in New Places: Low-Income Black Families in Suburbia." In X. de Souza Briggs, ed., *The Geography of Opportunity.* Washington, D.C.: Brookings Institute, pp. 150–175.

Rosenthal, R., and L. Jacobson. 1968. *Pygmalion in the Classroom: Teacher Expectations and Pupils' Intellectual Development.* New York: Holt, Rinehart & Winston.

Rossell, C., and K. Baker. 1996. *Bilingual Education in Massachusetts: The Emperor Has No Clothes.* Boston: Pioneer Institute.

Rotermund, S. 2007. *Educational and Economic Consequences for Students Who Drop Out of High School.* Santa Barbara: California Dropout Research Project. http://www.lmri.ucsb.edu/dropouts.

Rothstein, R. 2004. *Class and Schools: Using Social, Economic, and Educational Reform to Close the Black-White Achievement Gap.* New York: Teachers College, Columbia University.

Roug, L. 2007. "Few Migrants, Much Opposition." *Los Angeles Times,* December 6, p. A23.

Rouse, C. 2007. "Consequences for the Labor Market." In C. Belfield and H. Levin, eds., *The Price We Pay,* p. 110. Washington, D.C.: Brookings Institution Press.

Ruiz, R. 1984. "Orientations in Language Planning." *Journal for the National Association for Bilingual Education* 8, no. 2: 15–34.

Rumbaut, R. 1995. "The New Californians: Comparative Research Findings on the Educational Progress of Immigrant Children." In R. Rumbaut and W. Cornelius, eds., *California's Immigrant Children: Theory, Research, and Implications for Educational Policy.* La Jolla: Center for U.S.-Mexican Studies, University of California, San Diego.

Rumberger, R. 2003. "The Causes and Consequences of Student Mobility." *Journal of Negro Education* 72: 6–21.

Rumberger, R., and M. Brenner. 2002. *Can Mentoring Improve Academic Achievement? An Evaluation of a Four-Year, Early Adolescent Program.* Santa Barbara: Gevirtz Research Center, University of California, Santa Barbara.

Rumberger, R., and P. Gándara. 2004. "Seeking Equity in the Education of California's English Learners." *Teachers College Record* 106, no. 10: 2031–2055.

Rumberger, R., P. Gándara, and B. Merino. 2006. "Where California's English Learners Attend School and Why It Matters." *UCLMRI Newsletter* 15: 1–3. http://www.lmri.ucsb.edu/publications/newsletters/v15n2.pdf.

Rumberger, R., and K. Larson. 1998a. "Student Mobility and Increased Risk of High School Dropout." *American Journal of Education* 107: 1–35.

———. 1998b. "Toward Explaining Differences in Educational Achievement among

Mexican American Language-Minority Students." *Sociology of Education* 71, no. 1: 69–93.

Rumberger, R., and G. Rodriguez. 2002. "Chicano Dropouts: An Update of Research and Policy Issues." In R. Valencia, ed., *Chicano School Failure and Success: Past, Present, and Future.* New York: Routledge.

Rumberger, R. W., and L. Tran. 2006. *Preschool Participation and the Cognitive and Social Development of Language Minority Students.* Los Angeles: Center for the Study of Evaluation, Graduate School of Education and Information Studies, University of California, Los Angeles.

Rumberger, R., and L. Tran. 2008. "State Language Policies, School Language Practices, and the EL Achievement GAP." Paper presented at U.C. Linguistic Minority Research Institute, 21st Annual Conference, Sacramento, May 2–3, 2008.

Rutter, M., B. Maughan, P. Mortimer, and J. Ousten. 1979. *Fifteen Thousand Hours: Secondary Schools and Their Effects on Children.* Cambridge: Harvard University Press.

Saenz, V. B., L. Oseguera, and S. Hurtado. 2007. "Losing Ground: Exploring Racial/Ethnic Enrollment Shifts in Freshman Access to Selective Institutions." In G. Orfield, P. Marin, S. M. Flores, and L. M. Garces, eds., *Charting the Future of College Affirmative Action: Legal Victories, Continuing Attacks, and New Research.* Los Angeles: Civil Rights Project at University of California, Los Angeles.

Salinas, M. F., and J. Aronson. 1998. *Stereotype Threat: The Role of Effort Withdrawal and Apprehension on the Intellectual Underperformance of Mexican-Americans. Dissertation Abstracts International* 59(06), 1908A, UMI no. AAT98-38106.

Sanders, W. L., and J. C. Rivers. 1996. *Cumulative and Residual Effects of Teachers on Future Student Academic Achievement.* Research Progress Report. Knoxville: University of Tennessee Value-Added Research and Assessment Center. http://www.mccsc.edu/~curriculum/cumulative%20and%20residual%20effects%20of%20teachers.pdf.

Sax, L., and C. Harper. 2005. *Origins of the Gender Gap: Pre-College and College Influences on Differences between Men and Women.* Paper presented at the annual meeting of the Association for Institutional Research, San Diego.

Scheckner, S., S. A. Rollin, C. Kaiser-Ulrey, and R. Wagner. 2002. "School Violence in Children and Adolescents: A Meta-Analysis of the Effectiveness of Current Interventions." *Journal of School Violence* 1, no. 2: 5–32.

Schlesinger, A. 1991. *The Disuniting of America: Reflections in a Multicultural Society.* New York: Norton.

Schmader, T., and M. Johns. 2003. "Converging Evidence That Stereotype Threat Reduces Working Memory Capacity." *Journal of Personality and Social Psychology* 85: 440–452.

Schmidt, R. 1998. "The Politics of Language in Canada and the United States: Explaining the Difference." In Thomas Ricento and B. Burnaby, eds., *Language and Politics in the United States and Canada: Myths and Realities,* pp. 37–70. Philadelphia: Lawrence Erlbaum.

———. 2000. *Language Policy and Identity Politics in the United States.* Philadelphia: Temple University Press.

Schneider, B., and D. Stevenson. 1999. *The Ambitious Generation: America's Teenagers, Motivated but Directionless.* New Haven: Yale University Press.

Seligman, M. E. P. 1990. *Learned Optimism.* New York: Pocket Books.

Seligman, M. E. P., K. Reivich, L. Jaycox, and J. Gillham. 1995. *The Optimistic Child: A Revolutionary Program That Safeguards Children against Depression and Builds Lifelong Resilience.* Boston: Houghton Mifflin.

Short, D. 2007. *Double the Work: Challenges and Solutions to Acquiring Language and Academic Literacy for Adolescent ELLs.* Washington, D.C.: Center for Applied Linguistics.

Shulock, N., ed. 2006. "Practitioners on Making Accountability Work for the Public." *New Directions in Higher Education* 135.

Shulock, N., C. Moore, T. Gage, and M. Newman. 2005. "Assessing the Mismatch Hypothesis: Differentials in College Graduation Rates by Institutional Selectivity." *Sociology of Education* 78, no. 4: 294–315.

———. 2006. *Improving Facility Planning for California Higher Education.* Sacramento: Center for California Studies, Faculty Research Fellows Program.

Simcox, D. 2002. *Another Fifty Years of Mass Mexican Immigration: Mexican Government Report Projects Continued Flow Regardless of Economics or Birth Rates.* Washington, D.C.: Center for Immigration Studies. http://www.cis.org/articles/2002/back202.html#author.

Simon, J. L. 1996. "Public Expenditures on Immigrants to the United States, Past and Present." *Population and Development Review* 22, no. 1: 99–109.

Slavin, R. E., and A. Cheung. 2004. "How Do English Language Learners Learn to Read?" *Educational Leadership* 61, no. 6: 52–57.

———. 2005. "A Synthesis of Research on Language of Reading Instruction for English Language Learners." *Review of Educational Research* 75: 247–284.

Slavin, R. E., and O. S. Fashola. 1998. *Show Me the Evidence! Proven and Promising Programs for America's Schools.* Thousand Oaks, Calif.: Corwin Press.

Slavin, R. E., and N. L. Karweit. 1985. "Effects of Whole Class, Ability Grouped, and Individualized Instruction on Mathematics Achievement." *American Educational Research Journal* 22, no. 3: 351–367.

Slavin, R. E., and N. Madden. 2006. *Success for All: Summary of Research on Achievement Outcomes.* Baltimore: Johns Hopkins University, Center for Research and Reform in Education.

Smith, P. J. 2003. "Assimilation across the Latino Generations." *American Economic Review* 93, no. 2: 315–319.

Snipes, J., G. I. Holton, and F. Doolittle. 2006. *Charting a Path to Graduation: The Effect of Project GRAD on Elementary School Student Outcomes in Four Urban School Districts.* New York: MDRC Publications. http://www.mdrc.org/publications/432/full.pdf.

Snipes, J., G. I. Holton, F. Doolittle, and L. Sztejnberg. 2006. *Striving for Student Success: The Effect of Project GRAD on High School Student Outcomes in Three Urban School Districts.* New York: MDRC Publications. http://www.mdrc.org/publications/433/full.pdf.

Snow, C. 1992. "Perspectives on Second-Language Development: Implications for Bilingual Education," *Educational Researcher* 21: 16–19.

Snow, C., M. Burns, and P. Griffin, eds. 1998. *Preventing Reading Difficulties in Young Children.* Washington, D.C.: National Academy Press. http://books.nap.edu/html/prdyc.

Snow, C., and M. Hofnagle-Hohle. 1978. "The Critical Period for Language Acquisition." *Child Development* 4: 1114–1128.

Snyder, T., S. Dillow, and C. Hoffman. 2006. *Digest of Education Statistics, 2006.*

Washington, D.C.: U.S. Department of Education, National Center for Education Statistics.

Solorzano, D., and A. Ornelas. 2004. "A Critical Race Analysis of Latina/o African American Advanced Placement Enrollment in Public High Schools." *High School Journal* (February/March): 15–26.

Somers, P., J. Cofer, and J. Vanderputten. 2002. "The Early Bird Goes to College: The Link between Early College Aspirations and Postsecondary Matriculation." *Journal of College Student Development* 43, no. 1: 93–107.

Sommers, C. H. 2000. *The War against Boys: How Misguided Feminism Is Harming Our Boys.* New York: Touchstone.

South, S., E. P. Baumer, and A. Lutz. 2003. "Interpreting Community Effects on Youth Educational Attainment." *Youth and Society* 35: 3–36.

South, S., K. Crowder, and K. Trent. 1998. "Children's Residential Mobility and Neighborhood Environment following Parental Divorce and Remarriage." *Social Forces* 77: 667–693.

Stanton-Salazar, R. 1997. "A Social Capital Framework for Understanding the Socialization of Racial Minority Children and Youths." *Harvard Educational Review* 67: 1–40.

Steele, C. 1997. "A Threat in the Air: How Stereotypes Shape Intellectual Identity and Performance." *American Psychologist* 52: 613–629.

Steele, S. 1999. *A Dream Deferred: The Second Betrayal of Black Freedom in America.* New York: Harper Perennial.

Steinberg, L. 1996. *Beyond the Classroom: Why School Reform Has Failed and What Parents Need to Do.* New York: Simon & Schuster.

Steinberg, L., S. Dornbusch, and B. Brown. 1992. "Ethnic Differences in Adolescent Achievement: An Ecological Perspective." *American Psychologist* 47: 723–729.

Strenta, A. C., and R. Elliott. 1987. "Differential Grading Standards Revisited." *Journal of Educational Measurement* 24: 281–291.

Suárez, A. 2003. "Forward Transfer: Strengthening the Educational Pipeline for Latino Community College Students." *Community College Journal of Research and Practice* 27, no. 2: 95–117.

Suárez-Orozco, C., and M. Suárez-Orozco. 1995. *Transformations: Migration, Family Life, and Achievement Motivation among Latino Adolescents.* Stanford, Calif.: Stanford University Press.

Suárez-Orozco, C., M. Suárez-Orozco, and I. Todorova. 2007. *Learning a New Land: Immigrant Students in American Society.* Cambridge: Harvard University Press.

Suárez-Orozco, M. 2007. *The Education of Immigrant Students after "Plyler": International Reflections on Immigration and Education.* Presentation at the Annual Meeting of the American Educational Research Association, Chicago.

Suárez-Orozco, M., and M. Páez, eds. 2002. *Latinos: Remaking America.* Berkeley: University of California Press.

———. 2003. *Latinos Remaking America.* Berkeley: University of California Press.

Sunderman, G. L., and G. Orfield. 2006. "Domesticating a Revolution: No Child Left Behind and State Administrative Response." *Harvard Educational Review* 76, no. 4: 526–556.

Swail, W. S. 2004. *Value Added: The Costs and Benefits of College Preparatory Programs.* Virginia Beach, Va.: Educational Policy Institute.

Swail, W. S., A. F. Cabrera, and C. Lee. 2004. *Latino Youth and the Pathway to College.* Washington, D.C.: Pew Hispanic Center.

Swanson, C. 2004. "Sketching a Portrait of Public High School Graduation: Who Graduates? Who Doesn't?" In G. Orfield, ed., *Dropouts in America*. Cambridge: Harvard Education Press.

Swanson, C., and D. Chaplin. 2003. *Counting High School Graduates When Graduates Count: Measuring Graduation Rates under the High Stakes of NCLB*. Washington, D.C.: Urban Institute.

Sweet, J., S. Rasher, B. Ambromitis, and E. Johnson. 2004. *Case Studies of High Performing, High-Technology Schools: Final Research Report on Schools with Predominantly Low Income, African American or Latino Student Populations*. Naperville, Ill.: North Central Regional Educational Laboratory.

Tate, W. 1997. "Race-Ethnicity, SES, Gender, and Language Proficiency Trends in Mathematics Achievement: An Update." *Journal for Research in Mathematics Education* 28, no. 6: 652–679.

Tatum, B. 1997. *Why Are All the Black Kids Sitting Together in the Cafeteria? And Other Conversations about Race*. New York: Basic Books.

TCC Group (The Conservation Company). 2004. Evaluation of the National Posse Program. New York: Posse Foundation.

Telles, E., and V. Ortiz. 2008. *Generations of Exclusion: Mexican Americans, Assimilation, and Race*. New York: Russell Sage Foundation.

Teranishi, R., W. Allen, and D. Solorzano. 2004. "Opportunity at the Crossroads: Racial Inequality, School Segregation, and Higher Education in California." *Teachers College Record* 106, no. 11: 2224–2245.

Terenzini, P. T., A. F. Cabrera, and E. M. Bernal. 2001. *Swimming against the Tide: The Poor in American Higher Education*. New York: College Board.

Thernstrom, A., and S. Thernstrom. 2002. *Beyond the Color Line: New Perspectives on Race and Ethnicity in America*. Palo Alto: Hoover Institution Press.

Thernstrom, S., and A. Thernstrom. 1997. *America in Black and White: One Nation Indivisible*. New York: Simon & Schuster.

———. 1999. "Reflections on the Shape of the *River* Book Review." *UCLA Law Review* 46: 1583–1631.

Thomas, W., and V. Collier. 1997. *A National Study of School Effectiveness for Language Minority Students. Long-Term Academic Achievement*. Santa Cruz, Calif.: CREDE. http://www.usc.edu.dept/education/CMMR/CollierThomasComplete.pdf (accessed June 16, 2007).

Thornburgh, N. 2007. "The Case for Amnesty," *Time*, June 18, p. 42.

Tienda, M. 1989. "Puerto Ricans and the Underclass Debate." *Annals of the American Academy of Political and Social Science* 501: 105–119.

Tienda, M., and F. Mitchell. 2006. *Multiple Origins, Uncertain Destinies: Hispanics and the American Future*. Washington, D.C.: National Academies Press.

Tinto, V. 1993. *Leaving College: Rethinking the Causes and Cures of Student Attrition*, 2d ed. Chicago: University of Chicago Press.

Tornatzky, L., R. Cutler, and J. Lee. 2002. *College Knowledge: What Latino Parents Need to Know and Why They Don't Know It*. Claremont, Calif.: Tomás Rivera Policy Institute.

Trasviña, J. 2006. *Examining Views on English as the Official Language*. Written testimony for the U.S. House of Representatives, Committee on Education and the Workforce, Subcomittee on Education Reform, July 26.

Trejo, S. J. 2001. *Intergenerational Progress of Mexican-Origin Workers in the U.S. Labor Market*. IZA Discussion Paper 377. http://ssrn.com/abstract=137328.

Trostel, P. 2008. "High Returns: Public Investment in Higher Education." *Communities and Banking* (Spring): 19, 31–34.

Tucker, J. T. 2007. "Waiting Times for ESL Classes and the Impact on English Learners." *National Civic Review* 96, no. 1: 30–37.

UCLA IDEA/UCACCORD. 2007. *Latino Educational Opportunity Report.* Los Angeles: University of California Los Angeles Institute for Democracy, Education and Access, and University of California All Campus Consortium on Research for Diversity.

University of California Latino Eligibility Study. 1997. *Latino Student Eligibility and Participation in the University of California: YA BASTA!* Oakland: University of California Latino Eligibility Task Force.

Unmuth, K. L. 2007. "Educators Split on Bilingual Classes." *Dallas Morning News,* March 18. http://www.dallasnews.com (accessed March 19, 2007).

Unz, R. 1997. "Bilingual Is a Damaging Myth." *Los Angeles Times,* October 19, p. A20.

U.S. Census Bureau. 2008. *Current Population Survey (CPS).* Washington, D.C. U.S. Government Printing Office, table 216.

U.S. Commission on Civil Rights. 1974. *Toward Quality Education for Mexican Americans.* Washington, D.C.: U.S. Commission on Civil Rights.

U.S. Department of Commerce, Census Bureau. 2005. *Current Population Survey (CPS): Annual Social and Economic Study Supplement, 1971–2005.* Previously unpublished tabulation (November). http://nces.ed.gov/pubs2007/minoritytrends/tables/table_5.asp?referrer=report (accessed May 1, 2008).

———. 2006. *Current Population Report, P60-231: Money and Income of Families—Number and Distribution by Race and Hispanic Origin, 2005,* table 672. http://pubdb3.census.gov/macro/032006/faminc/new07_000.htm. (accessed May 1, 2008).

———. 2007a. *American Community Survey.* http://www.census.gov/prod/2007pubs/acs-08.pdf.

———. 2007b. *Current Population Survey (CPS).* October Supplement, 1972–2005. Washington, D.C.: U.S. Government Printing Office.

U.S. Department of Education. 2007. *The Nation's Report Card, 2007.* http://NCES.ed.gov/nationsreportcard/nies/nies_2007/n0029.asp.

———. 2005. *Digest of Education Statistics.* http://nces .ed.gov/programs/digets/d05/tables/ (accessed February 20, 2008).

———, Institute of Education Sciences. 2000. *National Center for Education Statistics, High School Transcript Study* (HSTS). Washington, D.C.: Institute for Information Sciences.

———, National Center for Education Statistics. 1999. *The Condition of Education, 1998.* Washington, D.C.: U.S. Government Printing Office. http://nces.ed.gov/pubs98/98013.pdf.

———. 2000. *Digest of Education Statistics, 2000.* Washington, D.C.: U.S. Government Printing Office.

———. 2003–2004. Table 3.7: Number and Percentage Distribution of Public Elementary and Secondary School Teachers, by Locale and Selected Characteristics. http://www.nces.ed.gov.

———. 2005. *Indicators of School Crime and Safety, 2005.* http://www.nces.ed.gov/Pubsearch/pubsinfo.asp?pubid=2006001.

———. 2006. *The Condition of Education, 2005* (NCES 2005–094). Washington,

D.C.: U.S. Government Printing Office. http://nces.ed.gov//programs/coe/2005/section1/indicator05.asp (accessed September 29, 2005).

———. 2007. *The Condition of Education, 2006* (NCES 2006–071). Washington, D.C.: U.S. Government Printing Office.

Useem, Elizabeth L. 1992. "Middle Schools and Math Groups: Parents' Involvement in Children's Placement." *Sociology of Education* 65: 263–279.

Vaden-Kiernan, N., and J. McManus. 2005. *Parent and Family Involvement in Education: 2002–2003.* http://nces.ed.gov/pubsearch/pubsinfo.asp?pubid=2005043.

Valdés, G. 1997. "Dual-Language Immersion Programs: A Cautionary Note concerning the Education of Language-Minority Students." *Harvard Educational Review.*

———. 2001. *Learning and Not Learning English: Latino Students in American Schools.* New York: Teachers College Press.

Valenzuela, A. 1999. *Subtractive Schooling: U.S.-Mexican Youth and the Politics of Caring.* Albany: State University of New York Press.

Vasquez Garcia, H., C. García Coll, S. Erkut, O. Alarcón, and L. Tropp. 2000. "Family Values of Latino Adolescents." In M. Montero-Sieburth and F. Villaruel, eds., *Making Invisible Latino Adolescents Visible: A Critical Approach to Latino Diversity,* pp. 239–264. New York: Falmer Press.

Vernez, G., and L. Mizell. 2001. *Goal: To Double the Rate of Hispanics Earning a Bachelor's Degree.* Santa Monica, Calif.: RAND Corporation. http:// rand.org/pubs/documented_briefings/2005/DB350.pdf.

Vigil, J. D. 2004. "Gangs and School Membership: Implications for Schooling," In G. Gibson, P. Gándara, and J. Koyama, eds., *School Connections: U.S.-Mexican Youth, Peers, and School Achievement,* pp. 87–106. New York: Teachers College Press.

Villaruel, A. M. 1998. "Cultural Influences on the Sexual Attitudes, Beliefs, and Norms of Young Latina Adolescents." *Journal of the Society of Pediatric Nurses* 3: 69–79.

Walberg, H. 1993. "Productive Use of Time." In L. Anderson and H. Walberg, eds., *Timepiece: Extending and Enhancing Learning Time.* Reston, Va.: National Association of Secondary School Principals.

Warschauer, M., M. Knobel, and L. Stone. 2004. "Technology and Equity in Schooling: Deconstructing the Digital Divide." *Educational Policy* 18, no. 4: 562–588.

Waters, T., and R. Marzano. 2006. *School District Leadership That Works: The Effect of Superintendent Leadership on Student Achievement.* Working paper. Aurora, Colo.: Mid-Continent Research for Education and Learning.

Weinstein, R. 1989. "Perceptions of Classroom Processes and Student Motivation: Children's Views of Self-Fulfilling Prophecies." In R. Ames and C. Ames, eds., *Research on Motivation in Education: Goals and Cognition,* pp. 187–221. New York: Academic Press.

Werner, E., and R. Smith. 2001. *Journeys from Childhood to Mid-Life: Risk, Resilience and Recovery.* Ithaca, N.Y.: Cornell University Press.

West, J., K. Denton, and E. Germino-Hausken. 2000. *America's Kindergartners: Findings from the Early Childhood Longitudinal Study, Kindergarten Class of 1998–1999.* Washington, D.C.: National Center for Education Statistics.

Whalen, S. 2002. *Report of the Evaluation of the Polk Bros. Foundations' Full Service Schools Initiative.* Chicago: University of Chicago Chapin Hall Center for Children.

Wiley, T., and W. Wright. 2004. "Against the Undertow: Language-Minority Education Policy and Politics in the 'Age of Accountability.'" *Educational Policy* 18, no. 1: 142–168.

Wilhelm, T., D. Carmen, and M. Reynolds. 2002. *Connecting Kids to Technology.* Baltimore: Annie E. Casey Foundation.

Williams v. State of California. 2005. No. 312236 (Cal. Sup. Ct.).

Willig, A. 1985. "A Meta-Analysis of Selected Studies on the Effectiveness of Bilingual Education." *Review of Educational Research* 55: 269–317.

Wilson, W. J. 1996. *When Work Disappears: The World of the New Urban Poor.* New York: Vintage Press.

Wong-Fillmore, L. 1985. "Learning a Second Language: Chinese Children in the American Classroom." In J. Alatis and J. Staczek, eds., *Perspectives on Bilingualism and Bilingual Education.* Washington, D.C.: Georgetown University Press.

———. 1991. "When Learning a Second Language Means Losing Your First." *Early Childhood Research Quarterly* 6: 323–346.

Wong-Fillmore, L., and C. Snow. 2000. *What Teachers Need to Know about Language.* Washington, D.C.: U.S. Department of Education, Office of Educational Research and Improvement.

Woolfolk, A. E., B. Rosoff, and W. K. Hoy. 1990. "Teachers' Sense of Efficacy and Their Beliefs about Managing Students." *Teaching and Teacher Education* 6: 137–148.

Yettick, H. R. 2006. "Unz Reduz: A Literature Review of Research on the Unz Initiatives." Unpublished paper, University of Colorado, Graduate School of Education, Boulder.

Zarate, M. E., and H. P. Pachón. 2006a. *Gaining or Losing Ground? Equity in Offering Advanced Placement Courses in California High Schools, 1997–2003.* Los Angeles: Tomás Rivera Policy Institute. http://www.trpi.org/PDFs/ap_2006.pdf.

———. 2006b. *Perceptions of College Financial Aid among California Latino Youth.* Los Angeles: Tomás Rivera Policy Institute. http://www.trpi.org/PDFs/Financial_Aid_Surveyfinal6302006.pdf

Zehler, A., H. Fleischman, P. Hopstock, T. Stephenson, M. Pendzick, and S. Sapru. 2003. *Descriptive Study of Services to Limited English Proficient Students.* Washington, D.C.: Development Associates.

Zehr, M. A. 2007a. "NCLB Seen a Damper on Bilingual Programs." *Education Week,* May 9, pp. 5, 12.

———. 2007b. "States Lag in ELL Curriculum Guidance." *Education Week,* July 5. http://www.edweek.org/ew/articles/2007/07/05/43guidance_web.h26.html?print=1.

Zhou, M., and S. S. Kim. 2006. "Community Forces, Social Capital, and Educational Achievement: The Case of Supplementary Education in the Chinese and Korean Immigrant Communities." *Harvard Educational Review* 76, no. 1: 1–26.

Zigler, E., and S. Styfco, eds. 1993. *Head Start and Beyond: A National Plan for Extended Childhood Intervention.* New Haven: Yale University Press.

Zill, N., M. Collins, J. West, and E. Germino-Hausken. 1995. *Approaching Kindergarten: A Look at Preschoolers in the United States.* Washington, D.C.: U.S. Department of Education, National Center for Education Statistics. http://nces.ed.gov/pubsearch/pubsinfo.asp?pubid=95280.

Zwick, R. 2002. *Fair Game? The Use of Standardized Admissions Tests in Higher Education,* 1st ed. New York: Routledge/Falmer Press.

———. 2004. *Rethinking the SAT: The Future of Standardized Testing in University Admissions.* New York: Routledge/Falmer Press.